Adobe®
After Effects® 7.0
STUDIO TECHNIQUES

Mark Christiansen

ADOBE
PRESS

Adobe

Adobe After Effects 7.0 Studio Techniques

Mark Christiansen

Copyright © 2006 Mark Christiansen

This Adobe Press book is published by Peachpit. For information on Adobe Press books, contact:

Peachpit
1249 Eighth Street
Berkeley, CA 94710
(510) 524-2178
Fax: (510) 524-2221
www.adobepress.com

To report errors, please send a note to errata@peachpit.com

Peachpit Press is a division of Pearson Education

Project Editor: Karen Reichstein
Development and Copy Editor: Linda Laflamme
Production Editor: Lisa Brazieal
Technical Editor: Alexandre Czetwertynski
Proofreader: Haig MacGregor
Compositor: Kim Scott
Indexer: Rebecca Plunkett
Cover design: Charlene Charles-Will
Cover illustration: Alicia Buelow

ISBN 0-321-38552-7

9 8 7 6 5 4 3 2 1

Printed and bound in the United States of America

Contents at a Glance

Introduction   xiii

Section I   Working Foundations   1

Chapter 1   The 7.0 Workflow   3

Chapter 2   The Timeline   57

Chapter 3   Selections: The Key to Compositing   103

Chapter 4   Optimizing Your Projects   135

Section II   Effects Compositing Essentials   161

Chapter 5   Color Correction   163

Chapter 6   Color Keying   209

Chapter 7   Rotoscoping and Paint   247

Chapter 8   Effective Motion Tracking   275

Chapter 9   Virtual Cinematography   311

Chapter 10   Expressions   349

Chapter 11   Film, HDR, and 32 Bit Compositing   381

Section III   Creative Explorations   415

Chapter 12   Working with Light   417

Chapter 13   Climate: Air, Water, Smoke, Clouds   455

Chapter 14   Pyrotechnics: Fire, Explosions, Energy Phenomena   483

Chapter 15   Learning to See by *Stu Maschwitz*   507

Index   525

What's on the DVD?   547

Contents

Introduction   xiii

Section I   **Working Foundations**   1

Chapter 1   The 7.0 Workflow   3

Workspaces and Panels   5

Making the Most of the UI   10

Settings: Project, Footage, Composition   20

Previews and OpenGL   31

Effects & Presets   45

Output: The Render Queue   47

Study a Shot like an Effects Artist   54

Chapter 2   The Timeline   57

Organization   59

Animation Methods   68

Keyframes and The Graph Editor   70

Über-mastery   85

Transform Offsets   88

Motion Blur   90

Manipulating Time Itself   93

In Conclusion   101

Chapter 3   Selections: The Key to Compositing   103

The Many Ways to Create Selections   104

Compositing: Science and Nature   108

Alpha Channels and Premultiplication   111

Masks   116

Combining Multiple Masks   119

Putting Masks in Motion   122

Blending Modes: The Real Deal   124

Track Mattes   132

Chapter 4   Optimizing your Projects   135

Navigating Multiple Compositions   137

Precomposing and Nesting   141

Adjustment and Guide Layers   148

Understanding Rendering Order   152

Optimizing After Effects   158

Onward to Effects   160

Section II   **Effects Compositing Essentials**   161

Chapter 5   Color Correction   163

Optimizing Plate Levels   165

Color Matching   192

Beyond the Basics   207

Chapter 6	Color Keying	209
	Good Habits and Best Practices	211
	Linear Keyers and Hi-Con Mattes	213
	Blue-Screen and Green-Screen Keying	219
	Understanding and Optimizing Keylight	228
	Fixing Typical Problems	238
	Conclusion	245

Chapter 7	Rotoscoping and Paint	247
	Articulated Mattes	249
	Working Around Limitations	256
	Morphing	260
	Paint and Cloning	265
	Conclusion	274

Chapter 8	Effective Motion Tracking	275
	The Essentials	277
	Optimizing Tracking Using 3D	292
	Extending a Track with Expressions	301
	Tracking for Rotoscoping	303
	Using 3D Tracking Data	305
	Conclusion	309

Chapter 9	Virtual Cinematography	311
	2.5D: Pick Up the Camera	313
	Storytelling and the Camera	326
	Camera Blur	332
	The Role of Grain	337
	Film and Video Looks	343
	Conclusion	347

Chapter 10	Expressions	349
	Logic and Grammar	351
	Muting Keyframes	353
	Linking Animation Data	355
	Looping Animations	361
	Smoothing and Destabilizing	365
	Offsetting Layers and Time	368
	Conditionals and Triggers	372
	Tell Me More	378

Chapter 11	Film, HDR, and 32 Bit Compositing	381
	Film 101	385
	Dynamic Range	388
	Cineon Log Space	390
	Video Gamma Space	393
	Battle of the Color Spaces	394

Floating Point 398
32 Bits per Channel 400
Conclusion 414

Section III Creative Explorations 415

Chapter 12 Working with Light 417
Light Source and Direction 419
Creating a Look with Color 426
Backlighting, Flares, Light Volume 432
Shadows and Reflected Light 441
HDR Lighting 445
Conclusion 453

Chapter 13 Climate: Air, Water, Smoke, Clouds 455
Particulate Matter 457
Sky Replacement 463
The Fog, Smoke, or Mist Rolls In 466
Billowing Smoke 469
Wind 475
Water 478
Conclusion 482

Chapter 14 Pyrotechnics: Fire, Explosions, Energy
Phenomena 483
Firearms 486
Sci-Fi Weaponry 492
Heat Distortion 494
Fire 498
Explosions 505
In a Blaze of Glory 506

Chapter 15 Learning to See *by Stu Maschwitz* 507
Why Doesn't This Shot Look Real? 509
All Hail Reference 513
Rolling Thine Own 522
Not a Conclusion 523

Index 525
What's On the DVD 547

About the Authors

 **Mark Christiansen**'s diverse creative career has somehow never strayed far from compositing in general, and After Effects in particular. He has created visual effects and computer-generated animations for feature films, television, computer games, and various other formats clients occasionally dream up. Feature effects credits at The Orphanage, where Mark learned many of the finer points of visual effects production, include *The Day After Tomorrow* and a pair of Robert Rodriguez films. He is currently a freelance artist based in San Francisco and can be located via http://christiansen.com. His independent directing and design work has been featured at festivals including the 2004 Los Angeles International Short Film Festival; his television work has appeared on HBO, the History Channel, and ABC.

Co-author with Nathan Moody of *After Effects 5.5 Magic,* and a longtime contributing editor for *DV Magazine,* Mark has made guest speaking appearances at NAB, DV Expo, and GDC, as well as for professional groups in the Bay Area. Officially named the "number one beta tester" by the developers for After Effects 6.0, Mark has also been contracted directly by Adobe to support related development and training efforts.

Mark's production career began in the art department at LucasArts Entertainment, culminating in the role of Lead Artist on the innovative *Behind the Magic* which was honored with *Entertainment Weekly*'s pick of Number 1 of 1998 in the "Multimedia" category. He was hired to pioneer LucasArts' short-lived venture into the use of live-action video in games, single-handedly compositing over 100 shots in After Effects for *Rebel Assault II*—the first live-action Star Wars shoot of the 1990s. Like the rest of the world, Mark is relieved that most games no longer contain live-action video.

Mark is a Phi Beta Kappa graduate of Pomona College. He and his wife have two amazing kids.

 **Stu Maschwitz** is a director, visual effects supervisor, renowned technologist and founding partner of The Orphanage, where his credits include mind-bending effects for award-winning commercials, as well as such feature films as *Sin City*, *Spy Kids 3-D: Game Over*, and *The Adventures of Sharkboy and Lavagirl in 3-D*. An innovator in filmmaking technology, he is also the creator of The Orphanage's Magic Bullet software. Prior to joining up with his fellow co-conspirators to start The Orphanage, Maschwitz spent five years at George Lucas' Industrial Light + Magic, where he supervised space battle sequences on *Star Wars, Episode One: The Phantom Menace*. His other visual effects credits include the blockbusters *Twister*, *Men in Black*, *Deep Impact* and *Mission: Impossible*.

Acknowledgments

Thanks are due once again to the good people of The Orphanage in San Francisco, and in particular Stu Maschwitz and Brendan Bolles, two of the most knowledgeable After Effects users in the world; although they did not play as active a role in writing the book this time around, there would have been no book without them. Most of Brendan's excellent groundwork for Chapter 11 has been retained this time around, simply because it was one of the best things about the previous book. I'm only sorry that I had to turn down opportunities to work with these and other Orphans to get this new edition done properly.

A huge thank you this time around goes to the Pixel Corps (www.pixelcorps.com) and its founder and main man, Alex Lindsay, who let me pick and choose from their Sony F900 HD footage in order to include what the last book lacked: hands-on examples with professional caliber footage. They have since upgraded to the F950 HD; look for more great resources from them in the future. Likewise, a huge thank you to Julie Hill and Artbeats for generously providing valuable HD footage for inclusion this time around; they are a great resource for professionally shot stock.

Jeff Almasol (www.redifinery.com) is a constant contributor to the After Effects community in his role as one of the few full-fledged After Effects scripting programmers in the world, and he contributed two scripts at my request, scripts which he generously elected to distribute only via this book's disc.

Clients gave me the firsthand experience that went into this book, and some were willing to commit time (and even money) to secure elements or final shots for use in this book's figures despite no benefit to themselves: Christina Crowley, President of The Kenwood Group, Rama Dunayevich and Marc Sadeghi at The Orphanage, Coral Petretti at ABC Photography, David Donegan at Red Bull USA, Tim Fink of Tim Fink Events and Media, Gary Jaeger and Cameron Baxter at Core Studio, Jonathan Barson at The Foundry UK, Fred Lewis and Inhance Digital, Boeing and the Navy UCAV program, Patrick Campbell of Suburban Imageworks, and Matthew Ward and the wacky goofiness that is markandmatty.com.

I mined http://flickr.com/creativecommons/ for a few difficult-to-find source stills; a huge thank you to the gifted photographers who voluntarily chose to add the Creative Commons tag to their work: Micah Parker, Jorge L. Peschiera, Shuets Udono, and Eric E. Yang. And while I'm at it, thank you to Creative Commons and Laurence Lessig (http://creativecommons.org) for innovating flexible copyright law in an era in which overzealous rights management threatens creativity itself.

To the people at Adobe who've made After Effects what it is, in particular Dave Simons, Dan Wilk, Erica Schisler, and Steve Kilisky, and to some of the developers who've helped me understand it better over the years, including Michael Natkin and Chris Prosser.

Thanks to the companies that contributed to the book's DVD: Peder Norrby, who *is* Trapcode, Russ Andersson of Andersson Technologies, Sean Safreed of Red Giant Software, Andrew Millin of ObviousFX LLC, Marco Paolini of SilhouetteFX, and Pierre Jasmin of RevisionFX. These were my choices for inclusion because they all provide something vital to effects compositing in After Effects.

Other people who were helpful e-mailing their feedback on various topics include Bruno Nicoletti at the Foundry UK, Dan Ebberts (www.motionscript.com), Scott Squires (www.effectscorner.com), Tim Dobbert at The Orphanage, Don Shay at *Cinefex Magazine*, and Matt Silverman at Phoenix Editorial.

A huge thank you to Peachpit, who collectively show a strong commitment to producing the highest quality books, from full color imagery to careful indexing and proofreading. This time around I had the honor and pleasure of working with Karen Reichstein, whose hundreds of e-mails, long hours, and careful read-throughs to manage the details made this book what it is. It was a pleasure to work again with Linda Laflamme, who is no doubt thankful I sold my dictation software before beginning this version. Lisa Brazieal put extra effort at the beginning of the layout process to make sure that the images would read well, and Kim Scott laid out a great looking book. Marjorie Baer and Kelly Ryer helped get everything underway and keep things running, as did Rachel Charlton Tiley, who gets a special mention for pulling me into the fun and memorable Peachpit party at Macworld '06, in which I learned their dark secrets (thanks to the fully hosted bar).

As if that wasn't enough, I even had a dedicated Technical Editor in Alexandre Czetwertinski (whose name I am proud to have spelled from memory). Alex got the nod because he was already doing the job, helpfully sending me very specific questions and comments about the previous edition. He completed the job despite traveling from New York to Paris to Brazil and Central America while the book was being written and edited.

On that note, thanks to all of the thoughtful folks who dropped me a line at aestudiotechniques@gmail.com the last time around; the positive and constructive feedback is a huge part of what makes doing a project like this worthwhile.

A special acknowledgement to my childhood friend and former editor at *DV Magazine*, Jim Feeley, who had been urging me to write a book like this for years. Thanks to my former students at the Academy of Art and to *The Day After Tomorrow* compositing crew at The Orphanage. Helping experienced compositors as well as novice students work with After Effects for the first time offered a lot of insight that went into this book.

Finally, thanks to my mom, who remains always supportive and loving, and my father, who told me—much too late to make any difference—how grueling and tedious he found writing his own textbook a few years back.

Introduction

If you aren't fired with enthusiasm, you will be fired with enthusiasm.

—Vince Lombardi

Introduction

Why This Book?

After Effects 7.0 Studio Techniques fills a unique niche among After Effects books: It is focused on the art (and, to a certain extent, the science) of compositing realistic visual effects. Other After Effects resources tend to focus predominantly on motion graphics, touching only briefly on topics that make up the core of visual effects compositing. Pressed to define it, I would say that effects compositing is the art of blending disparate elements into a shot so that it appears as if it was taken live with a single camera, with no post-processing whatsoever.

Because every shot is different, this book relies very little on step-by-step tutorials, although many hands-on examples are included with this edition. And although every shot is different, the secret is that most of them rely on the application of techniques that need not be devised from scratch; those are the techniques this book attempts to cover in detail.

Until recently, not much information was available on the process of creating visual effects at the feature film level, and it all seemed very complex and mysterious (which is not to say that it's not). A code of silence existed around this type of work similar to the one that has surrounded the work of stage magicians since nearly a century ago, during the time of Harry Houdini and the heyday of the Magic Castle (headquartered, perhaps coincidentally, perhaps not, in Hollywood).

One of the great novels of the past decade is Michael Chabon's *The Amazing Adventures of Kavalier and Clay* (Random House). If you enjoy stories about magic in the days of Houdini, stories about the birth of comics, or just an extremely well-written novel, I highly recommend this Pulitzer Prize winner.

The Cult of Magic

Back in the early days of magic, before you could go to your local bookstore or magic shop and buy a copy of David Pogue's *Magic for Dummies* (Hungry Minds), magic was a dark art practiced by masters sequestered in private clubs, using techniques shared only with a handful of apprentices. The word "magic" is rooted in the Magi, members of the Zoroastrian priesthood. It doesn't get much more sequestered than that.

Visual effects, those skillful re-creations of reality, have themselves been an art form since the beginning of filmmaking; just watch 1900's *Trip to the Moon* by George Meliés (**Figure I.1**). In fact, the earliest films capitalized on two phenomena above all others: the startling realism of the medium and the ability to make up scenes that were impossible to create any other way.

But until the 1990s, special effects post-production for movies was a craft known only to a few hundred practitioners *worldwide*, and the dark art of its practices (often photochemical, sometimes crude, sometimes sophisticated, almost always labor-intensive and fraught with treacherously little room for error) was largely known only to them, passed on in a guild-like fashion to those few apprentices who found their way to this strange specialization (**Figure I.3**).

Figure I.1 *Trip to the Moon* is sometimes called the first visual effects film.

The earliest public motion picture display by the Lumière brothers (**Figure I.2**) reputedly included footage of a train pulling into a station that had the poor naive audience diving to the floor in panic, believing a real train was headed their way. Louis Lumière evidently grew quickly tired of this spectacle, famously declaring a short time later, "The cinema is an invention without a future."

Figure I.3 A torture device? Only to the operator. An optical printer such as this one was the sole means of compositing film prior to the digital age, a painstaking and perfectionistic practice.

Figure I.2 The Lumière borthers. Louis Lumière famously declared, "The cinema is an invention without a future."

Enter the color desktop computer, then Adobe Photoshop, then After Effects, and suddenly anyone with a few thousand bucks for equipment, or access to borrow it, could have a go at creating a visual effects shot. And have a go people did, creating visionary low-budget videos (as well as hundreds of *Star Wars* tribute films) and growing the professional visual effects community exponentially.

Yet the old cultish attitudes in many ways prevailed during the early digital era. Sure, lots of kids proved that they could produce a convincing lightsaber battle on the family computer, but try to learn how to create an elaborate effects shot by reading up on it and the response was made up of smoke, mirrors, vagaries, and what has quickly become a cliché of *Cinefex* magazine (once full of nitty-gritty details, in the pre-digital era): the use of "proprietary software." Visual effects work might as well have *been* magic because it seemed to be made up of a bunch of exacting techniques crafted by super-geniuses and jealously guarded as trade secrets.

Fast forward to today, and a recent survey by an Adobe product manager turned up over 250 Hollywood features that had relied on After Effects, despite that it may not be the first compositing application that comes to everyone's mind for feature film work. Stu Maschwitz, author of Chapter 15, "Learning to See," led the Rebel Mac group at Industrial Light + Magic for several years in the 1990s; their use of After Effects on big-budget, Academy-nominated effects films was largely unpublicized, mostly due to the perception (even among film studios) that only "big iron" was up to work of that caliber.

Truly Challenging

Ironically indeed, visual effects artists themselves often underestimate (and underbid) the complications involved in crafting a shot; once a difficult shot is declared a final, one's memory is often a blur of long days spent making subtle corrections to create dozens of takes of a few seconds of film. The individual steps seem at that stage almost unremarkable and trivial, but a complex shot might

NOTES

Metaphorically speaking, this book teaches the fundamentals of magic tricks, the visual effects equivalents of hiding a card or palming a coin. If your goal is to be the Harry Houdini or David Blaine of compositing, begin by mastering the basics that come up again and again, those effects that are often ingredients in the most original and fantastic visual sequences.

consist of hundreds or even thousands of such steps, many of which were, at some stage, surprising and revelatory to any artist, no matter how smart and sophisticated. Nobody is born knowing how to do this stuff.

Also, each visual effects shot seems to be unique, and in many ways, it is. Explaining the exact steps to create one shot may be of little use when it comes time to create the next one. Some bread-and-butter techniques, however, are done similarly at every studio and are no one's trade secret. These come up all the time, sometimes as a component of a larger and more complex shot, sometimes as the main focus of a simple shot. Every compositing artist should know how to do them.

This book is about those kinds of effects; ultimately, it is about the process of building them up to create a shot that is greater than the sum of its parts and fools the eye of the viewer.

All visual effects can be broken down into comprehensible components (although, to comprehend some of the components might very well also require an understanding of wave dynamics or Fourier transforms). Moreover, very few (even simple) effects can be called complete without being refined much further than the novice artist is typically willing to go.

This brings us to the keys to creating the best visual effects, those that are often pretty close to invisible and call no attention to themselves whatsoever. They do not detract from the story, but enhance it, and only later on do you wonder, "How the heck did they do that?"

The Keys

You do it by following some simple guidelines—simple, yet so important in delineating your success or failure as an effects compositor. The keys are

- ▶ **Get reference.** You can't re-create what you can't see clearly and in great detail. Great artists recognize many features of the world that the untrained eye fails to see.

▶ **Simpler is often better.** Effects compositing is complicated enough without the addition of convoluted processes and needless extra steps. To very loosely paraphrase Einstein, a robust effects pipeline should be made up of solutions that are as simple as possible, but no simpler.

▶ **Break it down.** More than anything, novices try to solve problems using a single solution, applied globally to the whole shot or one of its elements. For example, beginners (and even many pros) do not examine individual color channels when matching foreground and background colors; looking at the individual channels is demonstrated in Chapter 5, "Color Correction," to be essential to a realistic composite. And if this advice applies to something so fundamental as color matching, you'd better believe it applies to more complex effects as well.

▶ **It's not good enough.** My old colleague Paul Topolos (at this writing employed in the art department at Pixar) used to say that "recognizing flaws in your work doesn't mean you're a bad artist. It only means you have taste." Remember that flawed intermediate versions of any work of art are almost always part of the journey to the version that the public is allowed to see.

Plus, if you let your guard down and settle for "good enough," someone's going to say it…

"That Looks Fake"

No doubt you've heard that utterance, perhaps blurted out flatly by a teenage kid sitting behind you at the multiplex? That kid is not always even correct (I've heard this label slapped on a shot that I knew had no visual effects), but to fool the skeptical viewer, you may as well welcome the sentiment.

A little bit of that petulant teen lives in all of us, after all. Ideally the statement will evolve to "That looks fake because…" with you able to complete the phrase using your eyes, your observations of the world and those of your colleagues, and information from a source like this book.

A somewhat more civilized version of that rude teenager shows up at dailies on a feature film effects project, but with the title of Visual Effects Supervisor. Here's how dailies generally go: At the start of a workday, a bunch of people get some coffee, stumble into a dark screening room, watch a shot more times in a minute or two than the average audience will watch it in a lifetime (unless of course it's a shot from *Star Wars*), and you are told why it doesn't look right. It sounds like a harsh way to start the day, but actually, this is absolutely where the real process of doing great work is rooted.

Relentless dissatisfaction, then, is one of the keys to successful visual effects. Try not to confuse it with actual discouragement, no matter how harsh your own (or someone else's) criticism.

What Compositing Can (and Can't) Do

The type of full visual effects pipeline used to produce a big-budget feature film contains many roles and specializations; depending on your point of view and on the shot in question, the compositor's role can be considered the most crucial. Typically, with the possible exception of a colorist, the compositor is the last one to touch the shot before it goes in the movie.

To a large extent, a composite is only as good as the sum of its elements. The best compositors have a reputation for producing gold out of dross, building a great-looking shot despite poorly shot plates and slap-dash 3D elements. But compositors still need elements to do their work, and poorly shot or created elements typically lead to an equally poor result.

If you're still learning how to composite, you may be working solo, and creating all of your elements yourself. That's great practice even if you end up specializing as a compositor. For example, it's essential that you understand how the camera gathers images so you can mimic the reality created by a camera. If you're comfortable as a 3D animator, those skills will help you navigate the 3D capabilities of After Effects. Knowing both skills can save lots of time by allowing you to fine-tune computer-generated shots in 2D, rather than tweaking them endlessly in 3D render after 3D render. For that reason in particular, there is often an overlap between 3D lighting and compositing; many artists are good at both.

This book teaches you techniques to faithfully re-create phenomena from the world around you, such as a camera would gather, but it also teaches you how to cheat in order to make your shot even more believable.

About This Book

After Effects 7.0 Studio Techniques will help you toward more believable shots in many ways, but it is not intended to help you create your first After Effects project. It is the textbook that I didn't have when I taught the Introduction to Visual Effects course at the Academy of Art University in San Francisco. My students were familiar with how to use After Effects but had not yet put it to work finishing shots.

If you're new to After Effects, first spend some time with its excellent documentation or check out one of the many books available to help beginners learn to use After Effects, such as *After Effects 7 for Windows and Macintosh: Visual QuickPro Guide* (Anthony Bolante, Peachpit Press), *Adobe After Effects 7 Hands-On Training* (Lynda Weinman, Peachpit Press; available in summer 2006), and *Adobe After Effects 7.0 Classroom in a Book* (Adobe Press).

If, however, you're moderately comfortable with After Effects, or with compositing in general, and you want to take your visual effects work to the next level, read on. This book was written for you.

After Effects 7.0 Studio Techniques is organized into three sections:

▶ **Section I, "Working Foundations,"** reviews fundamentals of After Effects to help you to work smarter and more efficiently. You'll explore how to make the best use of the program's core features, including the new Graph Editor, and how to optimize your workflow. Even if you already are an experienced After Effects artist, skim this section for tips and tricks you might not have known or have forgotten.

▶ **Section II, "Effects Compositing Essentials,"** focuses on the core techniques required for effects compositing: color matching, keying, rotoscoping, motion tracking, and emulating a physical camera. For example, there is deep discussion of how the Levels effect and Keylight contribute to the essential work of visual effects. This section also tackles a couple of topics that other books would consider too complicated for average users: the use of expressions and how to work with film source and linear floating point compositing using new 32 bit-per-channel features.

▶ **Section III, "Creative Explorations,"** demonstrates actual effects and looks at the phenomena you might wish to re-create, taking observations of how these things look in the natural world. Most importantly, you'll learn how to apply that understanding to your shot.

What you won't find in these sections are menu-by-menu descriptions of the interface or step-by-step tutorials that walk you through projects with little connection to real-world visual effects needs.

Understanding Is Preferable to Knowledge

The goal of *After Effects 7.0 Studio Techniques* is to help you understand how the world within After Effects works and how it corresponds to the physical world you are attempting to re-create.

Your goal should be to apply what you learn here to your own shots and continue to expand your knowledge. By understanding how things work, not by mimicking prearranged steps, you will truly learn to do this work on your own. Compositing is the methodical buildup of individual component steps, steps that recur in unique combinations on each individual shot and project. This book offers advice on those steps. Putting them all together for your individual shot is up to you and your team.

If You've Used Other Compositing Programs

The impetus to write this book grew largely from my experience as "The After Effects Guy" on various projects. On *The Day After Tomorrow*, for example, I joined a team of veteran freelance compositors at The Orphanage, few of whom had ever used After Effects. They were far more experienced with Apple's Shake, Digital Domain's Nuke, and Discreet's Flame. My role was not only to complete my own shots but also to help debug their problems using After Effects, freeing the compositing supervisor's time.

This double duty helped me gain a perspective on what is confusing about After Effects to people who otherwise understand compositing well. Believe it or not, compositing programs do not vary as much in their fundamental workflow as, say, 3D animation programs do. Although After Effects appears to operate completely differently than Shake, Nuke, Flame, Toxic, and other node-based applications, the fundamental differences are relatively few. To summarize, they are

▶ **Render order in After Effects is established on the Timeline and via precomposing.** The clearest distinction between After Effects and its node-based brethren is its lack of a tree/node interface. Open Project Flowchart view and you see that, under the hood, After Effects tracks rendering order works the same way as these other applications (**Figure I.4**). After Effects, however, doesn't let you interact this way. (See Chapter 2, "The Timeline," and Chapter 4, "Optimizing Your Projects.")

▶ **Transforms, effects, and masks become part of a layer and render in a set order.** In After Effects, layers have properties that belong only to them. To an After Effects user, the Shake method of applying a transform to a clip, rather than simply animating a layer's Position property, is a little hard to get used to (**Figure I.5**). On the other hand, as is explained in Chapter 4, After Effects sometimes enforces a specific order in which certain properties render, and you need to know what that is.

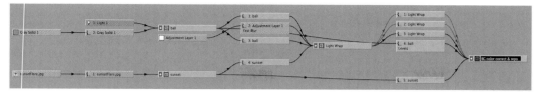

Figure I.4 Project Flowchart view is perhaps the least familiar After Effects view; many users hardly know it even exists.

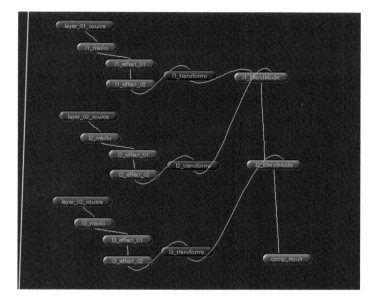

Figure I.5 A Shake node flow re-creates the set order (masks, effects, transforms, and finally Blending modes) in After Effects for a three-layer composite. (Image courtesy Stu Maschwitz.)

▶ **After Effects, like other Adobe applications, tends to "think" in terms of four channels: red, green, blue, and alpha (or transparency).** This is a subtle one, but the distinction plays out as soon as you start creating selections for layers (see Chapter 3, "Selections: The Key to Compositing"). Node-based applications tend to encourage you to think of mattes as luminance data, which they are. Like Photoshop, however, After Effects retains through its pipeline the persistent idea of a fourth color channel, the alpha channel, which controls transparency. You will have more success working with After Effects if you are willing to work on building alpha channels rather than combinations of luminance data for transparency.

▶ **After Effects operates natively in straight alpha mode, and it handles the conversion from straight to premultiplied alpha internally.** Not only does After Effects have a persistent idea of an alpha channel, but internally, it is always working with that alpha in straight mode. Chapter 3 covers the few provisions available to deal explicitly with premultiplication inside of After Effects.

▶ **There is, alas, no direct equivalent in After Effects to macros.** If you've never used an application like Shake, you don't know what you're missing. If you've gone far enough with the node-based application to write your own macros, however, After Effects may leave you scratching your head. It offers little in the way of direct pixel calculation and no way to batch process images via a script. The workarounds typically involve effect plug-ins and precomposing.

▶ **Temporal and spatial settings tend to be absolute in After Effects.** Many differences between After Effects and the node-based applications contain both benefits and pitfalls. If you need to carefully manage timing and spatial data (animation), the After Effects Timeline offers huge advantages. On the other hand, all layers contain spatial and timing information relative to their composition. In other words, if you create a cool effect on the adjustment layer of a video resolution comp, and then copy the adjustment layer to a longer film-resolution comp, the layer won't cover the whole frame, nor will it last the duration of the new comp. This is something you don't typically have to think about in a node-based application.

Of these differences, some are arbitrary, most are a mixed bag of advantages and drawbacks, and a couple of them are constantly used by the competition as a metaphorical stick with which to beat After Effects. The two that come up the most are the handling of precomposing and the lack of macros.

This book attempts to shed light on these and other areas of After Effects that are not explicitly dealt with in its user interface or documentation. The truth is that Shake, Nuke, and others require that you understand their own rules, such as the need to manage premultiplication in your pipeline, in order to master them. After Effects spares you details that as a casual user, you might never need to know about, but that as a professional user you should understand thoroughly. This book is here to help.

What's On the DVD

If you want to find out more about some of the plug-ins and software mentioned in this book, look no further than its DVD-ROM. For example, the disc includes demos of

- Adobe After Effects 7.0
- Andersson Technologies' SynthEyes (3D tracking software)
- Plug-ins from Trapcode, including Particular and Lux
- Red Giant Software's Primatte, Magic Bullet, Knoll Light Factory, Key Correct, Instant HD, and Film Fix
- SilhouetteFX (rotoscope, paint, and tracking software)
- Reel Smart Motion Blur from Revision FX
- Erodilation and CopyImage from ObviousFX

You'll also find HD footage from Artbeats and Pixel Corps with which you can experiment and practice your techniques; for more such footage, see www.artbeats.com and www.pixelcorps.com. Finally, there are dozens of example files to help you deconstruct the techniques described.

The Bottom Line

Just like the debates about which operating system is best, debates about which compositing software is tops are largely meaningless—especially when you consider the number of first-rate, big-budget, movie effects extravaganzas that were created on three or four different platforms, with half a dozen 2D and 3D programs. If the proof of the pudding is in the eating, the consistent quality of effects in such films as *The Day After Tomorrow*, which used a variety of programs and effects houses, should show that it is the *artists* not the tools who make the biggest difference.

I like using After Effects, because I have come to think in the same way the software lays out my shots; it's no longer work, it's instinct. The goal of this book is to help you reach that point as well.

To install these files, simply copy each chapter folder in its entirety to your hard drive. Note that all .aep files are located in the Projects subfolder of each chapter folder on the disc, while .ffx files can be found in the animation Presents subfolders.

If you have comments or questions you'd like to share with the author, please e-mail them to AEStudioTechniques@gmail.com.

SECTION I

Working Foundations

Chapter 1   The 7.0 Workflow   3

Chapter 2   The Timeline   57

Chapter 3   Selections: The Key to Compositing   103

Chapter 4   Optimizing Your Projects   135

1

The 7.0 Workflow

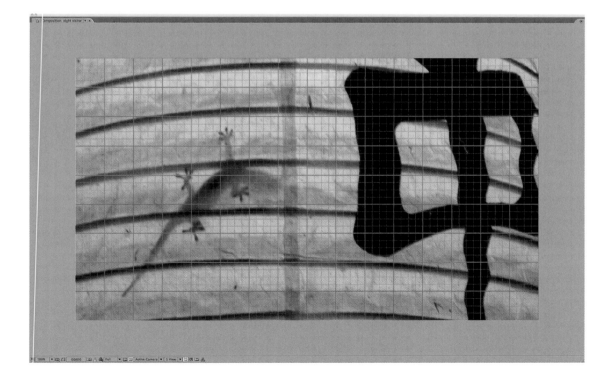

Good surfing is power, speed, and flow. The rest of it doesn't matter to me at all.

—Gary Elkerton, Australian surfer

The 7.0 Workflow

Version 7.0 may be remembered as the most radical upgrade to Adobe After Effects to date, because it includes a complete overhaul of the user interface. Although this new version of After Effects will not be completely unfamiliar to anyone who has used previous versions of the application, everything will, at first, seem a little bit different in this version.

Like every other compositing program available today, After Effects is a project-based, non-destructive image editor. In other words, the basic workflow of After Effects is that you import such resources as footage, still images, and audio and work to create compositions, which are combinations of those resources. When you save, the resources themselves are unaffected; you create new shots by rendering them to an entirely new file.

The big advantage of After Effects 7.0 is that it is more streamlined, and this chapter focuses on how to make your own workflow habits more efficient and effective within it. This first chapter is a different beast from the openers of most other books out there; it assumes you already know your way around the basics of After Effects and are ready to learn to work smarter. So, even if you're an experienced After Effects artist, keep reading. You may discover techniques and options you did not even know were available to you. I encourage you to look through this chapter and the rest of Section I carefully for new ideas about working with After Effects.

TIP

If this book opens at too advanced a level for you, check out *Adobe After Effects 7.0 Classroom in a Book* (Adobe Press) and *After Effects 7.0 for Windows and Macintosh: Visual QuickPro Guide* (Peachpit Press), two helpful beginner's resources.

Workspaces and Panels

When you see After Effects 7.0 for the first time, the most surprising thing is what you don't see, especially if you're familiar with previous versions. Parts of your desktop or other open applications no longer can peek in between various floating windows and palettes; instead, the user interface is unified into a single, coherent environment that is fully customizable.

Before we look at how to use this new interface, it is helpful to define what is here. **Figure 1.1** shows the Standard workspace that appears when you first open After Effects 7.0. The interface consists of one main *application window*; on the Mac, this window contains the name of the open project, and on Windows it also includes the menu bar. It is possible to create additional *floating windows*; more on this in a bit.

Both types of windows contain *frames*, separated by *dividers*. Each frame contains one or more *panels*. If a frame contains multiple panels, the tab of each panel can be seen at the top, but only the contents of the forward tab can be seen. To bring a panel forward, you click on its tab.

Some panels are *viewers*; these include a pull-down menu in the tab that lets you choose the content displayed. These also include a *lock* option (specified via a small lock icon, also in the tab) that prevents that panel from switching to a different display automatically; more on this feature follows further on.

Now, to put these definitions in context, look more closely at Figure 1.1. The Standard workspace contains the bones of an entire project:

▶ **Project panel:** Contains all of the resources used in your compositions (source footage, stills, solids that you create, audio, even the compositions themselves).

▶ **Composition panel:** Is the viewer where you perform the predominant visual work of assembling a shot.

▶ **Timeline panel:** Organizes the elements that go into the individual composition (otherwise known as a shot).

▶ **Info, Audio, Time Controls, and Effects & Presets panels:** Help you work with your compositions.

How much time and effort was wasted over the years by After Effects artists moving palettes around to see what they needed? We'll never know, but the days of juggling windows are banished to the sands of time for anyone who upgrades to 7.0.

All available panels in After Effects are listed under the Window menu; some even list preset keyboard shortcuts for rapid access. These panels used to be actual floating windows, but Adobe decided not to change the name of the menu, as it is standard across many applications.

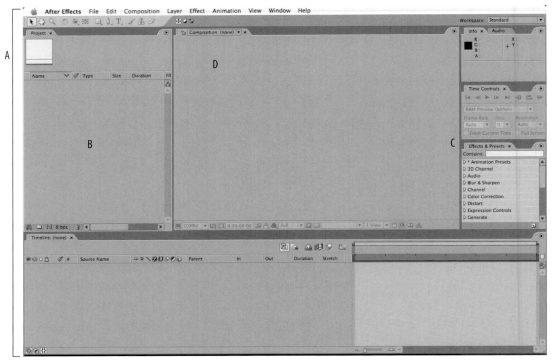

Figure 1.1 The Standard workspace layout is all contained in a single application window (A). The frame containing the Project panel (B) is currently active, as indicated by the yellow highlight around the panel's border. Dividers such as the long one (C) between the Composition panel and the smaller panels at the right separate the frames. The tab of the Composition viewer (D) includes a pull-down menu for choosing a particular composition, and a lock icon for keeping that composition forward regardless of what else is clicked.

Figure 1.1 uses darker user interface colors than are displayed in After Effects by default. The User Interface Brightness control resides in Preferences > User Interface Colors.

The basic workflow of After Effects, then, is to create a new composition, typically containing items from the Project panel, and to work with it in the Composition and Timeline viewers.

To see the full story of the After Effects workflow, however, you can use the Workspace pull-down to switch to the All Panels layout. This reveals lots of little collapsed panels for various tools such as the paint tools (Paint and Brush Tips), the type tools (Character and Paragraph), the motion tracker (Tracker Controls), and so on.

Look closely at the workspace, and you will see the other key pieces of the After Effects workflow: the Effect Controls, for adding specific effects to layers; the Layer and Footage palettes, for working with an individual layer in a composition or viewing source footage; the Flowchart view, which provides a node-based overview of a project; and the Render Queue, where you output your work. All of these are empty now, and so they give you no context for what they do; this chapter will provide that context.

The All Panels layout is not particularly useful—it's crowded with panels you may never use—but it provides a glimpse of what all is available in the After Effects user interface. Adobe set other default workspaces to antici- pate common usages of After Effects: Animation, Effects, Motion Tracking, Paint, and Text. The Minimal workspace consists only of Timeline and Composition panels (where you'll do most of your work).

There is even something of an escape hatch back to the After Effects of old. The Undocked panel floats the three main informational panels, and it is possible to make floating windows of all of the panels in After Effects for those stubborn souls who desperately miss the full 6.5 (and earlier) experience. Before you make a big mess for nostalgia's sake, however, consider what comprises the interface and how you go about customizing it, whether for a tiny laptop or multiple monitors.

Customizing Your Workspace

Workspaces used to be an underused feature in After Effects, but now they have taken center stage. Quite likely, however, you will end up customizing your workspaces to differ, slightly or radically, from what ships with version 7.0. The best way to do this is to mess around with the user interface yourself, but here are some pointers you might miss with such an approach.

Docking, Grouping, Rearranging, Resizing Panels

In case you haven't already figured it out, each panel in After Effects is labeled via a tab at the upper left, which contains the title of the panel, an x to close the panel (to the right of the title), and a little grip area at the left of the title (**Figure 1.2**). At the upper right is a smaller tab with another grip area and a triangular icon for the panel's context menu.

In this discussion, it is assumed that you have not yet customized any of the After Effects Workspaces. If what you see when you choose a Workspace doesn't match what is described here, you can use Window > Workspace > Reset to bring a given workspace back to its previous settings (although if you have saved over any of the defaults, you will see the saved version).

To make any panel a floating window, hold down the Ctrl/Cmd key while dragging its tab away from its host panel.

TIP

Although overlooked in the documentation, the four drop zones at the edges of the After Effects window cause the panel being dragged to occupy that entire side of the interface. So if, for example, you want the Timeline to fill the bottom portion of your screen, even below several other panels, move it down to the very bottom of the application window until you see a teal-colored drop zone appear across the bottom edge, and drop it.

Figure 1.2 The active tab, for the Effect Controls panel, includes grip areas at the left of each tab section for dragging the panel and an x to close it. At the far right is the panel menu icon, which reveals a context menu. Because this panel is used to contain effects for any layer, it includes a pull-down menu (to specify which one) and a lock (to keep the current one active). Also in this frame is the Project panel, which does not contain these extras.

Those grip areas are your target for clicking and dragging a panel to another location in the user interface (UI). In any workspace, try dragging a panel. (Don't worry, instructions to reset your workspace follow.) As you move it over another panel, you see geometric shapes like those in **Figure 1.3**. These are the drop zones, allowing your panel to occupy the space directly above, below, left, or right of the panel. If you drop at the center or in the zone at the very top, along the tabs, it is grouped with the target panel.

If you hold your pointer on the border between two panels, you will see it become a divider dragger (**Figure 1.4**). This allows you to resize the adjacent panels. But if you want the panel you are working with to take up a much larger amount of space for a moment, there is a better option.

The tilde key (~) toggles whichever panel is currently active (indicated by the yellow line around its border) to take over the entire After Effects window. You will use this shortcut a *lot* as you work with compositions, regardless of your monitor size; its most prominent use is to reveal more of the image in your Composition or Layer view, free of the rest of the interface.

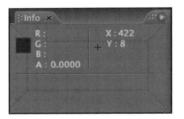

Figure 1.3 Six possible drop areas are shown over the Info panel. Dropping on the center or along the top has the same result: grouping the dropped panel in the same frame as Info; dropping in any of the other four positions the dropped panel just to that side of Info.

Figure 1.4 The border icon appears to indicate that you can offset the border between sets of frames, causing some panels to expand and others to contract.

Figure 1.5 Highlighted is the scrollbar, which subtly appears atop a frame that contains too many panels to be displayed together horizontally. There is no vertical equivalent in 7.0.

Floating Panels and Multiple Monitors

Because I typically prefer a multiple-monitor setup for After Effects, I was dismayed (at first) that After Effects is now self-contained in a single window. Two monitors are not always the same dimensions, and even when they are, spanning two displays with a single window usually becomes a real pain.

That's why I was relieved to discover that you can tear off any panel and make it float, the way all of the windows and palettes of After Effects used to do. Holding down the **Ctrl/Cmd** key as you drag a panel causes it to occupy a floating window.

If you are really nostalgic for the way After Effects used to work, you can even tear off every panel, giving each its own floating window. I don't recommend it, but there are bound to be diehards. More useful is to tear off a window that you only use occasionally—say, the Render Queue (**Figure 1.6**)—so that it only appears when you request it (using the keyboard shortcut **Ctrl+Alt+0/Cmd+Option+0** in the case of the Render Queue).

When too many panels are grouped together in one area to see all of their titles, a slider bar appears above them, allowing you to scroll back and forth among them. It's very small and can easily escape notice (**Figure 1.5**).

When dragged to an area of your desktop beyond the After Effects window, the panel will tear off without the need for any modifier key.

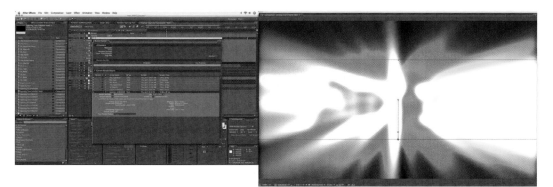

Figure 1.6 Even if you are using two monitors of differing sizes, you can smoothly make use of both of them by tearing off one or more panels into a separate floating window that occupies the second monitor. You can also make the Render Queue, which is typically used only when you are done working, its own floating window, closed during normal use.

CLOSE-UP

Full Screenery

When you tear off a panel and move it to a second monitor as a floating window, you may notice that it lacks the Zoom button along the top to send the window to full screen.

The shortcut **Ctrl+\ (Cmd+\)** can zoom the window instead. If the selected floating window is not occupying the full borders of the screen (or has been moved or offset), pressing the shortcut keys maximizes the window. If you press again, the shortcut toggles off the top menu bar, filling the entire screen with the window. This also works with the main UI window; if you don't like seeing the top of your monitor taken up by the After Effects menu bar, you can use **Ctrl+\ (Cmd+\)** to maximize the entire UI.

It is not uncommon these days to preview to a monitor that shares at least one dimension with your footage. For example, I often work with HD footage (1920 x 1080) on a set of 1920 x 1200 monitors. To see my Composition panel at 100% on one of those monitors, I make it a floating window and then use this shortcut.

As is noted later, you can always RAM Preview in full-screen mode by checking the Full Screen box in the Time Controls.

Saving and Resetting Workspaces

There is no undo available when you rearrange panels. You can reset any given workspace, however, by choosing the Reset option at the bottom of the Workspace menu.

If you've switched back and forth between custom workspaces, you have probably noticed that all of the changes you make to a given workspace persist with it. If you make a complete mess of Standard and switch to Effects, then back to Standard, it's still the exact mess that you left it. If you're used to the old workspaces of version 6.5 and earlier, this is at first dismaying, until you notice that Reset option.

If you never choose Reset, your customizations will remain, at least until your preferences are reset or you inadvertently change them. For that reason, if you come up with a customization you like, save it (using the New Workspace option in the Workspace menu). You'll probably want to save at least one workspace whose proportions and orientation to your monitor setup suits you best, and if you change your mind, you can always save over it or delete it.

Those are the basics of the new user interface; in other contexts, you will investigate some of the cooler enhancements that have been added to it, such as multiple views in a single composition viewer (Chapter 9, "Virtual Cinematography"), the viewer lock, and "ETLAT" (Chapter 4, "Optimizing Your Projects").

Making the Most of the UI

Because this book is tailored toward the experienced digital artist, the focus turns now to some of the nicest workflow enhancements in After Effects. These are the features and work habits that are routinely missed by beginners, but for experts, they are some of the features we would be most reluctant to give up, because they make using the program more effortless.

Often, the complaints lodged by artists who are used to a competing application result from the fact that they are trying to work the same exact way they would work in Apple's Shake or eyeon Software's Fusion. This is a similar mistake to translating words directly to another language in order to speak it; it ignores the colorful, time-tested idioms that are particular to the new system.

Well, you get the idea.

Importing Source

The way to get started in After Effects is generally to import source footage—stills, sequences, and movies, as well as other types of source such as audio tracks or Photoshop compositions—and then to place that footage into a composition, which is where much of the real work is centered in After Effects.

There are several methods to import source. The most obvious of these is to use File > Import; new in After Effects 7.0 is the File > Import Recent Footage option, which remembers the last 10 items imported into After Effects.

Unlike some other video and compositing applications, After Effects does not recognize an image sequence as being a single clip, but version 7.0 is smarter about sequences than previous versions. By default, a numbered sequence of still images causes the Sequence box in the Import File dialog to be checked. However, if you make a habit of unchecking this box several times in a row, After Effects will memorize this as a preference and leave the box unchecked.

The Force alphabetical order option available with sequences in Import File causes After Effects to fill in placeholder files for any numbered stills missing from the sequence; thus, if the sequence contains only odd-numbered stills, the even numbered ones will be added as placeholders (and the clip will in that case be twice as long as it would be without this option). This is useful when you are using a temporary render (say, at half frame rate) that will be replaced later on.

The most popular shortcut for importing is to drag footage directly into After Effects, and in 7.0 this will work no matter where in the open project you drag the footage—it doesn't have to be dragged specifically to the Project panel. To drag a sequence into After Effects, drag in the folder containing the sequence while holding the control (command) key.

TIP

You can delete any workspace (except the one you have currently selected) with the Delete Workspace command in the Workspace menu. If you inadvertently blow away one of the ones that ships with After Effects, you can either create a new one with the same name (which will restore its shortcut, if it had one) or reset your preferences (hold down **Shift+Ctrl+Alt/ Shift+Cmd+Option** at startup, but remember that **all** of your preferences will be reset).

TIP

You can use Force alphabetical order to make a full-length placeholder for a sequence that hasn't even been rendered. All you need are representations of the first and last numbered files and this option will fill in placeholders for the rest. That way, if you know that a sequence is going to be rendered overnight and ready in the morning, you can get your project ready for it.

Figure 1.7 Look closely at how this project is organized and you will see a few helpful decisions that have been made. The main folders are numbered to show in which order they are used in the overall process, and they and their items are color coded. Source footage is placed directly into source compositions, which contain only that footage (for easy replacement as needed); likewise, special output compositions contain the settings (work area, dimensions, and so on) needed for output to specific formats (although for some artists this may seem like overkill, it can avoid rendering mistakes).

The Well-Organized Project

Okay, so admittedly, this section sounds like the "keep your room clean" segment. However, if you work with other people, and you want to work with them again, sharing projects that are clearly organized is one sure-fire way to get invited back. Beyond that, by maintaining a clearly organized project you can:

▶ Avoid frustration and wasted time hunting for an element in your project.

▶ Help (and gain the respect of) someone else who might have to inherit your project or refer back to it.

▶ Help yourself think clearly through the steps of your composition. In a complex project, a well-organized Project panel can actually help you in the same way that a disciplined crew helps you on a film shoot.

▶ Prevent rendering errors (more on this in "Output: The Render Queue").

Suppose that a simple project uses some source footage, a main composition, a couple of pre-comps, some reference footage, and at least one solid layer. For this project, I might propose a project organization along the lines of the one shown in **Figure 1.7**; each type of item resides in its own folder. Only the main composition resides in the root area of the project, and its main components are organized according to how they are used. An artist unfamiliar with the project could immediately begin investigating it in this hierarchical fashion. Projects included with this book follow an organization something like this.

On larger and more ambitious projects shared by several artists, it is typical to create a project template that anticipates a certain workflow, so that items are easy to find in predictable locations. Chapter 4 offers an example of such a template and demonstrates how to work with multiple compositions.

Context-Clicking (and Keyboard Shortcuts)

Throughout this book you will see references to *context-clicking* on interface items. I would prefer to call it right-clicking, but the Mac has only just begun to ship with a multi-button "Mighty Mouse" (although pretty much every

Mac-based artist I know has one). Therefore, on the Mac, to get the same effect without a right mouse button, you must hold down the Control key while clicking. I myself face this issue when working on a vintage Powerbook.

After Effects does not let you take your hands off the mouse very often; many important operations are not possible with keyboard shortcuts alone. Although I highly advocate learning and using keyboard shortcuts wherever possible and offer effective keyboard shortcuts throughout the book, I advocate context-clicking just as strongly because it keeps the mouse always in your hand, engaged in the process.

Between keyboard shortcuts and context menus, an advanced user may almost never visit the menu bar in After Effects. The amount of mouse dragging and clicking I've saved might not stretch from my studio to the moon, but it certainly does add up.

I actively encourage you to choose context-clicking and shortcuts over the menu bar whenever possible. There are dozens of context menus available, too many to discuss in detail without boring the pants off of you. **Figures 1.8a, b,** and **c** display some of the menus I use all of the time in the Project and Timeline panels.

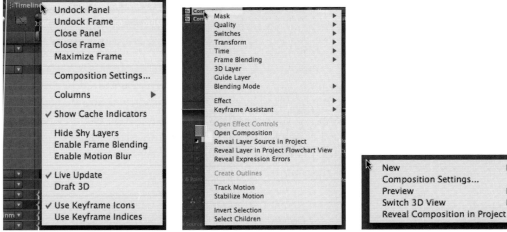

Figures 1.8a, b, and c Context menus are everywhere your cursor is, and for that reason, very effective. Context-click the tab of the Timeline panel (a), and you will see very different selections than if you context-click a layer in that panel (b), or the empty space below the layers (c). Depending on whether a layer is a camera, a solid, or footage, different options will appear, as well.

Besides context menus, After Effects also includes panel menus; these are the ones you reach via the little triangular icon at the upper right of each panel. I don't believe there is any function that is contained only in those menus, but you may find them an intuitive place to look for settings related to that palette.

Redundancy is a great thing about the After Effects interface that is often overlooked. There is almost always more than one way to get at the same setting or command, allowing you to develop your own preference.

Keeping Sources Linked

Because After Effects requires the presence of source footage files to operate properly, it's necessary to understand what to do when source footage files become unlinked. This problem arises particularly when you move a project from one location on your drive to another, to another drive, or to another computer or server altogether.

Should a footage item become unlinked, and you know where the source is located, or you can search for it on your drive, the solution is fairly simple. To try this on your own, drag any .aep file from the book's disc to your drive without any of its accompanying source footage.

You can choose your favorite method to bring up the Replace Footage File dialog among these:

> ▶ Double-click the missing footage item in the Project panel

> ▶ Context-click the missing footage, choose Replace Footage, and then choose File

> ▶ Highlight the missing footage, and press **Ctrl+H/Cmd+H**

In the Replace Footage File dialog, navigate to and choose the missing footage item (**Figure 1.9**). True, you are replacing a file with what it should have been all along, but After Effects understands this and will even help you by relinking other files in the same folder if it notices them.

TIP

To reload footage that was updated in the background after you opened your project, highlight the item and choose Reload Footage from the context menu (or **Ctrl+Alt+L/Cmd+Option+L**). After Effects avoids, where possible, re-reading a file on your drive or server, caching it instead. This command refreshes the cache.

NOTES

Probably for your own protection, you are not allowed to apply Replace Footage to multiple items; you must replace them one at a time.

Figure 1.9 Missing footage appears with a small color bar icon. In the File Path column, After Effects also displays the path where the file was expected to be, which can help when searching on a drive or network for a missing, unlinked file.

Should you receive a warning on opening a project that a file or files are missing, but you don't know which ones (sometimes a project is too big or complex to spot them easily), use the binoculars icon at the bottom of your Project panel (**Figure 1.10**). Leave the text field blank but check the Find Missing Footage box, and After Effects will search through your project for items that have become unlinked. Repeat as needed. It's not sophisticated, but it works.

Should a file refuse to relink (the selected item is gray and cannot be highlighted in the Replace Footage File dialog), After Effects is somehow not recognizing the footage as its intended format. There are a few potential causes, but the most common is simply moving a project from Mac to Windows, or vice versa. The simplest solution is to add a missing three-character extension to the file (for example, .jpg for a JPEG file). Note that this problem is not limited to Windows; when the headers are stripped from a file by transferring it via FTP or e-mail, OS X will fail to recognize it until the extension is restored.

If the file refuses to relink, even with the proper extension, it may have become corrupted, or it may be a file type that does not work equally well on Mac and Windows. For example, Mac PICT files don't read properly on Windows. To avoid this, it's best to use formats that are universally understood on all platforms, such as TIFF, TGA, PNG, or JPEG. (For more on choosing formats, see the section "Footage and Composition Settings.")

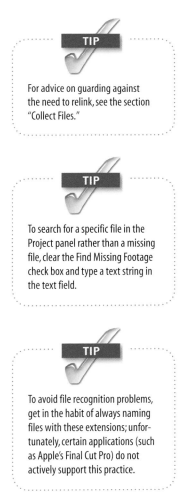

Figure 1.10 Click the binoculars icon at the lower left of the Project panel. In the dialog box that appears, check Find Missing Footage, entering nothing in the Find field. After Effects will sequentially search for unlinked files in your project, one at a time.

TIP

For advice on guarding against the need to relink, see the section "Collect Files."

TIP

To search for a specific file in the Project panel rather than a missing file, clear the Find Missing Footage check box and type a text string in the text field.

TIP

To avoid file recognition problems, get in the habit of always naming files with these extensions; unfortunately, certain applications (such as Apple's Final Cut Pro) do not actively support this practice.

Editing and Replacing Source

Perhaps you are working away in After Effects and notice a change that is needed in source material created or edited in another application. There is a shortcut for opening that file in the program that created it (according to its file tag): **Ctrl+E/Cmd+E.** You make your edits in the other application and save the result; After Effects checks to see if the file has been updated (by looking at the modification date, so remember to save after making your edits—unsaved changes will not appear) and imports the result. To try this out with a multiple-layer Photoshop source, open colors. aep in the accompanying disc's CH01 folder; apply the shortcut to one of the layers within the colors Layers folder. Make a simple change to the layer in Photoshop and save; the change should appear in After Effects.

Note, however, that several things can prevent this update from occurring. If you change any other layer and save, the update does not occur automatically but only on reloading; it is as if each layer of a multilayer document is a separate file. Furthermore, if you use Save As instead of Save for the external edit, you must replace the source to see it in After Effects.

Collect Files

Of course, a better approach is to avoid having to relink files at all, and elegant options are available for preparing After Effects projects and their source files to be moved or backed up. The old-fashioned way was to place the After Effects project in a master directory and all of its source files in subdirectories because this is how the program automatically searches for linked files (using relative, rather than absolute file paths). If you don't want to organize your files this way, however, consider the Collect Files alternative, which does this for you automatically. To try this feature, drag a number of source files into a project (or open one that already contains various sources) and choose File > Collect Files.

The Collect Files command was originally designed to support the Watch Folder command, which enables you to render an After Effects project on several machines (see Chapter 4). If you leave all the default settings for Collect Files and click the Collect button, you can select the location for creating a new folder that contains a copy of the project and all of its source files (**Figure 1.11**).

Figure 1.11 The Collect Files dialog includes several options. It's useful to select the final rendering composition prior to activating Collect Files if the project is complete— by then selecting Collect Source Files: For Selected Comps (and checking Reduce Project) you don't collect files you don't need. In the lower-left corner, is a summary of what will be collected, what is missing, and how many effects are employed; note that you can add comments.

This is incredibly useful for transporting or archiving After Effects projects and their source files, a "no file left behind" policy for your workflow. To streamline even further, you can reduce your project down to only the files that are used in existing compositions. Instead of leaving Collect Source Files set to All, choose a subset of files—only those used in comps in this project or in comps in the Render Queue, for example. Or you can select a composition prior to choosing Collect Files and reduce the project to only the files used in that one composition.

Import One Project into Another

The only way to join two separate .aep projects together in After Effects 7.0 is to import one project into the other. The imported project appears in its own folder (**Figure 1.12**) with the complete organization of its Project palette intact. Therefore, if you've been organizing your projects as is encouraged above, you will have overlapping folders (for source, precomps and solids, say) that you will have to integrate into the master project yourself.

Reduce Project and Consolidate All Footage

Reduce Project is available as a command under the File menu, in addition to being part of the Collect Files process, so you can engage its services at any time to clean up a project. Given a project with multiple compositions, select one of them and choose Reduce Project; After Effects removes all of the source files in the project that are not used in that comp (**Figure 1.13**). After Effects even lets you know (in a dialog) how many files were removed and reminds you of the ability to undo.

TIP

The Consolidate All Footage command always keeps the first instance of any recurring source file; therefore, to eliminate duplicate source elements before integrating an imported project, add a z at the beginning of its master folder name so that it moves to the bottom of the Project list.

Figure 1.12 The imported project folder contains subdirectories that are redundant to those in the master composition. After Effects offers no built-in quick fix to reorganize these.

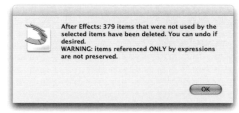

Figure 1.13 Do not be alarmed. After Effects is merely reminding you that the Reduce Project operation will remove items from the project (but not actually delete them from the source disk). The extra warning regarding expressions is pertinent only if you have linked a property's expression to a separate composition that is not otherwise used (a somewhat rare case).

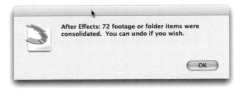

Figure 1.14 A similar warning appears when you choose File > Consolidate Footage, which looks for duplicate instances of the same source file in the project and chooses the first of these (in top-to-bottom order in the Project panel) to represent all instances.

But wait, that's not all. Just above Reduce Project in the File menu are a couple of other highly useful tools for cleaning up your project: Consolidate All Footage and Remove Unused Footage. Consolidate All Footage looks for two or more instances of the same source file and combines them, choosing the first instance, top to bottom, in the Project panel to replace all other instances (**Figure 1.14**). To try this, open any project and import that same project, so that all files have one redundant copy.

Alas, Consolidate All Footage does not eliminate solids clutter—the presence of several identical solids in the Solids folder of your project. After Effects assumes that you are keeping each instance unique so as not to inadvertently edit them all by changing one (despite also offering a check box in the Solid Footage Settings dialog to Affect All Layers that Use This Solid).

Remove Unused Footage does exactly as it says, ridding your project of all footage that is not included in any composition, regardless of what is selected when you activate the command.

Advanced Save Options

After Effects offers a couple of unique methods for saving your project, beyond a simple Save, Save As, or Save a Copy command.

The Increment and Save option attaches a version number to your saved project, or increments whatever number is at the end of the file name (before the .aep extension). This is a fantastic option if you are about to do something risky and potentially destructive with your project, although some artists are in the habit of always incrementing their saves, and never saving over a project file. There's little harm in that approach because .aep files tend to be small (unless they have a lot of paint effects in them), but it does yield quite a lot of files.

New with version 7.0 is the Project Auto-Save option. You won't find this option in the File menu with the other save options; instead, you control it via Preferences > Auto-Save, where it is toggled off by default (**Figure 1.15**). Check the box marked Automatically Save Projects and specify the period of time between automatic saves.

This feature works a little bit more elegantly than you might expect. Let's say you work a modest 10-hour day in After Effects; choosing the default 20-minute interval for Auto-Save would therefore save 30 versions of your file, which sounds like it would leave a big mess to clean up at the end of the day.

However, After Effects automatically creates a new folder called Adobe After Effects Auto-Save within the folder where your main project is saved. The project is incremented and saved within that folder, but the file you have open remains separate. The total number of incremented versions is limited depending on the value you enter for Maximum Project Versions; when you reach the specified maximum, After Effects deletes the oldest (lowest-numbered) file. Also, After Effects notices if you haven't made any changes to the project during the specified time period, and doesn't restart the clock until you do make changes, so you don't end up with a bunch of useless files if you forget to close the project during lunch.

Figure 1.15 A new feature in 7.0, easily missed, is housed in Preferences > Auto-Save; when activated, this feature creates auto-saved versions of the currently open project after the specified interval. There is very little reason not to use this feature, provided you don't mind some redundant copies of your project (which can easily be deleted when the project is completed).

At the end of the day, you still save over your master project, at which point you can pretty much ignore the Auto-Saved versions. They are there in case disaster strikes—a power outage, a tech support person kneeling into your reset button, a power supply suddenly failing. All of these have happened to me, and at The Orphanage, for example power outages seem to occur only at the most crucial times, in strict adherence to Murphy's Law (the full text of which, as my father likes to remind me, is "Anything that can go wrong will go wrong *at the worst possible moment*."). It's at such times that you realize how many artists, even seasoned pros, can work for several hours without remembering to save.

Settings: Project, Footage, Composition

Why devote a section to settings if After Effects does its best to automate them and keep them out of your direct attention? Because although automation is great, only you can get settings right every time. A misinterpreted alpha channel, nonsquare pixel footage interpreted as square, undetected scan lines, and similar issues will leave you fighting an uphill battle if you don't manage settings properly before you ever start assembling a composition. And new and changing formats merely increase the number of possible variables, some of which are completely new to version 7.0.

Project Settings

The Project Settings dialog (**Ctrl+Alt+Shift+K/Cmd+Option+Shift+K**) is easily overlooked by novice users. It controls the following within your project:

▶ The Timecode Base (default frames per second)

▶ How time is displayed (as timecode, frames, or the old-school filmic feet and frames option)

▶ Color Depth (8, 16, or 32 bits per channel), as well as new settings for the Working Space and handling of linear light (these are addressed in Chapter 11, "Film, HDR, and 32 Bit Compositing")

New to After Effects 7.0 is an Auto setting for Timecode Base; this is now the default setting. It used to be that you could choose only one Timecode Base setting for an entire project; if you imported 29.97 fps footage into a project set to 24 fps, the timelines would display 24 frames per second only, even in a 29.97 fps composition. This is no longer the case, and in this particular situation automation is a good thing.

Besides the Color Settings options (which are the tip of a rather large iceberg whose depths are plumbed in Chapter 11), the option worth knowing about here is the choice of displaying Timecode or Frames (Feet + Frames we will leave to those few souls still working with reels of physical film, probably for Scorsese or Spielberg). Most film-based projects will choose frames, while video people tend to think in terms of timecode. Furthermore, with the Frames option, you can specify a number at which the frames begin (the default is 0 but some crews prefer 1).

Even when you choose the Frames option, the timecode base of your individual composition displays beside the frame counter in the Timeline (**Figure 1.16**).

Interpret Footage

This book generally eschews the practice of taking you menu by menu through After Effects, but sometimes the UI perfectly encapsulates a given set of production challenges. The Interpret Footage dialog is one such case, a section-by-section checklist of all that can go wrong when you import footage: misinterpreted Alpha, incorrect frame rate, misadjusted Fields and Pulldown settings, incorrect Pixel Aspect Ratio, even misinterpreted ITU-R601 Luma Levels (which is quite a mouthful even on the printed page). To bring up the Interpret Footage dialog for a given clip, select it in the Project panel and press **Ctrl+F/Cmd+F** or context-click and select Interpret Footage > Main.

Alpha

Alpha settings are more complicated than you might think when it comes to compositing; most After Effects users have no idea just how complicated, in fact. **Figure 1.17** shows the most common symptom of a misinterpreted alpha

TIP

Why set Timecode Base to anything but Auto? It could be useful in situations where you want to compare times or durations for items with differing frame rates. With the Auto setting, you don't know if 0:00:01:15 means 1.5 seconds or 1 15/24 seconds without knowing the underlying frame rate.

00047 (24.00 fps)

Figure 1.16 The Timeline provides a constant reminder (in parentheses) of what frame rate is being used in the current project, regardless of how time is displayed (in this case, in frames, which tends to be standard for film work while timecode is more often used for video).

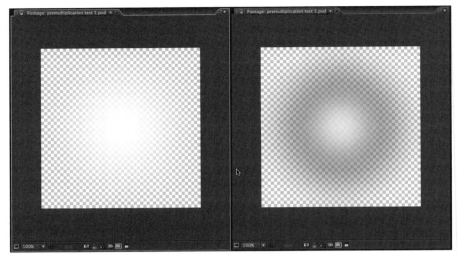

Figure 1.17 It's typically easy to distinguish a properly interpreted (left) from an incorrect alpha channel (right). The give-away is fringing, caused in this case by the failure to remove the background color from the edge pixels by unmultiplying them (with black). The left image is premultiplied, the right is straight.

channel, fringing. To try this example for yourself, import premultipliedAlpha.tif from the CH01 folder; try changing each from the correct "Premultiplied" setting to the incorrect (in this case) "Straight" setting.

For the time being, here are a couple pointers and reminders:

▶   If you're unclear about which type of alpha channel you're working with, click Guess in the Interpretation dialog that shows up when you import footage with alpha. This will often, but not always, get the setting right.

▶   Under Preferences > Import is a setting for how you want After Effects to handle footage that comes in with an alpha channel. Beware of setting this to anything besides Ask User until you are certain you know what you are doing with alpha channels and that circumstances aren't likely to change without you noticing.

For a more in-depth discussion of alpha channels and how they operate in the After Effects pipeline, see Chapter 3, "Selections: The Key to Compositing."

Frame Rate

The clearest symptom of an incorrectly set frame rate is footage that does not play smoothly in a composition with the target frame rate. Interpreting frame rate properly is an issue only when you import image sequences, which, of course, is the most common way that you will import moving footage in a visual effects setting. Image sequences are preferred to formats such as QuickTime (.mov) or Windows Media (.avi) in a production setting because

▶ If something goes wrong with a rendered image sequence, only the missing frames need to be replaced. With a movie file, the whole file typically has to be discarded and replaced, potentially costing hours of render time.

▶ Movie file formats are not as universally recognized and standardized across various platforms and programs as still image formats. QuickTime is the most robust and flexible of the moving image formats, yet many Windows-based programs do not even natively support it.

Therefore, when importing still image sequences to use as moving footage, remember

▶ Just because you've set your Project Settings to the proper frame rate (say, 24 fps for a feature film project), your image sequences may still import at 30 fps by default. You can change this default setting under Preferences > Import.

▶ You can assign whatever frame rate you like to a footage sequence if you determine the default setting is not correct.

▶ Just because an imported moving image file (such as QuickTime) has its own frame rate does not mean you cannot override this rate as needed by checking Assume This Frame Rate and entering a value. Be certain, however, that this is really what you want to do; typically, it is only a correction for outputs that were set incorrectly in another application.

Figure 1.18 Useful information about any file can be found in the Project panel. Adjacent to the thumbnail image at the top, you'll find frame rate, duration, color depth, pixel aspect, and any sound info, as well as how many times the clip is used in the project. To see and select specific comps in which it is used, click the carat to the right of the file name. Below, the file listing itself also tells you the size, type and disk location of the source asset.

Keep in mind that you can highlight any clip in your Project panel and see its current frame rate, along with other default settings, displayed at the top of the panel (**Figure 1.18**).

Fields, Pulldown, Pixel Aspect Ratio (PAR)

Most of the rest of the Interpret Footage dialog has to do with settings specific to broadcast video formats. Fields are the result of footage interlacing, which I wish I could say was going to be a thing of the past with high definition formats, but alas, it has evolved with them, as well.

Fields essentially allow a broadcast format to get two frames out of one, by interlacing the two frames together. The result is that each field has only half as many vertical pixels as it otherwise should, but there can be twice as much motion detail in the clip. **Figure 1.19** shows a simplified version of how this works.

Therefore you must guard against symptoms such as those depicted in **Figure 1.20.** The best way to avoid field artifacts in moving footage is by making sure your Field setting matches that of your incoming footage; Separate Fields unweaves the two fields embedded in a single frame to be two separate frames (as far as After Effects is concerned), allowing you to add transforms and distortion effects without creating a complete mess. Furthermore, it can be vital to remove fields prior to masking and rotoscoping (covered further in Chapters 3 and 7).

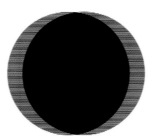

Figure 1.19 The ball is traveling horizontally, creating clear interlaced fields. This describes two frames' worth of motion via every other vertical pixel of a single frame.

Figure 1.20 The foreground pickup truck spells trouble if you're planning on doing much more than a simple color correction; fields were not removed for this clip. If you see a problem like this, check your Interpret Footage settings immediately.

Related to fields is 3:2 pulldown, which uses fields to convert 24 fps film footage to 29.97 fps by repeating one field every five frames. The question of which field is repeated is determined by the patterns listed in the Remove Pulldown menu, and After Effects will accurately guess them for you (using the buttons labeled "Guess") if there is sufficient motion in the first few frames to make the pattern obvious. If not, you must use trial and error, trying each pattern in Remove Pulldown until the footage plays at 23.976 fps with no visible field artifacts.

Pixel Aspect Ratio (PAR) is yet another compromise intended to improve the appearance of broadcast formats, and it has only proliferated with the advent of high definition video (**Figure 1.21**). The basic concept is to display video using pixels which are non-square, so that fewer of them are required along one axis where they are stretched upon display.

Any clip with a non-square PAR will look odd displayed via your monitor's square pixels; therefore After Effects includes a toggle along the bottom of the composition and

footage panels to stretch the footage so that its proportions look correct (**Figure 1.22**). This introduces error into the image fidelity and can cause smooth diagonals to appear jaggy. To accustom yourself with non-square pixels and how they appear in After Effects, try opening d1circle.tif from the CH01 folder and experiment with the PAR toggle.

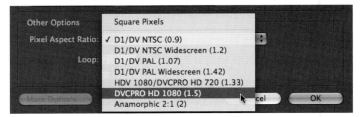

Figure 1.21 There are more non-square pixel video formats than ever these days; thankfully, After Effects 7.0 keeps up with them. All of the formats with values above 1.0 use pixels which are wider than they are tall, making the image appear anamorphic—a.k.a. too skinny—when displayed using square pixels, without compensation.

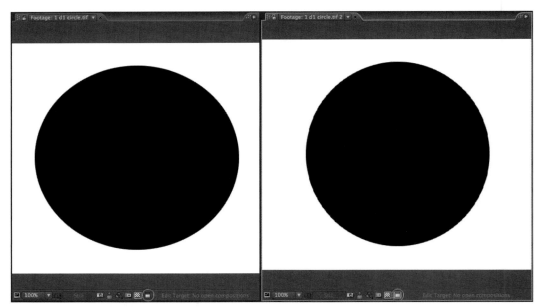

Figure 1.22 The same non-square pixel D1 aspect source, displayed with Pixel Aspect Ratio Correction toggled off (left) and on (right). The toggle for each is highlighted in red.

With standard digital formats such as DV, the process of setting field order and pixel aspect is standardized and automated; After Effects knows what to do by default if it sees. For other formats, you need to know not only whether your footage is coming in with fields but also whether the upper or lower field is first. Furthermore, with film footage you may have to deal with pulldown, which interleaves 24 fps footage into a 29.97 fps NTSC broadcast video-ready frame rate.

Digital Source Formats

After Effects is capable of importing and exporting a wide array of footage formats, yet only a small subset of these recur typically in visual effects production. Here are some of the most popular raster image formats and their advantages (for a summary, see **Table 1.1**):

- ▶ **TIFF (.tif):** In many ways the most flexible of formats, with the possible exception of PNG, TIFF is longstanding enough to be supported by most applications. It can be compressed effectively (and losslessly) by enabling LZW compression, which looks for recurring instances and patterns in the image and encodes them. New to After Effects 7.0 is native support for 16 bit per channel (bpc) and 32 bpc TIFF files; more on high bit depths can be found in Chapter 11.

- ▶ **Targa (.tga):** This format has the dual advantages of being universal to most computer graphics applications and offering lossless RLE (run length encoding) compression, which looks for sets of identical pixels that can be losslessly grouped together (such as a solid color in the background or alpha channel).

- ▶ **PNG (.png):** In many ways the most misunderstood of formats, PNG natively supports images of 8 or 16 bits per channel in Photoshop, and it often does the most effective job of losslessly keeping file sizes small. Because PNG has a reputation as a Web-oriented format, users sometimes mistakenly assume that it automatically adds lossy compression, as is the case with JPEG files.

One oddity about the PNG format is that, although it does permit saving an alpha channel, the alpha will always be saved and interpreted as Straight; the API of the format apparently does not allow for a premultiplied alpha.

▶ **Cineon (.cin)** and **DPX (.dpx):** Common formats for transferring digitized film images, these operate exclusively in nonlinear, 10-bit color and are examined in greater detail in Chapter 11.

▶ **Photoshop (.psd):** Although a universally supported format with many built-in extras, such as support for individual layer transparency, these files can be huge, as Photoshop offers no lossless compression options.

▶ **Camera Raw (.crw):** At this point only still (not video) cameras produce Camera Raw images, which contain all of the data that was captured from the camera with minimal processing. Camera Raw images allow you to adjust many characteristics of the image losslessly, as if you were making the adjustments (to exposure or light balance) directly in the camera.

▶ **Open EXR (.exr):** This is an advanced format for use solely with high dynamic range imaging (HDRI), source that has been taken in bit depths higher than linear 16 bit. With version 7.0, After Effects supports it natively, although specialized plug-ins take greater advantage of its extensible options, such as the ability to save Z depth data and motion vectors. If this all sounds like gobbledygook but you still want to learn more, have a look at Chapter 11 or www.openexr.com (where you can also download sample EXR files).

NOTES

In the case of Table 1.1, the term "8 bit" means 8 bits per channel, for a total 24 bits in an RGB image or 32 bits in an RGBA image. The Targa format includes a 16-bit option that actually means 16 bits total, or 5 per channel plus 1. Avoid this.

TABLE 1.1 Raster Image Formats and Their Advantages

Format	Bit Depth	Lossless Compression	Alpha Channel
TIFF	8, 16, or 32 bit	Y	Y (multiple via layers)
TGA	8 bit	Y	Y
PNG	8 or 16 bit	Y	Y (straight only)
CIN/DPX	10 bit		
PSD	8, 16, or 32 bit		Y (multiple via layers)
CRW	8 or 16 bit		
EXR (non-native)	16 bit floating point, 32 bit (integer and floating point)	Y	Y

So which format should you use? TIFF is useful overall, but 16-bit PNG will save substantial file space. Cineon is the only choice for 10-bit log files, and there's nothing particularly wrong with Targa (except perhaps slow run length encoding) or Photoshop (except the huge file sizes). EXR is the wave of the future for high dynamic range imaging because it was designed from the ground up for twenty-first century imaging.

Camera Raw will only come into play if your shot includes source from a digital SLR camera; importing a .crw image into After Effects activates the Camera Raw application, which is also included with Adobe Photoshop; it allows you to adjust and pre-set the characteristics that remain variable in this format. Photoshop books typically dedicate an entire chapter (if not the whole book) to this format, and because it does not yet come up regularly in After Effects work, use of Camera Raw is beyond the scope of what can be thoroughly covered in this book (although related issues are discussed in depth in Chapter 11).

Adobe Formats

After Effects supports some special features for dealing with files created by other Adobe applications. For effects work, the most handy one is support for multilayer Photoshop images, including layer names, transfer modes, and transparency settings.

To take advantage of this feature, import the Photoshop source as a composition, which leaves all of the properties of each individual layer editable in After Effects. The alternative is to import only a single layer or to flatten all layers and import the entire file as one image.

The ability to import a Photoshop file as a composition means you can set up a shot as a Photoshop still and import it with everything already in place. This is particularly useful with matte paintings that include separate elements, such as multiple planes of depth.

If you don't need the elements ready to go as layers of a composition, however, I would forego this option because it makes editing and updating the source trickier. Each

Moving Images

Moving image formats, such as QuickTime and Windows Media, almost never come into play in professional effects work, except perhaps as reference and dailies files transmitted to and from the editorial department.

These files can easily become huge at film resolution, and one corrupt frame can render an entire movie file unusable. Corrupt frames do, alas, occur, and being able to single them out for replacement is key; re-rendering an entire movie is simply not practical.

layer becomes a separate element that must be updated separately, and it's wasted effort if you never edit the associated composition.

New to After Effects 7.0 is the ability to create a Photoshop file directly from After Effects (File > New > Adobe Photoshop File). The file you create is a blank slate whose dimensions match that of the most recently opened composition, including title-safe and action-safe guides, and it automatically populates your After Effects project. In the context of a composition, you can create a new Photoshop layer by choosing Layer > New > Adobe Photoshop File.

Composition Settings

There are a couple of reliable methods for ensuring that your composition settings are exactly as they should be:

▶ Use a prebuilt project template that includes compositions whose settings are already correct

▶ Create new compositions by dragging a clip to the Create a New Composition icon and using only clips whose settings match the target output size and frame rate (**Figure 1.23**)

The crucial settings to get correct in the Composition Settings panel are the pixel dimensions, Pixel Aspect Ratio, Frame Rate, and Duration. (Actually, even Duration is negotiable so long as it is not too short.) If you're working with a footage format that isn't accurately described in any of the Preset options and you're going to be using this format again and again, then by all means create your own Preset setting by clicking on the small icon adjacent to the Preset pull-down menu, the icon that looks like a little floppy disk (**Figure 1.24**).

Figure 1.23 Dragging a source background clip to the highlighted icon at the bottom of the Project panel creates a new composition with the clip's duration, pixel dimensions, pixel aspect, and frame rate. It's a reasonably foolproof way to set up a new composition if you are working with a master background clip.

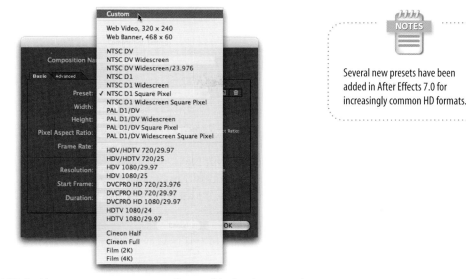

Figure 1.24 Feel free to create your own preset if none of the listed ones match one that you will be using continually for your project.

NOTES

Several new presets have been added in After Effects 7.0 for increasingly common HD formats.

The Advanced tab in the Composition Settings dialog pertains to options for specifying composition temporal and spatial settings (Chapter 4) and for working with motion blur and 3D (Chapter 9).

Previews and OpenGL

Nothing sets you apart as a visual effects pro more than the way you examine footage. A tax accountant who dealt solely with artists encouraged me a decade ago to write off my VCR and any movies I rented or purchased. She said that the IRS has no idea of the way that effects people look at movies—back and forth over the same section, frame by frame, and so on—nor the wear and tear it puts on video equipment.

Obviously, the way you look at a clip in After Effects is much different than the way your audience will look at it once it's in the finished movie. So to get to the heart of the matter: How exactly does a professional work with footage in After Effects? This section offers some of the habits of highly effective compositors, to paraphrase a popular productivity guru.

The strategies outlined here are particularly helpful when working with typically large format footage such as 2K film plates (film resolution typically footage measuring approximately 2000 pixels, or more precisely 2048, horizontally), but they're not bad habits for speeding you along regardless of format (or the speed of your workstation).

Resolution and Quality

After Effects 6.5 finally made it standard for any new layers in a composition to be set to Best quality in the timeline (with a check box for the setting in Preferences > General). Long ago, in the era of truly slow desktop computers, Draft quality was an effective hedge against slow previews, but in this day and age there are far more effective ways to manage preview speed without creating inaccurate previews, as Draft quality does.

There are several other effective ways to speed up previews and interactivity without ever resorting to Draft quality:

► Change Resolution/Down Sample Factor to Half; or in extreme cases, change it to Quarter

► Preview a Region of Interest (ROI)

► Change the way controls update using Preview settings and the Option key (for more on this, see the section "Caching and Previewing")

► Enable the Caps Lock key to prevent further updates to rendered views; use only in cases of extreme slowdown

Production monitors with a horizontal resolution of 1920 pixels or more are more common than they used to be, but they're far from universal. Artists working at film resolution tend to use this to their advantage by leaving the footage at 50% magnification and Half resolution, which keeps things moving more quickly (**Figure 1.25**).

NOTES

Avoid Draft quality, because in most cases the potential pitfalls (forgetting that it is set when making fine adjustments) are no longer outweighed by the benefits (which can be gained by reducing overall resolution, sampled area, frame rate, and so on, all detailed here).

TIP

In Preferences > Display is an option to "Auto-Zoom When Resolution Changes" but most artists leave it off, preferring to manage these separately. I find it can be handy with specific tasks such as rotoscoping.

Figure 1.25 It's generally good practice to keep the resolution (highlighted, right) matched to the current magnification setting (highlighted, left); this prevents over-rendering the current view (wasting your time) and helps RAM Previews to play at full speed.

This setup allows four times as much data to fill a RAM preview, and preview renders are created in a fraction—sometimes one half or, in extreme cases, one tenth—of the time required for Full resolution, which is reserved for cases in which it is necessary to zoom in and look closely, and for final render preparation.

To quickly change the display resolution in the Composition panel, use the keyboard shortcuts shown in **Table 1.2**.

TABLE 1.2 Keyboard Commands for Display Resolution/Size

Resolution/Size	Keyboard Shortcut
Full	Ctrl+J/Cmd+J
Half	Ctrl+Shift+J/Cmd+Shift+J
Quarter	Ctrl+Shift+Alt+J/ Cmd+Shift+Option+J
Fit in viewer	Shift+/
Fit up to 100%	Alt+/ / Option+/

You have probably noticed the lack of scrollbars in the Composition and Layer panels. Hold down the Spacebar or activate the Hand tool (**H**) to move your view of a clip around. To zoom in and out, you can use:

▶ **Ctrl+=/Cmd+=** and **Ctrl+-/Cmd+-**.

▶ Zoom tool (**Z**); press **Alt/Option** to zoom out.

▶ Comma and period keys.

▶ Does your mouse have a scroll wheel? Merely by moving the cursor over a viewer panel, you can zoom in and out by scrolling (no need to activate the panel first).

Reducing Things Further

When you really need to look at something at full resolution in full motion, consider whether you need to see the full frame or just some area of it, as is often the case. In such a situation, use the Region of Interest (ROI) tool (**Figure 1.26**).

NOTES

New to 7.0 is the ability to fit the Composition view to the size of the viewer. Choose Fit from the Magnification ratio pop-up at the bottom of the Composition viewer (or pressing **Shift+/**), or even more useful, Fit up to 100% (**Alt+/**, **Option+/**) which maintains the fit even as you scale the panel.

Figure 1.26 Activating the Region of Interest akin to cropping your composition, to preview only the activated region. You can even Crop Comp to Region of Interest (in the Composition menu) should you like what you see. ROI previews save render time and preview space (RAM).

> **TIP**
>
> If the ROI tool results in a crop of your image that you want to maintain, you can choose Composition > Crop Comp to Region of Interest.

Clicking the ROI tool turns your cursor into a set of crosshairs that you use to define the rectangular region you wish to isolate. Now as you preview, only the layer data that you need to render is calculated, and only this area of the screen buffers into physical memory, lengthening the temporal capacity of RAM previews (detailed further in "Caching and Previewing").

Maintaining Interactivity

One major gotcha in After Effects occurs in heavily render-intensive projects that need a lot of tweaking (say, fine adjustments of effect controls). As the processor becomes heavily loaded updating the frame display, UI interaction itself is slowed down—so much so in some cases that dragging a slider or a layer position stutters and becomes non-interactive.

In some cases, deactivating Live Update is enough to prevent the problem (**Figure 1.27**). If you're working with high-resolution footage on a machine that feels sluggish, you can toggle this off so that waiting for updates does not drive you crazy.

In extreme cases—say, on a network with heavy traffic, or in a huge composition—your panic button is Caps Lock. Activating it (**Figure 1.28**) prevents all further updates to any viewer. My own worst-case scenario was a movie with a server load so heavy that it was necessary to work "blind" in this manner for several consecutive edits before bravely reactivating the update and going to get some coffee.

Figure 1.27 Live Update is activated by this switch in the timeline; it is active by default. When it is active, the Composition and Layer panels update in real time, as you adjust sliders. Holding down Alt/Option as you adjust a slider prevents the views from updating. If Live Update is not activated, then holding down Alt/Option updates the view (the functionality is reversed).

TIP

Hold down Alt/Option as you make adjustments in the UI to toggle the Live Update setting; you can either set Live Update on (the default) and to hold down Alt/-Option to freeze updates, or vice versa.

Figure 1.28 Desperate times call for desperate measures. Pressing the Caps Lock key prevents view windows from updating and draws a big red border with a reminder in the corner that it's on.

Caching and Previewing

One key to optimal After Effects performance is to get the application to cache as much footage as possible into physical memory. This is something that After Effects does automatically as you navigate from frame to frame (Page Up and Page Down keys) or load frames into memory for a RAM preview (0 on your numeric keypad). The green line atop the timeline shows which frames are loaded.

Given that the maximum RAM accessible by After Effects on either platform is 4 GB, you can do better. To extend the cache from physical memory (RAM) to physical media (a high-speed local drive), enable Disk Cache in Preferences > Memory & Cache. This locks away a portion of your drive for use only by After Effects. Just as the green line shows frames that are cached to RAM, a blue line shows frames loaded in the Disk Cache.

When you check Enable Disk Cache, you are asked for a folder to use; if in doubt just create a folder somewhere handy on a drive with sufficient space, and name it something intuitive like "AE Scratch." Even the default 2 GB (2000 MB) setting greatly extends available cache without occupying permanent disk space (no drive should be full beyond 90% of capacity for more than a brief period of time).

Two main questions usually arise in regards to the Disk Cache:

▶ How can I ensure that the application caches as much material as possible?

▶ How can I preserve the cache once it is loaded?

The goal is to get as close to real-time performance as possible. Disk Cache exists only to save the time required to re-render a frame, if round-tripping a rendered frame to disk and back will be faster. Thus it is not designed to deliver real-time playback, and often is not invoked when you might think it should be. Likewise, After Effects is reasonably clever about deciding what can be preserved in the cache, but trial and error reveals that the cache will sometimes disappear when you might reason that it should not have done so. There are too many variables with this feature set to be any more specific in responding to these questions.

Figure 1.29 The panel menu of Time Controls contains the menu options for revealing the RAM Preview and Shift+RAM Preview options.

If RAM previews are taking too long to render and refined motion is not critical to preview, take advantage of the option to skip frames in RAM preview. This feature resides in the Time Controls panel. Choose Shift+RAM Preview Options in the pull-down menu (**Figure 1.29**). To preview every second frame, saving half the render time, set Skip to 1 (or 4 to render only every fifth frame, etc.). The short-cut for Shift+RAM Preview is, naturally enough, **Shift+0** (on the numeric keypad).

Preview Settings

By default, RAM Preview caches and previews all frames in the work area, from beginning to end. If you prefer, enable From Current Time in the Time Controls panel. This setting ignores the work area and begins the preview from the current time, continuing to the end of the composition (even if the work area ends before that point).

If you prefer to preview without the user interface, toggle Full Screen in Time Controls. Note that From Current Time and Full Screen have individual toggles for RAM Preview and Shift+RAM Preview—toggling one does not affect the other.

If you have any kind of external monitor attached to your workstation—even a second RGB monitor—it's worth checking in Preferences > Video Preview to see what options are listed under Output Device. Depending on your system, you may be able to see your composition previewed full-screen on a wide variety of devices, including a miniDV camera (connected via FireWire) or a broadcast or HD monitor (connected via a third-party PCI card such as Kona or Blackmagic).

The options here are mostly self-explanatory and subject to personal preference. Regardless of how you set them, you can update the preview to display the current frame simply by pressing the / key.

What's Your Background?

Custom backgrounds that contrast with foreground layers are valuable for a lot of effects work, such as keying and masking. You probably know that you can customize the background color of your compositions (**Ctrl+Shift+B/ Cmd+Shift+B** or Composition > Background Color). No doubt you also know about the Toggle Transparency Grid icon at the bottom of the Composition panel.

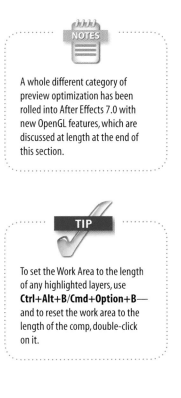

A whole different category of preview optimization has been rolled into After Effects 7.0 with new OpenGL features, which are discussed at length at the end of this section.

To set the Work Area to the length of any highlighted layers, use **Ctrl+Alt+B/Cmd+Option+B**—and to reset the work area to the length of the comp, double-click on it.

New to 7.0 is a check box called Scale and Letterbox Output to Fit Video Monitor. Turning this on allows you to preview a composition on the external monitor even if its dimensions don't match those of the comp.

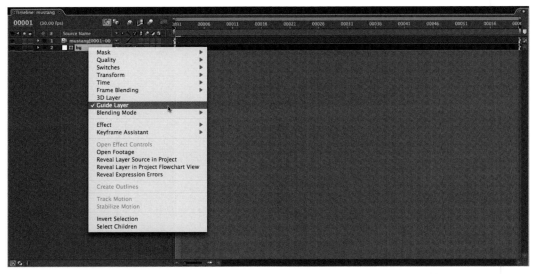

Figure 1.30 Guide Layer has been set for the background layer, evident by the second icon, a box of four small cyan guides, that appears beside the layer name.

When that's not enough, *guide layers* become handy. To insert background plate footage into a composition which will never appear in any subsequent comp or the final render context-click and choose Guide Layer (Layer > Guide Layer) (**Figure 1.30**). This is a special kind of layer that will show up only here, in the composition view—not when you render it, nor when you nest it in another comp (detailed in Chapter 4).

Using this feature you can create custom backgrounds for the sole purpose of previewing. For example, a gradient can help reveal qualities that are difficult to spot against a solid color or the Transparency Grid, particularly when you're refining a matte. Apply the Ramp effect to a solid, then toggle Guide Layer and you have an optimal preview background (**Figure 1.31**).

To the Fore

After Effects offers several modes and toggles to help control what you see in your Composition viewer.

Some toggles are common to all Adobe applications. Highlight the Composition panel and choose View > Show Grid

Figure 1.31 You can often more effectively see edge detail using a gradient background (left), rather than a solid color or a checkerboard. Guide Layer prevents the gradient from appearing in any subsequent comp or render; here it is nested into a main comp that shows only a checkerboard background (right).

(**Ctrl+"/Cmd+"**) to display an overlay grid. The default settings are almost never what you want, either for color or size, so you will make liberal use of Preferences > Grids & Guides to customize the color and size of the grid.

I tend to find a large grid with few subdivisions in a light gray least obtrusive. I also like to choose a Gridline value that multiplies evenly into the width (or both dimensions) of my composition; for example, with 1920 × 1080 footage I might choose a gridline every 80 pixels with 2 subdivisions. If gridlines are too prominent for your tastes, note that Grids & Guides preferences also include a Dashed Lines and a Dots option.

Other conventions which co-exist in other Adobe applications are View > Show Rulers (**Ctrl+R/Cmd+R**) and the various Guides options under the View menu. I don't make use of guides much in After Effects, but I like the fact that, for example, when you create a new Photoshop file with After Effects, it includes guides showing the safe areas.

The Title/Action Safe overlay can be useful even if you're not doing broadcast video. Standard definition television does not display the full digital frame the way digital

NOTES

Title/Action Safe also has the benefit of displaying a crosshair at the exact center of frame. If you want only the crosshair, new in 7.0, you can set the Action-safe and Title-safe both to 0% in Preferences > Grids & Guides.

Proportional Grids scale across any size of composition and can help show basic proportions. They (and other options including Rulers and Guides) are accessible via the Grid and Guides options at the bottom of the Composition panel (**Figure 1.32**).

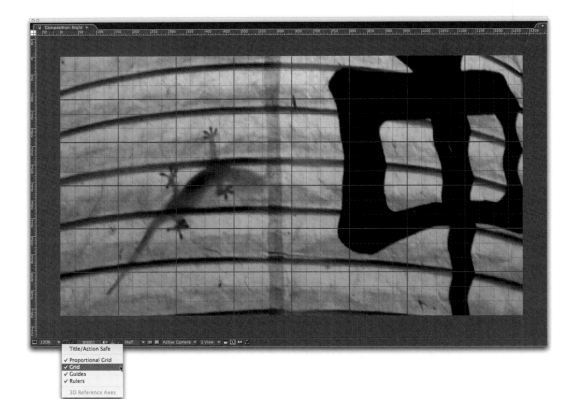

Figures 1.32a and b All measurement options are selected for this viewer, although one would typically choose either Grid or Proportional Grid (a). The difference is that a Grid is laid out by pixel dimensions, whereas a Proportional Grid draws a specific number of dividers on the horizontal and vertical axes. You can specify how these grids are drawn, and in what color for the Grid, in Preferences > Grids & Guides (b).

formats such as HD do, and the default settings in Preferences > Guides & Grids are preset for television "safe" areas
for displaying text and action. You can, however, customize
these, so that if you're working with film and you know
that you have a padding area at the edge of frame, you can
lower one of the safe areas to 1 or 2 percent and turn the
other one off by setting it to 0.

As you work with more complex compositions that include
3D elements and masks, you may find that the vector outlines showing these elements in your Composition panel
become too much. You can toggle them off individually in
View > View Options (**Ctrl+Alt+U**/**Cmd+Opt+U**, or via the
panel menu), but if you're just looking for a fast way to hide
them all, use View > Hide Layer Controls (**Ctrl+Shift+H**/
Cmd+Shift+H) which toggles them off and on.

The Toggle View Masks button next
to Grid and Guide Options at the
bottom of the Composition viewer
will toggle only your masks on and
off. More on masks in Chapters 3
and 7.

Change the Channel

Another way in which you will want to continually check
your work is by studying footage one color channel at a
time, including the alpha channel. The icon containing
overlapping colored disks at the bottom of the Composition
panel exists for this purpose, and a line in the color of the
channel you've chosen helpfully appears around the edge
of the panel when one of them is selected on (**Figure 1.33**).
The corresponding keyboard shortcuts—**Alt**/**Option+1**
through **Alt**/**Option+4**—accomplish the same end.

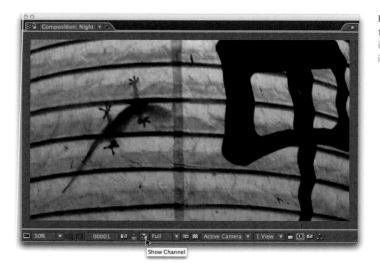

Figure 1.33 The green lines along
the edges of the Composition panel
indicate that only the green channel
is displayed.

Why preview on a single channel? Section II, "Effects Compositing Essentials," explores this in some depth.

New in After Effects 7.0, it is possible to RAM Preview while displaying a single channel mode. You have even more expanded previewing options in 7.0 if your display card is powerful (and up-to-date) enough to support the many new OpenGL features.

OpenGL

Advances in OpenGL display are certainly one of the top ten new features in After Effects 7.0, if only because there was so little that your 3D display card could do in previous versions. On the other hand, depending on your hardware setup and how you like to use the application, you may find that you don't use OpenGL previewing much, if at all, in effects compositing work. Thus, what follows is a brief outline to get started using OpenGL optimally in your compositions. If the result seems less than optimal, you can at least be satisfied that you have investigated all options.

First of all, for OpenGL options to be available at all, your system must include a display card capable of delivering the features. There's a relatively simple way to check this in After Effects: go to Preferences > Previews (or choose "Fast Previews Preferences" under the Fast Previews pulldown menu, **Figure 1.34**) and click OpenGL Info to see a list of advanced 3D capabilities that your display card can theoretically emulate (**Figure 1.35**). If your list is incomplete, you may need a new card, or you may simply need to update your system (particularly on a Mac, where OpenGL 2.0 is a more recent development).

A couple of important settings are tucked away in Preferences > Previews. Within the OpenGL Info dialog, you can specify the amount of Texture Memory—this is how much actual image data will be sent to the display card, and your target setting should be 20–30 MB less than the actual capacity of the card to leave room for non-texture image data. On the Mac, this is detected automatically, but on Windows, you must know the number or check it using the System Information accessory. Also, if Enable OpenGL isn't checked in the Previews dialog, the features won't be available. Finally, if the Quality setting (below Texture Memory in OpenGL Info) is set to More Accurate, you get the new OpenGL 2.0 features available with version 7.0. At the Faster setting, the style reverts to the more basic After Effects 6.0 style.

Once you have OpenGL properly configured, you can select your preferred preview method in the Fast Previews pulldown along the bottom of a viewer panel (Figure 1.34). Here is where your mileage will vary greatly, so to speak, depending on what and how much you are trying to preview.

The allure of OpenGL is that it is capable of bypassing the core processor and rendering imagery (including the sophisticated features on the preferences list, shown in Figure 1.35, and further detailed in the sidebar "What OpenGL Does") directly on the card. That makes it sound

Figure 1.34 The Fast Previews icon in any viewer panel offers easy access to OpenGL-related preferences. When OpenGL is active the icon displays a yellow lightning bolt (and the "OpenGL" text hint appears at the upper left of the viewer). In this instance, Freeze Layer Contents is also active, which prevents the footage itself from advancing while other animations (in this case, a 3D rotation) are advanced using Spacebar preview or by dragging the Current Time Indicator.

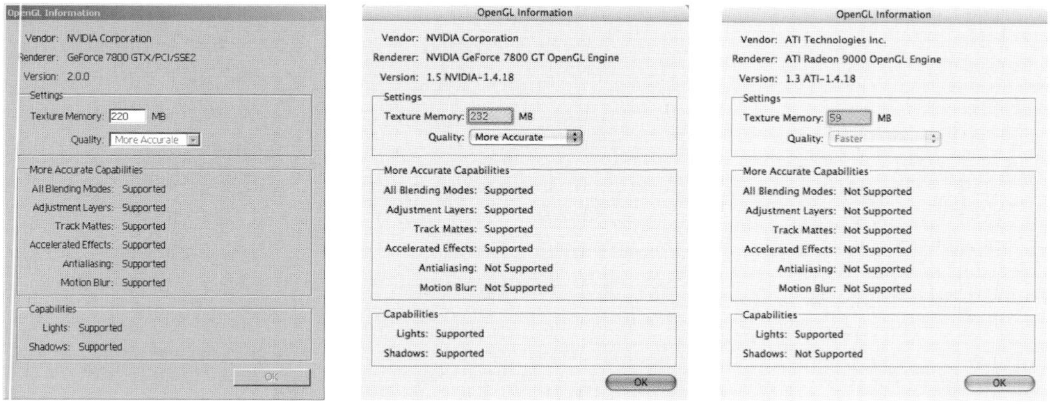

Figure 1.35 Shown are OpenGL settings for three different systems with varying degrees of OpenGL support. The Windows box (a) offers full OpenGL 2.0 support, while a Mac with the same display card (b) lacks anti-aliasing or motion blur support, due to limitations in OS X 10.4 (which are likely obviated by the time you read this). Users of older systems will be sad to see a dialog more like the one from a Powerbook (c), which does not even offer full OpenGL 1.0 support via its ancient (three-year-old) ATI Radeon 9000 card.

as though the result will be real-time, or at least faster than rendering on the processor (using one of the non-OpenGL options, "None" or "Adaptive Resolution" in Fast Previews).

The reality is that Open GL still requires time to process and store images, and this will often be slower than is necessary to stream your frames in real-time. Furthermore, the appearance, while similar, will not be identical to the non-OpenGL frame in most cases (depending on which features your card supports). Testing out how well this works for you is simple, once you've configured it. Choose OpenGL—Always On in Fast Previews and then press the spacebar; is your composition playing in real time? How does it look?

If the answers are "no" and "not good enough" respectively, don't fret—OpenGL is really intended for fast previewing, although there is an option to render with it (**Figure 1.36**). What you may want to do, in certain cases where it is taking a long time to page an animated source clip off of a slow drive (or server) is to choose Freeze Layer Contents. The layer continues to animate as keyframed, but the frame itself doesn't update until you release the Current Time Indicator (it does not apply to a spacebar preview).

It's fairly satisfying to load up a 2K HD clip and spin it around in greater than real-time with the Freeze Layer Contents setting on, but as to how often you will actually

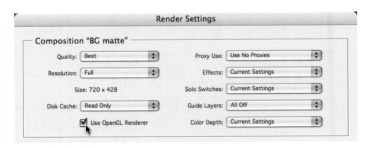

Figure 1.36 Are you sure you want to do that? If for some reason you fall in love with the way your composition looks in OpenGL mode, you are free to enable OpenGL for the final render. Beware, however, that the appearance of the render may change based simply on the hardware of the machine that renders it.

use this in your every day work, it depends of factors such as how many layers and how much animation (particularly transforms) you are adding. OpenGL won't help a bit when it comes to rendering complex effects (although it will do many color correction and blur effects), keying a matte, etc., but we all look forward to the day when it does.

Effects & Presets

It's a wry joke in the effects world that you can create any shot using only two effects: Levels and Fast Blur. This sentiment is very punk rock and like most such joking generalizations, while grossly exaggerated, it does contain a grain of truth:

▶ Most After Effects artists may never use the majority of effects in the Effect menu. Many effects, in fact, are there only to support old, otherwise outdated projects created in previous versions of the application.

▶ After Effects artists can get a bad rap in the visual effects community for seeking an effect plug-in to do for them what can actually be done with the core tools, if the artist knows how the effect is achieved.

One thing that has improved a great deal with version 7.0 is the categorization of effects. The number of categories overall has been reduced, and effects that relate to color correction now all live in the Color Correction category (which used to be divided between Adjust and Image Control, neither of which had as intuitive a title.

However, you don't ever have to use the Effect menu. The Effects & Presets palette has options for displaying effects without their categories (**Figure 1.37**). Once you know what you're looking for, listing effects in alphabetical order and searching for them in the palette's Contains field can speed things along a bit. You then apply the selected effect by double-clicking it (if the target layer is selected) or by dragging it to the target layer in the Timeline panel (or to its Effect Controls panel).

CLOSE-UP

What OpenGL does

The OpenGL feature set was originally designed to accelerate real-time 3D graphics, and much of the terminology belongs more to that world than to the world of compositing. Fundamentally, if you have an up-to-date card with 256 MB or more of video RAM (a.k.a. texture memory), you can think of your display card as a texture cache, where every frame of every clip or sequence is a texture. Once a texture is on the card, After Effects does everything possible to keep it there and process the image there, allowing the GPU (graphics processor unit) to do its magic of releasing the load on the main CPU (core processor unit).

The major display card manufacturers (ATI, nVidia, 3DLabs) have all adopted OpenGL 2.0, as have the Windows and Mac operating systems, all to varying degrees—meaning that all of the following can be accelerated by the GPU:

▶ Blending Modes (except dissolves)
▶ Color Corrections: Alpha Levels, Brightness & Contrast, Color Balance, Curves, Tint, Hue & Saturation
▶ Blur & Sharpen: Fast Blur, Channel Blur, Directional Blur, Gaussian Blur, Sharpen
▶ Noise
▶ Adjustment Layers
▶ Track Mattes
▶ Anti-aliasing & Motion Blur
▶ 3D rendering features: Lights & Shadows

Figure 1.37 Looking for all of the blur options in After Effects? Type "Blur" in the field labeled "Contains" in Effects & Presets and only effects with "blur" in the name are revealed.

Version 7.0 contains more Animation Presets than its predecessors. These are collections of presets configured by Adobe to create particular types of animation automatically, mostly for motion graphics use. The folder containing them begins with an asterisk, holding its place at the top of the list. Typing "blur" in the Search field yields a long list of presets containing various blur effects. To prevent this, use the Effect & Presets panel menu to turn off Show Animation Presets (or reduce its occurrence by turning off Show Preset Contents.

Types of Effects

You may have noticed the icons that appear next to the effect names in the Effects & Presets palette. There are six main types: 8-, 16- and 32-bit effects, Animation Presets, Audio, and one you may rarely see, Missing Effects. You may not be working at higher bit depths yet, but it is worth noting which effects are 32-bit ready; for the most part, those are the core After Effects plug-ins, the ones you'll consider using first and most often.

Effects that are capable of supporting 16 or 32 bits also operate at the standard 8 bits per channel. Chapter 11 contains more about the difference between bit depths and how to work with them.

The panel menu allows you to specify which type of effect to list (**Figure 1.38**). For example, you can show only 16-bit or only 32-bit effects, or you can see the contents of an Animation Preset (what it actually does, step by step). Beware if you set this option, however, because you may find yourself looking for an effect that is unexpectedly hidden from the palette.

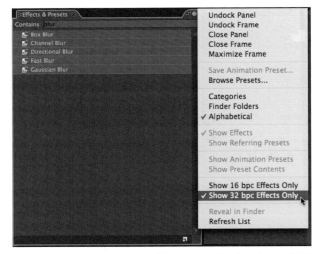

Figure 1.38 Wondering which types of blur are capable of working at 32 bits per channel? Type "blur" in the Contains field with the specified options in the panel menu and find out.

Animation Presets

Animation presets are particularly useful when you're working with a team and sharing standardized practices. You can recognize an animation preset file in your system by its .ffx file suffix; they can be found in the Plug-ins folder, within the same folder where the application itself is found (on Windows, this is a shortcut to the folder, which is stored one level deeper in the Support Files folder).

In the Effect Controls window or the timeline, select whatever effects and properties you want to save and choose Animation > Save Animation Preset. You can save the preset wherever you like, but for it to show up in the Effects & Presets palette automatically, save it to the Presets folder (the default choice for After Effects, also found in the folder where the application itself resides). In a studio situation, a preset can be distributed to a number of users via this folder. The next time they restart After Effects or update the palette (using the Refresh List command in the wing menu), the preset appears, ready for use.

Output: The Render Queue

The Render Queue itself is not terribly puzzling, but like many other key portions of the After Effects UI it contains a few features that many users miss, and a few gotchas that loom from time to time.

There are two key sections for each Render Queue item: Render Settings and Output Module. You can click on each to adjust settings, but I find that almost immediately you will want to get into the habit of choosing a preset, or template, from the pull-down menu. And in the altogether likely case that one does not already exist, you choose the selection at the bottom of each menu: Make Template.

Why make a template for each render? Render Settings tends to be standardized across a project, and you likely will use one of just a few output modules throughout the duration of the project. So why waste time thinking about settings each time you render, when that only leads to a higher likelihood of careless errors (which are, if you ask me, the bane of a compositor's existence)?

Browsing via Bridge

Prominently new in the 7.0 File menu are the Browse and Browse Template Projects commands. These activate Adobe Bridge, the file browsing utility that was introduced with Adobe Creative Studio.

You may have seen demonstrations in which it can be used to browse for animation presets and template project (.aet) files. If you have the functional content installed, you can try this for yourself (the Browse Template Projects command takes you straight to the templates whereas Browse takes you wherever you were last). The ability to see animated previews of effects presets in Bridge is pretty cool, and the idea of providing a special .aet template format that can be previewed and that cannot be inadvertently edited and saved seems useful.

In After Effects 7.0, however, the use of Bridge with After Effects is clearly in its introductory or 1.0 stage. You can preview video and audio file formats such as QuickTime and MP3, but file sequences do not appear as what they are, an animated clip. Instead, Bridge parses them as a series of individual files, each of them getting its own thumbnail. And those cool animated previews are not available to the populace at large in this version; you only get them with the shipped presets, not with those you create.

Bridge includes the ability to tag files with metadata that can be searched later in various ways; this means it may be worth keeping in mind for very specific uses. More likely you will be keeping your eye on future versions of Bridge to make substantial use of it with After Effects.

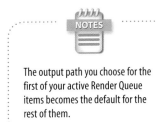

The output path you choose for the first of your active Render Queue items becomes the default for the rest of them.

Placing an Item in the Queue

After Effects is flexible about how you add an item to the Render Queue. You have a choice of two keyboard shortcuts: **Ctrl+M**/**Cmd+M** and the one I always tend to use, **Ctrl+Shift+/** (**Cmd+Shift+/**). You can also select a number of items in the Project panel and drag them to the Render Queue. If you drag footage without a comp to the Render Queue, After Effects makes a default comp for you to render the footage as is, which can be handy for quick file conversions such as creating a QuickTime output from an image sequence.

Render Settings: Your Manual Overrides

There's probably one set of parameters from the Render Settings dialog that you will prefer throughout a given project; in many cases it will simply be the default Best.

The Render Settings dialog consists mostly of manual overrides for the settings in your composition itself (**Figure 1.39**). It contains three sections:

Figure 1.39 The Render Settings dialog has three sections: overrides for the composition settings (top), specific time sampling overrides and settings (center), and two extra options for where and how files are rendered (bottom).

▶ The Composition section (top) includes a series of options to override Quality and Resolution settings for the composition, Disk Cache settings for the project, and layer-by-layer Proxy, Effects, Solo, and Guide Layer toggles. The Best setting ignores proxies, hidden effects, and guide layers, but respects current solo settings, with Quality forced to Best and Resolution at Full.

Disciplined artists who never leave an effect that they don't intend to have on and never solo a layer and intend to render it that way may prefer to override the current settings, but most people (myself included) will curse such a decision.

Proxy settings are trickier. An investigation into the ways you can employ them (as well as guide layers) is found in Chapter 4.

▶ The Time Sampling section (center) contains settings that override decisions that exist for the overall composition: the Frame Blending and Motion Blur switches for the composition (not individual layers), plus the Shutter Angle setting overriding the composition's motion blur setting (more on that in the next chapter). Field Render and 3:2 Pulldown pertain only to preparing the comp for broadcast video output; on projects you will either use them all the time or not at all for final output. The Time Span setting comes into play in situations where you need to re-render some portion of your total comp (otherwise, Work Area or Length of Comp should be preferable).

▶ The Options section (bottom) contains precisely two mutually exclusive options: If you check Use Storage Overflow then the overflow volumes that you can specify in Preferences > Output come into play (**Figure 1.40**). If the first one fills up, the second is used, and so on. If you do not check this option, you can let After Effects look in the destination folder and skip any files that it finds whose output names match files already in that folder. This is designed specifically for the Watch Folder option, but you can use it in any case where you are creating an image sequence and have some, but not all, of the rendered images already completed.

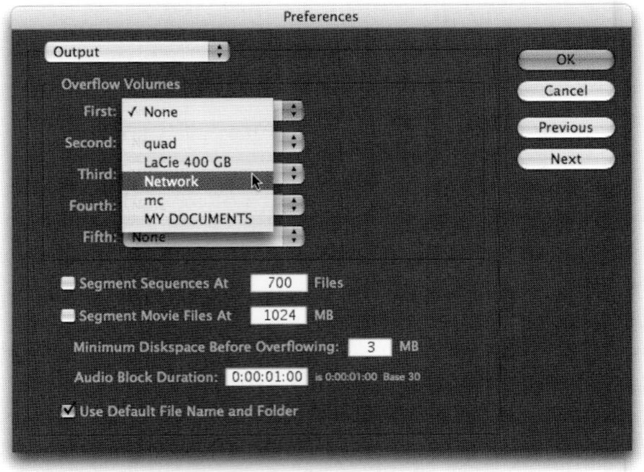

Figure 1.40 Storage overflow is insurance against failed planning; if you run out of space on the primary rendering drive, the volumes specified in this Preference dialog can be set to handle the overflow. With ample disk space, you should not need this, but it's preferable to a failed overnight render.

The way to use Render Settings overall is as a checklist of all the things you need to think about to get your output footage to look the way you want. It may work to simply use Best settings and walk away, or you may be reminded of something specific that needs to be custom set.

Output Modules: As Many as You Need

Throughout the course of your After Effects career you will probably create a large number of Output Module templates. The settings themselves are not so tricky if you know what you're after: Once you've chosen a format, and set the appropriate options (under Video Output), you have the additional options of stretching or cropping the output, and adding audio.

Note that Output Module appears after Render Settings, item by item. This is with good reason: As you will see in detail in Chapter 4, the order in the user interface shows the rendering order, and so Render Settings are applied to the render prior to the application of the Output Module settings.

This becomes important, for example, when scaling output: To scale down a clip and retain the highest quality, you will in most cases want to apply the scaling as a Stretch setting in the Output Module rather than a Resolution setting in the Render Settings (unless speeding up the render is more important than quality, in which case the inverse advice applies).

There are several elegant problem-solving tools embedded in the Output Module setup, some of which many users tend to miss. Among the most significant are

▶ You are allowed more than one Output Module per Render Queue item (**Figure 1.41**).

▶ You can change the Output Module of all of your Render Queue items by selecting the Output Module (rather than the Render Queue item itself) of the first item and then Shift-selecting the Output Module (again, rather than the item itself) of the last item (**Figure 1.42**).

▶ You can start numbering an image sequence using the integer of your choice (**Figure 1.43**).

▶ Stretching and cropping your output is often a quick, elegant solution to an otherwise thorny rendering problem.

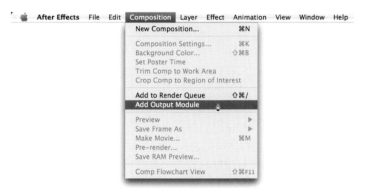

Figure 1.41 So many users—and not just beginners, by any means—fail to notice that you can add multiple **Output** Modules to a single render queue item, v a Composition > Add Output Module. This can be an immense timesaver, as several versions of a render can be created in one pass (for example, one at full resolution stills and a Web-compressed version).

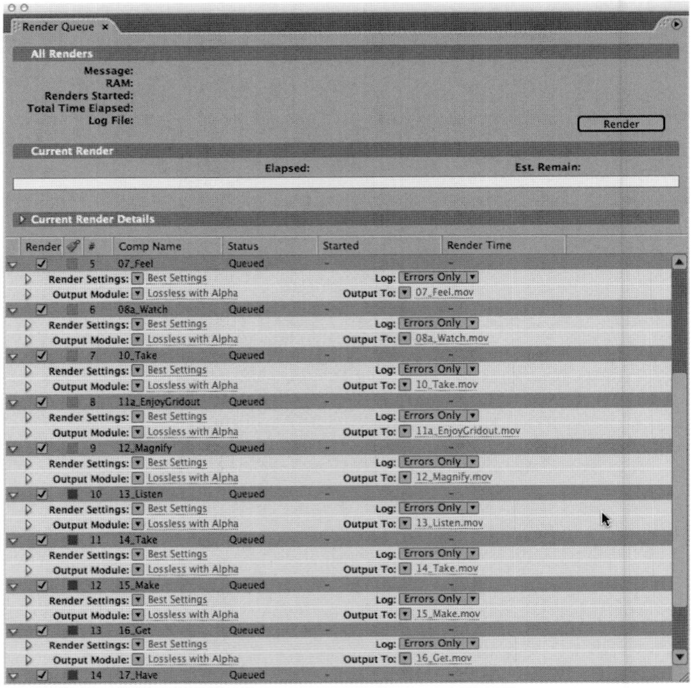

Figure 1.42 Oh no, I have to change all those? Fear not, you can select any number of consecutive Output Modules to change them, but don't select the render queue items themselves. Instead, select the first Output Module in the group and Shift-select the last, then change any of the selected ones and they all follow.

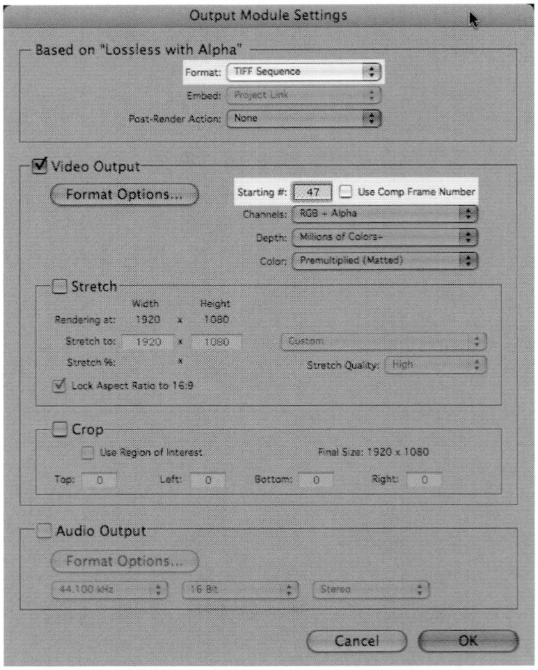

Figure 1.43 To custom-number your frame sequence, clear Use Comp Frame Number and enter your own.

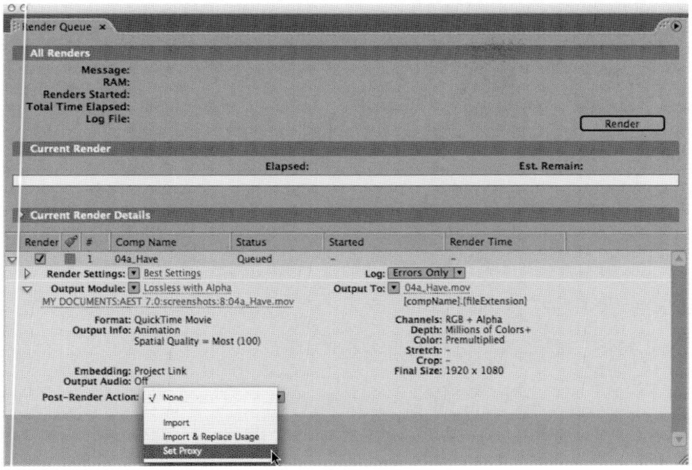

Figure 1.44 Post-Render Actions save you steps, if you intend to view your render in After Effects (Import) or replace a pre-comp with the render permanently (Import & Replace Usage) or just temporarily (Set Proxy).

▶ Included in the Output Module Settings, and also hidden under the twirl-down arrow (**Figure 1.44**) is an extra option, to perform one of three Post-Render Actions to import or replace the composition that was the source of the render. Chapter 4 contains more about how to use these.

▶ The shorthand for creating a numbered image sequence is simple if you follow the rules: After Effects replaces the string [###] within the overall output name with a three-digit sequential number. The number of # characters in this string corresponds to the amount of digits in the sequential number; if you want extra padding, add extra # characters.

Paying attention to the options available with Output Modules and taking the time to customize and apply presets that you can use again and again are big parts of getting optimum output out of After Effects.

Optimizing Output Settings

Here are some general guidelines for the output settings (Render Settings and Output Modules) that you can use in specific situations:

▶ **Lossless output:** Interframe compression (QuickTime with Animation/Most) is acceptable for movie files, lossless encoding (TGA with RLE, TIFF with LZW, or PNG) and for still images.

Whenever rendering to a format that adds compression, be aware that colors and overall gamma (brightness) can shift noticeably in a clip that otherwise shows few, if any, compression artifacts.

▶ **Low-loss output:** QuickTime with Photo-JPEG at 75% is ideal for creating test renders that are relatively small at full resolution yet show little in the way of compression artifacts. The newcomer in this territory is QuickTime H.264, which is also quite stunning at similar settings.

▶ **Web review:** This is a fast-changing area, subject to many variables. At this writing, QuickTime with MPEG-4 or H.264 offer some of the best results, but some studios prefer to use the Sorenson compressor that is supported on systems that haven't been recently updated to the latest versions of QuickTime. In some cases, QuickTime will not be the answer and Divx or another encoding scheme will be preferred, particularly among Windows and Linux users.

▶ **DV/HDV:** If working with these or other compressed source formats, remember that they recompress prerenders, so make all of your edits to the source file and render once!

Obviously, there is much more to choosing your output settings than is covered here; the intention is to help you get started. In many cases, the settings you need to use will be dictated by your delivery format or by what is needed by the next person after you in the production pipeline.

Study a Shot like an Effects Artist

The last chapter of this book is a take on how visual effects artists look at the world around us. Here, I'd like to focus for a moment on how you study a given shot in After Effects most effectively.

If you've never had your work reviewed in dailies at an effects studio, your first time in that setting may be a bit of a shock. Seasoned visual effects supervisors miss nothing, and in some cases they do not even need to see a clip twice to tell you what needs to change—even if it is only 40 frames long. In other cases, your shot will loop on and on for several minutes while the whole team gangs up on it, picking it apart.

Typically, however, footage is examined in dailies the same way that you want to look at it in After Effects, but in After

Effects, you have a huge advantage—extra tools at your disposal to show you what is going on, and no surly supervisor sitting near you!

Throughout the book, and in your work, as you preview your shot you are encouraged to

▶ Check your Info palette (**Figure 1.45**)

▶ Loop and rock and roll previews (**Figure 1.46**)

▶ Zoom in and take a close look

▶ Examine footage channel by channel

▶ "Slam" your levels to see your work in extreme contrast; this is the practice of temporarily (via a top level Adjustment Layer) applying high-contrast to your composition to make sure that blacks, midtones, and highlights still match (introduced in Chapter 5, "Color and Light: Adjusting and Matching")

▶ Keep looking for the thing you cannot initially see, and remain critical of the result (without being unfair to yourself)

▶ Expect that you will make careless errors; many final takes are lost to this factor. Effects compositing is a little like computer programming: a series of exacting decisions, where one careless error can invalidate the whole effort.

Were I teaching you this subject in person, I would probably remind you of these practices constantly; because doing that throughout a book isn't practical (and could get downright annoying), I encourage you to remind yourself. You will reap the benefits: a shot that is final in fewer takes, thanks to few careless mistakes, resulting in a pleased effects team who lauds your efforts and awards you with trickier, even more impressive shots (and an occasional break).

Figure 1.45 Whoops! You thought your background level was pure black, but a glance at the Info palette while your cursor is over the background shows that it is actually 2% gray, which can cause problems further down the line.

TIP

Does your mouse have a zoom wheel? If so, you can use it to zoom in and out on your Composition and Layer views. If you hold down Alt/Option as you mouse-wheel, the zoom will center around your pointer—a very useful extra for an effects artist hunting for details.

Figure 1.46 The three available settings for looping previews are highlighted in blue: loop (the default, top), ping-pong (center), or play through once (bottom); toggle these by clicking on the icon.

The Timeline

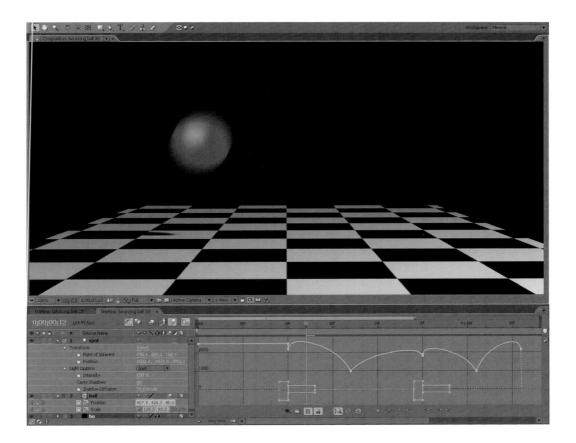

I've been a long time coming, and I'll be a long time gone. You've got your whole life to do something, and that's not very long.

—Ani DiFranco (American singer, songwriter, and guitarist)

The Timeline

The Timeline is After Effects' killer application. It is the reason above all others that After Effects is equally effective for motion graphics or visual effects work. Node-based compositors make it easy to see render order, but they can make coordinating the timing of events more difficult.

In 7.0, the Timeline has only become even better with the addition of the Graph Editor, a new user interface for editing multiple animation curves at once.

With the Timeline as the center of your compositing process, you can always investigate how elements and timing relate. You could argue that render order is more significant than timing for visual effects work, but once you get the hang of managing the Timeline well, render order is no longer as much of an issue.

The Timeline panel is also a relatively user-friendly part of the application, albeit one packed with hidden powers. By unlocking those powers and mastering them, you can streamline your workflow a great deal, setting the stage for more advanced work.

One major source of hidden powers is the Timeline's set of shortcuts: A lot of what you can accomplish in the Timeline can be accomplished more efficiently and effectively using keyboard shortcuts and context menus. My feeling is that these are not extras to be learned once you're a veteran, but small productivity enhancers that you can learn gradually all the time, enhancers that collectively offer you a good deal of extra momentum and confidence as an After Effects artist.

NOTES

The Timeline even makes render order explicit if you know how to view it; 2D layers render beginning with the lowest in the stack and ending with the top. Properties of each layer (visible by twirling down) render in top-to-bottom order. Chapter 4, "Optimizing Your Projects," further explores the render pipeline.

Organization

The Timeline is a dynamic environment; as you work with it, you constantly alter not only its contents, but also your view of the environment itself. Thus a good number of the tips offered in this chapter are workflow improvements (views and shortcuts) designed to speed you on your way.

The Timeline panel's top-level customizable views are its columns. Right-clicking on any column heading shows a menu list containing all of the possible views. You won't work with all of them revealed, however, as it's a pointless waste of space (even on a huge monitor); there are much better organized ways to keep what you need in front of you as you work.

Column Views

After Effects 7.0 has streamlined the ways in which you can organize your Timeline panel without rendering it unfamiliar to users of previous versions. Many UI elements are gone, yet no essential functionality has been lost.

You can context-click on any column heading to see and toggle all the different columns of data available in the Timeline, but there are smarter ways to turn these on and off. We begin with a setup as shown in **Figure 2.1,** the most minimal column setup that would ever be useful. I can't imagine why you would ever turn off the first four items in the Columns menu; these require minimal space and are useful all of the time. From there, you have a few useful contextual options:

▶ **Lower-left icons:** You can access most (but not all) of the extra data you need via the three toggles found at the lower left of the Timeline (**Figure 2.2**). More

Figure 2.1 This is a good minimal column layout if screen real estate is at a premium. All columns other than Parent and Comment are available via a single left-click or a shortcut.

Figure 2.2 These icons at the lower left of the Timeline expand (or collapse) the most used panes: Layer Switches, Transfer Controls, and the various timing controls for a layer.

about how, exactly to use all of the various controls they contain follows throughout this chapter and the rest of Section I; for now, focus only on revealing and concealing these controls.

▶ **Layer Switches/Transfer Controls:** You can save space by reversing the toggle between those first two switches. Enable one of them, and either press F4 or simply click in the space at the bottom of the displayed column (where the "Switches/Modes" label used to appear), and the toggle is reversed.

▶ **Layer/Source:** Another toggle lives atop the Layer Name column, the one you can never hide. Click on the column heading to toggle from Layer Name to Source Name. Source Name is always the name of the source file itself (typically as it appears in the Project panel). Layer Name defaults to the Source Name, in brackets (to show that it's unchanged); assign your own name by selecting the layer, pressing Return (don't use Enter on the numeric keypad), and typing.

▶ **Time Stretch:** The third icon at the lower left toggles In, Out, Duration, and Stretch together. It's easy to forget these are here, because there are other more visual ways of setting everything besides Stretch, whose most useful function is to time-reverse a layer, giving it a stripy appearance. (See "Manipulating Time Itself," ahead.)

If both Layer Switches and Transfer Controls are displayed, you can use the **F4** toggle to hide both of them, regaining the maximum amount of horizontal space to view keyframes and the Graph Editor.

Even if your source names are unwieldy or hard to distinguish, or you are reusing the same source for multiple layers, you can develop a logical system for naming each instance (**Figures 2.3a** and **b**).

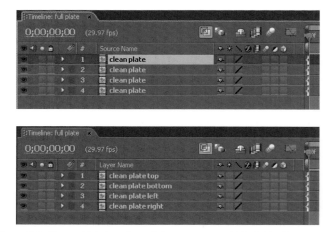

Figure 2.3 Give multiple iterations of the same source (a) individual layer names (b) in order to make them easier to distinguish as you work with them.

▶ **Parent:** The odd-man-out with the toggles is the Parent column, which is often left on in compositions that use no parenting, wasting horizontal space. (More on putting it to use in "Transform Offsets" later in this chapter).

▶ **AV Features/Keys:** Why anyone would ever hide A/V Features, or show the Keys column when these controls appear below A/V Features in the same column (**Figure 2.4**), is beyond me.

No matter how big a monitor you have for the Timeline, the game is always to preserve as much horizontal space as you can for keyframe data, keeping only the relevant controls in front of you.

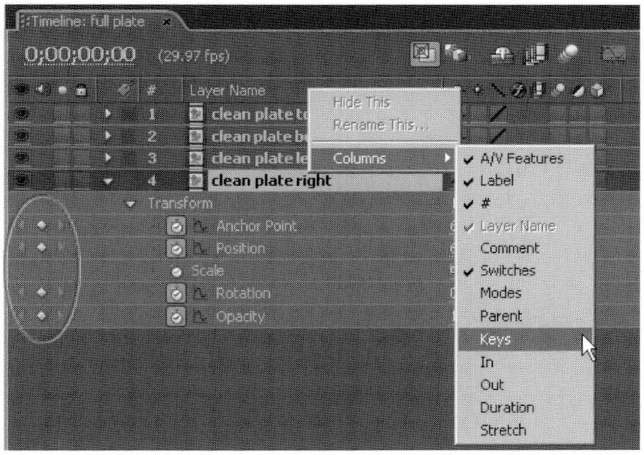

Figure 2.4 Don't bother choosing to view the Keys column separately; the data from this column tucks in nicely underneath A/V Features (circled).

Comments and Color

Ever try to make sense of someone else's project? As with computer programming, it's almost like looking at the way someone thinks.

Everyone prefers to work with clear thinkers, and you can be one for your coworkers by color-coding your layers and using plenty of comments (again, just like computer programming).

Choosing a distinct color for each layer can provide intuitive visual clues. It can even help *you* find and group items more quickly as you work. How you handle colors is really up to you; **Figure 2.5** shows an example of a Timeline with several layers that are color coded by type.

Figure 2.5 A unique color is assigned to each type of layer, so you can easily and quickly discern among them.

The manner in which label colors are assigned by default is specified in Preferences > Label Defaults; these make more sense in the Project panel context, and you will develop criteria of your own (not listed here) in the Timeline. For example, you may wish to call out special types of layers, such as track mattes and adjustment layers, with particular colors.

Comments may be the most neglected column in the Timeline, but if you know that you're going to be handing your project off to another artist, or you are creating a template for several people to use, you can offer full contextual explanations of what's going on.

A more useful and obvious way to show comments is to add them via a layer marker. With a target layer highlighted—and, if desired, at a specific time—press the * key on your numeric keypad. Double-click the layer marker, and a Marker dialog appears; enter text in the Comment field and click OK. The Comments column can be hidden, but if the layer is visible, the result appears right on it.

Solo, Lock, and Shy

Several toggles on the A/V Features and Switches columns pertain to how layers are edited and viewed (or heard) as you work. Because I've seen users who should know better miss or forget them, here's a refresher.

The round, white icon (**Figure 2.6**) in A/V Features is the Solo switch. Solo a layer, and you see only it; render a comp with a layer toggled solo, and the Solo Switches menu in Render Settings determines whether it outputs that way.

The Lock toggle is useful in situations when you know a layer is done and should not be touched; you can't even select a locked layer.

Shy is (literally) a more elusive feature; toggle a layer to shy and nothing happens, until you also activate the Shy toggle for the entire composition (**Figure 2.7**). Suddenly, all shy layers disappear from view in the Timeline, although they still display in the comp itself, as before. Because you might not always have as much vertical space to display the Timeline as you might like, this helps keep only the layers you're editing in front of you.

Figure 2.6 You may already use the Solo switch, engaged here for three individual layers; remember that leaving a layer solo in a subcomposition displays it that way in the main comp, a common gotcha.

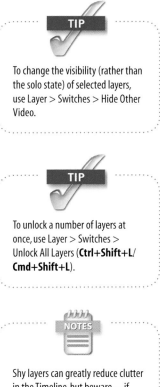

Figure 2.7 Hey, what happened to layers 2, 5, and 7? The track matte and background layers have been set to shy (and thus are hidden) by enabling the Shy toggle at the top of the Timeline (highlighted). Very useful for showing only the layers you're still adjusting, but don't forget about those hidden layers.

Navigation and Shortcuts

More than anywhere else in After Effects, the Timeline is *the* place where keyboard shortcuts—lots of them—come into play. There's plenty you can do via either a single keyboard shortcut or a single click of the mouse, where a beginner might use several clicks of the mouse.

Time Navigation

Many users—particularly those with an editing background—learn time navigation shortcuts right away. Others seem content to drag the time needle around all of the time, a policy opposed on the grounds that it quickly becomes tedious. Here are your time navigation shortcuts:

TIP

To change the visibility (rather than the solo state) of selected layers, use Layer > Switches > Hide Other Video.

TIP

To unlock a number of layers at once, use Layer > Switches > Unlock All Layers (**Ctrl+Shift+L/Cmd+Shift+L**).

NOTES

Shy layers can greatly reduce clutter in the Timeline, but beware—if you're scratching your head wondering where that layer went, take a close look at the Index numbers. If they are no longer in sequential order, then the missing number belongs to a layer that is now shy.

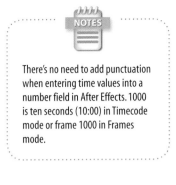

There's no need to add punctuation when entering time values into a number field in After Effects. 1000 is ten seconds (10:00) in Timecode mode or frame 1000 in Frames mode.

Figure 2.8 Setting this value to –48 would set the current time to that negative frame value, probably not what you want. But entering +–48 adds an offset of –48 frames, which might very well be useful.

The add-a-negative number offset operates in several types of number fields in the program. For example, you can subtract 30 degrees to Rotation by entering +–30; you can multiply or divide as well, using the * and / symbols, respectively. This feature works throughout number fields in the Timeline, as well as the Effect Controls and Render Queue, but not everywhere (not, for example, Duration in Composition Settings).

▶ The **Home**, **End**, **Page Up**, and **Page Down** keys correspond to moving to the first frame, the last frame, one frame backward, and one frame forward. **Shift+Page Up** and **Shift+Page Down** skip ten frames backward or forward, respectively. Press **Shift+Home** or **Shift+End**, and you are taken to the In and Out points of the Work Area.

▶ Click on the blue time status at the upper left of the timeline to open the Go to Time dialog (press **Ctrl+G/Cmd+G**). This is the way to navigate to a specific point in time.

▶ To navigate an arbitrary but precise number of frames or seconds (say, 48 frames following the current time), in the Go to Time dialog, replace the current time with your increment, in the format +48, click OK, and After Effects calculates the increment for you.

If instead you need to navigate *backward* in time 48 frames, you can't simply enter –48 in the Go to Time dialog. If you do, you're transported to negative 48 (frames or seconds, either of which probably moves the time needle right off the timeline—very confusing). Instead, you must use the format "+–48" to enter the offset; think of it as adding a negative number, rather than subtracting. It's weird, but it works (**Figure 2.8**).

Make Layers Behave

I was reviewing film-outs of shots from *The Day After Tomorrow* with the other artists at The Orphanage when my shot looking out a window at stragglers making their way across a snow-covered plaza, featuring a beautiful matte painting by Mike Pangrazio, began to loop. About two-thirds through the shot came a subtle pop. At some point, the shot had been lengthened, and a layer of noise and dirt I had included at approximately 3% transparency (for the window itself) had remained shorter in some subcomposition.

This is a primary reason some effects artists don't like to work with a timeline-based application; in other compositing programs, such as Shake, this would not inadvertently happen because static elements don't have a length.

After Effects 7.0 offers one significant improvement: Any static element you add to a composition (a single frame, a solid, an adjustment layer, and so on) is automatically added at frame 0 and extends the full length of the composition.

If you want to add a layer beginning at a specific time, you can drag the element below the Time Ruler (to the area containing the layers/Graph Editor) and you'll see a second Time Indicator appear that moves with your cursor (horizontally). This determines the layer's start frame. If other layers are present and visible, you can also determine the depth of the added layer (vertically).

Here are some other useful tips and shortcuts:

▶ Set the current frame to the previous or next keyframe (or layer marker) by pressing **J** and **K**, respectively. This works for any visible keyframe or layer marker.

▶ Navigate to the beginning or end frame of the Work Area by pressing **Shift+Home** or **Shift+End**, respectively.

▶ To reset the Work Area to the length of the composition, double-click it; to set it to the exact length of the currently active layer, press **Ctrl+Alt+B/ Cmd+Option+B**.

▶ Besides clicking on a layer to select it, you can enter the layer's index number using the numeric keypad.

▶ To select an adjacent layer without touching the mouse, use **Ctrl+Up Arrow** (**Cmd+Up Arrow**) to select the next layer up, and **Down Arrow** to select the next layer down.

▶ Add the **Alt** (**Option**) key to move a layer up or down in the stack, which you can also do with **Ctrl+]** and **Ctrl+[** (as in other Adobe applications). **Ctrl+Shift+]** moves a layer to the top of the stack and **Ctrl+Shift+[** moves it to the bottom.

▶ You can invert the layers currently selected: Context-click on a selected layer, and choose Invert Selection. (Locked layers are not selected, but Shy layers are selected even if invisible.)

NOTES

To avoid the gotcha in which a layer ends up too short for its host composition if either is edited, some users prefer to make all of their comps longer (in duration) than they ever expect to need, and manage their length using only the Work Area.

TIP

The keyboard shortcut **Ctrl+/** (**Cmd+/**) adds selected items as the top layer(s) of the active composition.

TIP

To trim a composition's Duration to the current Work Area, choose Composition > Trim Comp to Work Area.

TIP

It can be annoying that the Work Area controls both which frames preview and, by default, which frames render, because the two are often used exclusively of one another. If you employ a separate "Render Final" composition that contains all of the settings for the final render, you can leave that one untouched and mess with your other composition Work Areas as much as you want.

▶ Duplicate any layer (or virtually any selected item) using **Ctrl+D** (**Cmd+D**). If you duplicate a layer and its track matte (Chapter 3, "Selections: The Key to Compositing"), they retain proper orientation, both moving above the source.

▶ For various reasons you might instead wish to split a layer (**Ctrl+Shift+D**/**Cmd+Shift+D**); the source ends and the duplicate continues from the current time. This is useful, for example, when you need one layer to straddle another.

▶ To move a layer In point to the current time, use the [key, or press] to move the Out point. Add the **Alt** (**Option**) key to *set the current frame* as the In or Out point, trimming the layer.

▶ To slide a trimmed layer, preserving the In and Out points but translating the footage and its layer markers (but *not* keyframes), drag using the double-ended arrow you see over the area outside the In and Out points.

▶ To nudge a layer forward or backward in time (including its keyframes) use **Alt+Page Up**/**Page Down** (**Option+Page Up**/**Page Down**).

Often, you may add elements whose size or pixel aspect doesn't match those of the composition, yet which are meant to fill the frame (or one axis). No need to break open the Scale controls and guess; you can use the Fit to Comp shortcuts (which are included in the Layer > Transform menu).

The standard Fit to Comp, **Ctrl+Alt+F** (**Cmd+Option+F**) can be dangerous in that it ignores the aspect ratio of the layer, stretching X and Y scale individually to match each to the comp itself.

More commonly useful are the shortcuts for Fit to Comp on a single axis (X or Y), which retain the aspect ratio to scale the non-dominant axis. You can Fit to Comp Width (**Ctrl+Alt+Shift+H**/**Cmd+Option+Shift+H**), or Fit to Comp Height (twisting your fingers around **Ctrl+Alt+Shift+G**/ **Cmd+Option+Shift+G**).

There is even a preference controlling whether split layers are created above or below the source layer (Preferences > General; the toggle is labeled Create Split Layers Above Original Layer).

To memorize the H and G options for Fit to Comp, notice that they are adjacent on your keyboard to the standard command: F G & H.

Timeline View Options

And what about working with keyframe data? This has changed drastically with the Graph Editor, but some useful workflow enhancements remain, whether or not you're in Graph Editor mode:

▶ The **;** key toggles between a fully zoomed-in view of the current frame and a fully zoomed-out view of the whole Timeline.

▶ The slider at the bottom of the Timeline zooms in and out more selectively (**Figure 2.9**).

▶ If your mouse includes a scroll wheel, there's a cooler option: Not only can you scroll up and down the layer stack, and Shift-scroll left and right in a zoomed Timeline view, but Alt-scrolling (Option-scrolling) dynamically zooms you in and out of time. Shift-scrolling navigates back and forth. Position your cursor over the Timeline panel to try these.

At the right edge of the Timeline is the Comp button (**Figure 2.10a**), which brings the Composition view associated with that Timeline forward. The Composition panel similarly has a Timeline button for the same purpose in reverse (**Figure 2.10b**). Neither of these is necessary, however; if you need to make either panel appear, or toggle between the two of them, use the backslash (\) key.

Just above the Comp button is the Comp marker bin, where you can drag out a marker to a point on your Timeline. Markers are numbered sequentially. Holding down the Shift key as you drag the time needle snaps the needle to any comp or layer markers present.

Figures 2.10a and b Need to get to the Timeline related to the displayed composition, or vice versa? Each shortcut button is shown here, in respective order, but if you can remember the \ key, you don't need either of them. Just above the cursor in 2.10b is the Comp marker bin, from which you can drag up to 10 numbered markers.

Figure 2.9 Unless your mouse includes a scroll wheel, this click-and-drag interface at the bottom of the Timeline panel is probably the fastest method of zooming in and out.

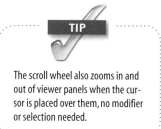

TIP

The scroll wheel also zooms in and out of viewer panels when the cursor is placed over them, no modifier or selection needed.

TIP

The Current Time Indicator is capable of going where your Timeline panel cannot: to time frames previous to the first frame of the composition or beyond the last frame (usually because the trimmed area of a layer extends there). In such cases, the indicator disappears from the Timeline entirely. Have no fear. Clicking in the Time Ruler to place the indicator, or using any of the time shortcuts outlined above recovers it.

TIP

To add a specific numbered comp marker, press Shift and one of the numbers at the top of your keyboard (not the numeric keypad): 1 through 0.

Replacing Layers

You will often want to replace the source of a layer with an alternate take or a different element in the Project panel, while keeping all of the settings you have added to it thus far.

You can easily do this by highlighting the layer to be replaced in the Timeline and holding down the Alt (Option) key while dragging the new source to the Timeline. An even easier method is to select both the existing layer and the new source and then press **Ctrl+Alt+/** (**Cmd+Option+/**). All of the settings from the previous layer, along with any applied effects, translate to the new layer automatically.

How do you neutralize a layer that is taking up a disproportionate amount of render time? Replacing it on the fly is not the recommended method; Chapter 4 covers some much more elegant methods for assigning proxies and pre-rendering embedded compositions.

NOTES

Beware if you are replacing with source material of a different size or aspect, as the mask and transform values may no longer work properly. Mask values are relative and will scale to the dimensions of the new layer; other values (transforms and effects settings) are absolute and, generally speaking, do not.

Animation Methods

Twirl down any layer in the Timeline, and the Transform controls are revealed. On a typical layer, transforms are spatial data related to Position and its cousins Anchor Point, Scale, Rotation, and, um, Opacity. Opacity isn't really spatial transform data, but apparently Adobe decided to sort of grandfather it in here as an essential layer property; and "Transforms" evidently has a snappier ring to it.

▶ The keyboard shortcuts to reveal individual transforms are the first letter of each type: **P**, **A**, **S**, **R**, and, um, **T**—Opacity is the oddball again, because O is already in use as the Out point of a layer (mentioned above).

▶ To reveal additional properties, hold down **Shift** when typing the letter shortcut; you can also toggle a property to hide in this manner.

A *property* in After Effects is a data channel found in a twirled-down layer. Typically a property can be animated and has a stopwatch icon beside it which, when clicked, sets a keyframe at the current time.

That by itself is simple enough. But there are, in fact, many different ways to animate a property in After Effects. How many can you think of? As an example, if you wanted to move a layer 200 pixels along the X axis over 24 frames, after setting the first keyframe and moving the time indicator forward 24 frames, you could

- Drag the layer to the new position in the Composition panel (with the Shift key held down, constraining it to one axis)
- **Shift+Right Arrow** 20 times to move the layer exactly 200 pixels
- Enter the new value by highlighting the X Position numerical value and typing in the new number
- Drag the X Position numerical value to the right until it is 200 pixels higher (perhaps holding down Shift to increment it by ten pixels)
- Enter a numerical offset by highlighting the X Position numerical value and typing +200 (as was done with time, above)
- Copy and paste the Position keyframe from another layer, or another point in time (assuming there is a keyframe with the needed Position value)

And those are just the options to keyframe that one property. You could also create the animation without keyframing a new Position value, and transform the layer 200 pixels on the X axis over 24 frames by

- Keyframing an anchor point offset in the opposite direction (negative 200 pixel X value) over 24 frames
- Enabling 3D for the layer, adding a 50mm camera, and animating the camera moving 200 pixels, again in the negative X direction
- Parenting the layer to another layer that has the transform
- Replacing the layer with a composition that already contains the layer and transform
- Assigning an expression to the Position channel that performs the animation without keyframes

NOTES

Don't worry, you're not going to be tested on these. But you can understand that there are many approaches to a given problem in After Effects, and the more of them you know, the more prepared you'll be for whatever comes your way.

NOTES

The Transform effect exists for one reason only: to allow you to change the order in which Transforms occur. Normally, they occur before all effects, but this plug-in lets them occur after an effect is applied as well, without the need to precompose.

TIP

When dragging text in the Timeline or Effect Controls, hold down **Shift** to increment values at ten times the normal amount, or hold down **Ctrl+Alt** (**Cmd+Option**) to increment at one tenth the normal amount. The "normal amount" is typically, but not always, 1 for any given property; it depends on the slider range, which you can edit by context-clicking on the value in Effect Controls and choosing Edit Value.

If that's not crazy enough, you could even

▶ Apply the Transform effect to the layer and animate the effect's Position value

▶ Animate in real time via the cursor using Motion Sketch (I did say "crazy")

▶ Paste in a path (perhaps using a Mask or a Path from Photoshop or Illustrator) to the Position channel, adjusting timing as needed (this method defaults to creating a two-second animation)—again, crazy, but possible

The last two options, in particular, are clearly designed for other, more complicated situations. Parenting is useful to transform several layers in the same manner, while expressions link two animations together, or create one from scratch.

Note that there is even a variety of ways to enter values while animating. You can

▶ Drag with the Selection tool (shortcut: **V**)

▶ Drag the Pan Behind tool to move the anchor point (shortcut: **Y**)

▶ Drag the Rotate tool (shortcut: **W**, which the official documentation even points out is for "wotate")

But you can also work directly with the values found in the Timeline, and you can do so by highlighting and entering values, or by dragging on them without highlighting.

Keyframes and The Graph Editor

In the last edition of this book, I began the Keyframes section saying, "The After Effects keyframe interface is fairly highly evolved, meaning you can create quite complex animations." With version 7.0, keyframes are more accessible and powerful thanks to the addition of the Graph Editor.

Sometimes called a "curve editor" in other applications, the Graph Editor is hardly an invention unique to After Effects, which was in fact among the last major animation packages to lack one. If you have animated using a curve editor before, much of what is included with this feature set may seem familiar and intuitive; my goal is to provide a context for all of the options this new toolset offers.

It's not as if the Graph Editor completely supersedes the layer bar view, which is what you see when it's toggled off. You can still more easily see where keyframes are placed on several layers and the overall structure of the composition in that view. The purpose of the Graph Editor is to give you maximum control over fine-tuning an animation, whether it consists of one animated property or several.

Learn to Use The Graph Editor

The simplest way to get started with the Graph Editor is to examine a sample project and to try messing around with it. To demonstrate the many features of this tool set, 02_graphEditor.aep in the accompanying disc's Chapter02 directory contains a simple animation, "bouncing ball 2d." If you preview the one composition in this project, you will see a ball bounce across the frame, with a little bit of squash and stretch animation occurring from where it hits the bottom of the frame. I recommend you begin by studying the existing animation and then try creating your own version.

To enable the Graph Editor, click its icon in the Timeline (**Figure 2.11**); you'll now see a grid in the area previously occupied by the layer bars. At the bottom of this grid are the Graph Editor controls, which are labeled in **Figure 2.12**.

Figure 2.11 Click this icon in the Timeline to access 7.0's new Graph Editor.

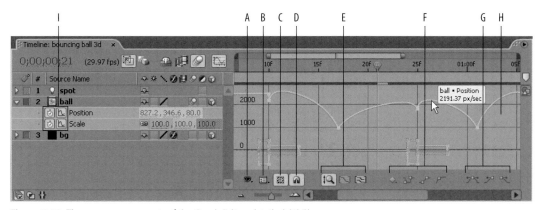

Figure 2.12 The many components of the Graph Editor, detailed: (A) Show Properties, (B) Graph Options, (C) Show Transform Box, (D) Snap (E) Zoom controls, (F) Keyframe controls, (G) Ease controls, (H) properties graphs, and (I) Graph Editor Set toggles.

Show Properties

At this point, if nothing is selected, you will not see any animation data; if you select an animated property you will probably see animation data, but what you see depends on the settings in the Show Properties menu (the eyeball at the lower left). Three toggles in this menu control how animation curves are displayed:

▶ Show Selected Properties displays animation data for any selected properties

▶ Show Animated Properties displays all animated properties in a selected layer

▶ Show Graph Editor Set displays properties whose Graph Editor Set toggle (next to the stopwatch and labeled I in Figure 2.12) is enabled

Here's how it works. Select any component of any layer, or the layer itself, and all animated (keyframe) properties for that layer are displayed. If you want to see only one property from that layer—say, only Position in the ball layer—deselect the layer (**F2** or **Ctrl+Shift+A**/**Cmd+Shift+A**) and enable the Graph Editor toggle for Position.

That way, if a property inadvertently becomes deselected, it doesn't disappear, and if you want an overview of all animation for a layer, you simply select that layer.

Graph Options

Now, how to understand all of that data that shows up and focus only on what you need? The Graph Options menu (labeled B in Figure 2.12) controls which components of the properties are displayed. For example, display only the Position data for ball and you might see something like the keyframe data in **Figure 2.13**.

Okay, what's going on here? By default, Auto-Select Graph Type and Show Reference Graph are enabled in the Graph Options. Therefore you see one curve (white or light magenta) with editable vertices (the little squares at each keyframe); this is the Speed Graph for Position. You also see a red and a green curve with no selectable vertices; these are the Value Graphs for X and Y position.

The most intuitive way to set Show Properties might seem to be to enable Show Selected Properties and disable the other two, but by default a new copy of After Effects has the opposite configuration (only Show Selected Properties is disabled), which is actually a more powerful (less annoying) way to work.

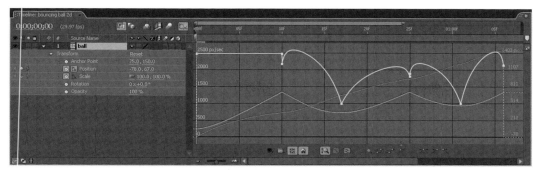

Figure 2.13 The 2D version of the bouncing ball animation is shown with the Speed Graph active and the Value Graph shown as a Reference Graph. Although After Effects does not allow you to keyframe individual axes independently of one another, they are both displayed (and if made active, can be edited) in the Graph Editor.

Spatial properties such as Position have two types of values in After Effects: Value (the actual position) and Speed (the rate of transition from one position to the next). Auto-Select Graph Type correctly assumes that with Position it is more useful to adjust speed in the Graph Editor, and position in the composition itself, so it displays Speed as the editable curve (and Value as a reference).

You can, of course, override this by choosing Edit Value Graph instead, and there is one compelling reason to do so: This offers you explicit control over a single axis (X or Y in a 2D composition; X, Y, or Z with 3D). However, it is important to understand that After Effects does not allow you to keyframe spatial axes individually. Notice that if you select a vertex on the red X axis, the vertex on the green Y axis is also selected, and although adjusting its value doesn't affect the other, adjusting its timing does.

The Reference Graph shows whichever graph type is not selected, along with corresponding values (in gray) at the right edge of the Graph Editor (look again at Figure 2.13). If you're finding it hard to wrap your head around even seeing spatial values in the graph, toggle Show Reference Graph off and you'll see only the Speed graph (**Figure 2.14**).

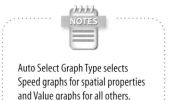

Auto Select Graph Type selects Speed graphs for spatial properties and Value graphs for all others.

A relatively simple method for separating X, Y, and Z axes for animation using parenting is explored later in this chapter. You can also apply the Separate XYZ Position preset (in Animation Presets, in the Effects & Presets panel) to set up separate axes with expressions.

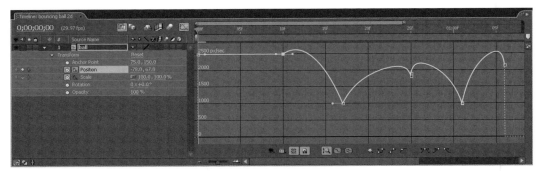

Figure 2.14 Displaying a reference graph as in Figure 2.13 is overkill in many cases; here is a simpler and more typical view of the Speed graph only. The graph shows the rate at which the layer travels at any given point of time; the low points at the bottom of each "v" shape show eases into a keyframe transition (the slowest points in the animation, which in this case are still 1000 pixels per second).

TIP

Show Graph Tool Tips is an especially useful feature to leave on; move your cursor over any animation data and you see relevant values at that exact time, including animation values at points other than keyframes.

NOTES

The Snap button causes any keyframe you drag to snap to virtually any other visible marker in the Graph Editor, but it does not snap to whole frame values if Allow Keyframes Between Frames is on.

The second set of Graph Options (from Show Audio Waveforms down to Show Expression Editor) are more self-explanatory; most of them pertain to features discussed elsewhere in this chapter. It's worth scanning these to notice, for example, that you can display an audio waveform or an expression in the Graph Editor.

At the bottom of the Graph Options menu is the Allow Keyframes Between Frames toggle. With this off, keyframes that you drag snap to precise frame values (as you would expect); turn it on and you can drag a keyframe to any point in time (should you wish to time a keyframe between two frames for some reason). When you scale a set of keyframes using the Transform Box, keyframes can fall in between frames whether or not this option is on.

The Transform Box

With the Transform Box, things really start to get interesting in the Graph Editor. Toggle this on and select more than one keyframe, and you see a semi-opaque white box with handles around the selected frames. Grab the handle at the right side and drag it left: You are scaling the entire animation to occur more quickly. Select all keyframes in the example composition and drag the right handles to the left; the relative timing of the animation is all the same, but it happens more quickly.

This is generally intuitive to artists used to editing free-transforms with mask shapes (the same controls used with Masks in After Effects, covered in Chapter 3). To simply translate a set of keyframes, you just drag inside the box. There are additionally a few unique things you can do with this control worth knowing about:

▶ To offset the center of the Transform Box and scale around the bounding box's anchor point, first move the anchor from the center to wherever you want it, then Ctrl-drag/Cmd-drag and the box scales around that point.

▶ To reverse keyframes, drag beyond the opposite (left/right) edge of the box.

▶ Speed graphs can only be adjusted horizontally, but value graphs have handles on all corners and sides of the bounding box. To scale the box proportionally, Shift-drag on a corner. To taper values at one end, Ctrl+Alt-drag (Cmd+Option-drag) on a corner (**Figure 2.15**). To move one side of the box up or down, Ctrl+Alt+Shift-drag (Cmd+Option+Shift–drag) on a corner. You can even skew the contents of the box by Alt-dragging (Option-dragging) on a corner handle.

Figure 2.15 Artists often wonder how to scale values proportionally; here's how. By Ctrl+Alt-dragging (Cmd+Option-dragging) on the corner of the Transform Box, you can taper (or in this case, expand) values at one end of the selection area.

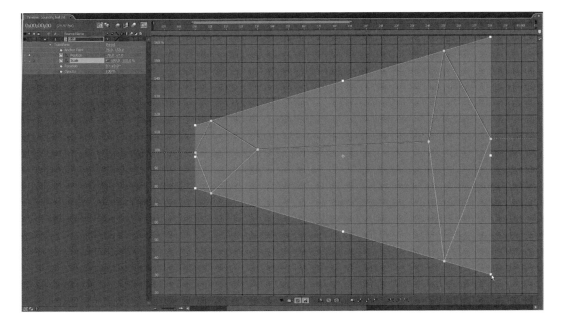

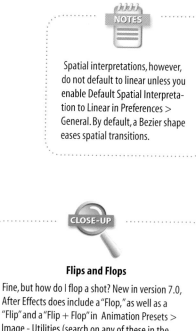
Temporal Data and Eases

Before you go completely crazy manipulating keyframe data with a bounding box, however, it's worth looking at the basics of how individual keyframes can be set, because you'll make these types of adjustments much more often.

A typical way that keyframes are used in an effects situation is to say, about a given value, "I want it to be this value at this point in the shot, and this value here." By default, After Effects sets linear temporal transitions; in other words, you travel from keyframe A to keyframe B at a steady rate, then from keyframe B to keyframe C at a separate but still steady rate.

Many basic animations are greatly aided by adding eases. Experienced animators and anthropologists alike will tell you how rare it is that anything in nature proceeds in a linear fashion; nature is full of arcs and curves. A classic example of this is a camera push: In most cases, with a real camera operator, a push would start and stop gently, moving at a steady rate only at the middle of the transition.

Figure 2.16 To flop a shot, be sure to uncheck Constrain Proportions before setting the X value to –100%.

CLOSE-UP

Flips and Flops

Fine, but how do I flop a shot? New in version 7.0, After Effects does include a "Flop," as well as a "Flip" and a "Flip + Flop" in Animation Presets > Image - Utilities (search on any of these in the Effects & Presets panel). To "flop" a shot means to invert it horizontally, on the Y axis (a "flip" occurs on the X axis). The preset employs the Transform effect, which unfortunately is not compatible with 32 bpc mode; you can instead toggle Constrain Proportions for Scale and add a minus sign beside the X value (**Figure 2.16**).

Easy Ease

A quick way to create eases is to apply the Easy Ease keyframe assistants. These can be applied as follows

▶ Context-click a keyframe and choose one of the Easy Ease options under the Keyframe Assistant submenu

▶ Use the keyboard shortcuts: **F9** applies Bezier interpolation, creating eases in and out of a keyframe, while **Shift+F9** creates an ease into the keyframe only, and **Ctrl+Shift+F9** (**Cmd+Shift+F9**) creates an ease out

▶ Use one of the Easy Ease buttons at the lower right of the Graph Editor

For the camera push example, you might ease out of the first frame and ease in to the final frame, adding an ease in both directions to any keyframes in the middle (for example, if the speed of the push changed at some point).

To see the result, twirl down the property to which the eases were applied. **Figures 2.17a** and **b** show the difference between a default linear camera push and one to which eases have been applied. The keyframes have changed from linear to Bezier type, and rate of motion is described by a curve instead of a straight line.

Now suppose you want to customize that ease. The Graph Editor makes this—pardon the expression—easier. Select any keyframe and you see yellow handles extending to its left and right. To make a transition ease more, drag the yellow handle away from the keyframe; to reduce the ease, drag it inward toward the keyframe. You can even create eases in this manner without having to set Easy Ease in the first place.

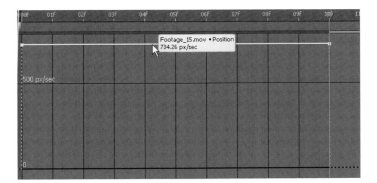

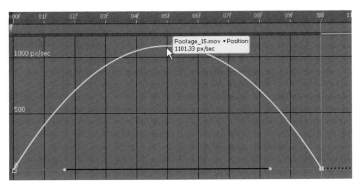

Figures 2.17a and b With no eases, the Speed: Position graph is flat, moving at a steady rate (a). Add eases (b), and it arcs from 0 (at the beginning and end of the move) to a higher value at the center peak of the ease.

Holds

You must set Hold keyframes deliberately, via one of the following

▶ Context-click on the keyframe and choose Toggle Hold Keyframe

▶ Use the shortcut **Ctrl+Alt+H** (**Cmd+Shift+H**)

▶ Choose the Hold button below the Graph Editor (the one with the graph lines all at right angles)

A Hold keyframe's value does not interpolate to the next keyframe. In layer bar mode this is indicated by the square appearance on one or both sides of the keyframe. In the Graph Editor this appears as a flat horizontal line to the right of a keyframe.

To reposition a layer over time with no transitions (no keyframe in-betweening whatsoever) begin by setting the first frame as a Hold keyframe; all keyframes that follow it in time will be Hold keyframes, signaled by their completely square appearance in layer bar mode or a series of right angles in the Graph Editor (**Figures 2.18a** and **b**).

Hold keyframes solve problems any time you see unwanted in-between information creep into an animation; beware of this particularly with spatial animations.

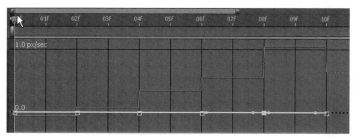

Figures 2.18a and b A series of Bezier keyframes have been converted to Hold keyframes, evident by the square shape at the right of each keyframe in the layer bar view (a) and right angles in the Graph Editor (b).

Spatial Data and Curves

If you are called upon to create a complex animation, the After Effects interface is up to it. I can't teach you to be a great animator, but I can focus on what you need to know to keyframe effectively and to avoid common pitfalls.

As you saw above, when keyframing Position (or Anchor Point) data, there are in fact two ways you can adjust keyframes: temporally (via the Speed graph) and spatially (via the Value graph, but more likely by adjusting the same keyframes as they appear in the Composition and Layer panels). A closer look at the simple bouncing ball reveals a lot about animating spatial keyframes (**Figures 2.19** to **2.22**).

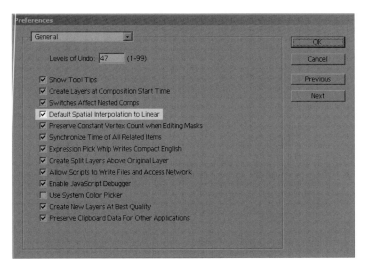

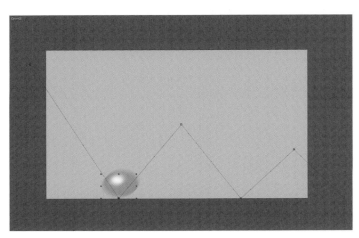

Figure 2.19 Under Preferences > General (**Ctrl+Alt+;** or **Cmd+Option+;**), the option Default Spatial Interpolation to Linear is off by default, producing this result when you create three or more position keys. After Effects also applies an automatic Bezier shape to any point that falls between two other points—the opposite of what you want for a bouncing ball.

Figure 2.20 Click the check box for Default Spatial Interpolation to Linear, restart After Effects, and this is the result: three keyframes that are linear in both time and position. This is in many cases preferable to movements that always arc through keyframes, and you may want to leave this preference on, but it does not create the realistic arcs of a bouncing ball.

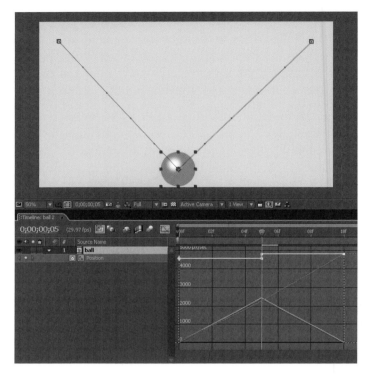

Figure 2.21 Hold down the Ctrl/Cmd key while clicking the middle keyframe to activate its Bezier handles, then Ctrl/Cmd-click on one of the handles to "break" them, enabling you to form the V-shape shown here, which naturally causes curved arcs to and from the bounce point.

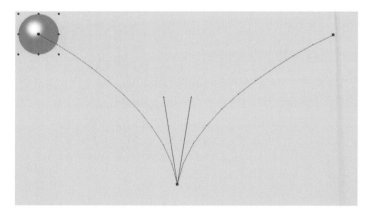

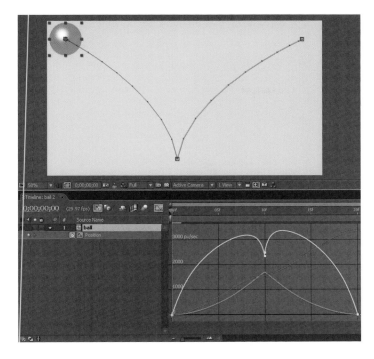

Figure 2.22 Temporal eases create a more realistic variation in motion speed. Selecting the first and last frame and pressing **F9** (or selecting an ease shortcut below the Graph Editor) causes eases to those frames and an effective acceleration in and out of the keyframe in between them. Look closely. The dots are spaced further apart (traveling faster) at the bottom and closer together at the top, where the eases are.

In the (somewhat likely) case you never need a bouncing ball animation, what does this example show you? Let's recap:

▶ You can take control of the shape of your motion path in the Composition panel, using the same shortcuts to adjust Beziers as with the Pen tool (described in detail in the next chapter).

▶ Realistic motion often requires a combination of shaping the motion path Beziers and adding eases to keyframes; you can perform the two actions independently on any given keyframe.

So, even though there is an infinite variety of position animations available to you in After Effects, they are just elaborations on the basic constraints covered here. True, it can get a little trickier in 3D, but mostly it's just trickier to see what you are doing.

Roving Keyframes

Suppose your animation must follow an exact path, hitting precise points, but progress steadily, with no variation in the rate of travel. This is the situation for which Roving keyframes were devised. **Figure 2.23** shows a before and after view of the application of a roving keyframe to the animation in Figure 2.22; the path of the animation is identical, but the keyframes are now evenly spaced.

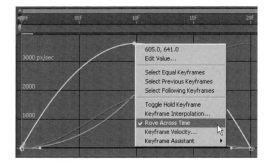

Figure 2.23 The middle keyframe was set to rove (by turning off the tiny toggle below the keyframe) and is now positioned in between frames 15 and 16; the keyframe's interpolation setting is no longer taken into account, and it moves to keep the curve created by the other keyframes smooth and steady.

Each keyframe can have one of three basic transition types, each of which has a shortcut at the bottom of the Graph Editor: Hold, Linear, and Automatic Bezier. If you adjust the handles or apply Easy Ease, you create a Custom Bezier Shape.

Copying and Pasting Trickery

There's a bit of a gotcha laying in wait when copying and pasting keyframe data. You must clearly recognize which item is active when you copy, and which is active when you paste, and this is not always as easy as you might think.

By default, After Effects tries to make things clear and automatic. If you copy keyframes from a particular property, then simply paste them to another layer, After Effects pastes them to that layer's corresponding property, beginning at the current time.

If that target property doesn't exist, because it's part of an effect applied only to the source layer, After Effects adds the effect as well as the keyframes. So far, so good.

However, it is also permissible to copy keyframes from one property and paste them to a different, similar property. For example, to apply a 2D Position keyframe to the Flare Center position of a Lens Flare effect, you simply select the Flare Center property in the timeline before pasting (otherwise those keyframes are copied to the Position property).

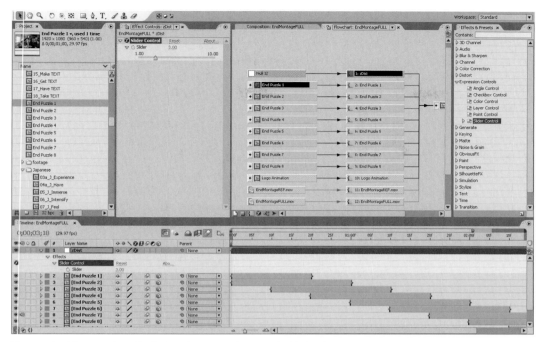

Figure 2.24 It's easy to be tricked when six separate items are highlighted (darker) in the Project, Timeline, Effect Controls Effects & Presets and Flowchart views. Press Delete, and what disappears? Hint: check which panel is active—it's the Slider Control effect in Effect Controls.

Therein lies the danger for any artist not paying attention, or failing to recognize which item is currently selected when copying or pasting. **Figure 2.24** shows a classic example, where a layer's properties are not twirled down, making it easy to miss that the Effect Controls panel is forward and has an effect highlighted. That effect only is copied, instead of the entire layer.

If the result of a copy and paste seems strange, immediately undo and try the copy operation again, selecting exactly the thing you want to copy and copying it with no intervening steps.

Real-World Graph Editor

This section has offered an introduction to the many features of the Graph Editor, but the question remains: How exactly should you use it? Should it ideally be active most

NOTES

New in After Effects 7.0 is a small lock icon that appears on the Effect Controls tab. Enable this toggle, and that effect remains visible even when you select a different layer. (This toggle also resides on the Composition and Layer tabs; its full use is described in Chapter 4.)

of the time, or only when refining an animation? For which types of animations is it most helpful?

Call me old-fashioned, but I don't recommend working in the Graph Editor constantly until you are at the refinement stage of your animation. Basic timing and the decision as to whether a given keyframe should be linear or include eases is more clearly and simply undertaken in the Layer view; the Graph Editor, by and large, is there when you need to go beyond what is possible in that view.

Try recreating a bouncing ball animation of your own from scratch (or anything with natural, specific motion), beginning in the Layer view and moving to the Graph Editor once the basic timing and movement are roughed in. It should only be a couple of minutes before you're ready to activate the Graph Editor, but you may also find that you want to return to the Layer view to simplify the animation—say, to reset a keyframe to be linear (by Ctrl/Cmd-clicking on it).

Overall, Layer view will be preferable when

▶ Blocking in keyframes with respect to the overall composition

▶ Timing needs are broad (Linear, Easy Ease, and Auto-Bezier are sufficient)

▶ Making editorial/compositing decisions with layers (layer start/stop/duration, splitting layers, determining layer order, and so on)

The Graph Editor is essential in cases when

▶ Refining an individual animation curve

▶ Comparing spatial and temporal data

▶ Scaling animation data, especially around a specific pivot point

▶ Timing is extremely specific (for example, a keyframe is needed between frames)

Either will do when

▶ Editing expressions

▶ Changing keyframe type (Linear, Hold, Ease in, and so on)

On the whole, although the Graph Editor is certainly one of the top three changes in After Effects 7.0, you will find that the majority of compositing and even animating is best accomplished in Layer view.

Über-mastery

With a nod to Friedrich Nietzsche, who hypothesized the *übermensch* (literally the "over-man" a.k.a. superman), let's focus in on the shortcuts that will make you a rapid-fire animator. This section is not only about the überkey, which is among the most useful shortcuts in all of After Effects, but also about taking control of keyframe data in general.

The überkey is available in two delicious flavors: **U** and **UU**. In the same 02_graphEditor.aep project, highlight the ball layer, and press **U**. All properties with keyframes (Position and Scale in this case) are revealed. Press **U** again to toggle, and they are concealed. You could arrive cold at an animation you've never seen and immediately find out what's been animated and where.

But wait, there's more. Now highlight the bg layer, which contains no keyframes whatsoever, and press **UU** (two Us in quick succession). All of the properties that have been set to any value other than their default—including those with keyframes (of which there are none in this case)—are revealed.

The utility of the **U** shortcut is immediately obvious: It's a quick way to get at keyframes to edit them or to find a keyframe that you suspect is hiding somewhere. But **UU**—now *that* is a full-on problem-solving tool all to itself. It allows you to quickly investigate what has been edited on a given layer, is helpful when troubleshooting your own layer settings, and is priceless when investigating an unfamiliar project. Highlight all of the layers in your comp, press **UU**, and you have before you all of the edits that have been made to all of the layer properties.

TIP

To reveal only applied effects on a selected layer, use the **E** key. Or, if the überkey reveals effects and transforms and you want only the transforms, use **Shift+E** to toggle off revealed effects.

NOTES

What's missing from the **UU** shortcut's reach? Any settings in nested compositions cannot be seen, other than by Alt-clicking (Option-clicking) to open them and **UU** on their layers as well. Locked layers are not affected by **UU**, and shy layers remain shy (and thus potentially hidden, although their properties are revealed). Key settings that affect a layer's appearance but are not properties, such as Blending Modes and Motion Blur (discussed later) are not revealed by **UU**.

Figure 2.25 What node-based compositing application is this? Why, the decidedly non-nodal After Effects. You cannot interact with this view the way a Shake user might expect, although you can open (or even delete) compositions (or even footage and layers) from this view.

Dissecting a Project

If you've been handed an unfamiliar project and need to make sense of it quickly, there are a couple of other tools to help you.

The Flowchart view offers a broad overview of the project's structure; it can be enabled with the right-most button along the bottom of the Composition panel, via Window > Flowchart or using **Ctrl+F11/Cmd+F11**. You have to see it to believe it: a nodal interface in After Effects (**Figure 2.25**), the least nodal of any of the major compositing applications.

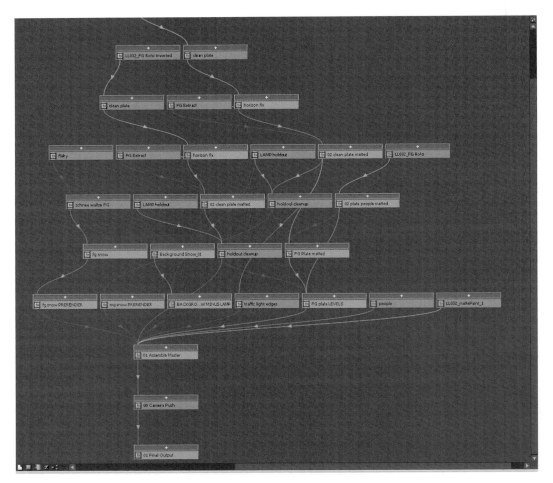

This view shows how objects (layers, compositions and effects) have been used and how they interrelate. The + button above a composition reveals its components; for the cleanest view, toggle layers and effects off at the lower left.

In the panel menu you can choose your view; Left to Right fits well on a typical monitor. Whether you choose straight or curved connecting lines is up to you, but you can clean up the view by clicking this toggle holding the Alt/Option key.

You can open any comp by double-clicking it in the Flowchart. Turn off the Shy toggle at the top if it's on, highlight all of the layers (**Ctrl+A/Cmd+A**), and enter **UU** to reveal all altered properties. Now preview the composition, stopping at any frame where you have questions and investigating which settings and animations apply to that point in time. If you find a nested composition, open it and investigate in the same manner.

It's most effective to start with the top-level compositions (those not contained in other compositions) and work your way backward. I wouldn't call this process speedy with a complex project, but if you approach it in this logical manner, you can escape feeling like you're in that dream where you showed up to work without any pants on.

Keyframe Navigation and Selection

Although no shortcut can hold a candle to the überkey, there are several other useful animation shortcuts:

- **J** and **K** keys navigate backward and forward, respectively, through all visible keyframes (and layer markers, and Work Area boundaries).

- To select all keyframes for a property, click that property's name.

- Context-click on a keyframe to Select Previous Keyframes or Select Following Keyframes. There is even an option to Select Equal Keyframes (those with an identical value).

- You can use **Alt/Option+Shift+**the shortcut corresponding to a transform property (**P**, **A**, **S**, **R**, or **T**) to set the first keyframe.

TIP

J and **K** hit all revealed keyframes, so to navigate in one channel only, you can click the arrows that appear under A/V Features (the Keys column). Or reveal only the keyframes in that channel; **J** and **K** will ignore the rest.

Multi-selection works differently with keyframes in the Layer Bar view than anywhere else in the application. To add or subtract a single frame from a selected group, Shift-click. Ctrl/Cmd-clicking on keyframes converts them to Auto-Bezier mode. This is not the case in the Graph Editor view.

▶ You can also use any stopwatch in the Effect Controls to set the first keyframe for an effect property at the current frame.

▶ To add a keyframe in Effect Controls without changing any values, context-click on the stopwatch and choose Add Keyframe.

Read on; you are not a keyframe Jedi—yet.

Keyframe Offsets

To offset the values of multiple keyframes by the same amount, select them all, *make certain that the Current Time Indicator is resting on a frame with one of the selected keyframes*, and drag the text value of one of them by your offset amount. If instead, you edit one of these by typing in a new value, all keyframes will be set to that value—not, in most cases, what you want.

Other tips for working with multiple keyframes include

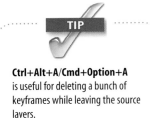

Ctrl+Alt+A/Cmd+Option+A is useful for deleting a bunch of keyframes while leaving the source layers.

▶ Nudge selected keyframes (one or many) forward or backward in time using **Alt+Right/Left Arrow** (**Option+Right/Left Arrow**), respectively.

▶ Deselect keyframes using **Shift+F2** *only*. Select all visible keyframes (without selecting their layers) using **Ctrl+Alt+A** (**Cmd+Option+A**).

▶ Delete a bunch of keyframes (using the Delete key), and the value of the *first* keyframe remains; turn off the stopwatch to clear them, and the *current* value remains.

Transform Offsets

The two most common ways to offset a transform animation—to edit its position, rotation, or scale from a point other than its center—are intuitive, easy to use, and well documented. In an individual layer, move the anchor point from the center to a specific point in the frame, typically using the Pan Behind tool (keyboard shortcut: **Y**). Details can be found in the "Editing the Anchor Point" section.

Although the transform box in the Graph Editor offers a clear visual method for scaling keyframes in time, you can do this in Layer view as well. Select a set of keyframes, Alt-drag (Option-drag) on a keyframe at either end of the set, and the entire set is scaled proportionally in time (with the opposite end of the selected set acting as the stationary anchor).

You can center several layers around a single layer by parenting them to that layer. The children take on all of the transforms of the parent layer (not Opacity, which, remember, isn't a real transform) plus whatever offsets they already have.

The number-one piece of advice when editing an anchor point or creating a parent-child relationship is to do so *before* animating, if at all possible. With Transform keyframes already in place, these settings work as offsets, and can change the current Position frame, messing up the animation as a whole.

The After Effects developers are consistent in their design of new features: Activating a feature should not change the appearance of the composition. Therefore editing an anchor point position with the Pan Behind tool triggers an equivalent offset to the Position, in the exact opposite direction. Similarly, when you parent a layer to another layer, the child layer does not move even if the parent layer is not at its default position.

That's all clear. But reset an offset anchor point in the middle of a Position animation, and the Position keyframe at that point in time changes. Or undo parenting at a frame other than the one where you set it, and its Position value changes so that it appears to remain in the same place. Weird.

TIP

You can override the default behavior described here. To adjust an anchor point or undo parenting without changing any dependent Position value, hold down the Alt (Option) key as you make the change.

Editing the Anchor Point

The most straightforward method to edit an anchor point in the Composition panel is to use the Pan Behind tool (**Y**); doing so offsets Position to maintain current appearance. For a similar result, you can edit anchor point values in the Timeline, but Position data is unaffected.

It is difficult to edit animated anchor point data in the Composition panel. Instead, activate the Layer panel. If you have animated the anchor point, change the View pulldown from Masks to Anchor Point Path (**Figure 2.26**).

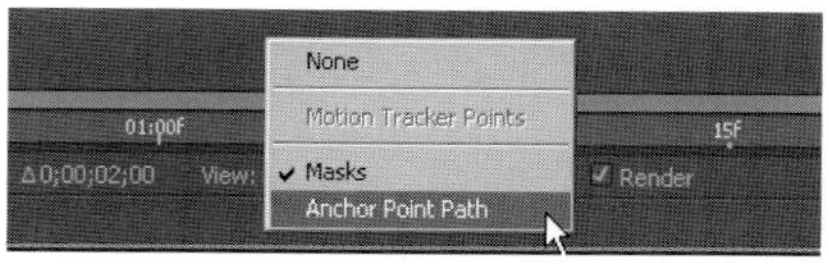

Figure 2.26 Masks, not Anchor Point Path, is the default Layer display mode. Change that as needed using this menu at the bottom of the Layer panel. Note that the bouncing ball examples included in 02_graphEditor.aep feature an offset (but not animated) anchor point, allowing squash and stretch animation to occur around the point of contact (at the base of the ball).

NOTES

The 02_graphEditor.aep project used for the bouncing ball animation earlier in this chapter includes an anchor point offset to the base of the ball; this allows the scaling involved for squash and stretch in the bounce to occur around the point of contact.

Editing the Parent Hierarchy

To set up a parent-child relationship, you can choose the target parent layer from the pull-down menu in the Parent column of the Timeline. Or, you can use the pickwhip control next to the pull-down menu, dragging it to the target parent layer. Either method will set multiple selected layers to the same parent.

Parenting "sticks" even when you change layer order or duplicate or rename the parent. You can select all of the children of a parent layer by context-clicking it and choosing Select Children. To remove parenting from all selected layers, choose None from the pull-down menu.

If you ever want to move layers relative to a point that is not represented in any current layer, you can add a null object (for the shortcut, go to Layer > New > Null Object. Null objects are actually 100×100 pixel layers that cannot be seen in a final render. They possess all of the normal transform controls and can contain effects (and Masks for that matter, which are completely useless in null objects). Contained effects can be used by expressions as reference for other settings; more on this in Chapter 10, "Expressions."

Motion Blur

Motion blur is essential to many of the illusions you can create with After Effects. If a layer animates at a sufficiently high velocity, and the Motion Blur toggle is enabled at the Layer and Composition levels, then you get this great illusion for free: The elements blur to match the apparent motion of the scene.

Motion blur is an artifact of motion occurring while a camera shutter is open. You might not notice motion blur with your naked eye, but it does occur—watch a ceiling fan in motion, and then follow the individual blades with your eye; depending on how closely you can follow its movement, you will see more or less blur.

Therefore motion looks very natural (and the lack of it, unnatural) for objects traveling fast. It complements the eye's persistence of vision, fooling your eye into seeing continuity when it actually sees a series of still frames. It can also look quite pretty, even in still photos. All of this helps explain why efforts to eliminate motion blur from a sampled image have tended to seem faddish and strange.

Some users don't realize that After Effects offers you control over how long and precisely when the camera shutter is open, via the Composition Settings dialog's Advanced tab (**Figure 2.27**). These settings are not intuitive until you know how to decipher them.

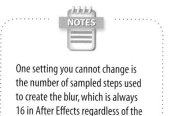

Figure 2.27 The Shutter Angle and Shutter Phase settings on the Advanced tab of the Composition Settings dialog control the appearance of motion blur.

The Shutter Angle setting controls how long the shutter is open; a higher number means more blur. Shutter Phase controls at what point, during a given frame, the shutter opens; at the default of 0, the shutter opens at the moment in time when the frame begins.

What the Settings Mean

A physical film camera typically has an angled mechanical shutter that can open in a circular motion anywhere between a few degrees and a full 360 degrees (an electronic shutter does not behave the same, but never mind about that). Theoretically, 360 degrees provides the maximum open aperture, and thus the greatest amount of blur a shot would contain.

NOTES

One setting you cannot change is the number of sampled steps used to create the blur, which is always 16 in After Effects regardless of the length of the blur being generated.

The Virtual Camera Shutter

Using a real, physical camera, the shutter setting (along with the aperture) determines the amount of light passed onto the film or video pickup. Low-lit scenes are blurrier because the shutter remains open longer, allowing it to gather more light. Other scenes will be deliberately taken with a slow shutter (and the aperture closed down) to produce nice, streaky blur.

After Effects is unconcerned with the need to gather light, and it does not produce (or even emulate) the lens effects associated with a high or low shutter angle setting (nor the Aperture setting on a 3D camera, explored in Chapter 9, "Virtual Cinematography"). Therefore, by opening the aperture, you create only the desirable part—the blur itself.

Setting Shutter Phase to −50% of Shutter Angle is useful when motion tracking and should probably be the default. When motion blur is added to the tracked layer, the track stays centered, instead of appearing offset.

After Effects, however, cheats by offering you double the blur overhead of a fully open shutter. The maximum setting for Shutter Angle in the Composition Settings dialog is 720, an impossibility in the real world.

A camera report can help you decide on this setting, although it's typically possible to carefully eyeball it by zooming in on an area where background and foreground elements both have blur and matching them (**Figures 2.28a and b**). If your camera report includes shutter speed, you can calculate the Shutter Angle setting using the following formula:

$$\text{shutter speed} = 1 \; / \; \text{frame rate} * (360 \; / \; \text{shutter angle})$$

This isn't as gnarly as it looks, but if you dislike formulas, think of it like this: If your camera takes 24 frames per second, but Shutter Angle is set at 180 degrees, then the frame is exposed half the time ($180/360 = \frac{1}{2}$) or $\frac{1}{48}$ of a second. If the camera report shows a $\frac{1}{96}$ of a second exposure, Shutter Angle should be 90 degrees.

Shutter Phase determines when the shutter opens—not necessarily at the beginning of the frame (although that is the default). Shutter Phase is meaningful as an offset of the Shutter Angle.

So, if 0 opens the shutter and starts the blur at the beginning of the frame, a −90 setting with a 180° Shutter Angle means that half the blur starts before the frame (blurring the previous frame) and half follows it.

Figures 2.28a and b In 2.28a, the default Shutter Angle setting of 180 degrees is too heavy for this white solid masked over the front hubcap, which has been tracked to match the shot motion. In 2.28b, Shutter Angle was cut down by 50% to 90 degrees. In this case, there was no camera report to guide the decisions; they are based on blur that can be observed on the rest of the moving truck.

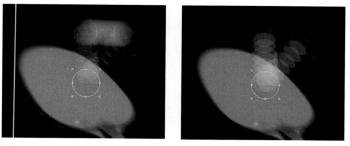

Figures 2.29a and b These two images should look the same, but you have to force After Effects into getting the result in 2.29b by adding a slight bit of rotation. The other key is setting the Shutter Phase to –50% of the Shutter Angle, which causes the motion blur to be sampled right at the middle of the motion.

Manipulating Time Itself

After Effects has the advantage of being quite flexible when working with time. You can retime footage or mix and match speeds and timing. Because it's not always obvious how to handle situations in which source footage needs retiming, it's worth looking at the overall approach to time in After Effects and the ways in which timing can be edited, highlighting which are useful and for what situations.

Absolute (Not Relative) Time

Here's the key: Internally, After Effects measures time in absolute (not relative) terms, using seconds (rather than frames, whose timing changes according to how many there are per second). If time was measured using the total number of frames, or frames per second, changing the frame rate would pose a problem. Instead, at the very deepest level, After Effects doesn't care what the frame rate is, allowing you to fiddle with the rate as it counts out the seconds.

This means that you can change the frame rate of any comp on the fly, and the keyframes and other timing information will stay accurate relative to the counting of seconds. The timing will not appear to change although the frames play back at a faster (or slower) rate. The keyframes won't even be averaged to the nearest frame; they will rest between frames, if necessary, to hold their position relative to seconds (**Figure 2.30**).

Ricochet

A negative 50% Shutter Phase setting is particularly useful when tracking in an object that ricochets, such as a bouncing ball, allowing you to see the motion in both directions at the frame of impact. However, this effect doesn't work by default in After Effects 7.0, which averages the surrounding frames (**Figure 2.29a**). You can trick it into making the V-shape of the ricochet by adding a very slight rotation to the ricochet layer. This forces After Effects into sampling all of the frames necessary to create the ricochet (**Figure 2.29b**). High-speed effects such as this also reveal steps in the blur, due to the number of samples used to create it—another limitation of the current version with no available adjustment.

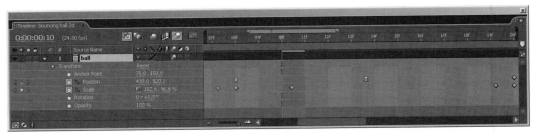

Figure 2.30 This composition has been changed from 29.97 fps to 24 fps. All frames following the first one now fall in between whole frames (visible as alternating light/dark stripes), and After Effects averages the data accordingly.

When Blur Is Needed Where None Exists

Motion blur is cool and automatic, if you animated the layer to receive the blur in After Effects. However, if the element comes in already animated but without sufficient blur—as can happen with 3D elements or when a scene is retimed to be faster—you need a different solution, because After Effects has no motion to sample to generate blur.

The painful way to deal with this is to apply directional blur to the elements in question. The problem is that that natural motion blur is rarely unidirectional.

In such cases, and when there's no possibility of reshooting or re-rendering, it's worth considering an investment in Real Smart Motion Blur by RE: Vision Effects (www.revisionfx.com). This plug-in can sample motion from other layers and enhance the amount of blur created by that motion. It's render-intensive and can require some tweaking, but it can be just the thing for such situations. A demo version is available on the book's disc.

Figure 2.31 This icon (highlighted) reveals and conceals the Time Stretch features.

The same methodology applies to footage (or a composition) whose frame rate does not match that of the main composition; After Effects simply displays the current frame in absolute time (whether it began at the same moment as the other frames or not).

This should make sense to musicians: in ¾ time, you can beat 3 against 4, or other polyrhythmic combinations, creating elaborate syncopation. Underneath it all, however, the metronome clicks on at the same rate.

Time Stretch

You may find the need to alter the duration and speed of a source clip; perhaps you need to lengthen and slow it down to cover the duration of the shot, or maybe it must be sped up to match the timing of another element. The solution in either case is Time Stretch, provided you don't need the frame rate to change during the course of the shot (in which case only Time Remap will do).

There are several ways to activate retiming, depending on what you want. The third of the three icons at the lower left of the Timeline reveals the In/Out/Duration/Stretch columns (**Figure 2.31**). You can

▶ Edit the In or Out point: **Ctrl+Shift+comma** (**Cmd+Shift+comma**) stretches the In point to the current frame, **Ctrl+Alt+comma** (**Cmd+Option+comma**) stretches the Out point to the current time

▶ Change the duration of the layer

▶ Change the stretch value from 100% to an alternate value

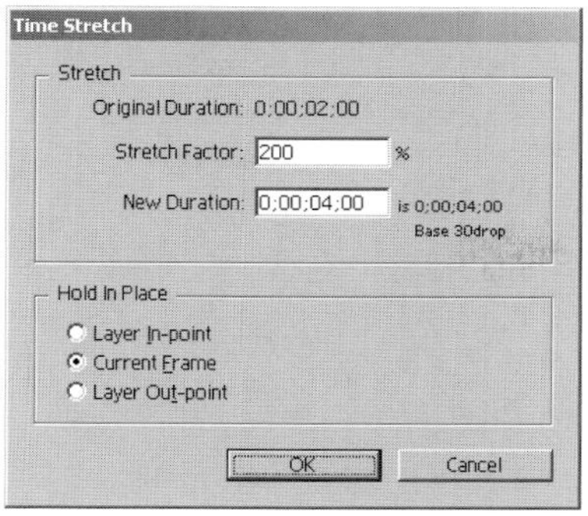

Figure 2.32 You can set an alternate Duration or Stretch Factor in the Time Stretch dialog. Here you can also specify the pivot point for the stretch: In point, Out point, or current time.

To display the Time Stretch dialog, you can click the Duration or Stretch value, or you can choose Layer > Time > Time Stretch (**Figure 2.32**).

Frame Blending

There is, of course, a noticeable side effect when lengthening a source clip (and even when shortening it): Frames repeat (or skip). Unless the stretch value factors evenly into 100% (say, 50% or 200%), the repeating or skipping occurs in irregular increments, potentially causing a herky-jerky motion.

Enable Frame Blending for the layer and the composition, and After Effects averages the frames together. This works not only on layers with time stretching but with any footage that comes in at a frame rate other than that of the composition.

With version 7.0, After Effects offers a more sophisticated method of averaging adjoining frames. Whereas previous versions could only overlay adjoining frames, essentially blurring them together (a mode now known as Frame Mix), the new Pixel Motion mode analyzes and tracks actual pixel data from frame to frame, creating new frames that sort of warp the adjoining frames together.

Figure 2.33 shows the location of the mode, and how the result might appear in each case. Essentially, the result will be acceptable based on a few typical criteria. It may appear

> **NOTES**
>
> Stretching a layer does not change the timing of any applied key-frames; you can use the Graph Editor to stretch keyframes as needed, or you can precompose the clip prior to Time Stretch, guaranteeing that the animation lines up.

Figure 2.33 These toggles allow you to enable Frame Mix, or the new Pixel Motion mode (instead of Whole Frames) for a retimed layer.

too blurry, too distorted, or contain too many noticeable frame artifacts.

In such a case, users of the Professional edition can try for a better result using the new Timewarp effect, explored below.

Time Reversal and Freeze Frame

Figure 2.34 The candy striping along the bottom of the layer offers a clear indicator that the Stretch value is negative and the footage runs in reverse.

You can reverse the timing of a layer with a simple shortcut: Highlight the layer, and press **Ctrl+Alt+R** (**Cmd+Option+R**) to set the Stretch value to –100%. The layer takes on a stripy appearance to remind you that its time has been set in reverse motion (**Figure 2.34**). Because you'll probably never remember that command, using it only once in a great while, it has also been added to the Layer > Time menu.

Also new to version 7.0 is the Layer > Time > Freeze Frame command. This is a one-step shortcut to what used to be a multiple-step process; it applies the Time Remap effect and sets a Hold keyframe at the current time.

Time Stretch and Nested Compositions

If you apply Time Stretch (or Time Remap) to a composition, After Effects, by default, recalculates the source composition's frame rate, re-slicing any keyframe animations to fit the new rate instead of adhering to the old one.

Be aware, therefore, that the frame values on any given frame will be different unless the underlying time values match exactly. After Effects does not round off to the nearest whole frame; again, it works in absolute time, even if that places current time between frames in the subcomposition.

You can override this behavior and force After Effects to round off, however. On the Advanced tab of the Composition Settings panel of the *nested* comp, toggle Preserve Frame Rate When Nested or in Render Queue (**Figure 2.35**). This forces After Effects to analyze only whole frame increments in the underlying composition, using its frame rate. If, for example, you ever needed the effect of showing an old movie (which might run at 15 fps) inside a composition with a higher frame rate, this is how you might do it.

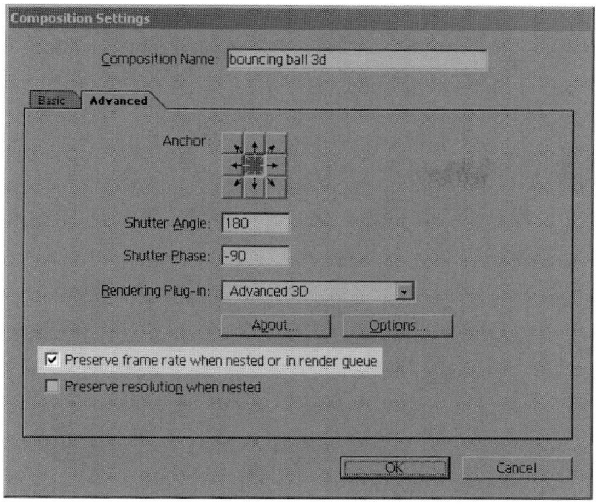

Figure 2.35 If you need a subcomposition to run at a different rate than the master composition, checking the highlighted box in the subcomp prevents After Effects from resampling keyframes at the master comp's rate.

Time Remap

You can do away with the Time Stretch feature set altogether if you are comfortable working with Time Remap instead. This feature may require a bit of practice just to wrap your head around it, but once you catch on, your powers increase.

The philosophy behind Time Remap is elusively simple: Time has a value, just like any other property, which means you can keyframe it, ease in and out of it, loop and ping-pong it, and do all of the other things you can do with any other animation data.

Figures 2.36a, b, and **c** show sample timelines that contain typical uses for Time Remap in an effects situation. The presumption is that you're not going completely nuts rolling footage back and forth, ramping the frame rate up and down, although you can of course do just that. Its applications for creating realistic effects, however, may be limited.

You can set Time Remap by selecting it under the Layer menu or using the shortcut (**Ctrl+Alt+T**/**Cmd+Option+T**). This sets (and reveals) two keyframes, one at the beginning and one at one frame beyond the end of the layer (not the layer In and Out points, should they have been edited).

If you've edited the layer In or Out points, a logical first step is to add Time Remap keyframes at the In and Out points, and perhaps delete the default ones.

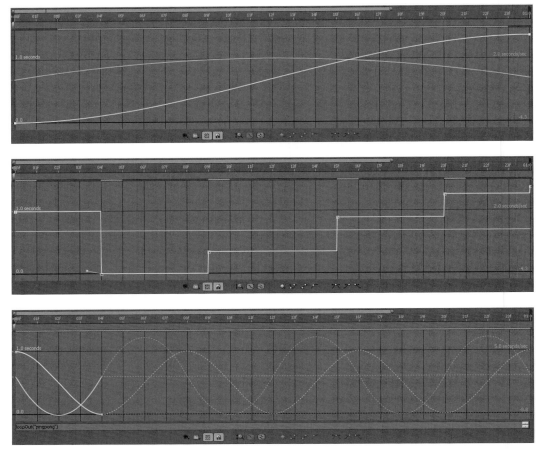

Figures 2.36a, b, and c Simple, everyday things you can do with Time Remap, shown with reference curves: speed up the source with eases (a), progress through a series of stills selected from the moving clip using Hold keyframes (b), and loop the source using a simple expression (c).

To reverse a clip via Time Remap, highlight all keyframes by clicking on the Time Remap property name. Next, context-click one of the highlighted keyframes, and select Keyframe Assistant > Time-Reverse Keyframes.

Time remapped layers have a theoretically infinite duration, and when you apply Time Remap to a layer whose duration is shorter than that of the composition, the layer automatically lengthens to the duration of the comp. If the final Time Remap frame has been passed, that frame is held for the remaining layer duration.

Time Remap can take a little while to understand in complex situations, but it is often used for simple eases, holds, loops (discussed in Chapter 10), and the occasional time reversal. If you find yourself in deeper, the same principles apply; you just have to pay closer attention.

Timewarp

New to After Effects 7.0 Professional is Timewarp. This effect allows you to fine-tune the results of frame blending using Pixel Motion (it also includes Frame Mix and even Whole Frames as output modes, but choosing these loses most of the benefits of Timewarp's controls).

Properly retiming footage can be a complex and processor-intensive procedure; Timewarp helps the process with a few customizations:

TIP

Beware when applying Time Remap to a layer whose duration exceeds that of the composition. Two keyframes are assigned when Time Remap is activated, and the second one can hide beyond the end of the Timeline. To get rid of it, set a new keyframe at the (visible) end of the composition, click Time Remap to highlight all of the keyframes, deselect the ones you can see, and then press Delete to get rid of that hidden final one.

- Fine-tuning of motion vectors (within the Tuning section) including a processor-intensive **Extreme** setting for Filtering for cases in which the normal method creates artifacts. Also processor-intensive is raising the **Vector Details** setting, but even a setting of 100, which produces one vector per pixel, may not improve the result. With fast motion, a lower setting is actually recommended.

- An **Error Threshold** setting that controls how much blending occurs between frames. A high setting increases blending and can reduce tearing along edges; a low setting can be helpful with a grainy image so that the grain is ignored.

- Control over what is sampled. You can set the **Weighting** to sample one color channel more than another. Even more useful, you can specify which portions of the footage are sampled using the **Matte Channel**, **Matte Layer**, and **Source Crops** options; so for example, if you are retiming only figures at the center of frame, you can avoid sampling all of the information in the garbage matte areas at the edges (**Figure 2.37**).

- Ability to sample one layer and apply the result to another using the **Warp Layer** control to set a target. This is vital if, for example, you are working with linear color footage that would appear very dark to Timewarp; you can apply the effect to a de-linearized layer instead and then send the result to the source linear layer (if that makes no sense, it should be clearer when you look at Chapter 11, "Film, HDR, and 32 Bit Compositing").

Figure 2.37 With a tracking shot such as this one, it would be a waste of time and effort to retime the areas of the frame outside of the mask. Timewarp allows you to specify a matte channel within which it will restrict resampling operations. In this case, you would typically garbage matte and then key the footage first, then apply Timewarp using the alpha channel generated by the key as the Matte Channel.

▶ Ability to create motion blur. Footage that moves faster should, naturally, produce more motion blur, and Timewarp can create it with **Enable Motion Blur** toggled on. With the Manual setting you can specify a Shutter Angle, or Automatic will attempt to choose a blur amount appropriate to the amount of motion being added. This setting increases render time.

A re-timing project included in the Chapter02 folder, 02_timewarp.aep, may help illustrate how Timewarp is used. Timewarp overrides any Time Remap settings that might exist on a layer; in the example, they are applied only to make the layer long enough to accommodate the slower motion.

Timewarp replicates a lot of options and settings previously available with Twixtor from ReVision Effects. Whether Timewarp completely obviates the need for Twixtor is dubious, given that the third-party effect is well beyond its third revision as Timewarp makes its debut in After Effects. In other words, if you are not satisfied with the results from Timewarp, you may be happier using Twixtor (a theory that you can test using the demo version of Twixtor).

In Conclusion

This chapter is an attempt to unlock some of the elegance and logic behind the After Effects Timeline, which is not always evident to the new user. Shortcuts and other workflow enhancements are designed to help streamline what might otherwise be tedious or exacting edits.

If the information seems overwhelming on first read, remember that most of it is tied to specific contexts. You don't need to memorize every shortcut or tip, but if you keep the working scenarios in mind, you can refer back to related advice as needed.

3

Selections:
The Key to Compositing

I'm fixing a hole where the rain gets in
And stops my mind from wandering
Where it will go.

—John Lennon and Paul McCartney

Selections: The Key to Compositing

A particle physicist works with atoms, bakers and bankers work with their own types of dough, and compositors work with selections—many different types of selections, each of them derived uniquely.

If compositing were simply a question of taking pristine, perfect foreground source A and overlaying it onto perfectly matching background plate B, there would be no compositor in the effects process; an editor could accomplish the job before lunchtime.

Instead, compositors break sequences of images apart and reassemble them, sometimes painstakingly, and usually including the element of motion. Often, it is one element, one frame, or one area of a shot that needs special attention. By the clever use of selections, a compositor can save fellow artists and camera operators, taking control of whatever part of the source footage is necessary.

In this chapter, we'll look at the foundation techniques that define how a layer merges with those behind it. Then throughout Section II, "Effects Compositing Essentials," and in particular in Chapters 6 and 7, we will focus on particular ways to refine selections, creating high-contrast mattes, and pulling keys from blue-screen footage.

The Many Ways to Create Selections

After Effects offers a number of ways to create selections, yet far fewer than exist in Photoshop. Why? To Photoshop's advantage, its selection tools must operate only with still images. This is a much simpler development problem, believe it or not, than creating selection tools for moving images, in which results must appear consistent across the changing array of frames that makes up a single clip.

So what are the After Effects methods for creating selections? Take a look.

Pull a Matte

You may think that pulling a matte refers to keying out the blue or green from an effects film shoot (**Figure 3.1**). True enough, but there are other types of mattes too. Even more common than blue-screen keys are high-contrast, or *hi-con*, *mattes*. You create these by maximizing the contrast of a particular channel or area of the image. There are other types of mattes possible as well, such as the elusive *difference matte*. Chapter 6, "Color Keying," discusses pulling mattes in depth.

Use an Existing Alpha Channel

Using an existing alpha channel sounds like a no-brainer, right? The source footage was created with an alpha channel (typically in a 3D animation program); just bring it in as is (**Figure 3.2**). No worries, done deal, right?

That's theoretically true, except that After Effects mostly conceals an issue that is quite explicit in other similar software packages (such as Apple's Shake): the interpretation of the alpha channel. Is the edge premultiplied or not, and

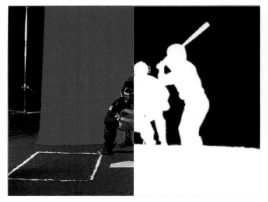

Figure 3.1 This split-screen image shows a blue-screen shoot (left) and the resulting matte. (All baseball images courtesy of Tim Fink Productions.)

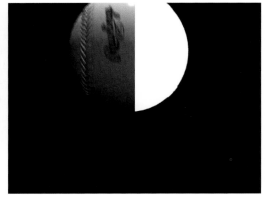

Figure 3.2 This close-up of a computer-generated baseball is split into color (left) and alpha channels.

what do you do in either case? The questions are raised not only when you import the initial image (as you do in After Effects) but also when applying effects to layers with an alpha.

How does After Effects get around this, and is it a good or a bad thing for compositors? For the answer, see the "Alpha Channels and Premultiplication" section later in this chapter.

Create a Mask (or Several)

A mask, by contrast, is a vector shape that determines the opaque and transparent areas of an image (**Figure 3.3**). Masks are generally created by hand, although After Effects does include a provision to generate them automatically by examining the raster data of an image.

The Layer > Auto-trace command is new and improved in version 7.0 of After Effects. With sufficient contrast on any channel you may find that it automatically creates detailed and accurate outlines. The downside of this approach is that, with all but the very simplest shots, it will create lots of overlapping outlines—dozens, typically—when you might want one or two. Combine this with changes over time and you can end up with far more than you can manage.

This chapter focuses on the basics of creating and combining masks. You can find a follow-up discussion in Chapter 7, "Rotoscoping and Paint," which focuses specifically on rotoscoping, the art of animating selections over time.

Use Blending Modes Instead

It's even possible to composite without selections at all, instead using blending modes (Add, Multiply, Screen) to combine color channels mathematically, pixel by pixel, in ways that mimic how light and shadow play out in the world (**Figure 3.4**). You can also use selections combined with blending modes to get the best of both worlds.

This chapter goes over the modes that are relevant to effects compositing and gets into the nitty-gritty of what these blending modes are actually doing as they combine pixel data.

NOTES

Because Auto-trace now also includes a Preview toggle, it's much easier to test values for its various settings and arrive at a useful result.

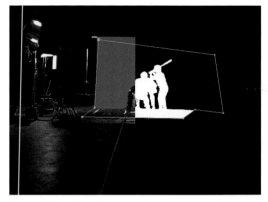

Figure 3.3 In this split-screen view, you can see the garbage matte mask that was added to remove areas of the stage that didn't have a blue screen.

Figure 3.4 Blending modes are the preferred way for compositing elements that are composed of light rather than matter, such as fire.

Use an Effect

Certain effects can be used to create transparency selections or to refine the ones you have. Section II discusses these in detail. Many common effects, such as Levels and Curves, include control of the transparency (alpha) channel, while most of the effects in the Channel menu permit you to create or alter the alpha channel directly.

Combine Techniques

As with blending modes, there is no reason not to combine techniques, using a garbage matte to clean up a color key or a hi-con matte to enhance the effect of a blending mode. This is very common in advanced effects work, where no two shots are exactly the same and where a single frame or clip can require a variety of approaches.

So What's the Big Deal?

The real skills here are knowing which approach to apply for a given situation, knowing how to apply it, and knowing when to try something else, either to enhance or to replace what you already have. None of these techniques or approaches is particularly sophisticated by itself, but applying them properly requires a clear vision of what the shot needs and how to supply it.

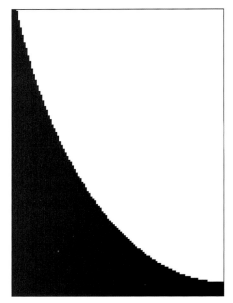

Figure 3.5 Using 400% magnification, you can see clearly how ugly a curved or angled shape is if it can be described by only bitmap pixels, pixels that are either fully off or fully on.

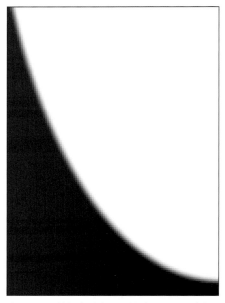

Figure 3.6 Ahh, that's better. With a proper alpha channel and a one-pixel feather adjustment, even at 400%, the edge does a much better job of describing a smooth, soft curve.

Compositing: Science and Nature

What exactly is happening in a simple A over B composite? You're just laying one image over another, right? Nothing to it—was obvious from the first time you used Photoshop, right?

For most people, the basic compositing operation is a completely intuitive process that is rarely questioned, but to deal with the crucial part of an A over B composite—the edge detail of layer A—it helps to know what is going on, not only in the world of software but also in the real world as well. The two worlds do not operate the same, but it is the job of the digital world to re-create, as faithfully as possible, what is happening in the natural world.

Bitmap Alpha

A *bitmap selection channel* is one in which each pixel is either fully opaque or fully transparent. This is the type of selection generated by the Magic Wand tool in Photoshop. You can feature or blur the resulting edge, but the default selection has no semitransparent pixels.

This type of selection has its place—say, isolating pixels of one particular color range to change them—but it does not reflect how nature works. An edge made up of pixels which are either fully opaque or invisible cannot describe a curve or angle smoothly, and even a straight line with no edge transparency looks unnatural in an image whose goal is realism (**Figure 3.5**).

Feathered Alpha

But although it's easy enough to see that a bitmap edge does not occur in nature, it's hard to imagine that a *feathered alpha* does occur—hard objects don't have semi-transparent edges, do they? Of course not. Look at the edge of this page, or anything in the foreground of your field of vision. Do you see semitransparent edge areas? No.

Not exactly, anyhow—but on the other hand, what you see isn't razor sharp in its hardness, either. It so happens that semi-transparent edge pixels are the best digital approximation we have for overlapping edges in nature

(**Figure 3.6**) because they solve two problems in translating the world of objects to the world of pixels:

▶ They come closer to describing organic curves.

▶ They approximate the physics of light as it bends around objects.

Say what? The first point is easy enough to see and appreciate, but the second one is a doozy, an observation that can be traced back a century to Einstein's *annus mirabilus*, in which he demonstrated how mass and light are interrelated. Light is bent—slightly—by any amount of mass that it passes. The greater the mass, the higher the amount of bending, right up to the extreme of black holes from which light cannot escape. With most objects, your eye sees a slight, subtle effect of the background light actually *bending around* the foreground object.

You can study this effect close-up in a digital photo with no compositing whatsoever (**Figures 3.7a** and **b**). In the digital image, you can see areas at the edge of objects that become a wash of color combining the foreground and background. This is caused by the influence of the mass of that object itself on the light (color) coming from behind it.

Figures 3.7a and b Consider a simple digital photo that is not composited (a). When you look closely, you can see that there is a natural softness at the edges of the sign despite that it is in sharp focus and hard-edged. The effect is even more evident close up, if you compare the sharpness within the sign itself to the softness of the edge (b). (Images courtesy of Nathan Moody.)

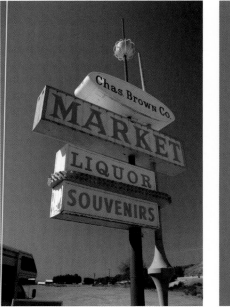

Geek Alert: The Compositing Formula

When you layer a raster image with semi-transparent alpha over an opaque background image, here's what happens: The foreground pixel values are multiplied by the percentage of transparency, which, if not fully opaque, reduces their value. The background pixels are multiplied by the percentage of opacity (the inverse of opacity), and the two values are added together to produce the composite. Expressed as a formula, it looks like

$$(Fg * A) + ((1-A)*Bg) = Comp$$

With real RGB pixel data of R: 185, G: 144, B: 207 in the foreground and R: 80, G: 94, B: 47 in the background, calculating one edge pixel only might look like

$$[(185, 144, 207) \times .6] + [.4 \times (80, 94, 47)] = (143, 124, 143)$$

The result is a weighted blend between the brightness of the foreground and the darker background.

Other effects compositing programs, such as Shake, do not take this operation for granted the way that After Effects and Photoshop do. You can't simply drag one image over another in a layer stack—you must apply an Over function to create this interaction. Is there a difference? Not until you add to the discussion the operations that go along with an Over, in particular premultiplication, which is detailed later in this chapter.

Opacity

But we're by no means finished discovering surprises with basic image combination; the way that Opacity edits work in After Effects often takes people by surprise as well, although they can work with it for years without coming face to face with what is counterintuitive about it.

Say you have two identical layers, no alpha/transparency information for either layer. Set each layer to 50% Opacity, and the result should look exactly like either one of the layers at 100%, right?

Wrong (**Figure 3.8**)! If you've ever heard of Zeno's Paradox, it describes a phenomenon that is something like how opacity is calculated in After Effects, but for good reason (where as Zeno's actual paradox is pure folly).

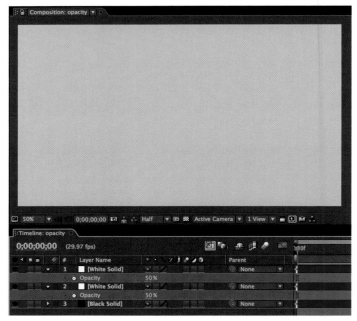

Figure 3.8 A series of white solids overlaid with Normal blending at 50% over a black solid at 100%. Each layer only adds 50% to the delta (difference) between current opacity and 100%, so only the center begins to approach pure white (but registers 91.25%). This is consistent with Photoshop, but not with many other compositing applications.

A lead developer on the After Effects team once described the program's opacity calculations as follows: Imagine you have a light which is 1, and place a 50% transparent filter (say, a sheet of vellum) in front of it. Half the total light is permitted through the vellum (0.5 * 1 = 0.5). Put another 50% transparent sheet of vellum on top of that. Now half of half the light shows through (0.5 * 0.5 = 0.25). You can theoretically repeat ad infinitum without reaching 0% light transmission, at least in a pure digital environment.

Hence, and in some tangential relationship to Zeno's Paradox, After Effects mimics how transparency behaves in the real world. This is *not* how opacity settings are handled in many alternative compositing applications, and so it often takes users of such programs as Shake by surprise, but the operation is by design.

Alpha Channels and Premultiplication

Clearly, you don't need to be able to write out the compositing formula to composite, any more than you need to be able to design a car in order to drive one. After Effects helps you by shielding this formula and many other mathematical portions of the compositing operations from your view.

Ignorance is not always bliss, however, when it comes to premultiplication, which After Effects also largely shields from view when you build a composition. Like Photoshop, After Effects uses non-premultiplied data for the compositing operation (that's how it operates internally), yet it never explicitly tells you (or even allows you to find out) how and when an image is premultiplied and unmultiplied as it makes its way through the image pipeline.

Fortunately, After Effects does an effective job of managing premultiplication under normal circumstances—fortunate because managing it yourself is a tedious process. You just need to know how things can go wrong, the symptoms that show you that something has gone wrong, and what to do to set it right.

NOTES

Zeno's Paradox goes something like this: Suppose I wish to cross the room. First, of course, I must cover half the distance. Then, I must cover half the remaining distance. Then, I must cover half the remaining distance. Then I must cover half the remaining distance, and so on forever. The consequence is that I can never get to the other side of the room.

Premultiplication Illustrated

Premultiplication exists for one reason only: so that source images look nice, with realistic, anti-aliased edges, *before they are composited.*

That's right, we have premultiplication just so that a matted object looks right against a black background when it comes out of, say, your 3D animation program. All premultiplication does is composite the foreground against the background, so that the edges and transparency blend as well into that solid color (typically black) as they would against the final background.

It is the color channels, not the alpha channel, that distinguish premultiplied and straight alpha images. When you ask After Effects to "guess" how to interpret the footage (on import, by choosing Guess in the Interpret Footage dialog, or using **Ctrl+F/Cmd+F**), it looks for a solid color background with edge pixels that seem to have had that color multiplied into them.

What does it mean to have the background multiplied into the edge pixels? Revisit "Geek Alert: The Compositing Formula," but imagine the background value to be 0,0,0. There's your answer. The effect is to darken semi-transparent edge pixels if the background is black, to lighten them if it's white, and to really wreak havoc with them if it's any other color.

The close-ups in **Figures 3.9a** and **b** show a section of the same foreground image with the alpha interpreted properly and with it misinterpreted. A misinterpreted alpha either fails to remove the background color from the edge pixels, or removes color that should actually be present.

Figures 3.9a and b Motion Blur clearly reveals the sins of improper premultiplication settings. Although there are dark areas in the blur of the properly interpreted foreground, they are consistent with the dark areas of the plane itself (a). The improperly interpreted version has dark matting all around it, including in the areas of the canopy that should be translucent, and around the blur of the propeller (b). You suspect it's wrong simply because it looks bad around the edges.

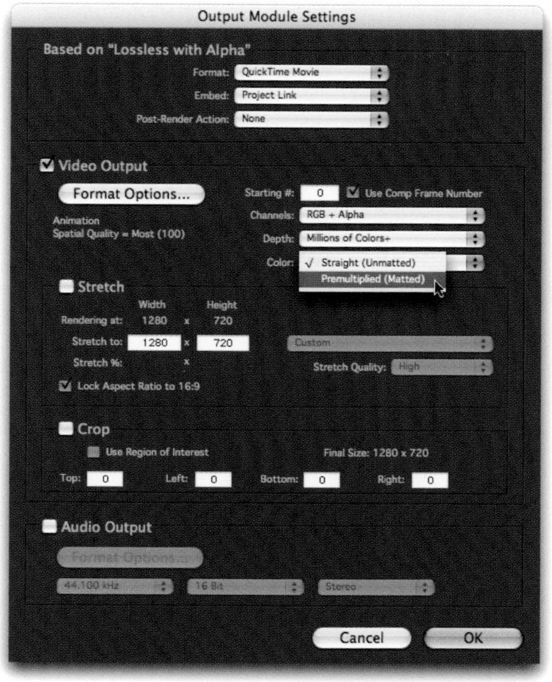

Figure 3.10 Although premultiplied alpha is typically the default setting, the Color pull-down menu in Output Settings will change the setting to Straight.

NOTES

Most computer-generated images are premultiplied, unless the artist takes specific steps to counteract the process. The Video Output section of the Output Module Settings for items in the Render Queue includes a pull-down to specify whether you render with Straight or Premultiplied alpha; by default, it is set to Premultiplied (**Figure 3.10**).

Why should you care about premultiplication? First of all, because incorrectly managing your alpha channels can produce undesirable fringe artifacts. But just as important, you may find yourself in a situation where those artifacts seem to be presenting themselves although you've carefully managed the process; Suddenly your composited elements have black edges around them. Your job depends on getting to the bottom of this. There are two basic ways it can happen:

- An alpha channel is misinterpreted on import (see "Getting It Right on Import")
- A matte is added within a composition and premultiplication isn't accounted for (see "Solving the Problem Internally")

Unfortunately, users who aren't confident enough to trace the underlying problem often end up resorting to all sorts of strange machinations to try to get rid of the black edge;

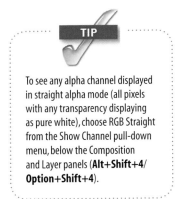

TIP

To see any alpha channel displayed in straight alpha mode (all pixels with any transparency displaying as pure white), choose RGB Straight from the Show Channel pull-down menu, below the Composition and Layer panels (**Alt+Shift+4/ Option+Shift+4**).

re-rendering the element against a different color, choking the alpha matte even though it comes from a 3D program and is accurate, and possibly even more frightening and desperate maneuvers.

Getting It Right on Import

Most people's ace in the hole if they don't really understand premultiplication is the Guess feature that sits next to the premultiplication settings in the Footage Settings dialog. A preference in Preferences > Import determines what happens when footage is imported with an alpha channel; if this is set to anything other than Ask User (the default), you may inadvertently import files without knowing what is happening to their alpha channels (**Figure 3.11**).

Is Guess ever wrong? Certainly it can be, if the factors it expects in a premultiplied alpha are there in a straight image or vice versa. Thus it is probably best not to automate this process. In the case of a premultiplied image, After Effects attempts to guess not only the setting but also the color of the background; generally this will be black or white, but watch out for situations where a 3D artist has become creative and rendered against canary yellow or powder blue. For that reason, there is an eyedropper adjacent to the Matted with Color setting (Figure 3.11). When in doubt, examine your footage without the alpha applied: If you see

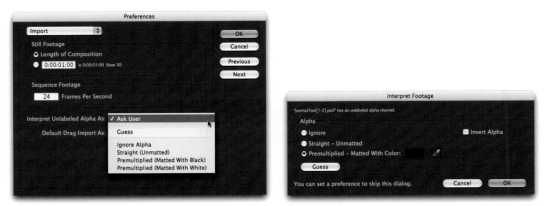

Figure 3.11 By default, the import preferences are set to ask the user how to interpret an alpha channel, which is a good thing, generally speaking, as a check against errors. If you're not sure about the appropriate setting, you can click on the Guess button, which typically can determine the type of channel. If it cannot guess confidently, it generates a beep.

a solid background that is neither pure black or white and After Effects isn't detecting it, use the eyedropper.

Fundamentally, though, as an effects compositor you need to be able to examine your images and spot the symptoms of a misinterpreted alpha: dark or bright fringing in the semi-opaque edges of your foreground.

Solving the Problem Internally

The really gnarly fact is that premultiplication errors can be introduced within the After Effects pipeline. Usually this happens when you apply a selection as a track matte to footage (described in more detail toward the end of this chapter), taking After Effects out of the loop; the application still assumes there is no premultiplication present.

If you see fringing in your edges and need to solve it internally in After Effects, there is a tool to help: the Remove Color Matting effect (**Figures 3.12a** and **b**). This effect has one setting only, for background color, because all it does is apply the unpremultiply calculation (the antidote to premultiplication) in the same manner that it would be applied in the Footage Settings.

Remove Color Matting will not work properly on a layer with a track matte; because this is the main situation in which it's useful, be sure to precompose the layer and its track matte prior to applying Channel > Remove Color Matting.

UnMult, originally created by John Knoll and available free from Red Giant Software (and included on this book's disc), is useful in tricky situations in which Remove Color Matting won't do the job because there is no alpha channel. It uses the black areas of the images to create transparency and remove premultiplied black from the resulting transparent pixels.

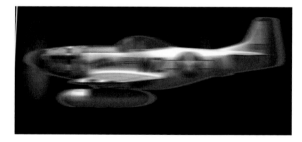

Figures 3.12a and b In 3.12a, the plane saved against a white background has transparency applied via a track matte, which does not unpremultiply, thus revealing evident white fringing against black. Remove Color Matting with Color set to pure white corrects the problem (b), but it is necessary to precompose the color and track matte layers first.

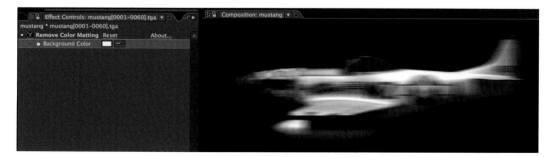

Masks

Although hand-created and animated for the most part, masks open up all kinds of possibilities in After Effects. Masks are the principal method for defining transparency regions in a clip without regard to actual pixels because they are vector shapes. This section lays down the basics for smart use of masks.

Typical Mask Workflow

There are three tools for creating masks: two basic shape tools and the Pen. To activate the Rectangular Mask tool, use the keyboard shortcut **Q**; press **Q** again to toggle the tool to the Elliptical Mask tool. If your mask doesn't conform well to a rectangle or an ellipse, you can draw it point by point with the Pen tool (**G**).

Whether you draw the mask in the Composition panel or the Layer window is up to you. It is somewhere between difficult and impossible to draw or see a mask accurately in the Composition panel if, say, the layer was offset and rotated in 3D space, but if you want to see the layer over its background, the Composition panel must at least be visible. Given sufficient monitor space, an ideal compromise is to keep both windows open side by side, working in the Layer window and watching the Composition panel for live updates.

Remember that your target shape doesn't have to be an ellipse to benefit from starting by drawing an ellipse. Indeed, if the shape calls for a perfectly circular curve on one side, you might do well to draw an ellipse (holding down Shift to make it perfectly circular) and then editing other sides of it with the Pen tool.

When drawing a rectangle or ellipse

- ▶ Double-click the Mask tool (in the Tools palette) to set the boundaries of the mask to match those of the layer.

- ▶ Use **Shift** to constrain the shape and/or **Ctrl/Cmd** to draw the shape from the center rather than from a corner.

TIP

If you're looking for other common primitive mask shapes—a rectangle with rounded corners, a hexagon, or the like—you may be best off drawing the shape in Adobe Illustrator (if you have it), then copying and pasting it. This, however, will not work unless the preferences in Illustrator are set properly. Under Illustrator's File Handling & Clipboard preference, choose AICB with Preserve Paths checked. This is not the default. You can also select and copy paths in Photoshop for use as masks.

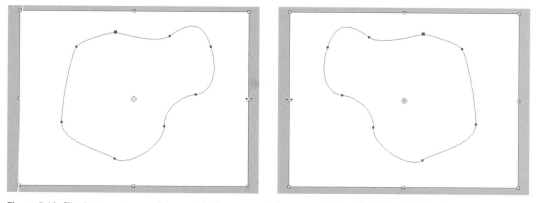

Figure 3.13 Flipping a custom mask symmetrically on one axis is no easy trick in After Effects. Holding down the Shift key scales both axes proportionally, flipping it on both axes. Instead, with View > Show Grid enabled and View Snap to Grid turned on, double-click the Rectangular Mask tool to create a second mask that is the size of the layer. Select both masks in the Timeline, and double-click a point on one of the masks to set the Free Transform tool. Now drag the handles at either side of the image and swap their positions, deleting the layer-sized mask when you're done.

▶ Try the Mask Shape dialog for those rare cases in which you must set the boundaries to exact dimensions and can't do it visually. Although this dialog's use is quite limited, you access it by clicking the underlined word "Shape" under Mask options (highlight the layer and click **M** to reveal it).

▶ Double-click a point on the shape to activate Free Transform mode, which enables you to offset, rotate, or scale the entire mask shape (**Figure 3.13**). As always, hold down **Shift** to keep the scale proportional, snap the rotation to 45 degree increments, or constrain movement to one axis.

Highlighting a layer with a mask and pressing **MM** (the **M** key twice in rapid succession) reveals the full Mask options for that layer. Some tips for those include

▶ Feather is set for the entire mask and operates in both directions (to the inside and outside of the mask shape); there is no way around these defaults. All kinds of lighting, smoke, and glow effects can begin with a masked solid that is heavily feathered. In other words, the feather setting is approximately half the width of the mask at its narrowest crossing, meaning the masked solid is now a big, soft gradient (**Figure 3.14**).

Figure 3.14 The Feather of this mask is set roughly equal to its radius, creating a big, diffuse gradient in the shape of the mask (in this case, elliptical), useful for many types of lighting effects.

▶ Pressing the **F** key reveals only the Mask Feather property in the Timeline.

▶ A hidden gem is Mask Expansion: You can use it to expand or, with a negative value, to contract the mask area. This has all sorts of uses, including creating an edge mask using one mask duplicated into two, each with a Mask Expansion value that is the inverse of the other, and the inner mask subtracted from the outer.

Keyboard shortcuts help eliminate a lot of the fuss and bother that comes with masking in After Effects.

Drawing Bezier Masks

By default, the Pen tool draws Bezier curves, and in After Effects you can do everything you need to create a mask by keeping the Pen tool active throughout the mask edit.

I sometimes draw a Bezier mask first as straight lines only, clicking to place points at key transitions and corners. Once I've completed the basic mask shape, with the Pen tool still active, I can go back point by point and edit the shape, because I have instant access to all of the mask shortcuts:

▶ Clicking on a point with the Pen tool active deletes it.

▶ Clicking on a segment between points with the Pen tool active adds a point.

- Alt/Option-clicking on a point with the Pen tool enables the Convert Vertex tool: Apply it to a point with no handles, and you can drag out to create handles. Apply it to a point with handles, and you cancel the handles.

- Clicking on a Bezier handle with the Pen tool breaks the center point of the Bezier, enabling you to adjust the handles individually; Alt/Option-clicking on a handle restores a linear connection between the handles.

- Context-clicking on the mask shape with the Pen tool (or the Selection tool, for that matter) enables the context menu of options for that mask, including all of its settings on the Timeline, the ability to specify a First Vertex, and Motion Blur settings for the mask, which can be unlocked from the layer itself.

Only when you want to double-click to free transform the entire mask is it necessary to switch to the Selection tool, which you can do either by pressing **V** or by holding down Ctrl/Cmd while you double-click a vertex. The **Ctrl/Cmd** key toggles back and forth between the Pen and Selection tools, regardless of which one is currently active.

Combining Multiple Masks

By default, all masks are drawn in Add mode, meaning that the contents of the mask are added to the layer selection, and the area outside all of the masks is excluded. There are other options for combining them, however; the five primary mask modes are

- **Add:** The default mode; adds the opacity values to the image as a whole, including masks higher in the stack (**Figure 3.15**)

- **Subtract:** Subtracts opacity values from masks higher in the stack or from the image as a whole if no other masks precede it (**Figure 3.16**)

- **Intersect:** Combines only the areas of opacity that overlap with masks higher in the stack (**Figure 3.17**)

- **Difference:** Subtracts overlapping areas (**Figure 3.18**)

- **None:** Has no effect on the image whatsoever; it can be useful as a placeholder or for effects that use masks (**Figure 3.19**)

> **TIP**
>
> As with most selectable UI elements in After Effects, pressing **F2** or **Ctrl+Shift+A** (**Cmd+Shift+A**) deselects the active mask. This is handy when you're done drawing one mask and want to create the next one without switching tools.

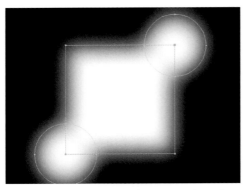

Figure 3.15 In Add mode, the luminance values of the overlapping masks are combined, increasing the masked area.

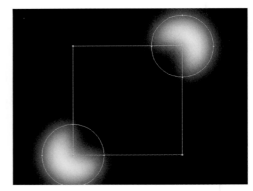

Figure 3.16 Subtract mode is the inverse of Add mode.

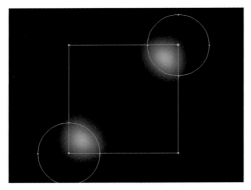

Figure 3.17 Intersect mode adds only the overlapping areas of opacity.

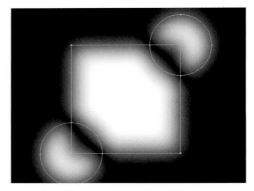

Figure 3.18 The inverse of Intersect, Difference mode subtracts overlapping areas.

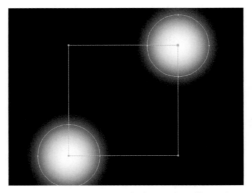

Figure 3.19 With None mode, the mask is effectively deactivated.

Particularly when rotoscoping (masking an animated shape), it is very wise to take advantage of using multiple masks, for one simple reason: The more points you have to keep track of on a given frame, the more likely you'll have to add a keyframe and the more likely you'll lose track of a point. With multiple masks there is far more forgiveness for small errors, and fewer keyframes per mask are needed to complete the job. This topic is explored in greater detail in Chapter 7.

Managing Density

"Density" is traditionally a film term describing how dark (opaque) the frame of film is at a given area of the image. It is therefore the inversion of opacity or alpha values; the higher the density, the less light is transmitted. In the digital world we sometimes speak of masks and alpha channels as having "density," and overlapping semi-transparent areas must be managed to avoid having the densities build up in undesirable ways.

When combining masks that have semi-transparent areas, either because the opacity of the masks is less than 100% or, as in the examples shown here, because the edges are heavily feathered, you may not want densities to have a linear relationship, building them up. That's when Lighten and Darken modes come into play.

Figures 3.20a and **b** show the result of using each of these modes; they prevent mask densities from building up the way that they do with the other modes. No pixel within the combined masks will have a value that is not already represented in one of the overlapping masks; either the lighter or the darker of the two will be represented.

Bug Alert, or Not?

Does a bug still count as a bug if the development team knows about it and has decided to leave it as is to be backward-compatible? I'll let you be the judge. Say there's one part of an overlaid element that you want to mask and reduce to partial opacity, perhaps 50%.

You create a mask for the area to be dialed back, set it to Subtract, and set Mask Opacity to 50%. But instead of the anticipated result, displaying the layer at full opacity and the masked area at 50%, the masked area is subtracted 100% and the rest of the layer displays at 50% opacity!

This is the identical result to applying the same mask in Add mode with Invert checked, although in that case the behavior is at least anticipated.

The workaround is to add a mask at the top of the stack, set to Add mode, giving the mask the dimensions of the entire layer (double-click the Rectangular Mask tool). The Subtract mask will now operate as expected if its opacity is lowered from 100%.

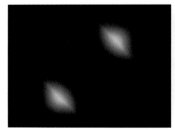

Figures 3.20a and b With a Lighten (a) or a Darken (b) mask, the transparency values are chosen either from the mask set to this mode or those overlapping it, depending on which has the lighter (higher) or darker (lower) values.

Keep these in mind when combining multiple feathered or semi-transparent masks. Remember that masks render from top to bottom, so each mask's mode applies to its relationship with the layers above it. Thus applying these modes to the top mask in the stack has no effect.

Managing Multiple Masks

A few features in After Effects exist specifically to help you manage multiple masks in a single layer.

One is Cycle Mask Colors, which is tucked away in the User Interface Colors section of Preferences. When Cycle Mask Colors is off, your masks are created in the same color (the mask itself and its swatch in the Timeline) each time. To change it, you click the swatch. With Cycle Mask Colors checked on, which I recommend, the mask colors vary on their own.

Also, when editing overlapping masks, you may find it helpful to use the context menu to lock and hide other masks. Context-click on the mask, and choose Lock Other Masks; now you can edit the active mask only. Context-click again, and choose Hide Locked Masks; this time your view is uncluttered as well.

Putting Masks in Motion

Putting masks in motion for visual effects work is also known as *rotoscoping* and is covered in greater depth in Chapter 7. Preceding that, consider this overview of some things to pay attention to when putting a mask in motion.

Interpolation Basics

You can set a temporal ease on a mask keyframe (and adjust it in the Graph Editor), but there is no corresponding spatial curve to adjust, as there is with Position keyframes. Each point will travel in a linear fashion to its next keyframed position. Thus in order to precisely mask an object traveling in an arc, you must set many more keyframes than for an object traveling in a single direction.

TIP

Don't forget that you can name masks by highlighting them in the Timeline, pressing Return, and typing in a new name. Under Preferences > User Interface Colors, you can also check Cycle Mask Colors so that each new mask is created with a unique color.

The real bummer about mask keyframes is that you can't select a group of them and translate the mask; as soon as you move, rotate, or scale it, your selection snaps to the current keyframe only.

There is a workaround. You can duplicate the layer being masked and use it as an alpha track matte for an unmasked source of the same layer, in which case you're free to transform (or even motion track) the duplicate using the normal layer transforms. It's not a perfect solution by any means, but it is often useful and hardly anyone thinks of it.

Moving, Copying, Pasting, and Masks

You can freely copy a mask shape from one source (a different mask, a different keyframe in the same mask animation, Illustrator, or Photoshop) and paste it into an existing mask channel, where it takes the place of the Mask Shape. You should, however, note some rather strict situational rules:

▶ **With no Mask Shape keyframes in the source or target:** Copying the mask and pasting it to another layer automatically either creates a new mask, or applies it to any mask that is selected.

▶ **Source mask contains Mask Shape keyframes, target has none:** Highlighting the mask (not the specific keyframes) and pasting creates a new mask as if pasting from time 0. Highlighting any or all Mask Shape keyframes pastes a new mask with keyframes starting at the current time.

▶ **Target layer contains masks (with or without keyframes):** To paste Mask Shape keyframes into a particular mask at a particular time, highlight the target mask before pasting. Highlighting the target Mask Shape property highlights any keyframes and replaces them (not usually what you want).

In all cases, if the target layer is a different size or dimension from the source, the mask stretches to maintain its relationship to the layer boundaries.

In many situations, pasting Mask Shape keyframes blindly in this manner is not what you're after, but a rather obscure feature in the Layer window *will* help you. The Target pulldown along the bottom of the window has a unique function: When you choose an existing mask as the target, you can start drawing a new mask anywhere in frame and it will replace the shape in the target mask layer (**Figure 3.21**).

First Vertex

When pasting in shapes or radically changing the existing mask by adding and deleting points, you may run into difficulty lining up the points. Hidden away in the Layer > Mask (or mask context) menu, and available *only with a single vertex of the mask selected*, is the Set First Vertex command. If your mask points twist around to the wrong point during an interpolation, setting the First Vertex to two points that definitely correspond should help straighten things out. This also can be imperative for effects that rely on mask shapes, such as the Reshape tool (described in Chapter 7).

Smart Mask Interpolation (available via a panel in the Window menu) is designed to smooth transitions between two radically different shapes. It's useful for stylized motion graphics of detailed masks transitioning from one to the next, but less useful for effects masking and rotoscoping because it's a bit too automated. The result, although sometimes pleasing, doesn't usually obviate the need to more carefully keyframe an accurate mask transition.

Figure 3.21 This pull-down menu along the bottom of the Layer panel makes it easy to create a new mask shape that replaces the shape in the target mask. If the target mask has keyframes, After Effects creates a new keyframe wherever the new shape is drawn.

Blending Modes: The Real Deal

After Effects includes 34 blending modes, each created with a specific purpose (**Figure 3.22**)—although no one is quite sure in what context Dancing Dissolve was ever useful (and I'm only half joking). For effects work, moreover, the majority of them are not particularly recommended. In fact, traditional optical compositing would effectively include only two of them: Add and Multiply.

So that's it? Use these two or none at all? Not quite—I'll point out a few other useful modes as well. Once you

"Traditional optical compositing" includes all effects films made prior to the 1990s. The optical compositor was capable of bi-packing (multiplying) and double-exposing (adding) two source frames (layers). Many sophisticated effects films were completed using these limited methods.

Figure 3.22 With 34 blending modes to choose from, it's virtually guaranteed that less experienced users will be easily overwhelmed and compelled to play hunt and peck. You will likely use a small subset of these 90% of the time.

These mathematical descriptions of blended pixel values use a color range normalized to 1; in other words, the full range of pixel values is described as 0 to 1 instead of 0 to 255, as it typically appears in your color controls. A medium gray on any channel is 0.5 instead of 128, pure white is 1, and pure black is 0 (**Figure 3.23**). This makes it much simpler to show the calculations that are actually used to create the blended pixels, because the internal math typically is based this way. For information about overbright values, which have a value greater than 1, see Chapter 11, "Film, HDR, and 32 Bit Compositing."

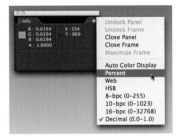

Figure 3.23 The Info panel can display pixel values in several optional modes (accessed via the panel menu). Shown here are decimal values with the cursor on medium gray. Visible decimal values are "normalized" to the range of 0.0 to 1.0, which makes calculations more straightforward than 0 to 255, the standard 8-bit range (or the even more obtuse 0 to 32768 for 16-bit). Select a color mode for the Info palette via its wing menu; whatever mode you select is thereafter also used by the Adobe Color Picker.

understand how your options work, you can make informed compositing decisions, rather than lazily playing Go Fish by trying one mode after the other until you see something you kind of like.

Remember, blending modes are all based on mathematical operations for combining pixels in the layer containing the given blending mode and the pixels behind it—either below it in the stack, if all the layers are 2D, or positioned behind it in 3D space, if all the layers are 3D.

To help you understand what the various blending modes are doing, **Figures 3.24** through **3.30** blend a grayscale gradient over a fully saturated background. Contextual examples using these blending modes follow in the next section.

Figure 3.24 Compare Figures 3.25 through 3.30 to this one, which shows a black-to-white gradient (created using the Ramp effects) over a gradient of fully bright and saturated color. Blending in this figure is set to Normal.

Figure 3.25 The same combination with Add mode applied to the foreground layer. Each background pixel is lightened by the brightness of the foreground pixel up to a value of full white (1.0). The darker the foreground pixel, the less the visibility. Figure 3.31c shows Add using photographed elements.

Figure 3.26 Screen mode is an attenuated Add, pushing fewer values to full white. Figure 3.32 further illustrates the difference between Screen and Add (Figure 3.31c).

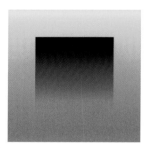

Figure 3.27 Multiply mode sends values toward 0.0, or full black. This is the equivalent of laying one frame of film over the other (a.k.a. "bi-packing"); the resulting combination is darker as the denser (darker) areas are built up. A practical example is shown in Figure 3.33.

Figure 3.28 Overlay combines Screen and Multiply; areas of the background below 50% brightness are multiplied, those above 50% are screened. A practical example is shown in Figure 3.34.

Figure 3.29 Hard Light is the inverse of Overlay; areas of the foreground below 50% brightness are multiplied, those above 50% are screened.

Figure 3.30 Difference bases the luminance of the foreground pixels on the amount of difference between the foreground and background source; the greater the difference, the brighter the value. Practical usage of Difference is demonstrated in Figure 3.36.

Add and Screen

Add and Screen modes both brighten the image. Screen typically yields a subtler effect than Add, which results in brighter values overall.

Add mode is every bit as simple as it sounds; the formula is

$$newPixel = A + B$$

where A is a pixel from the foreground layer and B is a background pixel (although they are obviously interchangeable in this formula). The result is clipped at 1 for 8- and 16-bit pixels (but can exceed 1 in 32 bpc mode); any pixels that add up to a value of more than 1 take the value of 1, full white.

In 32 bpc mode, this is likely to be your most commonly used blending mode. It generally brightens the overall image, but any black in the foreground acts transparent by adding a value of 0 to the background. It is useful for laying fire and explosion elements shot in negative space (against black) into a scene, adding noise or grain to an element, or any other element that is made up of light and texture (**Figures 3.31a**, **b**, and **c**).

Screen mode has an influence similar to Add mode's, but via a slightly different formula. The pixel values are inverted, multiplied together, and the result is inverted:

$$newPixel = 1-((1-A) * (1-B))$$

Note that with this formula, fully white pixels stay white, fully black pixels stay black, but a midrange pixel (0.5) takes on a brighter value (0.75), just not as bright as would be with Add (1).

NOTES

What is the difference between Add and Linear Dodge? The name! Open Photoshop and you'll notice it contains no blending mode called Add. Apparently Photoshop lacks the legal rights to use this term, hence Linear Dodge, which exists in After Effects only to match Photoshop. They are identical.

Figures 3.31a, b, and c Add mode takes the source foreground element, the fire shot against a black background shown in 3.31a, and adds its pixel values channel by channel to the background (b), causing the pure black pixels to disappear completely (c).

Figure 3.32 The difference between Screen and Add (**Figure 3.31**) may be subtle in printed figures until you look closely; notice there's less brightness in the "hottest" areas of the fire.

Technically speaking, Add mode doesn't work entirely correctly in 8 bpc and 16 bpc modes, where white values clip at 1, and Screen mode doesn't work at all in 32 bpc mode; more on this in Chapters 11 and 12.

You use Screen much like Add when working in 8 bpc and 16 bpc modes. Screen is most useful in situations where Add would blow out the highlights too much—glints, flares, glow passes, and so on (**Figure 3.32**).

Multiply

Multiply is another mode that is as simple as it sounds; it uses the formula

$$newPixel = A * B$$

This would seem to make the values *much* higher until you recollect that we are calculating values between 0 and 1; when you multiply by a fraction, the result is lower than the source value. Multiplying two images together, therefore, actually has the effect of reducing midrange pixels and darkening an image overall, although pixels that are full white in both images remain full white.

In optical compositing (the crude method used to do this stuff photochemically before we had computers that could manage it) the equivalent of multiply was layering two images, one over the other, combining their densities such that the dark areas of each image held out light from the other. This process was known as *bi-packing*.

Multiply literally has the inverse effect of Screen mode, darkening the midrange values of one image with another.

Figure 3.33 Dark smoke (actually a grayscale fractal noise pattern) is multiplied over the background, darkening the areas that are dark in either the foreground or background further.

It is useful in cases where you wish to emphasize dark tones in the foreground without replacing the lighter tones in the background, for example to layer in texture, shadow, or dark fog (**Figure 3.33**).

Overlay and the Light Modes

Overlay uses the bottom layer to determine whether to screen or multiply. Above a threshold of 50% gray (or .5 in normalized terms), it is screened. Below 50%, it is multiplied. Hard Light operates similarly, instead using the top layer to determine whether to screen or multiply, so the two are inverse effects. Reversing layer order and swapping Overlay for Hard Light yields an identical result.

These modes, along with Linear and Vivid Light, can be most useful for combining a layer that is predominantly color with another layer that is predominantly luminance, or contrast detail (**Figure 3.34**). This is how you create textures; for example, some of the lava texturing in the Level 4 sequence of *Spy Kids 3–D* was created by using Hard Light to combine a hand-painted color heat map with moving fractal noise patterns.

This type of usage is fine in 8 bpc or 16 bpc projects, but try to avoid fishing in the various Light modes when combining more detailed and specific elements. These methods don't work properly with 32 bpc overbright levels

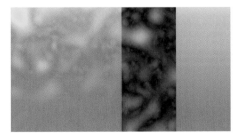

Figure 3.34 Overlay and its inverse, Hard Light, are useful for combining color and texture. Here, an instant lava lamp texture was created using the components shown at the right: a solid with Fractal Noise applied set to Overlay mode on top of a red-to-yellow gradient.

Figure 3.35 Difference mode can help you line up two layers that were shot at the same time, from the same camera setup. You know that the two layers are perfectly lined up when all of the pixels turn black.

Figure 3.36 Setting a deep-blue-colored solid to Color mode and overlaying it on the plate footage has the effect of tinting the colors in the image blue. Artistic uses of this mode are explored in Chapter 12, "Working with Light."

An effective use of both Stencil Alpha and Silhouette Alpha is the creation of a light wrap effect, detailed in Chapter 12.

(explored in Chapter 11), and this method of adjusting images is a warning sign that you haven't thought things through in terms of what you're trying to do.

Difference

Difference is a subtraction mode that inverts a pixel in the background according to how bright the foreground pixel is. There is one very specific use for Difference that has nothing to do with creating a blended look: You can line up two identical layers using this mode. When all of the pixels line up properly, layer details disappear (**Figure 3.35**).

HSB and Color Modes

The Hue, Saturation, and Brightness modes each combine the given value from the foreground layer with the other two from the background layer. Saturation applies the foreground saturation to the background hue and luminance values, Hue combines the foreground hue with the background saturation and luminance, and Brightness uses the foreground luminance in combination with the hue and saturation of the background.

Color takes both the hue and saturation of the top layer, using only the luminance from the underlying background (**Figure 3.36**).

Keep these modes in mind as shortcuts to channel operations in which you might want the color from a foreground combined with the detail (luminance) of the existing background.

Stencil and Silhouette

The Stencil and Silhouette blending modes apply transparency information to all of the layers below them in the composition. The Stencil modes use the light pixels, and Silhouette the dark pixels, of either the Alpha or Luminance values to determine the areas that remain visible in the layers below the current layer. You can keep these in mind for occasions in which they save you extra setup work.

Alpha Add and Luminescent Premultiply

Alpha Add and Luminescent Premultiply are special-case blending modes that affect semi-transparent edge pixels only.

Have you ever tried matting a layer with an alpha channel over the same layer with the alpha channel inverted? **Figures 3.37a** through **d** show the typical result: a semi-opaque line tracing the edge of the alpha, where the pixels remain semi-transparent because they are blended together in the same manner as semi-opaque layers. Alpha Add adds the actual values of the alpha pixels without compensating for the opacity effect, so two 50% opaque pixels become 100% opaque.

Why would you combine a layer with itself, inverting the alpha? You probably wouldn't. But you might combine two layers with overlapping transparency that would require this method—for example, two parts of the same layer.

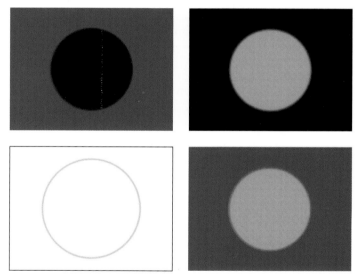

Figures 3.37a through d Placing a matted object over a background with the exact inverse matte (a, b) seems as though it should result in a fully opaque image. Instead, edge pixels form a semi-transparent halo in the alpha channel (c). Alpha Add does just what the title implies, adding the alpha values together so that inverse mattes total up to 100% throughout the image (d) (left to right).

Luminescent Premultiply is an alternative method of removing premultiplication from source footage, retaining bright values that would otherwise be clipped. Premultiplication over black causes all semi-transparent pixels to become darker; removing the black values while adding transparency, which is what removing premultiplication does, can cause them to appear dimmer than they should. This is useful for bright overlaid elements that come in with alpha channels and premultiplication, such as flares and explosions; you can set the footage to interpret as Straight on import and use this mode instead of Normal to overlay the element. It's another trick to keep in your arsenal should you ever see the symptoms (dim translucent elements) for which it is recommended.

Track Mattes

Track mattes allow you to use the alpha or luminance information of one layer as the transparency of another layer (**Figure 3.38**). This is actually the normal way to apply a matte channel in many compositing applications, which don't have the concept of the alpha channel so firmly integrated into the overall pipeline as After Effects.

Figure 3.38 A basic alpha track matte setup: The alpha of layer 1 is set as the alpha of layer 2 via the highlighted pull-down menu. The small icons just to the left of the layer names help remind you that this relationship has been set up, and which is the color layer and which is the matte.

The perceptual difference between an alpha channel and a track matte isn't, for the most part, too difficult to grasp. In both cases, you have pixels with a value (in 8-bit color space) between 0 and 255, whether they are color or grayscale alpha pixels. That any image would be interchangeable with the alpha channel shouldn't be too shocking; even if you're using the luminance of a full-color image, After Effects simply averages the 0 to 255 value of the three color channels into one value. The principle doesn't even change in 16-bit color—it's just the same range of values, with finer increments, being sampled.

You set a track matte by placing the layer that contains the transparency data directly above its target layer in the Timeline and choosing one of the four options from the Track Matte pull-down menu:

▶ **Alpha Matte:** Uses the alpha channel of the track matte layer as if it were the alpha of the underlying target layer

- **Alpha Inverted Matte:** Does the same as Alpha Matte but inverts the result, so that the lighter areas of the alpha are transparent and the darker areas are opaque
- **Luma Matte:** Uses the luminance data of the track matte layer (the relative brightness of the red, green, and blue channels combined) as if it were the alpha of the underlying target layer
- **Luma Inverted Matte:** Does the same as Luma Matte but inverts the result, so that the lighter areas of the alpha are transparent and the darker areas are opaque

By default, the source layer for the track matte (the upper of the two) has its visibility turned off when you set the track matte, which is almost always what you want. This sets the track matte with a single click to the Track Matte pull-down menu. If you need to adjust the source after setting it, you can always temporarily turn it back on; just remember to turn it back off when you're finished.

Why They're Useful

Track mattes are not the only way to apply alpha or luminance data to the transparency of a layer, but they're the clearest and most straightforward way. They help you out of a lot of jams in which creating a selection via other means would be inconvenient or in which mask or matte features constrain you.

For example, it's not possible to track a mask in After Effects. But it is possible to apply the mask to a track matte instead, and then to track that layer (instead of the mask itself). Chapter 8, "Effective Motion Tracking," discusses this in detail.

In Chapter 6 you will learn of the many ways to pull a key, including hi-con mattes. Some of these methods apply their results directly to the alpha channel of the target layer, but others cannot. Additionally, specific operations such as blue-screen keying can change the color of the source (automatically removing blue spill from the foreground); applying the key via a track matte to a duplicate clean source instead is an effective workaround if you want the matte but not the despill.

Figure 3.39 Selecting and duplicating the layers from Figure 3.37 creates two new layers that leapfrog above the previous layers to maintain the proper color/matte relationship in the source and duplicate layers.

NOTES

If the layer to which the track matte is applied already has an alpha channel, then the new selection area created by the track matte will be opaque only in the areas that are opaque in both mattes. So applying a track matte in this situation is like adding a subselection to the current selection.

NOTES

If there seems to be some doubt as to whether edits you are applying to the track matte are properly affecting the target, if possible, first crank up the effect applied to the track matte, so it's obvious whether it is applied or not. If it's not, you must precompose the track matte layer; this forces it to render prior to track matting.

Why They're Occasionally Tricky

Unlike with parented layers (described in Chapter 2, "The Timeline"), selecting a track matte layer does not lock it to the current layer. In fact, setting a track matte means that no matter which layer is next higher in the stack, that layer is the source of the matte. Thus, accidentally moving a layer in between a layer and its track matte can cause (easily solvable but nonetheless) disastrous results.

When you duplicate a layer with a track matte activated (**Ctrl+D**/**Cmd+D**), After Effects automatically duplicates it above the matte layer or two layers above the current layer. If you duplicate the matte layer at the same time, the duplicate will also move up two layers, so that all layers preserve their proper track mattes (**Figure 3.39**). That's good. What's bad is neglecting to duplicate both layers, because the track matte remains active in the duplicate layer. If it has been duplicated to the top of the stack, you can't even see that it's active, and it waits there like a ticking time bomb for you to position another layer above it, suddenly changing its transparency.

Render Order

Occasionally tricky is the render order of track mattes: In most cases, adjustments and effects that you apply to the matte layer are calculated prior to creating the target matte, but in other cases you must first precompose for applied effects and adjustments to activate prior to application of the track matte.

And what happens when you apply a track matte to another track matte? Generally speaking, this will not work and the practice should be avoided. It will work in some cases, however, and the user interface does not prohibit this behavior so you can try it. A better idea is certainly to precompose the first instance of track matting and apply the second track matte to that nested composition.

The next chapter, "Optimizing Your Project," looks in depth at solving issues related to render order such as these; you'll begin to see how After Effects can be a visual problem-solving tool for such situations.

Optimizing Your Projects

Build a system that even a fool can use and only a fool will want to use it.

— George Bernard Shaw

Optimizing your Projects

This chapter examines the flow of data through After Effects in specific detail. I realize that description might not sound utterly gripping, but once you learn to efficiently use the features that affect the order and conditions in which things happen, After Effects will help you work faster and solve thorny problems.

At times, you must be the digital compositor version of a master chef—someone who knows what has to be finished before something else can be started, and what can be prepped and considered "done" before it's time to serve the final result. At other times, you must think like a programmer. You have to isolate and "debug" elements of your project when the result doesn't look anything like what was planned. This chapter helps you reach both goals.

In the big picture, the keys to mastering the After Effects data pipeline are

▶ Understanding how to use multiple compositions

▶ Knowing when to precompose

▶ Optimizing your rendering time

This chapter will help you get After Effects running closer to real time, so that you're less likely to give your client the lame excuse that your shot is late because After Effects is still rendering. Efficient rendering, however, depends on well-organized compositions and plenty of advanced planning.

Navigating Multiple Compositions

When working with a complicated project, you can easily lose track of how everything is organized. This section will show you

▶ The benefits of designing and perhaps standardizing a project template with your specific project in mind

▶ Simple methods for keeping your compositions displayed so that you can visually remember their order or look at one while editing another

▶ Shortcuts that can help you when you've lost track of something

These tips have come in very handy when I've found myself working with artists who understood compositing quite well, but were nonetheless wrestling with tracking down and solving problems in After Effects.

Project Template Benefits

If you're working on your own, you're basically free to organize your projects however you like, just as if you live alone, you're free never to tidy your apartment. Successful collaborative projects at studios, however, make use of project templates that specify where different types of items live in the Project panel. Your personal value to those projects will in large part depend on your ability to play nicely with others by contributing to that organizational system.

Figure 4.1 shows a typical project template containing multiple compositions. It's a simplified version of a comp template used at The Orphanage for feature film work. Considering the days or even weeks that can be involved doing multiple takes of a visual effects shot, a template like this can be a lifesaver. Here are some of the template's useful attributes:

▶ The Master comps are numbered so that they show up in order at the top of a list (sorted by name) in the Project panel.

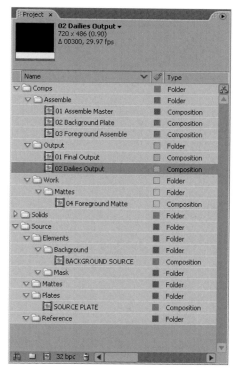

Figure 4.1 Here's a top-level look at the organization of an unpopulated composition template that could be used on a feature film effects shot. There are two basic categories of folders (Source and Comps) and numbered, preconfigured compositions listed in correct render order. This template and an even more simplified version are included in the CH04 folder on the book's disc.

▶ The Final Output comp is preset to the exact format and length specified for it to be filmed out for the movie. No work whatsoever occurs in this comp; previews are not done here, so its work area does not change, and no effects, animations, or expressions are created here that might inadvertently be left off at render time.

▶ There is a locked placeholder layer at the top of various comps reminding you how to use them.

▶ Helpful guide layers, such as masks for different formats and preset adjustment layers with Levels set to high contrast (for checking black and white level matches), are placed in ahead of time (**Figure 4.2**).

Figure 4.2 This default Assemble Master composition for a film project includes preset layers that would be specified by the comp supervisor. These might include non-rendering layers, showing the holdout areas for delivery formats as well as a Levels adjustment to "slam" the gamma (more about that in Section II). There is a color correction that is specified not to be edited, as well as pre-populated foreground and background layers.

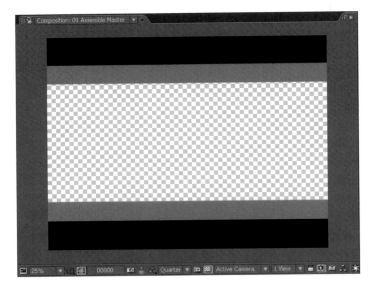

▶ A Source folder is organized with preset compositions to hold elements, such as the background plate, as well as reference items. These comps, rather than the footage items themselves, are used thereafter in the project. Like the Final Output comp, this seems to prevent careless errors that can occur when footage is replaced.

▶ Standardized organization means that anyone, a supervisor or someone coming in to help clean up, can much more quickly recognize where the elements of the project reside.

You can take this idea as far as you want. The basic concepts of a Master comp, source comps, and a render comp seem useful on just about any shot to which you will be devoting more than a couple of hours of work, but a template can include a lot more than that. The Orphanage designs a custom template .aep file for each film production, and the template alone can be 4 MB or more before any work has been added (big for an empty .aep file!), including custom expressions, camera rigs, log/linear conversions, and recurring effects setups.

Working with Tabs

Because your compositing operations are primarily done via the Timeline rather than a tree/node interface, it is incumbent upon you, the artist, to keep your Timeline panels organized in a way that makes sense to you. After Effects 7.0 offers a huge improvement over previous versions by having only one Composition panel by default, but it is still possible to have an unlimited number of Timelines open. If you've ever found yourself hunting around for a particular comp's tab in the Timeline panel, I have a couple of suggestions.

First of all, and most obviously, you may have too many tabs open. It can be helpful to close all Timeline tabs and start over (with any Timeline highlighted, choose **Ctrl+Alt+A/ Cmd+Opt+A**): Reopen your Master composition. Alt/ Option-double-click on the subcomp you want to work on, and if the specific composition you want is three or four layers deep, keep going until you've reached that one. Now your reopened tabs follow, right to left, the basic render order.

TIP

To navigate quickly forward or backward through a set of open comp tabs, press **Alt+Shift+comma** or **Alt+Shift+period (Option+ Shift+comma** or **Option+ Shift+period on a Mac)**. You can remember them as the < and > keys, as if they were arrows.

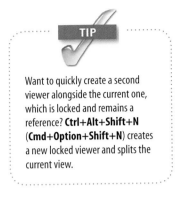

Want to quickly create a second viewer alongside the current one, which is locked and remains a reference? **Ctrl+Alt+Shift+N** (**Cmd+Option+Shift+N**) creates a new locked viewer and splits the current view.

If you're adjusting properties in the Timeline panel and nothing seems to be happening, it may be that you've closed the Composition panel but left its Timeline open (which you can do by Alt-clicking to close the Composition panel). Far more likely, however, is that you have a Layer panel open and have mistaken it for the Composition panel.

New in After Effects 7.0, you can context-click on the empty region of any Timeline panel (below the layers) and choose Reveal Composition in Project from the bottom of the context menu.

If you need to see two compositions at once, editing the viewer of one while you work in the Timeline of the other, you will be very happy you upgraded to version 7.0. At the upper left of the Composition tab is a lock icon. Click this to lock any composition, and that comp always is displayed in its Composition panel, no matter which Timeline is forward. This makes it easy to see the effect of subcomposition changes on a Master composition.

Alternatively, if it's only at preview time that you want to see the Master comp, remember the Always Preview This View toggle at the lower left of the Composition panel, which displays the toggled composition during a RAM Preview. Not everyone—myself included—uses this feature, because inevitably it will be left on after you no longer want it, showing you the same preview after you've moved on. Always Preview This View can be considered the old way of doing things, and locked viewers the new, preferred method.

Where Am I?

We all lose our bearings sometimes. For that reason, context menu shortcuts in the Timeline panel enable you to select a layer and reveal it, either in the Project panel or in Project Flowchart view.

Although you can use the Project Flowchart view to map out an existing project, I find it more helpful to keep the Project panel as clearly and hierarchically organized as is usefully possible, thereby continuing in the spirit of the templates. This might sound about as much fun as keeping your room clean, but if you think in terms of helping someone new to your project to understand it, you may find that you help yourself as well. For example, if you want to refer back to that project in a few months' time, you effectively are in the same shoes as that other artist arriving at the project completely cold.

Descriptive Names

It's rather obvious, but you can help yourself a lot by using descriptive names for your compositions. For example, if you want to keep track of composition order, you can number the Master comp 00, the first nested comp 01, and so on, using descriptive names after the numbers, for example 00_master and so on. Some After Effects veterans have joked that leaving the name of a composition at the default Comp 1 is a firing offense.

Precomposing and Nesting

Precomposing is sometimes regarded as a kludge, an ill-conceived solution to render order problems. I don't agree. To me, it is an effective way to solve problems and optimize projects in After Effects, provided you plan things out a little.

Just to get our terms straight, *precomposing* is the action of selecting a set of layers in a composition and assigning them to a new subcomp. Closely related to this is composition *nesting*, the action of placing one already created composition inside of another.

Typically, you precompose by selecting the layers of a composition that can and should be grouped together and choosing Precompose from the Layer menu. (You can also use the keyboard shortcut **Ctrl+Shift+C/Cmd+Shift+C**.) You are given two options: to leave attributes where they are or to move them into the new composition. One of the options is grayed out when multiple layers are selected, for reasons that are explained in the fine print of the dialog box (**Figure 4.3**). If you're wondering what constitutes an attribute that would be precomposed, it's pretty much anything that you've edited on the layer: an effect, a mask, paint strokes, or even layer In and Out points.

Debugging a Shot

Compositing is not altogether unlike computer programming, in that a complicated shot is made up of a series of individual decisions, any one of which can affect the whole. If you ever find yourself needing to troubleshoot a complicated shot, in which some unidentified variable seems to have crept in uninvited, you can attack the problem beginning from the Master comp. Solo layers one by one until you find the culprit, and if it's a comp, Alt/Option-double-click to open it, and repeat the process, until you've isolated the culprit and nailed it.

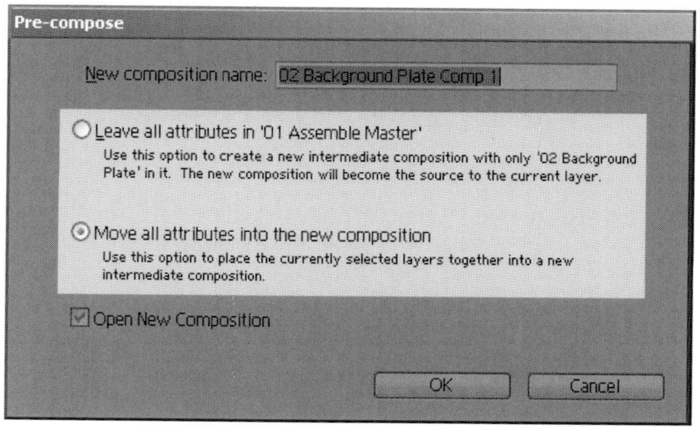

Figure 4.3 Select two layers for precomposing and the Leave All Attributes option is not available. It's hard to read the fine print in this figure, but look closely in the dialog and you'll see that it clearly tells you what will happen depending on which option you choose (when precomposing a single layer, that is).

Why Do It?

Depending on who you ask, precomposing is either the solution to most problems in After Effects or one of the most annoying things that you have to do in the program.

So why not just work in one big happy composition? The advantages of doing so would seem to be many. All of the properties and keyframes that you would want remain right there in front of you, you never have to go digging into some subcomp to fix a Levels setting, and there's no difficulty keeping track of composition order.

To wax poetic about it for a moment, there are almost as many reasons to precompose as the day is long. Here are a few of the most common:

▶ **To keep two layers in sync:** If you ever find yourself making the same adjustments to two different layers in the same comp, that may be a signal that those layers now comprise an element and you need to precompose.

▶ **As a fix for render order problems:** Sometimes it is simply not possible to make one render action occur prior to another without precomposing. For example, if you want to mask a layer after applying effects to it, you must apply the effects to a precomposition and then mask that.

▶ **To keep the Master comp tidy:** This one should be self-explanatory. A Master composition with six well-organized elements is far more useful than one with dozens of disparate elements (**Figure 4.4**).

▶ **To reuse an element:** If you've used a set of layers to create an element that you think might be used again or that your client might want to change globally in several locations, it makes a huge amount of sense to nest these layers as a composition. That way, to reuse the element, you need only drop it into a new Timeline.

▶ **Because an element or a set of layers is essentially done:** This, in case you didn't know it, is your big picture goal. If you can finish some part of your shot, particularly if it's a render-intensive portion, precomposing that part gives you the option of pre-rendering it.

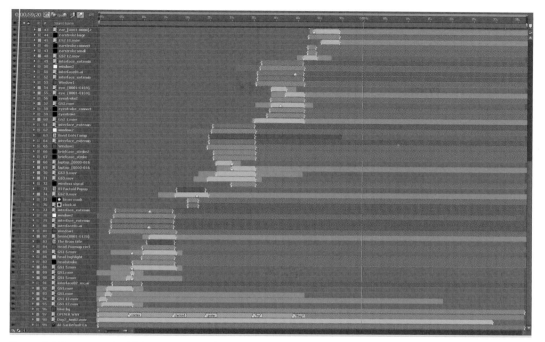

Figure 4.4 Try never to let this happen to one of your compositions.

If you're already comfortable with the idea of precomposing, the last point is probably the most important for you to keep in mind. As you'll see later in this chapter, there are huge advantages to changing your mentality from that of an artist who wants to keep all options open, to that of an artist who understands the benefits of finishing an element, if only for the time being.

Options and Gotchas

Precomposing a single layer using the Leave All Attributes option is relatively straightforward. Most of the time, however, you will find yourself precomposing multiple layers via the Move All Attributes option, a route that can be fraught with peril if you don't pay attention. Typical gotchas associated with this process include

▶ Changes in layer duration and offset as they appear in the Timeline.

▶ There is no provision for the need to precompose some attributes, but not all.

NOTES

Some other compositing applications, and in particular, Discreet's Inferno, seem to have cornered mind share in terms of perceived speed and power. Inferno is powerful, running on customized hardware, but people sometimes fail to notice that it is not truly real time; even Inferno has to render. Inferno artists will conceal this fact by rendering in the background or requiring that elements come in pre-rendered—often (and ironically) from After Effects.

143

▶ It is difficult to undo precompositions several edits further on.

▶ Behavior of precomposed Blending modes and 3D transforms changes depending on whether Collapse Transformations is on or off.

▶ Confusion about recursion: In what cases do motion blur, frame blending, and collapsed transformation switches affect nested comps?

Take a closer look at each of these situations, as well as some useful strategies for working with them.

Layer Duration Confusion

Figure 4.5 demonstrates the layer duration problem: Precomposing a set of layers that are not the same duration as the source composition puts them in a new composition whose duration matches that of the source composition, but not that of the layers. The result is that the precomposition layer includes empty frames at the top or tail of the shot.

You can trim the layer to match the original edits, but there's a better option. This works best if you have Synchronize Time of All Related Items checked in General Preferences, as it now is by default.

1. In the precomp, move the time needle to the first frame that contains any data.

2. Select all the layers, and with the Shift key held down move them so that that first frame lines up as the first frame of the composition.

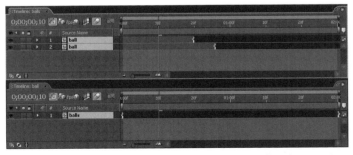

Figure 4.5 Precompose layers offset in time with the Move All Attributes option, and you may not notice that the offset is transferred to the precomposition, while the Master comp shows a layer that appears to begin at frame 0.

3. With the time needle still where the layers originally began, return to the main comp.

4. Press the [key to realign the first frame of the composition at the correct point.

If you like, you can trim the tail as well by going into the subcomp, putting the time needle on the last frame that contains any data, then returning to the Master comp and pressing **Alt+]** (**Option+]**) to trim the layer.

The Missing Option

There are, of course, situations in which the two options in the Precompose dialog don't cover everything you need. What if you want to move some but not all attributes into a new composition? Unfortunately, there is no automated solution for such a situation and all its variables.

The best way to handle this is probably to choose the Move All Attributes option, check the Open New Composition box, and then cut any attributes that belong in the Master composition, pasting them there. Or, if you're precomposing one layer only, you can do it the other way around: Leave the attributes in the Master comp, and then cut and paste the ones you want into the subcomp.

Data Pass Through

Finally, how do you know if 3D position data or Blending modes of a layer in the subcomp will be preserved and appear correctly in the Master comp? Or, if you turn on motion blur or frame blending on the subcomp layer in the Master comp, how do you know those elements you animated in the subcomp, or even in a subcomp of a subcomp, are going to take on those settings? To manage these situations properly, you should be aware of a couple of settings.

For motion blur and frame blending, the key is the Switches Affect Nested Comps check box in General Preferences. With this checked (as it is by default), turning on these features in the Master comp turns them on in any affected subcomps as well. Unless you specify otherwise in the Render Settings, this is also how this situation is handled when rendering.

TIP

Included on the book's disc is preCompToLayerDur.jsx. According to its full description at www.motionscript.com, "this script will precompose one or more selected layers with the Move All Attributes option and the resulting new comp's In point will be the earliest In point of the selected layers, and the comp's Out point will be the latest Out point of the selected layers." Load it via File > Scripts > Run Script File.

CLOSE-UP

Undoing a Precomposition

If you set a precomp and then change your mind immediately, you can, of course, undo the action. A problem emerges, however, when you progress further with your project and decide that precomposing was a bad idea. In that case, the only option is to cut the layers from the precomp and carefully paste them back into the Master comp, taking care that layer order is preserved and that such basic properties as Transforms remain correct.

Figure 4.6 This switch (highlighted) has two roles (and two names). With a nested composition layer, it is a Collapse Transformations toggle. Enable it, and Blending modes and 3D positions from the nested comp are passed through as if they were not precomposed at all. (Its other role, Continuously Rasterize, applies only to vector layers such as Adobe Illustrator files.)

Passing through 3D position data and Blending modes, on the other hand, is a question of enabling the Collapse Transformations toggle for any comp layer (**Figure 4.6**). Turning this option on causes these properties to behave as if the precomposed layers were still in the Master comp; turning it off prevents them from interacting with the Master comp.

The Cool Way Time Is Nested

After Effects is less rigid than many digital video applications when it comes to working with time. You are not forced to have all of the compositions in a given project use the same frame rate, and changing the frame rate of an existing composition is handled rather gracefully, with all of the keyframes retaining their positions relative to overall time.

CLOSE-UP

Grow Bounds

Sometimes enabling Collapse Transformations/ Continuously Rasterize is not desirable—for example, if you set up 3D layers in a subcomp and don't want them affected by a camera in the Master comp. This can lead to a gotcha where effects that expand the pixel area occupied by that layer (such as blurs and distortions) are cut off at the edges of the nested composition (**Figure 4.7a**). By adding the Grow Bounds effect prior to the effect that needs more pixel area, you avoid this problem (**Figure 4.7b**).

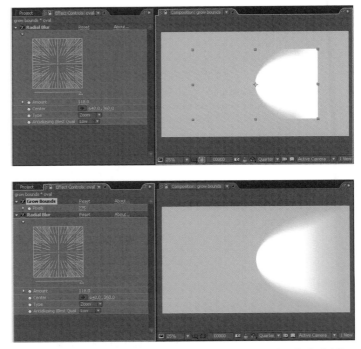

Figures 4.7a and b The half-oval layer has been precomposed, and a Radial Blur is cut off at the edges of the layer (a). Precomposing would restore the other half of the oval, but Grow Bounds (b) just enlarges the boundaries of the layer so the blur is not truncated.

That doesn't mean you can be sloppy, of course, it just means you have options. Artists familiar with other applications often forget to pay attention to frame rate settings when

▶ Importing an image sequence

▶ Creating a new composition from scratch

▶ Embedding a composition with a given frame rate into another with a different frame rate

In the third instance, by default, After Effects does its best to stretch or compress the frame rate of the embedded composition to match that of the Master composition. Sometimes, however, that's not what you want, which is when you need to examine options on the Advanced tab of the Composition Settings dialog.

The Advanced Tab

The Composition Settings dialog's Advanced tab contains a hodgepodge of extras that can come in handy. For example, Anchor Grid specifies how a composition is cropped if you adjust its pixel dimensions downward on the Basic tab. Shutter Angle and Shutter Phase affect motion blur (see Chapter 9, "Virtual Cinematography"). As for the rendering plug-in, you will fairly certainly just leave it at the default setting, Advanced 3D (**Figure 4.8**).

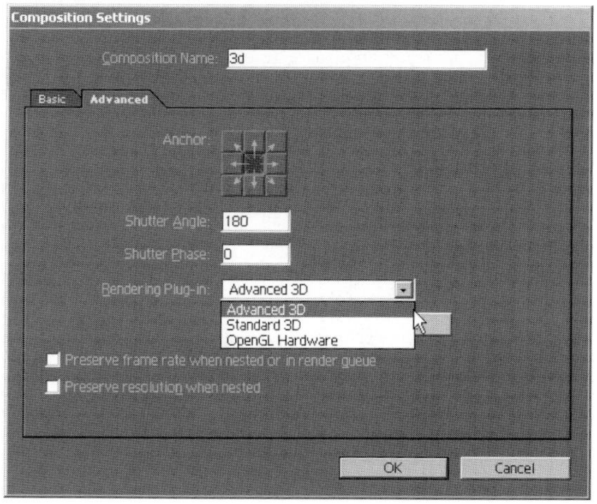

CLOSE-UP

Collapsing New Blendings

One limitation of turning on Collapse Transformations is that you're thereafter prevented from adding a blending mode on the collapsed layer. The Blending mode menu shows only a – symbol.

The workaround is to apply an effect to the layer that does nothing or that is even turned off. This forces After Effects to render the collapsed layer (making it what the Adobe developers call a *parenthesized* comp), a side benefit of which is that Blending modes become available.

The downside is that 3D layers are no longer passed through. But this workaround is helpful when you wish to precompose for the purpose of scaling.

Figure 4.8 Rare is the occasion when you would not use the default Advanced 3D rendering plug-in. The "plug-in" idea was devised offering third parties the ability to write their own 3D renderers for After Effects, but at this writing (and in several years) no developer outside of Adobe has offered one.

New in 7.0 is a third rendering plug-in option: OpenGL Hardware. This option is grayed out until you check Enable OpenGL in Preferences > Previews. As with all things OpenGL, this option is a matter of taste; it is likely to offer a more stylized video game look that may not render similarly on two different machines.

Maladjusted

There are only a couple of major gotchas to watch out for with adjustment layers. Always keep in mind that their timing and Transform properties still apply.

In other words, make sure that your adjustment layer starts at the first frame of the comp and extends to the last frame of the comp (or the start and end frames of the portion for which you need it), otherwise its effects will pop on and off unexpectedly. And if you set any transforms to the adjustment layer, make sure they are intentional, as the boundaries of these layers are still respected in the rendering process. Finally, if you enlarge a composition you will probably have to resize any adjustment layers as well.

And then there are the two Preserve check boxes. Preserve Frame Rate maintains the frame rate of the current composition no matter the frame rate settings wherever you might send it—into another composition with a different frame rate, or into the Render Queue with different frame rate settings. So if you've keyframed a simple cycle animation that looks right at 4 frames per second, and then place that composition into a 24 fps comp, After Effects will not try to stretch that composition across the higher frame rate, but will maintain 4 fps.

Ditto the Preserve Resolution When Nested option: Typically, if an element is scaled down in a precomp and the composition is scaled up in the Master comp, you will want After Effects to treat these two opposing scales as one operation, "concatenating" the transform operations (in computer parlance) so that no data loss occurs via quantization. If you want the data in the subcomp to appear as if it were scaled up from a lower-resolution element, however, toggle on Preserve Resolution When Nested and live it up with the big pixel look.

Adjustment and Guide Layers

As you may already know, versions 6.0 and 6.5 of After Effects introduced two new layer forms—adjustment layers and guide layers—that are easy to use and seem simple enough on the surface. Each has vitally useful applications, however, that might not be immediately apparent.

Adjustment Layers

Any layer in your Timeline can become an adjustment layer. An *adjustment layer* is itself invisible, but the effects applied to it affect all layers below it in the stack; it behaves just like an effect filter node in a node-based compositor such as Shake. This elegant, profound feature is too often overlooked, perhaps because it is fundamentally so simple, yet it has many uses.

To convert a layer to an adjustment layer, toggle the feature in the Switches column (**Figure 4.9**). The more typical approach, however, is to create a new layer specified as an adjustment layer from the get-go. Context-click in an empty area of the Timeline, and choose New > Adjustment Layer (or do the same from the Layer menu).

That's easy enough (although, alas, it has no keyboard shortcut). So what's so cool? What can you do with adjustment layers that you can't with normal effects?

For one thing, you can effectively dial back any effect in an adjustment layer using Opacity. An effective quick fix, this is the equivalent of a dissolve operation in a node-based compositing application. Most effects do not include the ability to be dialed back, even though it makes perfect sense to do so in many cases. Colorize your scene using Hue/Saturation, and the supervisor says, "Dial it back 50%." Set the adjustment layer's Opacity to 50%, or even dial it up and down before the supe's very eyes. Impressive.

You can also add mattes or masks to adjustment layers, delineating specific holdout areas for effects. This avoids precomposing in situations where it is undesirable. Instead, a track matte layer containing the necessary transparency information will do; the adjusted layers themselves can even serve as the track matte (**Figures 4.10a** and **b**).

Guide Layers

Like adjustment layers, *guide layers* are normal layers that behave differently when toggled on. In this case, a guide layer appears in the current composition but disappears in any subsequent compositions into which it is nested, nor does it render by default. Its visibility setting is not a worry if you want it never to appear in your output.

This feature is useful when you add anything to help your compositing process that you would never want to see in the final render. Examples include custom backgrounds that make it easy to judge edge detail or adjustment layers that "slam" the levels of the composition to see if its layers still match (more on that in Section II).

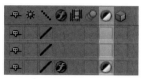

Figure 4.9 You can convert any layer, except a camera, to an adjustment layer by toggling this switch. Creating a new adjustment layer simply creates a white solid the size of the comp with this switch toggled on.

NOTES

Effects that work specifically with the alpha channel have no effect on adjustment layers. This is consistent with the general principle that an adjustment layer contains effects that change layers below the adjustment layer only, rendering no image data of its own.

TIP

There are lots of creative uses of guide layers. Is there something you always forget to do before rendering? Add a text layer with a big note to yourself in the Render Comp and make it a guide layer. Another great usage for guide layers is with intermediate view LUT's, which are discussed beginning in Chapter 11, "Film, HDR, and 32 Bit Compositing."

Figures 4.10a and b The highlights on the wing of the plane have been bloomed warmer by first creating a luma matte that isolates only them (a). This is then applied as a Luma Track Matte to an adjustment layer containing a colorization effect that makes the highlight areas rosy; this is then dialed back using the Opacity control of the adjustment layer (b).

NOTES

If you decide you want guide layers to appear at render time, there is a toggle to do so in Render Settings. This does, of course, sort of defeat the whole purpose, but at least the option exists.

You can toggle any type of layer into a guide layer either by context-clicking it or by choosing Guide Layer from the Layer menu. Within the current comp, you'll notice no difference (**Figures 4.11a** and **b**). You can still apply effects to this layer or have other layers refer to it, and it is fully visible. Nest this composition in another composition, however, and the guide layer disappears.

Figures 4.11a and b Shown are a couple of effective uses for guide layers: displaying a matted element against an gradient, without worrying that the gradient will show up when the element is used (a), and in combination with an adjustment layer to "slam" a composition (b), revealing flaws in the matte edges, whether the blacks match, and so on.

Understanding Rendering Order

To truly master After Effects and become an expert compositor, you must precisely understand the order in which actions occur. For example, you need to know whether a mask is applied before an effect and whether an effect is applied to a track matte. You must fully comprehend the render pipeline.

For the most part the render pipeline is plainly visible in the Timeline and follows consistent rules:

▶ 2D layers are calculated from bottom to top of the layer stack

▶ Masks, effects, transforms, paint, and type are calculated from top to bottom (as seen when twirling down layer properties)

▶ 3D layers are calculated based on their distance from the camera; coplanar 3D layers use stacking order just like 2D layers

So, in a 2D composition, After Effects starts with the bottom layer, calculates any adjustments to it in the order properties are shown, top to bottom, then calculates adjustments to the layer above it, composites the two of them together, and so on up to the top layer of the stack. If you want to know what order is used to calculate layer properties, you need only reveal them in the Timeline (**Figure 4.12**).

This, then, adds an extra advantage to adjustment layers. They behave just like other 2D layers in the stack, so that they are always rendered after all calculations on layers below them are completed. Effects within layers, on the other hand, always calculate prior to transforms.

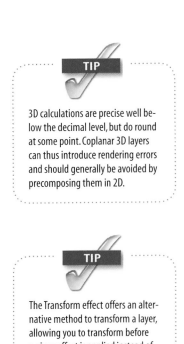

TIP

3D calculations are precise well below the decimal level, but do round at some point. Coplanar 3D layers can thus introduce rendering errors and should generally be avoided by precomposing them in 2D.

TIP

The Transform effect offers an alternative method to transform a layer, allowing you to transform before a given effect is applied instead of precomposing (because transforms otherwise always follow effects).

Figure 4.12 Just because After Effects lacks a tree/node interface doesn't mean you can't see the render order in the Timeline easily. Layer properties render in top to bottom order (as shown here: Motion Trackers, then Masks, Effects, and finally Transforms).

And what about track mattes? Track mattes (and Blending modes) are calculated after all of the other layer properties (masks, effects, and transforms) have been calculated. Of course, before track mattes are applied, their own mask, effect, and transform data are applied to them. Therefore, it should not be necessary to pre-render a track matte in order to see these edits affect the matte.

As I mentioned in the previous chapter, you are taking your chances if you try to apply two consecutive track mattes (in other words, you apply a track matte to a track matte). Sometimes the method works, and the UI does not specifically prohibit you from doing it; however, it's inconsistent. I recommend precomposing instead. Better safe than sorry.

Optimizing Previews and Renders

I sometimes surprise directors and supervisors with the speed and interactivity I squeeze out of After Effects, even at full 2K film resolution. Here's my secret: As I work, I organize portions of my master comp that I consider finished into their own subcomps, and if they require any render cycles at all, I pre-render them.

It is astonishing how many veteran compositing artists waste redundant rendering time by failing to commit to their own decisions, especially given how easy it is to make changes if you've guessed wrong. For example, on effects shots that begin with a blue-screen key, but develop into very complex shots, artists often fail to pre-render the keying results for fear that they might need to tweak them later. This can add several seconds to each individual frame update and minutes or even hours to a film-resolution render. Every time you want to see the result of a new color correction, you end up waiting for your keyer to redo its work. Collectively, you can waste hours of your day in this fashion.

After Effects does have a RAM cache (which is further optimized with each major upgrade of the application) to keep track of what has not changed when you make adjustments and avoid unnecessary re-rendering. This is a great feature, but you should not rely on that alone to speed your workflow.

NOTES

After Effects is often more clever than you might guess about optimizing what to calculate and what to ignore or cache. Portions of layers that are not visible (because they are occluded, masked, or otherwise outside of the visible frame) often will not be calculated. You can't control this process, but you often reap the benefits (via faster renders) without even realizing it.

TIP

Apply an Add mask to a layer set as a Luma Track Matte and the areas outside the mask contain the equivalent of solid black (transparent) pixels.

TIP

The Info panel can show you what exactly is rendering at any time. To view these descriptive updates, choose Preferences > Display and check Show Rendering in Process in Info Panel and Flowchart.

Post-Render Options

The After Effects UI anticipates the need to pre-render nested compositions and replace usage in the project, then potentially change your mind later. Tucked away in the Render Queue panel, but easily visible if you twirl down the arrow next to Output Module (**Figure 4.13**), is a menu of three post-render actions. After the render is complete, you can choose

▶ **Import:** Imports the result

▶ **Import & Replace Usage:** Does not eliminate the source comp from the project; only takes its place (or that of any other item you specify) in the project

▶ **Set Proxy:** Makes the rendered output a proxy (temporary substitute) of the source comp (or of any other item you specify)

If you choose either of the latter two options, the pickwhip icon appears adjacent to the menu. Click and drag from this icon to whatever item in the Project panel you wish to replace. By default, the rendered composition is replaced.

What if you choose Import & Replace Usage and change your mind? To change usage back to the comp, bypassing rendered footage, hold down the Alt (Option) key as you drag and drop the comp over the footage in the Project panel; this replaces usage throughout the project. The same method of Alt-drag into a Timeline panel replaces only that individual instance (useful in other cases).

If your intention is only to work faster, and you anticipate re-rendering everything from scratch when outputting the final version, you can use proxies.

Figure 4.13 Twirl down the arrow beside the Output Module settings for a Render Queue item and you reveal options to perform actions following the render. The last two options are particularly useful for speeding up future renders, if you apply them to subcompositions and render those.

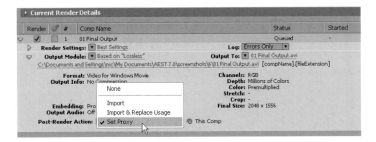

Proxies

Any visual item in your Project panel can be set with a *proxy*, which is an imported image or sequence that stands in for that item. Its pixel dimensions, color space, compression, and even its length can differ from the item it replaces; for example, you can use a low-resolution, JPEG-compressed still image to stand-in for a full-resolution, moving image background.

Figure 4.14 shows how a proxy appears in the Project panel. Although the scale of the proxy differs from that of the source item, transform settings within the comps that use this item remain consistent; that's the beauty of it.

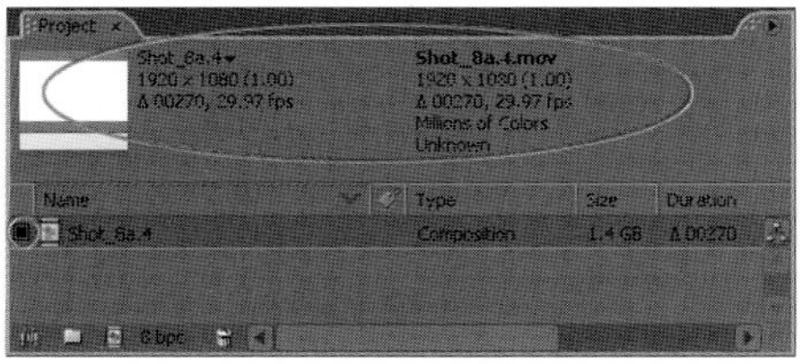

Proxies need not only be temporary stand-ins; you can use them to pre-render compositions, as long as you remember to manage their usage in Render Settings > Proxy Use. The Use Comp Proxies Only, Use All Proxies, and Current Settings options (**Figure 4.15**) will all use proxies in the final render. The source composition remains in place as a backup but no longer expends rendering resources.

Proxies are relatively easy to blow away when no longer desired. Select the items, context-click (or go to the File menu), and choose Set Proxy > None. Alternatively, you can simply rely on the default Proxy Use > Use No Proxies in Render Settings, which will ignore them.

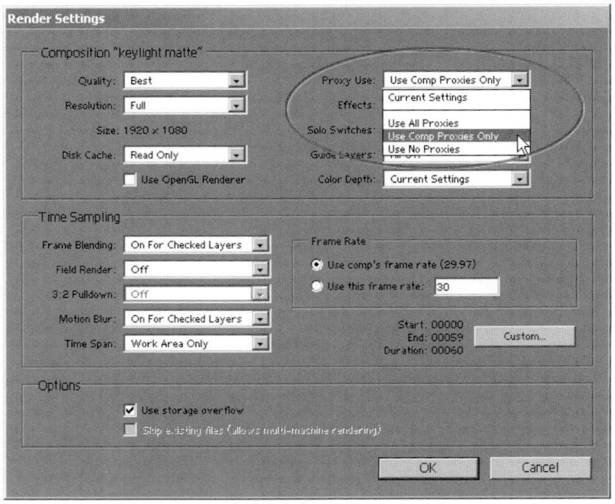

Figure 4.14 The black square icon to the left of an item in the Project panel indicates that a proxy is enabled; a hollow square indicates that a proxy is assigned but not currently active. Both items are listed atop the Project panel, the active one in bold.

Figure 4.15 Use Comp Proxies Only offers you the best of both worlds with proxies. Source footage can employ low-resolution stand-ins that do not appear in the final render, while source compositions use fully rendered stand-ins that can save gobs of rendering time thereafter. Some users prefer to use the Current Settings option and manage proxy use in the Project panel.

GridIron renders

New with After Effects Professional 6.5 was X-Factor, a plug-in developed by GridIron Software (www.gridironxfactor.com) that distributes the RAM previewing task over any number of peer machines (render nodes) that are available on the network.

Now, GridIron has added a plug-in to help users of a single multiprocessor/multicore system: Nucleo. Nucleo is designed to take over your previewing and rendering process and optimize it to make the most of what your system can do. It is relatively simple to install and try out, and you can enable or disable it via a menu in After Effects.

Network Renders

A single system, even one with multiple processor cores, can only do so much to render an After Effects project. If your studio is large enough that it includes a server network, it makes sense to look into network rendering, in which all available machines are used to render a shot—simultaneously.

There are two basic network rendering options. The built-in solution is File > Watch Folder, which looks in a given folder for projects ready to be rendered. This works reasonably well on small, intimate networks, but it has to be set up manually on each machine that will run it (by opening the application and setting it to watch a specific folder). This rapidly becomes impractical in a facility with a *render farm*, a rack (or room full) of servers dedicated only to rendering.

In such a case, it is easily worth the extra expense and effort to invest in a third-party rendering solution that takes advantage of After Effects' command-line rendering capabilities (aerender), such as Rush Render Queue (http://seriss.com/rush/). These programs run scripts that manage the process of rendering on multiple machines (**Figure 4.16**), and can manage many complicated rendering permutations, such as dependent or time-delayed renders, as well as managing error messages and machines that crash (as will inevitably occur with 150 machines on the job).

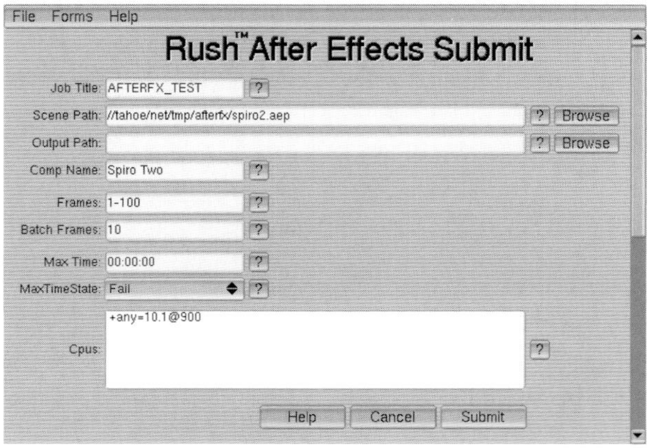

Figure 4.16 Rush Render Queue may not have a pretty front-end, but it's pretty sophisticated; This Submit panel allows you to specify which boxes will pick up the render, at what priority, how many to use, and how much time to give each of them to render before timing out. At big studios, this is indispensable.

Unfortunately this software is not plug-and-play, nor is it even implemented via a standard installer; required instead are the implementation skills of a system administrator or equivalent technical expert. Most larger facilities have such a person on staff, and many advanced After Effects users are themselves capable of setting this up in smaller studios.

If you want to use Watch Folder, and aren't certain how to do it, the online documentation provided by Adobe is complete and helpful. The help topic "Rendering" on the "Network: Using a Watch Folder" page includes everything you need to know, so there's no reason to reiterate it here.

Finally, you can simply run aerender from the command line on either platform; this is what Rush and all of the other render management applications are doing behind the scenes.

Multiple Copies of After Effects

A simpler way to hot-rod your machine so that you can render and keep working simultaneously is to run multiple copies of After Effects on a single system. This will almost certainly reduce system performance and can even cause the application to be less stable, but many After Effects consider this one of their most used tricks.

On a Mac, all you need to do is locate Adobe After Effects 7.0.app in the Finder (most likely in Applications/Adobe After Effects 7.0) and duplicate it (**Cmd+D**). You now have two versions of the application that will open separately, and you are free to render a project in one version while continuing to work in the other. One downside is that it can be hard to tell the two of them apart (unless you hack the icon of one of them), although the duplicate application will retain whatever name you give it (Adobe After Effects 7.0 copy.app by default).

On Windows, you can open a second version of After Effects from the command line, assuming you have some basic DOS navigation skills. From the Start menu, choose Run, type cmd, and click OK. In the DOS shell that opens, navigate to the location of AfterFX.exe and then enter AfterFX.exe −m (that's "m" as in "multiple"). Voila, a

You can run After Effects from the Terminal in OS X and the same −m flag operates in Unix. It's just simpler for most Mac users to work directly in the Finder.

second version initializes. If you know how to write a DOS batch script, you can create a .bat file that does all of this for you with a double-click.

Note that this is not an officially sanctioned activity, and that it's a good idea not to work on the same project that is rendering so that you don't trip yourself up inadvertently saving over your own work in the wrong application. Note also that you are not limited to running just two copies at a time, but for most systems, this is a sensible limit.

To prevent the two copies of After Effects from competing with one another, you can even lower the priority of the background copy of the application so that full interactivity is maintained as you continue to work in the forward copy. This is easily done on a Windows system: Open the Task Manager (**Ctrl+Alt+Del**), click on the Processes tab, locate the background application, and right-click to decrease the Set Priority setting. On the Mac, this involves use of the nice command in Terminal (man nice to learn more); the trick is getting the path to After Effects entered correctly, which, like DOS, is beyond scope for this book.

Optimizing After Effects

In the last edition of this book I rather bracingly inserted a list of optimal Preferences settings near the beginning of Chapter 1. This time around, many of these are embedded in context throughout other chapters, but as we have arrived at the end of Section I of the book it is time to mention a few optimizations that haven't come up yet. Not only preferences, but also settings for memory management and what do to if After Effects crashes.

Setting Preferences and Project Settings

The preference defaults have changed in version 7.0 and you may be happy with most of them. Here, however, are a few you might want to adjust that haven't been mentioned yet:

▶ **Preferences > Genera > Levels of Undo:** The default is now 32, which may be geared toward a system with less RAM than yours. I set mine to 47 so that I always know I was the one to set it; something around there usually gives me enough undos. Setting it to the maximum value of 99 won't bring the application to a grinding halt, but it may shorten the amount of time available in RAM Previews.

▶ **Preferences General:** You may also want to check Allow Scripts to Write Files and Access Network to use some of the scripts included with this book. Use System Color Picker may be preferable on a Mac, but not so in Windows XP.

▶ **Preferences > Display:** Go ahead, set Disable Thumbnails in Project Panel. If you never look at the thumbnails at the top of the Project panel, you might as well disable the feature. Otherwise, be prepared for situations in which you wait for it to update. If you're working on film-resolution files over a network, for example, you can expect delays while you wait for those updating thumbnail images.

▶ **Preferences > User Interface Colors:** You may wish to darken the UI using the User Interface Brightness slider. In the same dialog, consider turning on Cycle Mask Colors so that multiple masks applied to a layer automatically have different colors.

▶ **The Secret Preferences:** Hold down Shift while opening the Preferences dialog and you'll see an extra "Secret" category of Preferences at the bottom of the drop-down list. These relate to memory management, covered in the next section.

Memory Management

One area of major improvement in After Effects 7.0 is that the application can handle more physical memory (RAM) than previous versions.

In OS X, After Effects can now see and use more than 2 GB of RAM. Theoretically the amount of space available is 4 GB, but because the system reserves some of that space, it is more like 3.5 GB. Your machine may have more total memory than this, but most applications on a Mac are still limited to 32-bit 4 GB address spaces.

TIP

To restore Preferences to their defaults, hold down **Alt+Ctrl+Shift/ Option+Cmd+Shift** immediately after launching After Effects, and click OK on the prompt. Hold down **Alt/Option** while clicking OK, and you're asked if you want to delete your shortcuts file as well (otherwise, they remain).

On the Mac: Forcing a Crash

One benefit of After Effects has historically been that it is among the most stable applications in its category, and when it does crash, it attempts to do so gracefully, offering the option to save before it exits. The new auto-save options, if used properly further diminish the likelihood that you are ever likely in danger of losing project data.

For OS X users, there is an extra feature that may come in handy if the application becomes unresponsive but does not actually crash.

Open Terminal, and enter `ps -x` (then press Return) to list all processes. Scan the resulting list for After Effects and note its PID (Process ID) value.

Now enter `kill -SEGV ###` where "###" is replaced by the After Effects PID value. This causes the application to crash with a save opportunity.

On Windows XP, the maximum amount of memory supported for a single application is 4 GB (again, using 32-bit 4 GB address spaces). According to Microsoft, however, "The virtual address space of processes and applications is still limited to 2 GB unless the /3GB switch is used in the Boot.ini file." Editing this file is out of scope for this book, so check out www.microsoft.com/whdc/system/platform/server/PAE/PAEmem.mspx for specific information.

On either platform, extra memory (beyond what the application can use) will come in handy when running more than one version of the application, when using Nucleo (which simulates running multiple versions of After Effects), or, obviously, when running other applications simultaneously.

Some users have found in certain situations that renders that fail due to out-of-memory errors will succeed if the image cache is emptied more aggressively than usual. If you want to try this, hold down the Shift key when opening any category of Preferences, and the Secret category is revealed in the pull-down menu. You can check Disable Layer Cache and specify the number of frames after which the cache will be purged (1 being the most aggressive setting). You can also check Ignore Sequence Rendering Errors, which will continue rendering even if out-of-memory errors occur. Under normal circumstances, neither should be necessary; this option exists only for desperation situations in which renders fail due to memory errors.

Onward to Effects

You've reached the end of Section I (assuming you're reading this book linearly, that is) and should now have a firm grasp on getting the most out of the After Effects workflow. Now it's time to focus more specifically on the art of visual effects. Section II, "Effects Compositing Essentials," will teach you the techniques, and Section III, "Creative Explorations," will show you how they work in specific effects situations.

Avanti.

SECTION II

Effects Compositing Essentials

Chapter 5   Color Correction   163

Chapter 6   Color Keying   209

Chapter 7   Rotoscoping and Paint   247

Chapter 8   Effective Motion Tracking   275

Chapter 9   Virtual Cinematography   311

Chapter 10   Expressions   349

Chapter 11   Film, HDRI, and 32 Bit Compositing   381

Color Correction

I cannot pretend to be impartial about the colors.
I rejoice with the brilliant ones, and am genuinely
sorry for the poor browns.

— Winston Churchill

Color Correction

What is the pinnacle, the *sunnum bonum,* or (don't speak Latin?) the ultimate achievement for a compositor? Pulling the perfect matte? Creating a convincing effect seemingly from nothing? Leaving the last doughnut at dailies for the effects supervisor? Those are all significant, but none is as essential as the ability to authoritatively and conclusively take control of color, such that foreground and background elements seem to inhabit the same world, shots from a sequence are consistent with one another, and the overall look matches the artistic direction of the project.

Without color correction skills, you will not have earned the privilege of the compositor to be the last one to touch the shot before it goes into the edit. No matter how good your source elements are, they'll never appear to have been shot all at once by a real camera.

With this skill, however, you can begin to perform magic, injecting life, clarity, and drama into standard (or even substandard) 3D output, adequately (or even poorly) shot footage, and flat, monochromatic stills, drawing the audience's attention exactly where the director wants it to go, and seamlessly matching the other shots in the sequence.

Is this some sort of pure art, requiring that you have a "good eye" or some other capability no one can teach you? Of course not. It's a skill that you can practice and refine even if you have no feel for adjusting images—indeed, even if you consider yourself color blind.

And what is the latest, greatest toolset for this lofty job? For the most part, it is a trio of tools that have been part of After Effects and Photoshop practically since day one: Levels, Curves, and Hue/Saturation. You will use other tools in the Color Correction category in other situations, but for basic effects composites these no frills tools endure, and with good reason: They are stable and fast, and they will get the job done every time—once you fully understand how to use them.

If you remain skeptical, you may be asking:

▶ Why are we still using the same old tools, found in Photoshop since even before After Effects existed, when there seem to be so many cool newer ones such as Color Finesse and Auto Color?

▶ If I'm adjusting brightness and contrast, shouldn't I use the Brightness & Contrast effect, or Shadow and Highlight if it's the shadows and highlights I want to adjust?

▶ What do you mean I can adjust Levels even if I'm color blind?

This chapter holds the answers. You will begin by looking at how to effectively adjust a standalone source clip, focusing on optimizing brightness and contrast on individual color channels, as well as the more mysterious gamma. You'll then move into matching a foreground layer to the optimized background, and take your adjustment skills into all three color channels to balance color as needed.

This chapter is only the beginning of a discussion of color and light in this book. If you're curious about how color works in 32 bits per channel (bpc) mode; take a look at Chapter 11, "Film, HDR, and 32 Bit Compositing." More specialized color adjustments are in Section III, beginning with Chapter 12, "Working with Light."

Optimizing Plate Levels

Anyone reading this book has no doubt tried to make a good image look better or, at the very least, tried to make a poorly shot image look acceptable. Even if you've already moved beyond using that time-honored method of flailing around with the controls until arbitrarily arriving at a more-or-less acceptable result, this section may help you nail things down faster and more effectively.

We're going to start by balancing brightness and contrast of the *plate* footage. The term "plate" stretches back to the earliest days of optical compositing (and indeed, of photography itself) and refers to the source footage, typically the background onto which foreground elements will be composited. A related term, "*clean plate*," refers to the background with any moving foreground elements removed; its usage is covered later in the book.

Matching footage would seem to be absolute—either it's right or it's wrong—but optimizing footage is relative. What constitutes an "optimized" clip? What makes a color corrected image correct? Let's look at what is typically "wrong" with source footage levels and the usual methods for correcting them, laying the groundwork for color matching.

Levels

It's a wry joke in the effects world that you can create any shot using only two effects: Levels and Fast Blur. This sentiment is very punk rock, and like most such joking generalizations, while grossly exaggerated, it does contain a grain of truth: Those tools are used again and again in all sorts of permutations. Even if Levels is already your most used tool in After Effects, you may not be using it to full effect (pun fully intended).

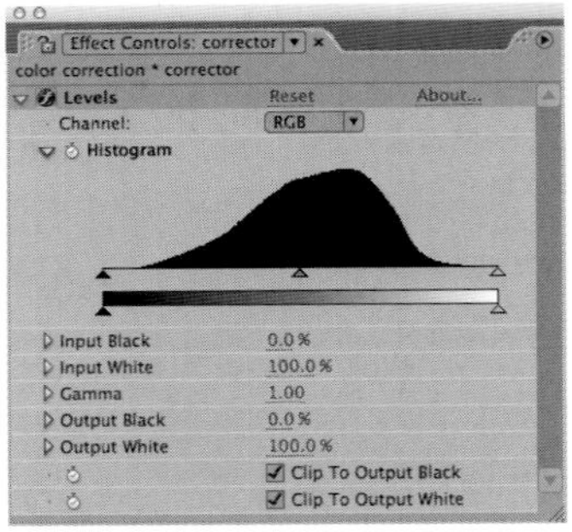

Levels consists of five basic controls, each of which can be adjusted in one of five channel contexts (you can apply them to the four individual image channels R,G,B, and A, as well as to all three color channels, RGB, at once). There are two different ways to adjust these controls: via their numerical sliders or by dragging their respective carat sliders on the histogram. The latter is the more typical method for experienced users.

Contrast: Input and Output Levels

Leaving aside gamma for the moment, let's examine what four of the five controls—Input Black, Input White, Output Black and Output White—actually do to the image when adjusted (**Figure 5.1**). Together they control the brightness and contrast, and as you'll see they can do

New in After Effects 7.0 are two check boxes at the bottom of the Levels effect controls; these specify whether black and white levels should be clipped on output. These are checked on by default, and until you reach Chapter 11 and start working in 32-bpc mode, you might as well ignore their very existence; they were added to allow Levels to work with levels that extend beyond the range that your monitor can display.

Figure 5.1 Possibly the most used "effect" in After Effects, Levels consists of a histogram and five basic controls per channel; the controls are typically adjusted using the triangles on the histogram, although the corresponding numerical/slider controls appear below. New in version 7.0 are the Clip to Output Black and Clip to Output White toggles, explained further in Chapter 11.

so with more precision than is possible with Brightness & Contrast.

When doing your own experiments to see what an effect does—a very useful habit for cases in which you're uncertain—it is helpful to have an image that will clearly show what is going on. In scientific experiments, this is known as a *control*; it prevents factors other than those being studied from affecting the outcome. In the case of color correction, the Ramp effect provides an effective control: a gradient that transitions evenly from black to white.

Figures 5.2a and **b** show a Ramp effect applied to a solid using the default settings, followed by the Levels effect. For the moment, leave the appearance of the histogram itself (odd in the case of a ramp, which is an even distribution of luminance values) alone and focus on what happens to the histogram as you adjust the settings.

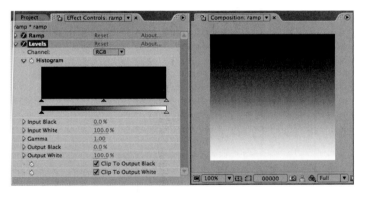

Figures 5.2a and b Levels is applied to a layer containing a Ramp effect at the default settings, which creates a smooth gradient from black to white (a); this will be the basis for understanding what the basic color correction tools do. You can create this for yourself or open 05_colorCorrection.aep, which also contains the image (b).

Begin by moving the black carat at the lower left of the histogram—the Input Black level—to the right. Pure blackness rolls across the gradient as values that were lighter than black are pushed toward pure black; the further up you move the carat, the more black values are "crushed" to pure black, below this specified threshold.

Now move the Input White carat at the right end of the histogram to the left, toward the Input Black carat. Watch the numbers beside the Input White value below, you should see them change as you adjust. The effect of bringing down the Input White value is just as with Input Black, except the effect is the opposite; more and more white values are "blown out" to pure white (**Figure 5.3**).

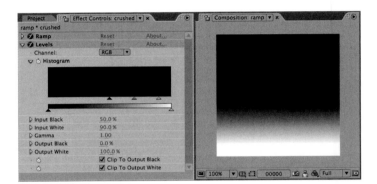

Figure 5.3 Raising Input Black and lowering Input White has the effect of increasing contrast at either end of the scale; at an extreme adjustment like this, many pixels are pushed to pure white or black (in an 8-bpc or 16-bpc project).

The net effect on your image of either adjustment is to increase the contrast. However, notice that (depending on what Input Black and Input White values you choose) you also change the midpoint of the gradient; in Figure 5.3 Input Black has been adjusted more heavily than Input White, causing the horizon of the gradient to move toward the white end as more of the image has been crushed to black. You can re-create a similar gradient using Brightness & Contrast (**Figure 5.4**) but not with the Contrast control alone, and not relative to a histogram, and not combined with a gamma adjustment (and the importance of the last two is yet to be explored).

Now reset Levels (click Reset at the top of the Levels effect controls) and try the same experiment with the Output Black and Output White controls, which are found along

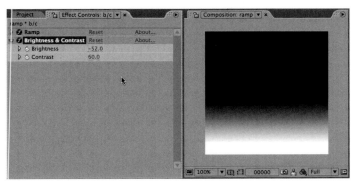

Figure 5.4 It's pushing the outer limits of the meager Brightness & Contrast just to match the look of Figure 5.3, due to the lack of a histogram; with a real image, or one that requires a gamma adjustment as well, this approach becomes less possible.

Figures 5.5a, b, and c The source (a) was balanced for the sky, leaving foreground detail too dark to make out. Raising Brightness to bring detail out of the shadows makes the entire image washed out (b); raising Contrast to compensate completely blows out the sky (c). Madness.

the short gradient below the histogram. Output Black specifies the darkest black that can appear in the image; at the default of 0.00, black can be pure black, but at higher levels, any pixel below that level is raised to a new, lighter minimum value.

Similarly, the effect of lowering Input White is something like dimming the image, cutting off the maximum possible white value at a level you specify. If you adjust both Output levels, you are effectively reducing the contrast in your image; push them close to one another and you will see your gradient become a solid gray (**Figure 5.6**).

Evidently the Input and Output controls have the opposite effect on their respective black and white values, when examined in this straightforward fashion. What happens if you use them together?

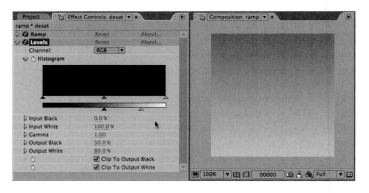

Figure 5.6 Raising Output Black and lowering Output White reduces contrast in the dark and light areas of the image, respectively; they will come into play in the Matching section.

Reset, and try raising both Input Black and Output Black levels. As is the case throughout After Effects, the controls are operating in the order listed in the interface. In other words, the Input Black level first crushes the blacks, and then the Output Black level raises all of those pure black levels as one (**Figure 5.7**). It does not restore the black detail in the original pixels; the blacks remain crushed, they all just become lighter. If you're thinking, "So what?" at this point, just stay with this—an understanding of the controls is being broken down before it is built up.

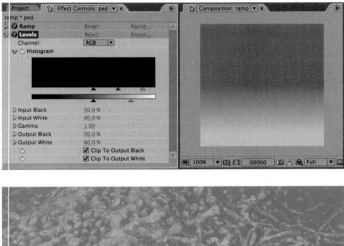

Figure 5.7 At the risk of seeming dry and pedantic, because the image is now looking worse and worse, I just want to point out that none of the black and white levels that were crushed by adjusting the Input controls are brought back by the Output controls, which instead simply limit the overall dynamic range of the image, raising the darkest possible black level and lowering the brightest possible white.

Geek Alert: What Is Gamma, Anyway?

It would be so nice simply to say, "gamma is the midpoint of your color range" and leave it at that. The more accurate the discussion of gamma becomes, the more obscure and mathematical it gets. There are plenty of artists out there who understand gamma intuitively and are able to work with it without knowing the math behind it or the way the eye sees color midtones. That's fine, but if you'd like to broaden your understanding, read on.

The point of gamma adjustment is to take the midpoint of color values and shift it without affecting the black or white points. This is done by taking a pixel value and raising it to the power of the gamma value, then inverting the value. The formula looks like this

$$newPixel = pixel^{(1/gamma)}$$

You're probably used to thinking of pixel values as being 0 to 255, but this formula works only if they are *normalized* to 1. In other words, all 255 values occur between 0 and 1, so 0 is 0, 255 is 1, and 128 is .5—which is the "normal" way the math is done behind the scenes.

Why does it work this way? Because of the magic of logarithms: Any number to the power of 0 is 0, any number to the power of 1 is itself, and raising a fractional value (less than 1) to a higher and higher power makes it closer and closer to 0. This value is then inverted, or subtracted from 1, so that the higher the gamma, the closer the value gets to 1 or pure white. The real "magic" of logarithms is that the values are described on a curve, hence a *gamma curve*.

Hmmm, was that simple? If not, look ahead to the Curves discussion for a visual example of gamma in action.

Brightness: Gamma

You've probably noticed that as you adjust the Input Black and White values, the third carat that sits between them maintains its place between them, at the same proportion. This carat controls gamma, which corresponds to the midtones—the middle gray point—of the image, all of the way out to black and white, which themselves remain unaffected. Try adjusting it over the gradient and notice that you can push the grays in the image brighter (to the left) or darker (to the right) with it, without changing the black and white levels.

Many images have perfect contrast levels yet need that extra bit of punch that boosting gamma slightly provides. Similarly, an image that looks a bit too hot may be instantly adjusted simply by lowering gamma. For now, this is a helpful way to think of gamma; as you progress through the book, you will see that it plays a crucial role not only in color adjustment but also in the inner workings of the image pipeline itself (more on that in Chapter 11).

In most cases, the histogram won't offer much of a clue as to whether the gamma needs adjusting or by how much. (For more on histograms, see the section "Problem Solving with Histograms.") The image itself provides a better guide for how to adjust gamma, which is why it's more useful to think of it in terms of real images (**Figure 5.8**).

So what is your guideline for how much you should adjust gamma, if at all? In my first professional color correction job, my supervisor told me that he had to see it go too far before he knew how much to dial it back. That's a good approach, especially when you are learning. For a more powerful approach to adjusting gamma, it's worth looking at a related tool that scares most novice artists away: Curves.

By mixing these five controls together, can we learn everything there is to know about using Levels? No—because there are not, in fact, five basic controls in Levels (Input and Output White and Black plus Gamma), but instead, five times five (RGB, Red, Green Blue, and Alpha).

Figure 5.8 It was tempting to set this up as a game of "match the histogram with the image," so surprising (and revealing) can a histogram reading be to artists who haven't worked with them. Here are two sets of seemingly similar images with distinct histogram readings.

Figure 5.9 Even if you've never worked with print files, you may be familiar with CMYK color, which is the system generally used by digital print professionals. Ignoring the "K" (which controls black for printing purposes), the letters "CMY" line up in the same order as "RGB," and they are the corresponding opposites on the digital color wheel.

Individual Channels

Now it's time to lay some initial groundwork in the area of color correction that separates the artists from the hacks: the habit of adjusting footage on individual color channels.

The vast majority of After Effects users completely ignore that pull-down menu at the top of the Levels control that isolates red, green, blue, and alpha adjustments, and even those who do use it once in a while may do so with trepidation; how can you predictably understand what will happen when you adjust the five basic Levels controls on an individual channel? The gradient again serves as an effective learning tool to ponder what exactly is going on.

Reset the Levels effect applied to the Ramp gradient once more. Pick Red, Green, or Blue in the Channel pull-down of Levels and try adjusting each of the four Input and Output carats. Color is introduced into what was a purely grayscale image. With the Red channel selected, by moving Red Output Black inward, you tint the darker areas of the image red. If you adjust Input White inward, the midtones and highlights turn pink (light red). If, instead, you adjust Input Black or Output White inward, the tinting goes in the opposite direction—toward cyan, in the corresponding shadows and highlights. As you probably know, on the digital wheel of color, cyan is the opposite of red, just as magenta is the opposite of green and yellow is the opposite of blue (**Figure 5.9**).

Okay, this is straightforward enough on a gradient, but how are you supposed to remember what the effect will be in a real image? The only way to make sense of this is to develop the habit of studying your image in its individual color channels as you work. This will become evident in the next section of this chapter as the key to effective color matching.

Along the bottom of the Composition panel, all of the icons are monochrome by default save one: the Show Channel pull-down. It contains five selections: the three color channels as well as two alpha modes. Each one has

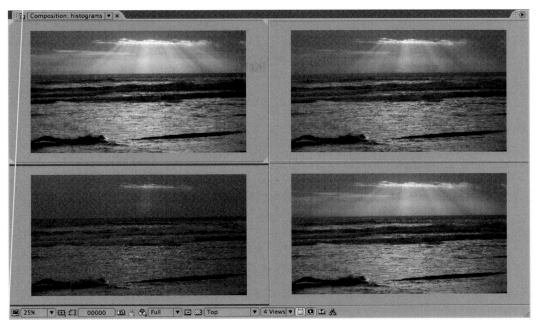

Figure 5.10 Here's an interesting use of the 4 Views layout (which is generally considered only for 3D channels): the red, green, blue, and RGB channels can be displayed simultaneously, with the stripes at the top and bottom of each viewer showing which channel is which. If you're wondering why this is useful, read on.

a shortcut that, unfortunately, is not shown in the menu: **Alt+1** through **Alt+4** (**Option+1** through **Option+4**) reveal each color channel in order. These shortcuts are toggles, so selecting the shortcut for the active channel sends you back to RGB. A colored outline around the edge of the composition palette reminds you which channel is displayed (**Figure 5.10**).

Try the same experiment, adjusting a single channel in Levels, but this time display only that channel as you work with it. Suddenly you are back on familiar territory, adjusting brightness and contrast of a grayscale image. This is how you will work with this effect until you are very confident with individual channel adjustments. Now take a look at what happens when you start to work with actual images instead of gradients, using the histogram to show you what is happening in your image.

TIP

An often overlooked feature of Levels, Alpha Channel mode allows direct adjustment of brightness, contrast, and gamma of the grayscale transparency channel. More on this in Chapter 6, "Color Keying."

TIP

You can reset any individual effect control by context-clicking it and choosing Reset. You know it's individual if it has its own stopwatch.

The Levels Histogram

You probably couldn't help but notice the odd appearance of the histogram in the preceding examples in which Levels was applied to a default Ramp. If you were to try this setup on your own, depending on the size of the layer to which you applied Ramp, you might see a histogram that is flat along the top with spikes protruding at regular intervals (**Figures 5.11a** and **b**).

The histogram is exactly 256 pixels wide; it is a bar graph with 256 single pixel bars, each corresponding to one of the 256 possible levels of luminance in an 8-bpc image (these levels are displayed below the histogram, above the Output controls). In the case of a pure gradient, such as Ramp generates, the histogram is flat because luminance is evenly distributed from black to white; the spikes occur because the image is not exactly 255 pixels high (or some exact multiple of 256, minus one edge pixel because the Ramp controls default to the edges of the layer), causing certain luminance values to occur one extra time.

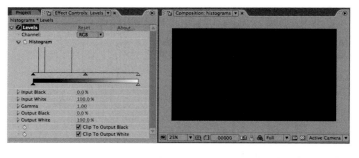

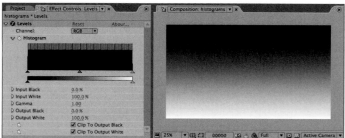

Figures 5.11a and b Strange-looking histograms such as these can actually help elucidate how the histogram works. The histogram of a colored solid (a) shows three spikes, one each for the red, green, and blue values, and nothing else. With a Ramp (b) the distribution is even, but the spikes at the top are the result of the ramp not being an exact multiple of 255 pixels, causing certain pixels to recur more often than others.

Don't worry too much about that explanation if it doesn't instantly make sense. It's much more useful to look at real-world examples, because the histogram is useful for mapping image data that isn't plainly evident. Its basic function is to help you assess whether the changes you are making are liable to help or harm the image. There is in fact no one typical or ideal histogram—they can vary as much as the images themselves, as seen back in Figure 5.8.

Despite that fact, there's a simple rule of thumb for optimizing contrast using Levels. Find the top and bottom end of the RGB histogram—the highest and lowest points where there is any data whatsoever—and bracket them with the triangle controls for Input Black and Input White. To "bracket" them means to adjust these controls inward so each sits just outside its corresponding end of the histogram (**Figure 5.12**). The result stretches values closer to the top or bottom of the dynamic range, as you can easily see by applying a second Levels effect and studying its histogram (**Figure 5.13**).

The histogram displayed when RGB is selected in Channel is a composite average of the red, green, and blue channels. It becomes no more accurate at higher bit depths, but always averages to 8 bits per channel.

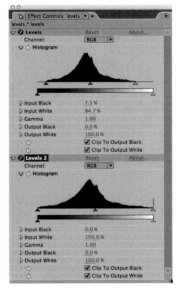

Figure 5.13 Adding a second Levels effect to this image's histogram only reveals the result of the prior adjustment; levels now extend to each end of the contrast spectrum. The stripes are the result of quantization, showing that values have been stretched. Although not severe in this case, they are a by-product of working in 8-bit color; 16 bpc will not produce them.

Figure 5.12 Here is a perfect case for bringing the triangle controls corresponding to Input Black and Input White in to bracket the edges of the histogram, increasing contrast without losing detail.

Bracketing the Input levels in this manner offers a similar result of the Auto Levels effect. If that by itself isn't enough to convince you to avoid use Auto Levels, or the "Auto" correctors, consider also that they are processor intensive (in other words, slow) and resample on every frame (so the result is not consistent from frame to frame). If you're curious about them, apply one, take a snapshot of the result, and see if you can match what you like about it using the techniques in this chapter.

Footage is by its very nature dynamic, so it is a good idea to leave headroom for the whites and foot room for the blacks until you start working in 32 bits per channel. Headroom is particularly important if something exceptionally bright—such as a sun glint, flare, or fire—enters frame.

Many current displays, and in particular LCD flat-panels and projectors, lack the black detail that can be produced on a good CRT monitor or captured on film. The next time you see a projected film, notice how much detail you can see in the shadows and compare.

Try applying Levels to any image or footage from the disc and see for yourself how this works. First crush the blacks (by moving Input Black well above the lowest black level in the histogram) and then blow out the whites (moving Input White below the highest white value). Subsequent adjustments will not bring back that detail—at least not until you start learning to work in 32 bpc mode (Chapter 11), which can store color data that has been pushed out of the visible range. Occasionally a stylized look will call for such a high-contrast result, but generally speaking and until you really know what you're doing, this is bad form (**Figure 5.14**).

Black and white are not at all equivalent, in terms of how your eye sees them. Blown-out whites are not pretty and are usually a sign of overexposed digital footage, but your eye is much more sensitive to subtle gradations of low black levels. These low, rich blacks account for much of what makes film look filmic, and they can contain a surprising amount of detail, none of which, unfortunately, would be apparent on the printed page.

The occasions on which you would optimize your footage by adjusting Output Black and Output White controls are rare, as this lowers the dynamic range and the overall contrast of the image (**Figure 5.15**). However, the effects applications of lowering contrast are many, once you begin to use levels to create high-contrast mattes, to soften overlay effects (say, fog and clouds), and so on. More on that in the latter part of this chapter.

Problem Solving with the Histogram

As you've no doubt noticed, the Levels histogram shows only incoming image data, not the results of Levels adjustments. After Effects lacks a panel equivalent to Photoshop's Histogram palette, but you can, of course, apply a second Levels effect just to see how the histogram changed from adjustments in the first instance of Levels, at least for the purposes of learning (as was done in Figure 5.13).

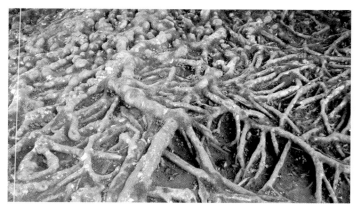

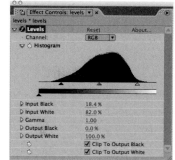

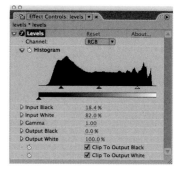

Figure 5.14 Here's how the histogram really helps: The same Levels adjustment can bring a rich dramatic quality to one clip, while totally ruining another. Note in the second histogram how much more of the image is affected by this adjustment, including most of the lower range and all of the highlight variation.

Figure 5.15 There are plenty of compositing situations in which you might want to make footage look like this—say, if it were meant to appear as if it were outside a window—but this is not how you would *optimize* this image.

Applied to the backlit shot from Figure 5.5, now adjusted with Levels to bring out foreground highlights, the resulting histogram reveals a couple of new wrinkles (**Figures 5.16a** and **b**). At the top end of the histogram the levels increase right up to the top white, ending in a spike. This may indicate that the white data has been crushed slightly, forcing too many whites to pure white and destroying image detail.

At the other end of the scale is the result of a Gamma adjustment: a series of spikes rising out of the lower values like protruding hash marks, even though the project is in 16 bpc mode which should prevent quantization. Raising Gamma moves the midpoint closer to black to raise midrange brightness. This in turn stretches the levels below the midpoint, causing them to clump up at regular intervals. As with crushing blacks and blowing out highlights—the net effect is a loss of detail.

In this case, the spikes are not a worry because they occur among a healthy amount of surrounding data—a curve of data across the range. In more extreme cases, in which there is no data in between the spikes whatsoever, you will see the result of too much level adjusting in the form of *banding* (**Figure 5.17**).

Banding is the result of limits associated with working in 8-bit color, and After Effects offers a ready-made solution: 16-bit color mode, which you can access by Alt-clicking

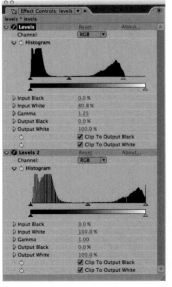

Figures 5.16a and b In the first instance of Levels (a), Gamma is raised and the Input White brought in to enhance detail in the dark areas of the foreground (b). The second instance is applied only to show its histogram.

Figure 5.17 Push an adjustment far enough and you may see quantization, otherwise known as banding in the image. Those big gaps in the histogram are expressed visible bands on a gradient. Switching to 16 bpc from 8 bpc is an instant fix for this problem in most cases.

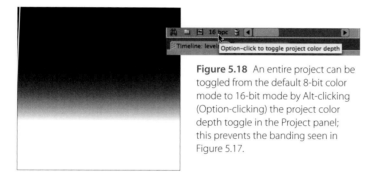

Figure 5.18 An entire project can be toggled from the default 8-bit color mode to 16-bit mode by Alt-clicking (Option-clicking) the project color depth toggle in the Project panel; this prevents the banding seen in Figure 5.17.

(Option-clicking) on the bit-depth identifier along the bottom of the Project panel (**Figure 5.18**). 16-bpc mode was added to After Effects for this very situation; to understand more about what 16-bit color is and how it differs from After Effects 7.0's new 32-bpc mode, see Chapter 11.

Perfecting Brightness with Curves

Curves rocks. I heart curves. Curves is particularly preferable for gamma correction, because

▶ Curves can be used to gently roll off adjustments, giving a gentler, more organic curve to the corrections they introduce, weighted more toward one or the other end of the curve.

- You can use Curves to introduce more than one gamma adjustment to a single image or to restrict the gamma adjustment to just one part of the image's dynamic range.

- You can often nail an image adjustment with a single well-placed point in Curves, whereas deriving the equivalent adjustment using Levels would require coordinated adjustment of three separate controls.

It's also worth understanding Curves controls because they are a common shorthand for color adjustments in visual effects work; this control recurs not only in all of the other effects compositing packages but also in more sophisticated tools within After Effects, such as Color Finesse (discussed briefly later in this chapter).

Curves does, however, have drawbacks, compared with Levels:

- It's not initially intuitive how to use Curves, and on any creative team there may be people who aren't as comfortable with Curves as with Levels.

- Unlike Photoshop, After Effects doesn't offer a value you can derive from the points you create. It's a purely visual control requiring your eyes rather than numerical data to adjust correctly.

- Without a histogram, you may miss obvious clues as to contrast adjustments (for which Levels will remain more suitable as you are learning).

The most daunting thing about Curves is its interface, which is simply a grid with a diagonal line extending from lower left to upper right. There is a Channel selector at the top, set by default to RGB as in Levels, and there are some optional extra controls on the right to help you draw, save, and retrieve custom curves. To the novice, the graph is an unintuitive abstraction that you can easily use to make a complete mess of your image. Once you understand it, however, you can see it as an elegantly simple description of how image adjustment works.

Figure 5.19a diagrams the Curves controls, showing that the gradient along the bottom corresponds to input, and

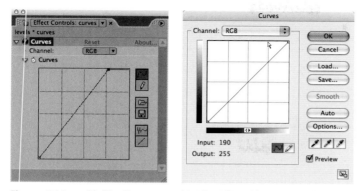

Figures 5.19a and b The Curves control in After Effects (a) isn't as helpful as Photoshop CS2's (b) in showing what is going on. The gradient along the left side of Photoshop Curves shows the output range, and the gradient along the bottom shows input; if you position the cursor on the arbitrary map, it even shows the input and output values that correspond to that position. The adjustment in 5.19a is exactly like raising Input White in Levels.

the gradient at the left output. Notice what happens to a given value when, for example, the overall brightness is raised by moving the point at the upper right to the left; all values raise proportionally, the exact equivalent of adjusting Input White in Levels.

Figures 5.20a through **f** show some basic Curves adjustments and their effect on images, as well as on a linear gradient, and the equivalent Levels settings. This is the best way I could conceive to show what is happening with Curves, and it's the kind of thing you can try easily on your own, using the Ramp effect to create a gradient if you want a neutral palette on which to see the result of the changes. I would even go so far as to say that performing these kinds of scientific explorations into how these tools work is one of the things that will separate you from the mass of artists who work more haphazardly.

More interesting than these basic adjustments (which are included only to give you a clear idea of what Curves is doing) are the types of adjustments that only Curves allows you to do—or at least do easily. I came to realize that most of the adjustments I make with Curves fall into a few distinct types that I use over and over, and so those are summarized here.

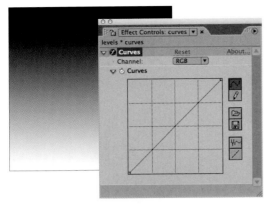

Figure 5.20a The default gradient and Curves setting

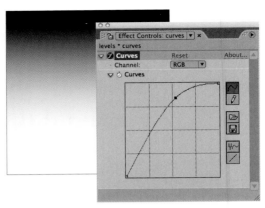

Figure 5.20b An increase in gamma

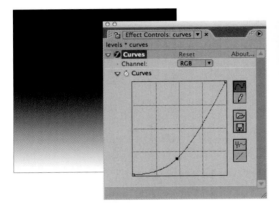

Figure 5.20c A decrease in gamma

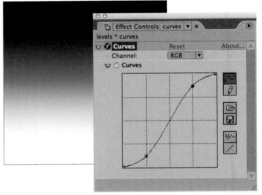

Figure 5.20d An increase in brightness and contrast

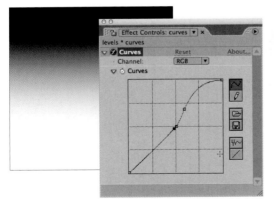

Figure 5.20e Raised gamma in the highlights only

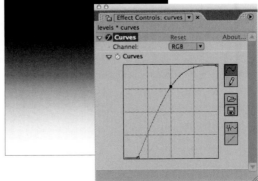

Figure 5.20f Raised gamma with clamped black values

Figures 5.20a through f This array of Curves adjustments applied to a gradient shows the results of some typical settings.

The most common adjustment is to simply raise or lower the gamma with Curves, by adding a point at the middle of the RGB curve and then moving it upward or downward. **Figure 5.21** shows the result of each. This produces a subtly different result from raising or lowering the Gamma control in Levels because of how you control the roll-off (**Figure 5.22**).

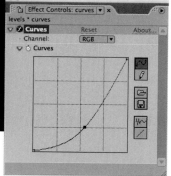

Figure 5.21 Two equally valid gamma adjustments employ a single point adjustment in the Curves control. Dramatically lit footage particularly benefits from the roll-off possible in the highlights and shadows.

Figure 5.22 Both the gradient and the histogram show that you can push the gamma much harder, still preserving the full range of contrast, with Curves than with Levels, where you face a choice between losing highlights and shadows somewhat or crushing them.

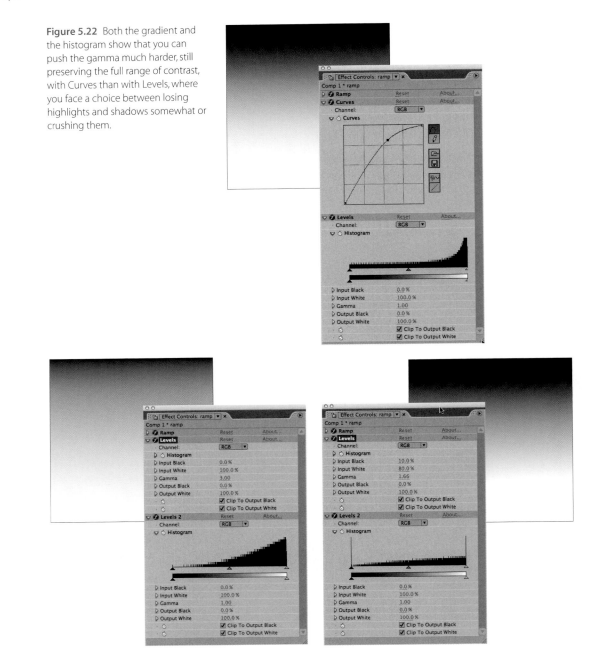

Take this idea further, and you can weight the adjustment to the high or low values of the image, pushing a nice roll-off into an image that might have appeared rather low in contrast (**Figure 5.23**). Combine high and low adjustments and you have a classic S-curve adjustment, which is universally understood to enhance brightness and contrast, but which additionally has the benefit of introducing roll-offs into the highlights and shadows (**Figure 5.24**). Keep in mind that you want to aim the curve to travel directly through the midpoint of your Curves grid if you don't wish to affect gamma.

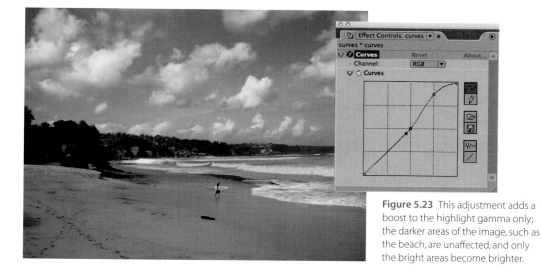

Figure 5.23 This adjustment adds a boost to the highlight gamma only; the darker areas of the image, such as the beach, are unaffected, and only the bright areas become brighter.

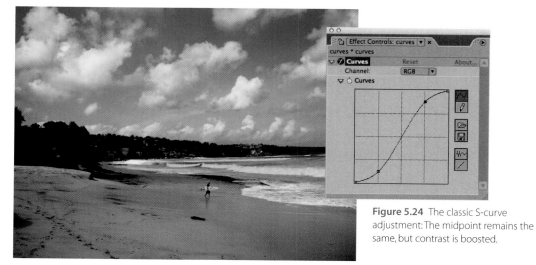

Figure 5.24 The classic S-curve adjustment: The midpoint remains the same, but contrast is boosted.

187

Some images need a gamma adjustment only to one end of the range—for example, a boost to the darker pixels, below the midpoint, that doesn't alter the black point and doesn't brighten the white values. Here you are required to add three points (**Figure 5.25**):

▶ One to hold the midpoint

▶ One to boost the low values

▶ One to flatten the curve above the midpoint

Figure 5.25 The ultimate solution to the backlighting problem presented back in Figure 5.5: Adding a mini-boost to the darker levels while leaving the lighter levels flat preserves the detail in the sky and brings out detail in the foreground that was previously missing.

A typical method for working in Curves is to begin with a single point adjustment to adjust gamma or contrast, then modulating it with one or two added points. More points quickly become unmanageable, as each adjustment changes the weighting of the surrounding points. Typically, I will add a single point, then a second one to restrict its range, and a third as needed to bring the shape of one section back where I want it. The images used for the figures in this section are included as single stills for your own experimentation; open 05_colorCorrection.aep to find them.

Just for Color: Hue/Saturation

Third in the troika of essential color correction tools is Hue/Saturation. This one has many individualized uses:

▶ Colorizing images that were created as grayscale or monochrome

▶ Shifting the overall hue of an image

▶ De-emphasizing, or knocking out completely, an individual color channel

▶ Desaturating an image or adding saturation (the tool's most common use)

All of these uses will come into play in Chapters 12 through 14, when you start to create monochrome elements, such as smoke, from scratch.

The Hue/Saturation control allows you to do something you can't do with Levels or Curves, which is to directly control the hue, saturation, and brightness of an image. The HSB color model is merely a different way of looking at the same color data as exists in the RGB model used by Levels and Curves. All good color pickers, including the Apple and Adobe pickers, handle RGB and HSB as two different modes that use three values to describe any given color, which is the correct way to conceptualize it.

In other words, you could arrive at the same color adjustments using Levels and Curves, but Hue/Saturation gives you direct access to a couple of key color attributes that are otherwise difficult to get at. For example, desaturating an image is essentially bringing the red, green, and blue values closer together, reducing the relative intensity of the strongest of them. With a complex image, this approach would be difficult and unnecessary when a single slider will do it.

Desaturating an image slightly—lowering the Saturation value somewhere between 5 and 20—can be an effective way to make an image adjustment come together quickly (**Figure 5.26**). This is a case where understanding your delivery medium is essential, as film is more tolerant and friendly to saturated images than television.

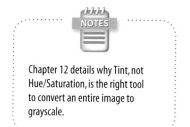

Chapter 12 details why Tint, not Hue/Saturation, is the right tool to convert an entire image to grayscale.

The other quick fix that Hue/Saturation affords you is a shift to the hue of the overall image or of one or more of its individual channels. The Channel Control menu for Hue/Saturation includes not only the red, green, and blue channels but also their chromatic opposites of cyan, magenta, and yellow. When you're working in RGB color, these secondary colors are in direct opposition, so that, for example, lowering blue gamma effectively raises the yellow gamma, and vice versa.

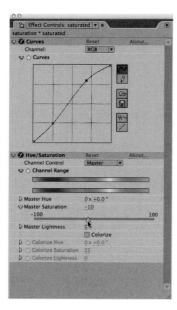

Figure 5.26 For footage that is already saturated with color, even a subtle boost to the gamma can cause saturation to go over the top. There's no easy way to control this with RGB controls, such as Levels and Curves, but moving over to the HSB model allows you to single out Saturation and dial it back.

But in the HSB model all six are singled out individually, which means that if a given channel is too bright or over-saturated, you can dial back its Brightness & Saturation levels, or you can shift its Hue toward the part of the spectrum where you want it (**Figures 5.27** and **5.28**), without unduly affecting the other primary and secondary colors.

More Color Tools and Techniques

This section has laid the foundation for color correction in After Effects using its most fundamental tools. The truth is that there are lots of ways to adjust the color levels of an image. Some alternatives for achieving a specific look—layering in a color solid, creating selections from an image using the image itself along with blending modes, and more—are discussed in Section III of this book.

Even with these basic tools, there are more usage alternatives. For example, you can apply these basic color correctors using an adjustment layer rather than directly to your footage. This gives you the added advantage of being able to dial back the correction by varying the opacity of the adjustment layer.

Will After Effects ever have a more sophisticated color correction system, and does the lack of one mean your output will be inferior? The answers are, it already sort of does, and in most cases, no, although more sophisticated

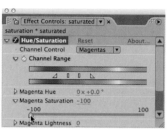

Figures 5.27a, b, and c Sometimes one color channel comes in much too strong (a), and you can get away with isolating that channel—in this case, magenta—and knocking its Saturation back heavily (b). Go too far, however, and you may not notice artifacts such as areas that have lost too much saturation (c).

Figure 5.28 When in doubt about the amount of color in a given channel, try boosting its Saturation to 100%, blowing it out—this makes the presence of that tone in pixels very easy to spot.

tools might offer particular shortcuts to a given look. Color Finesse is a sophisticated color correction system included with After Effects Professional; unfortunately, it runs as a separate application, and does not allow you to see your corrections in the context of a composite (**Figure 5.29**), making it more suitable for overall color adjustments. Furthermore, it is made up mostly of tools that resemble the ones described in the preceding section, so you'll still want to master them. And although I love the way it allows easy isolation and adjustment of specific secondary color ranges, I rarely use it for compositing (other ways of isolating color for adjustment are revealed throughout Section II of the book).

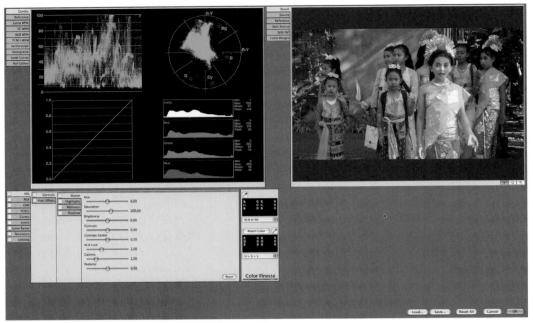

Figure 5.29 Do the controls in Color Finesse seem familiar? Although snazzier looking, they combine the fundamental tools covered in depth thus far in the chapter: Levels, Curves, and Hue/Saturation.

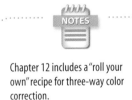

Chapter 12 includes a "roll your own" recipe for three-way color correction.

Meanwhile, owners of the Adobe Production Suite (Windows only) may have noticed that Adobe Premiere Pro includes a Three-Way Color Corrector, and for the sake of support across the suite, this is a hidden effect inside of After Effects (again, Windows only) that appears only when it has been applied in a Premiere Pro project that is then imported into After Effects. Unfortunately, the effect is less useful in After Effects because its graphical user interface (consisting of color wheels) is missing; hopefully, this tool will make its way fully into a future version of After Effects, but for now, trying to use it is probably not worth the trouble for those few users who even have it.

Color Matching

You've examined the color correction tools in depth; now it's time to move on to the bread and butter of compositing: matching foreground and background elements so that the scene appears to have been taken with the same basic light conditions.

Melding images together and eliminating all clues that they came from separate sources is as much science as art. Up to this point we've focused on optimizing source footage, which is a more subjective and artistic practice. Once the background has been properly graded, however, matching the foreground using the same tools is typically more objective (except in cases where essential clues are missing—more on that in a bit). The process obeys such strict rules that you can do it without an experienced eye for color. Assuming the background (or whatever source element you're matching) has already been color-graded, you even can satisfactorily complete a shot on a monitor that is nowhere near correctly calibrated.

How is that possible?

As with so many things in visual effects work, the answer is really a question of correctly breaking down the problem. In this case, the job of matching one image to another obeys rules that can be observed channel by channel, independent of the final, full-color result.

Of course, effective compositing is not simply a question of making colors match; in many cases that is only the first step. You must also obey rules you will understand from having done the kind of careful observing of nature described in the previous chapter. And even if your colors are correctly matched, if you haven't interpreted your edges properly (Chapter 3) or pulled a good matte (Chapter 6), or if such essential elements as lighting (Chapter 12), the camera view (Chapter 9), or motion (Chapter 8) are mismatched, your composite will not succeed.

These same basic techniques will work for other situations in which your job is to match footage precisely—for example, color correcting a sequence to match a hero shot, a process also sometimes known as *color timing*.

The Fundamental Technique

Integrating a foreground element into the color space of a background scene breaks down into three steps:

1. Match contrast without regard to color, using Levels. When matching the black and white points, pay attention to atmospheric conditions.

2. Study individual color channels and use Levels to match the contrast of each channel (as needed—not all images contain so fundamental a color imbalance).

3. Match the color of the midtones (gamma), channel by channel, using Levels or, preferably, Curves. This is sometimes known as "matching grays" and is easily done if there is an object in the background scene that you know is colorless gray (or something close).

4. Evaluate the result for other problems that may be interfering with the illusion that the elements belong in the same world—lighting direction, the role of atmospheric conditions, perspective, grain or other ambient movement, and so on (all of which are dealt with in subsequent chapters of this book).

The overall approach, although not complicated or even particularly sexy, can take you to places your naked eye doesn't readily understand when looking at color. Yet, when you see the results, you realize that nature beats logic every time.

The sad truth is that even an experienced artist can be completely fooled by the context of the image. **Figures 5.30a, b,** and **c** show an example in which seeing is most definitely *not* believing. Therefore you should not feel that the techniques described here are a crutch—instead, they are a necessary scientific advantage. The results of your color adjustments will be challenged by other members of your production team—it's pretty cool to be able to show them that you got it right.

Ordinary lighting

We begin with a simple example: inserting a 3D element lit with ordinary white lights into a daylight scene. As you can see in **Figure 5.31**, the two elements are close enough in color range that a lazy or hurried compositor might be tempted to leave it as is.

With only a few minutes of effort, you can make the plane look as though it belongs there. Make sure the Info palette is somewhere that you can see it, and for now, choose Percent (0–100) in that palette's wing menu to have your

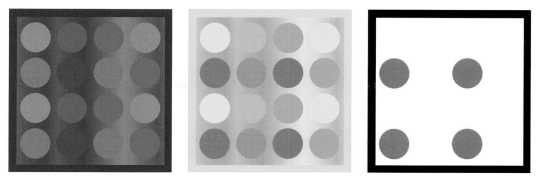

Figures 5.30a, b, and c There are no yellow dots in 5.30a, and no blue dots in 5.30b; the four dots shown in 5.30c are identical to their counterparts in the other two images.

Figure 5.31 An unadjusted foreground layer (the plane) over a daylit background.

values line up with the ones discussed here. You are free to choose any of the color modes in this menu; I advocate this one only for the purpose of standardizing the discussion.

This particular scene is a good beginner-level example of the technique because it is full of elements that would be monochromatic under white light; next we'll move on to scenes that aren't so straightforward. The background is dominated by concrete, which is generally flat, colorless gray, and the foreground element is an aircraft with a silver body that is lit from the top with white light with dark shadows underneath.

Begin by looking for suitable black and white points to use as references in the background and foreground. In this case, the shadow areas under the archways in the background, and underneath the wing of the foreground plane, are just what's needed for black points—they are not the very darkest elements in the scene, but they contain a similar mixture of reflected light and shadow cast onto similar surfaces, and you can expect them to fairly nearly match. For highlights, you happily have the top of the bus shelter to use for a background white point, and the top silver areas of the plane's tail in the foreground are lit brightly enough to contain pure white pixels at this point.

Figure 5.32 shows the targeted shadow and highlight regions and their corresponding readings in the Info palette. The shadow levels in the foreground are lower (darker) than those in the background, while the background shadows have slightly more red in them, giving the background a warmth that the unadjusted foreground lacks. The top of the plane and the top of the bus shelter

Figure 5.32 The target highlight and shadow areas for the foreground and background are outlined in yellow; levels corresponding to each highlight (in Percent values, as set in the panel menu) are displayed in the adjacent Info palette.

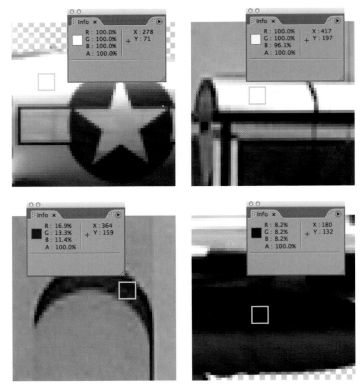

both contain levels at 100%, or pure white; the blue readings on the bus shelter, which are a few percentage points lower, give it a more yellow appearance.

To correct for these mismatches, apply Levels to the foreground and move the Output Black slider up to about 7.5%. This raises the level of the blackest black in the image, lowering the contrast, something we didn't expect to do when optimizing images earlier in the chapter.

Having aligned the contrast levels, it's time to correct for the differences in color. Remember the red levels in the background shadows are higher than blue or green, which is a clue that you should now switch the Composition panel to the red channel (click on the red marker at the bottom of the panel or use the **Alt+1/Option+1** shortcut). A thin red line around the outside of the display reminds you that you are looking only at red levels, and you can zoom in to an area that shows both of the regions you're comparing (**Figure 5.33**).

Figure 5.33 Evaluate and match black and white levels; start with RGB and then work on each color channel individually. In this case the image is "green matched:" The RGB adjustment is all that is needed for the green channel (often the best channel to match using RGB instead of its individual channel).

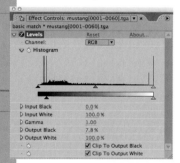

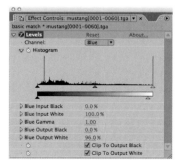

Now you can see clearly that the black levels in the red channel are still too low in the foreground, so raise them to match. Switch the Channel pop-up in Levels to Red, and raise Red Output Black slightly to about 3.5%. You can move your cursor from foreground to background and look at the Info palette to check whether you have it right, but the great thing about this method is that your eye usually gets variations in luminance correct when looking at a grayscale image.

Now for the whites. Because the background highlights have slightly less blue in them, switch to the blue channel (clicking the blue marker at the bottom of the Composition panel or use **Alt+3/Option+3**). Pull back slightly to where you can see the top of the bus shelter and the back of the plane. Switching Levels to the blue channel, lower the Blue Output White setting a few percentage points to match the lower blue reading in the background. Back in RGB mode (**Alt+3/Option+3** toggles back from blue to RGB), the highlights on the plane take on a more sunlit, yellow quality. It's subtle, but it seems right.

What about the midtones? In this case, they're taking care of themselves because both the foreground and background are reasonably well balanced and your corrections are mild.

Figure 5.34 displays the result, with the same regions targeted previously, but with the levels corrected. To add an extra bit of realism, I also turned on motion blur, without yet bothering to precisely match it (something you will learn more about in Chapter 8, "Effective Motion Tracking"). You see that the plane is now more acceptably part of the scene. Work on this composite isn't done either; besides matching the blur, you could add some sun glints on the plane as it passes, similar to those on the taxi. On the other hand, you can tell that you don't need to bother adding a pilot to the cockpit; the blur on the plane is too much to even notice that the pilot is missing.

TIP

The human eye is more sensitive to green than red and blue. Often, when you look at a shot channel by channel, you will see the strongest brightness and contrast in the green channel. For that reason, a sensible approach to matching color may be to get the overall match in the ballpark so that the green channels match perfectly, and then adjust the other two channels to make green work. That way, you run less risk of misadjusting the overall brightness and contrast of your footage.

Figure 5.34 This is a better match, particularly in the shadow areas; motion blur helps sell the color adjustment as well.

Dramatic Lighting

Watch contemporary feature films objectively for color and you'll notice that ordinary daylit scenes such as the plane example are relatively rare. Films (not to mention television and theater) use color and light to create the mood of the story (and to signify key characters and plot points). Novice viewers don't always take note of this, because in many cases your eye adapts to even extreme lighting choices if they complement the mood of the story (which is what they are designed to do).

Therefore a scene dominated by a single color, such as **Figure 5.35**, is much more commonly found in dramatic films than it is in your everyday family snapshots. One of the main reasons films take so long to shoot is that the cinematographer and lighting director require the time and resources to get the lighting the way it needs to be to create an image that is both beautiful and serves the story.

The foreground element added in **Figure 5.36** clearly does not belong in this scene; it does not even contain the scene's dominant color, and it has been lit with ordinary white light. That's fine; it will better demonstrate the effectiveness of this technique (although further adjustments, such as adjusting focus and adding a shadow, will be necessary at minimum to sell the shot).

Figure 5.35 This is the unembel-
lished source lighting of this shot.
(Image courtesy Shuets Udono via
Creative Commons license).

Figure 5.36 Not only is it clear that the can does not belong in the color
environment of the background, the mismatch is equally apparent on each color
channel.

Notice that both the foreground and the background elements have some areas that you would assume to be flat gray. The bridge has concrete footings for the steel girders along the edges of the road, while the can has areas of bare exposed aluminum.

To play along with this game, open the project 05_colormatching2.aep and apply Levels to the foreground layer in the "before" composition ("after" is the final comp to which you can refer as needed once you've tried this on your own).

Switch both your Compostion view (**Alt+1/Option+1**) and the Channel pull-down in Levels to Red. I'm warning you now that the most challenging thing about this technique will be remembering to keep both settings on the same color channel, which is why using a four-up setup as shown in Figure 5.36 is probably worth the trouble.

Now, let's pretend that the red channel is a black-and-white photograph in which you're using the red channel of the Levels effect to match the foreground to the background. Clearly, the foreground element is far too bright for the scene. Specifically, the darkest silver areas of the can are way brighter than the brightest areas of the concrete in the background. Therefore, adjust the gamma down (to the right) until it feels more like they inhabit the same world; in my example, I've adjusted Red Gamma way down to 0.67. Now cut down the red highlights a little; bring Red Output White down to about 92.5% or whatever looks right to you. The end result should look like a black-and-white photo whose elements match (**Figure 5.37a**).

Now move the Levels Channel and Composition view (**Alt+2/Option+2**) over to green. Green is the dominant color here, and its black contrast and brightness are much higher in the background. Therefore, raise Green Input Black to about 12.5% (for the contrast) and Green Gamma to something like 1.3 (**Figure 5.37b**). Better than copying my levels, try to find these on your own.

Finally, switch Levels and the Composition viewer (**Alt+3/Option+3**) to the Blue channel. Whoa; there is almost no

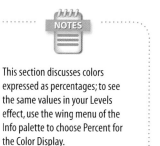

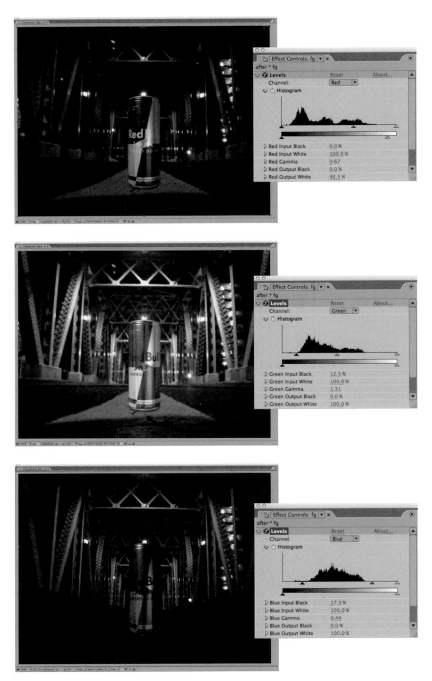

Figures 5.37a, b, and c It's actually fun to pull off an extreme match like this channel-by-channel. The Levels settings used were not really derived from the histogram, but by a mixture of looking for equivalent black/white/midpoints in the image, as well as just analyzing whether the result looks like a convincing black and white image on each channel.

match here. The can is way brighter and more washed out than the background. Again the Input Blue Level must come up, to about 17.5%, but this time gamma has to come way down, ending up at about 0.45%. Now the can looks believably like it belongs there (**Figure 5.37c**).

What's strange about this is that you've made all of these changes without ever looking at the result in full color. So now, go ahead and do that. Astoundingly, that can is now in range of looking like it belongs in that scene; defocus it slightly with a little fast blur and add a shadow and you start to believe it. Make any final contrast adjustments on the Levels RGB Channel, and you have an impressive result that required no guesswork whatsoever (**Figure 5.38**).

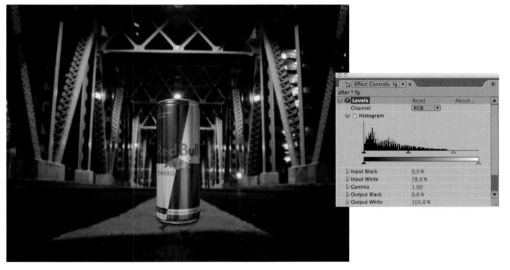

Figure 5.38 The result includes a subtle shadow that has also been color matched as well as a final adjustment to the white contrast.

When There's No Clear Reference

These examples have contained fairly clear black, white, and gray values in the foreground and background elements. Life, of course, is not always so simple.

Figure 5.39 is a scene that lacks any obvious gray values to match; the lighting is so strong, it's hard to tell what color anything in the scene was originally, or whether there were any neutral black, white or gray items in the scene.

Figure 5.39 What the heck is going on here? Again, the source image is as it was shot. Examine some of your favorite films and you may find scenes lit this dramatically; the eye quickly becomes accustomed to strong shifts of color, but the color can also be used to strike a subconscious chord. (Image courtesy Jorge L. Peschiera via Creative Commons license.)

NOTES

All kinds of studies show how taking a break once in a while helps your concentration and lets you stay healthy by stretching your body, but in this case there is a more specific use for turning away from your monitor for a minute or two. When you come back, even to a labored shot, you regain an immediate impression that can save you a lot of noodling. The process outlined in this section is designed to remove many variables to color correction, but it's still a question of whether the final shot looks right or not.

The technique still works in this case, but it may require more in the way of trial and error, or artist's intuition. Looking at each individual color channel, only green is even close to a plausible match right off the bat; the red channel contains blown-out whites, and the blue channel is so dark (and grainy) it hardly exists.

Once again, just try to get the brightness and contrast adjusted, working channel by channel, and you get an initial result something like **Figure 5.40**. Considering how subjective the adjustments have to be, this isn't half bad; and fine adjustments to the RGB channel can bring it where it needs to go.

The ability to match color without seeing an image in full color is so powerful that it can seem almost magical the first few times you try it. Why, then, do so few artists work this way? I would have to say that laziness and ignorance are the main culprits here. Switching channels seems like a pain, and few untrained artists clearly realize that color works like this.

Therefore, I must pose a rhetorical question: Which is more of a pain, switching channels in this manner, which can yield an impressive result in a couple of minutes, or fishing around for adjustments without being able to clearly see what's going on, which could take much longer?

Figure 5.40 This one requires as much intuition as logic, but adjusting it channel by channel still yields a striking result.

Gamma Slamming

Maybe you've seen an old movie on television—the example I think of first is *Return of the Jedi* (before the digital re-release)—in which you see black rectangular garbage mattes dancing around the Emperor's head, inside the cloak, that you obviously shouldn't be seeing. *Jedi* was made prior to the digital age, and some of the optical composites worked fine on film, but when they went to video, subtleties in the black levels that weren't previously evident suddenly became glaringly obvious.

Don't let this happen to you! Now that you know how to match levels, put them to the test by *slamming the gamma* of the image. To do this, you need to make a couple of adjustment layers. I usually call one slam up and the other slam down, as in the examples. Be sure that both of these are guide layers so that they have no possibility of showing up in your final render.

To slam up, apply Curves with the gamma raised significantly (**Figure 5.41**). This exposes any areas of the image that might have been too dark to distinguish on your monitor; if the blacks still match with the gamma slammed up, you're in good shape.

Similarly, and somewhat less crucial, you can slam down by lowering the gamma and bringing the highlights more into the midrange (**Figure 5.42**). All you're doing with these slams is stretching values that may be difficult for you to distinguish into a range that is easy for you to see.

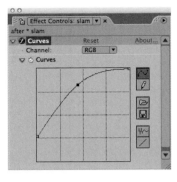

Figure 5.41 Slamming gamma is like shining a bright light on your scene. Your black and midtone levels should still match when viewed at these extremes.

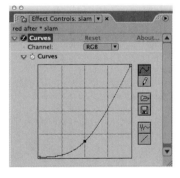

Figure 5.42 If in doubt about the highlights in your footage, you can also slam the gamma downward. Here, the slam makes it clear that the highlight reflected in the can is not as bright or bloomed as the overhead lights, and a lack of grain in the foreground becomes apparent. Grain matching is detailed in Chapter 9, "Virtual Cinematography."

This method is useful anywhere that there is a danger of subtle discrepancies of contrast; you can use it to examine a color key, as you'll learn in the next chapter, or a more extreme change of scene lighting.

Beyond the Basics

This chapter has covered some of the basics for adjusting and matching footage. Obviously there are exceptional situations, some of which occur all of the time: depth cueing, changes in lighting during the shot, backlighting, interactive light and shadow. There are even cases in which you can, to some degree, relight a shot in After Effects, introducing light direction, exchanging day for night, and so on. These topics and more are covered in depth in Chapter 12.

Color Keying

Juxtaposing a person with an environment that is boundless, collating him with a countless number of people passing by close to him and far away, relating a person to the whole world, that is the meaning of cinema.

— Andrei Tarkovsky (Russian film director)

Color Keying

Color keying is uses a big lie—pretending a solid color is negative space—to allow you to place human characters in virtually any location imaginable. Someday perhaps, when we have cameras that can perform full 3D scene reconstruction—not just what the lens lays down in a two-dimensional image, but a scan of the full spatial and temporal information of the scene—we'll laugh about the old days when we used to send actors out on to a mostly empty stage of saturated blue or green.

Not only does this artificial environment create an often challenging situation for the compositor, who must replace every trace of blue or green with subtle transparency, but in some cases it completely psyches out actors. (It's been compared to "acting in a void" or "acting in the desert" and was rumored to be a major reason Liam Neeson announced his intention to retire following *Star Wars, Episode One*, a statement of frustration he later recanted.)

Meanwhile, as they have for over half a century, blue screens (and their digital-era cousins, green screens) remain the state of the art for situations in which you want to shoot figures—usually actors—in one setting and composite them into another.

The process goes by many names: color keying, blue screening, green screening, pulling a matte, color differencing, and even chroma keying, a term that really belongs to television (think of a weather forecaster blowing storm clouds across the eastern seaboard—that is, Bill Murray in *Groundhog Day*).

NOTES

Novices often wonder if a background must be blue or green to be keyed. The answer is no. It just happens that blue and green are primary colors not dominant in human skin tones and can be differentiated clearly from most foreground colors, which contain a mixture of all three color channels.

This chapter covers not only color keying of blue- and green-screen footage but all cases in which pixel values (hue, saturation, and/or brightness) stand in for transparency, allowing compositors to effectively separate foreground from background based on color data.

All of these methods extract luminance information that is then applied to the alpha channel of a layer (or layers). The black areas become transparent, the white areas opaque, and the gray areas gradations of semiopacity, which is where the illusion usually succeeds or fails.

Good Habits and Best Practices

Before we get into detail about specific keying methods and when to use them, here is some top-level advice to remember when creating a matte:

▶ **Solo the matted foreground against a brightly colored background.** You can set the background of the composition (**Ctrl+Shift+B/Cmd+Shift+B**) to a saturated yellow, red, orange, or purple (**Figures 6.1a, b,** and **c**). If the foreground is going to be matted into a dark scene, you can employ a dark shade, but in most cases bright colors better contrast with the foreground, clearly showing any holes in the matte, or edge problems and noise in the background (**Figure 6.2**).

> **NOTES**
>
> If you're reading nonlinearly, this chapter extends logically from fundamental concepts about mattes and selections in Chapter 3, "Selections: The Key to Compositing." This chapter and the next move beyond fundamentals.

Figures 6.1a, b, and c The choice of background influences what you see. Against the default black, almost no detail is visible (a). With the checkerboard turned on, you can begin to see shadows (b). Flaws in the matte become clearest with a bright, solid, contrasting background (c). (Source footage courtesy Pixel Corps.)

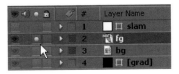

Figure 6.2 The keyed layer can be soloed at any time, revealing it against the background of your choice.

▶ **Protect edge detail at all costs.** Unless you're in a situation where your edges aren't discernable (say, because you're matting an image against itself), the game here is always to solidify opaque areas of the foreground, erase the background completely, but don't overdo either or your edge will suffer. Pushing edge pixels too far makes for crunchy, chewy mattes (**Figure 6.3**).

▶ **Keep it simple, and be willing to start over.** There is a Tao of keying: I have inherited mattes that involved hours or even days of labored work (with dozens of keyframes and hand-cut mattes) that I was able to redo in under an hour, because I knew where to begin. Until you have an expert level of experience, throwing in the towel and starting over can save you time in the long run.

▶ **Constantly zoom in and look hard at detail.** Otherwise, you're likely to get one frame looking perfect only to find that there's a problem as soon as the camera shifts or the actor moves. If possible, find a difficult frame and begin there; look for motion blur, fine detail, excessive color spill, and so on. And even on a single frame, use various methods to continually re-examine the frame: Check the Info panel, noting whether background alpha values are truly at zero, zoom in and out, and toggle alpha and color channels (**Figure 6.4**).

Figure 6.3 A coyote ugly, chewy matte is typically the result of clamping the foreground or background (or both) too far.

Figure 6.4 A glimpse of the alpha channel can reveal even more problems, such as faint holes in the foreground, which should be solid white. This is the matte from Figure 6.1.

▶ **Combine multiple passes.** This is the most important step that beginning artists skip; more about it is revealed further on. It's a common misconception to perceive keying as an automated process: Click a few buttons, check the result, and you're done. That can of course occur, but it is not the norm beyond the most straight-forward medium close-up. In many cases, a successful result includes a core matte whose foreground is 100% opaque and a second pass with refined edges.

Keep these basics in mind as you reveal the various keying options. You are also encouraged to review this list when it comes time to apply a key to your own shot, especially if you're new to keying.

Linear Keyers and Hi-Con Mattes

There are cases in which edge detail is not a factor because an element does not need to be completely isolated; perhaps you are merely creating a holdout area of an image using a *high-contrast* (*hi-con*) matte. For cases where you just need to specify one area of a clip to adjust it, a *linear key* will often do the trick.

We begin here before bringing out the big keying guns for a couple of reasons. Linear keyers are relatively simple and useful in a wide variety of cases, beyond just blue- and

TIP

Color Key and Luma Key offer no softness in the matte thresholds; they can only Edge Thin and Edge Feather, which are crude methods for choking, spreading, and blurring a *binary* matte (consisting of pixels that are only transparent or opaque). Subtleties of transparency are tacked on without reference to source data. There is no reason ever to use them—seriously.

CLOSE-UP

When, Exactly, Is Linear Keying Useful?

It's useful to key using a single channel (or the average of multiple channels) in order to

▶ Isolate a color range for the purpose of correcting it to a different color (because After Effects has no dedicated Three-Way Color Corrector).

▶ Create simple garbage mattes and holdouts (detailed later in this chapter).

▶ Matte elements shot over a pure black (or white) background. For example, fire is not typically photographed on a blue-screen stage, but outdoors at night, or in an unlit studio with black backdrops.

▶ Matte an element using its own luminance data, in order to hold out specific portions of the element for enhancement. For example, you duplicate a layer and matte its highlights to bloom them (see Chapter 12, "Working with Light").

green-screen shots. Their fundamental underlying concepts carry forward into more specialized keyers, such as Keylight, designed specifically to handle full color keying.

Linear keyers differ from dedicated matte tools in that they do not compare one channel or set of values against another (which is the key to effective blue- and green-screen keys); they are based merely on defining a range within a single set of values.

The most useful linear keyers are

▶ Extract

▶ Linear Color Key

The keyers to be avoided at all times are

▶ Luma Key

▶ Color Key

Linear Color Key and Extract

Although both are linear keying tools, Linear Color Key and Extract have different uses. Extract is most useful for *luminance (luma) keying*, using the black and white points of an image or any of its individual channels. Linear Color Key is more appropriate in cases in which you need to isolate a particular color (or color range).

Extract

Extract employs a histogram to help isolate the black and white cut-off points in the matte and then gradates the thresholds with black and white softness settings. It's not just for averaged RGB luminance, either, as it offers a pull-down menu to access histogram controls for all four color channels (red, green, blue, and alpha).

Keep in mind when luma keying, one of the three color channels often contains more initial useful contrast than overall luminance, which is merely an average of the three. Either green or red is typically the brightest and most contrasty channel, and blue is generally dimmest and often noisiest (**Figures 6.5a**, **b**, and **c**). If you work in full RGB instead of a single channel, keep in mind that the luminance values are weighted prior to image calculations that average them.

Figures 6.5a, b, and c Although the blue screen is dominant, the blue channel is comparatively dim and noisy (c), despite that the footage is uncompressed. The matte contains some green (b), and the greatest contrast is in the red channel (a). (Source footage courtesy Pixel Corps.)

Extract is interactive and easy to use; it's a cousin to Levels. It displays a histogram to show where the white or black values you're keying are; changing the Channel setting changes the histogram as well as the controls. The typical way to use it is to bring in the White Point or Black Point (the upper of the small square controls below the histogram), then threshold (soften) that adjustment with the White Softness or Black Softness controls (the lower of the small squares). It is intuitive and relatively easy to use.

Linear Color Key

Linear Color Key offers direct selection of a key color using an eyedropper tool. The default color is blue (ironic given that blue-screen keying is exactly what you don't want to do with this tool). The other odd thing about the defaults is the 10% Matching Softness setting, which is arbitrary and gives a rather loose range of matched tones. I often end up with settings closer to 1%.

Figure 6.6 This grayscale conversion (using Tint) of the channels shown in Figures 6.5a, b, and c weights the three channels according to how the eye sees them, and the eye is far less sensitive to blue than green, thus the background is far darker than it is in the blue channel.

CLOSE-UP

All Channels Are Not Created Equal

If you set an RGB image as a luma matte, the red, green, and blue channels are averaged together to determine the luminance of the overall image. However, they are not weighted evenly.

Compare **Figure 6.6** with **Figure 6.5c**, and you will note that the background of the averaged result is far less bright than the blue channel of the same image. In most internal color calculations, the three channels are weighted according to how brightly the eye perceives them: Red at 29%, Green at 59%, and Blue at 12% luminance (instead of 33.33% per channel, which would be an even distribution). This topic is explored in greater depth in Chapter 12, in the section on "Creating a Look with Color."

If you find yourself wanting to use a particular channel as a luma matte, you can employ the Shift Channels effect (**Figure 6.7**).

Figure 6.7 Here the Shift Channels effect is set to use Red for all channels. Alpha is set to Full On as a precaution against transparency data, which should not be used for a luma matte.

Note that there are, in fact, three eyedropper tools in the Linear Color Key effect. The top one replicates the Key Color eyedropper, and the other two add and subtract from the Matching Tolerance. You can click the eyedroppers directly on either of the adjacent thumbnail images, or if these are too small, you can open the Layer panel and choose the effect in its View pull-down, using the eyedropper there (**Figure 6.8**).

You can match the color using RGB, Hue, or Chroma values. In most cases, RGB will do the trick, but the best idea in unusual situations may be to sample each one before you start fine-tuning the controls. You can adjust the Tolerance, which specifies how close the colors have to be to the chosen value to be fully matted, and Softness, which then grades the threshold, softening the edges according to how close the color values are to the target range.

The default setting for the Key Operation is to Key Colors, which is straightforward enough. You might guess, therefore, that the other option, Keep Colors, would simply invert the result. In fact, Keep Colors was designed for cases in which the first instance of the effect eliminates something you want to bring back. First instance, you ask? That's right, you have the opportunity to recover foreground colors by adding a second copy of Linear Color Key targeting a second range, set to Keep Colors.

Figure 6.8 The Key Color eyedropper can be used in the Composition viewer, but the individual eyedroppers to refine the color range (in the Preview section of the effect) work in the Effect Controls panel or a Layer panel only. This tool is useful for matting a non-primary color range; in this case, the magenta sign on the bus is selected. The source clip, ext_busPassby_uncorrectedHD.mov, can be found on this book's disc (Source footage courtesy Pixel Corps.)

Difference Mattes

A *difference matte* sounds simple in principle: Frame two shots identically, the first containing the foreground subject, the other without it (commonly called a *clean plate*). Now, have the computer compare the two images and remove everything that matches identically, leaving only the foreground subject. Great idea.

Unfortunately, there are all sorts of criteria that preclude this from actually working very well, specifically

▸ Both shots must be locked off or motion stabilized to match, and even then, any offset—even of a fraction of a pixel—can preclude a clean key.

▸ The foreground element probably is not completely devoid of whatever is in the background; low luminance areas, in particular, are prone to appear as background to the Difference Matte effect.

▸ Even such subtleties as grain and slight changes of lighting can cause a mismatch to two otherwise identical shots. Raising the Blur Before Difference setting helps correct for this, but by introducing inaccuracy.

You can gauge the challenges involved yourself, using any locked-off shot with movement in it, ideally one in which a character enters the frame (such as the footage used for Figure 6.10, included on your DVD). Lock off a frame of the source shot; you can apply Time Remap and use a single keyframe with the time of the clean plate shot. Turn off visibility of that layer, and apply Difference Matte to the other layer. Viewing final output, adjust Tolerance and Softness to try to get the key you're after. If the result has noise in it, try raising the Blur Before Difference value.

Figures 6.10a, b, and **c** show the likely result of attempting to key this footage using only Difference Matte. It's not a terrible way to isolate something when clean edges are not critical, but it cannot compare with more sophisticated methods for removing a solid color background.

TIP

To set up a second instance of Linear Color Key to Keep Colors, you should turn off the first instance (set to Key Colors), so that you can set the color to keep (**Figure 6.9**). When you are done, enable both instances.

Figure 6.9 Two instances of Linear Color Key: The first is set to Key Colors, the second set to Keep Colors.

CLOSE-UP

Luma Mattes

In the interest of full disclosure, I often use track mattes (as detailed in Chapter 3) with a duplicate of the layer, instead of the luminance keys described here, applied directly to the layer. With a track matte, I can use Levels to work with color ranges on all channels, in order to refine transparency. Other artists may consider this approach more cumbersome, preferring to work with a single layer and an effect.

The hand-to-hand green-screen shots in this chapter (such as Figure 6.10) include tracking markers on the background. These are intended to provide dimensional perspective for 3D camera tracking (a.k.a. match moving), which otherwise might not be possible. More on match moving is included at the end of Chapter 8.

Figures 6.10a, b , and c This effects shot (a) includes a clean plate; (b) the alpha channel of a Difference Matte effect between them (c) demonstrates that this is not an effective way to key a foreground, but notice that other unwanted features such as the tracking markers—those little triangles on the background—are removed, making this matte useful if multiplied or otherwise combined with a regular green-screen key.

Blue-Screen and Green-Screen Keying

Back in the day, if you wanted to go beyond the rather pedestrian Color Difference Key in After Effects you needed a third-party keyer, and for a few years there were two choices: Ultimatte for After Effects (now AdvantEdge, Ultimate Corporation) and Primatte Keyer (Red Giant Software, formerly Pinnacle Systems, and before that, Puffin Designs).

Debuting with version 6.0 Professional was Keylight, a third well-known software keyer popular among Shake users. It remains part of After Effects 7.0 Professional (but as a separate installation, so make certain that you have it). The other keyers have by no means disappeared, and I personally remain a fan of Primatte, which offers a methodology very different from that of Keylight. Working on *The Adventures of Shark Boy and Lava Girl in 3D* after the previous edition of this book was released, I decided to use Keylight for all of my shots, however, and I never felt compelled to revert to Primatte. Because Keylight is what you have with After Effects Professional, let's focus on that.

Keylight is useful in many keying situations, not just studio-created blue- or green-screen shots. For example, you can use Keylight for removal of a murky blue sky (**Figure 6.11**). You wouldn't use Keylight to pull a luminance key, however, or when simply trying to isolate a certain color range within the shot.

NOTES

When I label Color Difference Key "pedestrian," I speak as someone who matted hundreds of shots with it, back before there were alternatives in After Effects. Its methodology is fundamental and can be replicated using basic channel math and Levels controls. It provides the exact methodology that was used for early digital composites (in such blockbuster films as *Terminator 2*), which itself is the digital equivalent of optical compositing (used in Hollywood classics from *The Ten Commandments* right through the original *Star Wars* trilogy).

Figure 6.11 In one pass, with no adjustments other than selecting the sky color, Keylight does an effective job of knocking out the background even around the motion-blurred bird in flight. The sky is nowhere near a perfect blue screen in this case, other than its uniformity: Blue saturation is around 50% and only about double the amount of red.

Keylight is most typically employed when the plate was shot against a uniform, saturated, primary color background, and when preserving edge detail is of utmost importance—in other words, most typically (but not exclusively) when working with footage that was specifically shot to be keyed, against a screen of blue or green.

Generalized Keying Methodology

Figure 6.12 shows a process tree that outlines the steps detailed below (also included on the book's disc as keyingFlowchart.pdf). No two complex shots are the same, but something like this approach should help you pull a good matte, regardless of the tools used. The next section reprises these steps, specifically using Keylight.

The basic steps are

1. **Garbage matte** any areas of the background that can easily be masked out. "Easily" means no articulated matte (don't animate individual mask points). It's whatever you can accomplish in about 20 minutes or less (**Figure 6.13**).

2. Attempt a **first pass** quickly, keeping this matte on the loose side (preserving as much edge detail as possible) to be refined later.

TIP

Just in case I'm not yet succeeding in beating you over the head with it, my overall message is: Break down plate footage into separate passes when keying. At the very least, a hard "core" matte to fill holes and an overlaid edge matte to recover detail will often improve radically on a single pass. Extra passes are then applied via masked layers to specific problem areas.

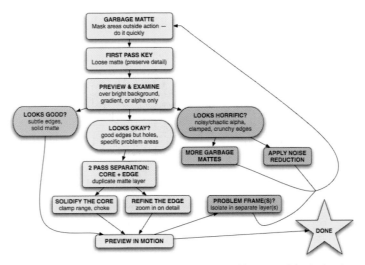

Figure 6.12 This chart summarizes steps that can yield a successful color key. It is also included as a PDF on the disc.

Figure 6.13 The quick-and-dirty garbage matte is your friend for eliminating unwanted parts of the stage.

3. **Preview** this at full resolution, in full motion, against a bright primary color. In rare cases, you will be done at this step. Switch to a view that clearly displays the alpha channel. Note any obvious holes in the foreground or areas of the background that have failed to disappear, as well as any noise in the solid areas of the matte (**Figure 6.14**).

If things look noisy and chaotic in the alpha channel or the edges are clamped and chewy, you can

- ▶ Start over and try a new pass
- ▶ Apply noise reduction to the plate, then start over (see "Noise Suppression" later in this chapter)
- ▶ Articulate or track garbage/holdout mattes to isolate problem portions of the footage (see "Fixing Typical Problems")

Figure 6.14 A quick diagnosis of Keylight's first pass at this shot: The shadows must be keyed out because they extend outside the garbage matte area (and right off the set). This in turn has an effect on fine detail such as motion blur and hair, so these areas (hands, hair) may require their own holdout mattes.

4. Decide about **separating the core and edge mattes.** Fix holes in the foreground by duplicating the matted plate layer. Solo the duplicated layer and clamp the matte to create a solid core matte with no holes. Now choke it far enough in that it does not overlap with the edges defined by the other matted plate layer.

5. **Refine the edge.** Zoom in on a challenging area of the foreground edge (200% to 400%), and refine the key to try to accommodate it, using strategies outlined in the following sections. Challenging areas may include

   ▶ Fine detail such as hair

   ▶ Motion blurred foreground elements

   ▶ Cast shadows

   You must also watch out for, and consider rotoscoping, foreground features that can threaten an effective key, such as

   ▶ Areas of the foreground that reflect the background color

   ▶ Edge areas whose color nearly matches the background

   ▶ Areas of poor contrast (typically underlit regions of the shot)

6. **Preview the shot in full motion.** Again, note holes and noise that crop up on individual frames, and now use strategies (outlined in "Fixing Typical Problems") to overcome these problems. Approaches you may employ at this stage are

   ▶ Adding holdout mattes (typically masks), either for the purpose of keying elements individually or rotoscoping them out of the shot (**Figure 6.15**)

   ▶ Holding out the matte edge only, for the purpose of refining or blurring it (see "Edge Matting")

This basic approach should work with any tool set. The real underlying point is that the attempt to key a plate in a single pass is typically too lazy. Ironically, it often results in much more work, overall, as you struggle to make all areas of your shot accommodate unified, one-size-fits-all settings.

Holdout Mattes

A *holdout matte* is an area of an image that is isolated for its own separate treatment. An effective key often involves the combination of two holdout mattes, one for the edge and another for the core.

The question then arises as to how these two mattes should be combined; with this method, it should be a simple matter either of overlapping the two layers or precomposing them so that they make a single alpha channel to be applied as a track matte.

In other compositing programs such as Shake, it's not unusual to employ a third holdout, for the background, but in After Effects this is typically avoided and is hopefully unnecessary. The difficulty is that this third matte must be subtracted, rather than added, and transparency (alpha) information is always combined additively in After Effects.

You can convert all of the alpha channels to RGB (using Shift Channels) and apply the Darken blending mode to the background holdout to subtract, but it is frankly a hassle in After Effects, useful only if no other method of holding out the background proves effective. I have seen ex-Shake users drive themselves completely batty working this way.

Figure 6.15 This is the step too many artists aren't willing to take soon enough. It may seem tedious and cumbersome to create individual holdout mattes for hair, heavy motion blur, and other such detail, but you could waste hours trying to eliminate the shadows while retaining the detail; a quick roto-matte can often be keyframed in 10 or 20 minutes on an average-length shot.

Using Keylight

The version of Keylight that ships with 7.0 is new, although the changes in version 1.1v1 of Keylight are relatively subtle.

The most significant of the Keylight parameters remains the Screen Colour selection (Keylight reveals its UK origins at Framestore CFC with that u). Choose the color to be keyed wisely, and you have a shot at a one-pass result. Otherwise, you may fight an uphill battle the rest of the way. More about how this selection works is found in "The Inner Workings of Keylight" section.

In the best-case scenario, after creating any basic garbage mattes as usual, you will

1. Use the Screen Colour eyedropper to sample a pixel that is roughly the median of the plate background. The View setting defaults to Final Result, so you can immediately examine the result of this one choice. To do so, set your background to a bright color and solo the plate layer, or examine the alpha channel (**Alt+4/Option+4**), or in Keylight, under View, choose the Status (more about that in a moment).

NOTES

You can follow along with the steps using the blueScrn_mcv_HD.mov footage included in this chapter's Pixel Corps folder on the book's disc. Completed versions of several of the examples from this chapter are contained in the 06_colorKey.aep project.

You can take a snapshot of each attempt (**Shift+F5** through **F8** to take four individual snapshots; hold down **F5** through **F8** to see each of them), but the method described holds each pass in the Undo buffer, allowing you to recover the best one.

The Eyedropper and the Info Panel

When you sample a pixel in After Effects, either using an eyedropper, such as the Screen Colour selector in Keylight, or simply by moving your cursor around the viewer and looking at the values in the Info panel, you are seeing the exact value of the exact pixel underneath the selection point of the cursor (the lower-left corner of the eyedropper, the upper-left corner of the pointer). But as with just about everything, there are exceptions.

If you hold the **Ctrl/Cmd** modifier key, the sample area increases and you get the average of the modified area. By default, this is 5 × 5 pixels, and hackers will even change it by editing the Adobe After Effects 7.0 Prefs file (searching for "Eye Dropper Sample Size With Modifier").

More significantly, in version 7.0 these sampling tools no longer necessarily give you the visible state of the pixel. As in Photoshop CS2, the *actual* state of the pixel is sampled, which means that with a semi-transparent layer, the value will be sampled as if the layer was opaque (straight transparency values).

Thus, if you sample any pixels in your matted plate, and they are not completely transparent, you get the color values the layer would have with its alpha channel turned off.

2. To try a different initial Screen Colour setting, click Reset at the top of Keylight (instead of using Undo) and try again. Repeat again as needed. Now you have multiple attempts saved in the Undo buffer. Choose the one that seems to have eliminated the most unwanted background (**Figures 6.16a**, **b**, and **c**), examining the alpha channel as needed.

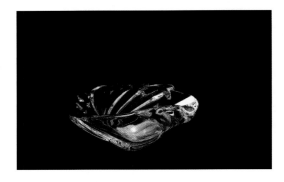

Figures 6.16a, b, and c Even when you use well-shot, high-definition source (a), it is imperative to get the Screen Colour setting right if you want to preserve all of the transparent detail in this shot. Choosing a darker background color (b) creates a more solid initial background, but a lighter color selection (c) preserves far more detail. (Source footage courtesy Pixel Corps.)

Now, as needed, seek out areas that want refining:

3. Switch View to Status. Opaque pixels become white, transparent pixels black, and those with any semi-transparency are gray (**Figure 6.17**). It's an exaggerated version of the alpha channel that shows where your matte is not solid.

4. Still in Status view, try Screen Balance at settings of 5.0, the default 50.0, and 95.0, and choose whichever one yields the best-looking matte. In this case, a Screen Balance of 95 looks good in Status view, but after switching to the Final Result it seems to generate a matte line (**Figure 6.18**).

Figure 6.17 Sampling a background pixel near the center of the image yields a good initial key, as seen in the Status matte. The black areas are already completely transparent, the white areas opaque, and the gray pixels constitute the areas of focus; they are the semi-transparent regions.

Figure 6.18 This initial result, with a Screen Balance of 95, would be fine but for the ugly black matte line that appears along the arm. Better in this case to stick with the default greenscreen setting of 50.

Figures 6.19a and b Screen Gain is raised to remove the gray in the background. It's tempting to go with a setting of around 120 to remove every last gray speck from the background (a), but a much looser setting (around 105) that leaves some speckling, particularly away from the foreground figure (b), is much preferable for maintaining edge detail. The noise in the corners can be eliminated either via a garbage matte or by raising Clip Black.

5. If the background is not solid black, boost Screen Gain until the gray mostly disappears in Status view. Try to preserve any gray that is at the edges of your foreground. If gray remains in the background, but separate from the foreground such that you can be easily garbage matted, do so (**Figures 6.19a** and **b**).

   This footage is well shot, and although the footage includes flowing hair (a challenge), it does not include the floor, which is usually much more of a challenge.

6. Now set the Despill Bias using its eyedropper (a new feature). Sample an area of the foreground that has no spill and should remain looking as is (typically a bright and saturated skin tone area). This shot does not have a lot of green spill, but notice as you try it that the color often appears richer (less contaminated) after this step.

   In this ideal scenario, your matte is complete without the need to go beyond these first four controls (Screen Colour, Screen Gain, Screen Balance, and Despill Bias), which comprise the heart of Keylight.

   However, a glance at the current alpha channel reveals a problem. The yellow stripes in the shirt are not fully part of the foreground matte (**Figure 6.20**) because yellow and green are so close to one another on the color wheel.

NOTES

Also included on the disc is a shot of this same model, wearing the same costume, but taken with a blue-screen background. Try an initial key on that plate (bluScrn_mcu_HD.mov, located on the disc's Pixel Corps folder) and you'll notice that the stripes in the shirt cause no problem—yellow and blue are virtual opposites—but other issues arise with the rim lighting in the hair.

This is the point at which you make the decision to separate out one (or even several) core mattes. Rather than ruining the nice edge detail by trying to get the yellow stripes on the same pass, you now create a separate core matte to take care of the shirt.

Keylight includes its own controls for adding holdout areas to mattes via the Inside Mask and Outside Mask controls. You draw a mask, set it to None, and then select it under Inside Mask or Outside Mask. This works for garbage mattes, but it's not a substitute for duplicating the layer to combine multiple keys.

7. Duplicate the layer with Keylight applied, so that the initial settings are now held by two layers, and solo the duplicate. You can rename the new layer Core and the original layer Edge. Select Core—don't adjust the wrong one or you'll be annoyed.

8. On the Core layer and still in Status view, twirl down the Screen Matte parameters. Adjust the Clip White value down until you start to see a matte that consists of entirely black pixels in the background, and turns the gray pixels in the shirt green. Green pixels indicate areas that contained some of the background color; these are not being color-corrected as part of the keying operation (**Figure 6.21**). For more on Keylight's spill suppression, see the "Spill Suppression" section.

9. Turn off soloing and toggle the core matte on and off in RGB and Alpha view. Yowch! The shirt is filled in, but the edges and hair are ruined. Use the Screen Grow/Shrink control to shrink the matte (using positive values) until you can toggle the core matte on and off and see no effect on the edges of the body (a value of around -3 may work); the hair troubles will have to be solved with a mask, as you can see if you try to lower this value to accommodate the hair as well (which doesn't work at all).

Figure 6.20 The yellow stripes on the shirt are not easily distinguished from the green matte.

Figure 6.21 The formerly gray pixels in the foreground are now green in Status view. These are the pixels that have been changed by clipping the matte. The spill suppression that occurred as part of the initial keying operation no longer applies to these pixels.

10. Add a holdout mask for the hair. It will need to be rotoscoped (animated over time) to accommodate the motion of the talent, but that is covered more thoroughly in Chapter 7, "Rotoscoping and Paint." For now just isolate the shirt or hair for one frame. Happily, the result is a good-looking matte (**Figure 6.22**).

Now what? The mask needs animating, and the discoloration to the shirt will have to be dealt with (see the "Color Spill" section). But without too much pain you have a mask that can be used to place this model and her long flowing hair over whatever background you choose.

Figure 6.22 In a perfect world, you could create a matte this good without the need for the holdout matte. But you and I don't live in that world, so you may as well be grateful this shot only requires one mask.

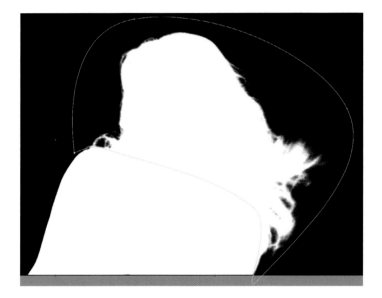

Understanding and Optimizing Keylight

If you're working on your own shot using this methodology, your composite is now either looking pretty good or has at least one obvious problem. If you think it's looking good, focus in on a few details, and note if there are any problems with the following in your full motion preview:

▶ Hair detail: Are all of the "wispies" coming through?

▶ Motion blur or, in unusual cases with a defocus, lens blur: Do blurred objects appear chunky or noisy, or do they thin out and partially disappear?

- ▶ Screen contamination areas: Do holes remain in the foreground?
- ▶ Shadows: Are they keying as desired (typically either all there or all gone)?

You are, of course, free to find niggling problems of your own and share them with your friends (**Figures 6.23a** through **d**).

Alternatively, you may discover something fundamentally wrong with your matte, including

- ▶ Ill-defined foreground/background separation or semi-transparency throughout the foreground or background
- ▶ *Crunchy, chewy,* or *sizzling* edges (these terms are common at The Orphanage; feel free to invent your own)
- ▶ Other noise in the matte

TIP

Version 7.0 allows you to switch the viewer containing your RAM Preview to the Alpha Channel view (**Alt+4/Option+4**) without blowing the cache. Not only that, but the alpha will preview at speed, in full motion.

Figures 6.23a through d Fun challenges you may encounter when pulling a color key include wispy hair (a), motion blur (b), contamination of foreground elements by the background color (c), and shadows (d).

▶ Edge fringing or an overly choked matte

▶ Errors in the spill suppression

Keylight anticipates these issues, offering specific tools and techniques to address them. Before delving into those (in the "Focusing In" section), take a look under the hood at how Keylight actually works.

The Inner Workings of Keylight

A few decisions are "key" in Keylight, and most of the other controls compensate for how effectively you made those few decisions. This section offers a glimpse into the inner workings of Keylight, which will greatly aid your intuition when pulling a matte.

The core of Keylight involves generating the *screen matte*, and as has been mentioned, the most essential step is the choice of screen color. From that, Keylight makes weighted comparisons between its saturation and hue and that of each pixel, as detailed in **Table 6.1**.

TABLE 6.1 How Keylight Makes Its Key Decisions

COMPARED TO SCREEN COLOR, PIXEL IS	KEYLIGHT WILL
Of a different hue	Consider it foreground, make it opaque
Of a similar hue and more saturated	Key it out completely, making it transparent
Of a similar hue, but less saturated	Subtract a mathematically weighted amount of the screen color and make it semitransparent

The lesson contained in Table 6.1 is that a healthy background color is of a reasonably high saturation level and of a distinct hue.

Those sound like vague criteria, not easily met—and it's true, they are somewhat vague, and often not met. That's why Keylight adds the Screen Gain, Screen Balance, and Despill and Alpha Bias controls. Screen Gain emphasizes

Screen Gain Versus Clip Black

These two controls seem to have a redundant effect; each makes the background more transparent. In many cases you can derive the same result from both. How do you know which one to use?

Screen Strength

▶ Is part of the basic screen matte calculation and adds no processing load

▶ Is not affected by edge rollback

▶ Does not trigger color replacement as the matte is made more or less transparent

Clip Black

▶ Is a post process requiring extra time and memory

▶ Is affected by edge rollback

▶ Triggers color replacement as the matte is made more or less transparent (generating the green pixels in Status view, as in Figure 6.21)

So although it is not crucial to choose one of these over the other at any given time, understanding the differences can certainly help you along.

the saturation of the background pixels, and Screen Balance delineates the background hue from the other primary colors. The Bias controls color-correct the foreground.

Screen Gain

One major enemy of a successful color key is muddy, desaturated colors in the background. A clear symptom that the background lacks sufficient intensity is when areas of the background are of a consistent hue, yet fail to key easily. Similarly, a clear symptom that your foreground is contaminated with reflected color from the background is that it appears semi-opaque. In either case, Screen Gain becomes useful.

Screen Gain boosts or reduces the saturation of each pixel before comparing it to the screen color. This effectively brings more desaturated background pixels into the keying range if raised or, if lowered, knocks back pixels in the foreground containing the background color.

Screen Balance

That takes care of saturation, but what about hue (the actual green-ness or blue-ness of the background and foreground) how pure is it? Keylight is designed to expect one of the three RGB color values to be far more prevalent than the other two in order to do its basic job. It is even more effective, however, if it knows whether one of the two remaining colors is more prevalent, and which one.

Screen Balance allows you to alert Keylight to this fact.

On this theory, you would employ a balance of 95% with blue screens and leave it at 50% for green screens, and in version 1.1v1 of Keylight, that is exactly how the plug-in sets Screen Balance depending on whether you choose a blue or green Screen Colour setting.

The more generalized recommendation from The Foundry, however, is to set it "near 0, near 100, and compare" these to the default setting of 50 to evaluate which one works best. In other words, imagine there are three settings (instead of 100) and try 5%, 50%, and 95%.

NOTES

These top five controls (from Screen Colour to Alpha Bias) differ from those below them in that they work on the color comparison process itself, rather than the resulting matte. You can adjust them without adding any processing load whatsoever, and they work together to yield the ideal matte; the rest of the controls merely correct the result.

NOTES

A Rosco Ultimatte Blue screen contains quite a bit of green—much more than red, unless someone has lit it wrong. Ultimatte Green screens, meanwhile, are nearly pure green (**Figure 6.24**).

Figure 6.24 The Rosco colors: Ultimatte Blue, Ultimatte Green, and Ultimatte Super Blue. The blue colors are not pure blue: Blue is double the amount of green, which in turn is double the amount of red. Ultimatte Green is more pure, with only a quarter the amount of red and no blue whatsoever. Lighting can change their hue (as does converting them for print in this book).

TIP

I have found, to my dismay, that keyed footage can become significantly granier as the result of adjusting Despill Bias. It is highly recommended that you compare before and after versions of foreground plate footage if you use this feature, and if the result is adding grainy noise to your footage, reset Despill Bias and try a different despill method (see "Spill Suppression").

TIP

Remember that with a scroll wheel on your mouse, you can hold down **Alt/Option** to zoom around the point where you place the cursor.

TIP

Increment and save your project after creating a good basic matte, should you wish to revert after further changes.

Bias

The Bias settings, Despill Bias and Alpha Bias, color correct the image in the process of keying, by scaling the primary color component up or down (enhancing or reducing its difference from the other two components).

As mentioned, a couple of things have changed with these settings in this new version. They are no longer tied together by default, and The Foundry recommends that in most cases you leave Alpha Bias at the default. They also both now operate via eyedroppers rather than value sliders, and it is recommended that you click the Despill Bias eyedropper on a well-lit skin tone that you wish to preserve; despill pivots around this value.

Focusing In: Clean-Up Tools

Once you are satisfied that you have as good an edge matte as possible, you are ready to zoom in on a detail area and work on solving specific problems.

If you see an area that looks like a candidate for refinement, save (so that you can revert to this as your ultimate undo point), zoom in, and create a region of interest around the area in question.

Now take a look at some common problems you might encounter and the tools built into Keylight to solve them.

Holes and Edges

The double-matte method (core and edge) shortcuts a lot of the tug of war that otherwise exists between a solid foreground and subtle edges. Even with this advantage, both mattes may require adjustments to the Clip White or Clip Black controls.

The game is to keep the largest possible difference (or *delta*, if you prefer) between these two settings. The closer the two numbers approach one another, the closer you are to a bitmap alpha channel, in which each pixel is pure black or white—a very bad thing indeed (**Figure 6.25**). The delta between the Clip values represents the area where all of your gray, semi-transparent alpha pixels live, so the goal is to offer them as much real estate as possible.

Figure 6.25 Here's how her hair would look if you hadn't separated an edge matte for the hair. This is the very definition of a "chewy" matte—you can see individual, contrasty pixels.

If you push the Clip controls too far and need a way out of that corner without starting over, raise the Clip Rollback value. This control restores detail only to the edge, and only what was there in the original matte operation (with those top five controls). Used in moderation, and with a close eye on the result, it can be effective.

Clip Rollback works as follows: Its value is the number of pixels from the edge that are rolled back. The edge pixels reference the original, unclipped screen matte. So if your edges were looking nice and soft on the first pass and removing noise from the matte hardened them, this tool can restore the subtlety.

Noise Suppression

Are your mattes sizzling? Keylight includes a Screen Preblur option that you should apply only in a zoomed-in view (to closely examine the result) and only with footage that has a clearly evident noise problem, such as source shot on miniDV. Essentially, this option blurs your source footage before keying it, so it adds inaccuracy and is something of a desperation move. The footage itself does not appear blurred, but the matte does.

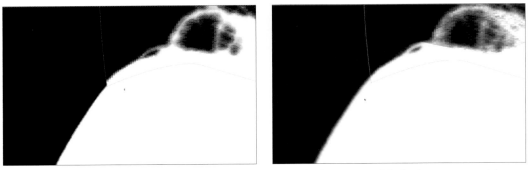

Figures 6.26a and b The softer hair matte and the harder matte around the torso don't line up, and the torso has an unrealistically hard border (a). Adding Screen Softness and a positive Shrink/Grow adjustment can fix this (b).

Chroma Sampling: The 411 on 4:1:1

Most digital video images aren't stored as RGB but Y'CrCb, the digital equivalent of YUV. Y' is the luminance or brightness signal; Cr and Cb are color-difference signals (roughly corresponding to red-cyan and blue-yellow).

The human eye is much better at noticing compression in contrast than in color, a fact compressed digital formats take advantage of by saving fewer chroma samples per line than luma samples. With a 4:2:2 format (employed by DigiBeta and DVCPro50), chroma has half the horizontal resolution of luma; one color pixel for every two brightness pixels. With 4:1:1 (the NTSC DV and PAL DVCPro ratio) the compression is even more drastic: One color pixel spans four brightness pixels.

Unfortunately, as you might imagine, this type of compression is less than ideal for color keying; hence the recommended approach here for softening the effect of color quantization particularly in common formats such as miniDV.

A better alternative for a fundamentally sound matte is Screen Softness, found under the Screen Matte controls. Screen Softness blurs the matte itself after the key has been pulled and the matte created, so it has a much better chance of retaining detail. As was shown in Chapter 3, edges in nature are always slightly soft; so used to a modest degree (considering that it is introducing error into your key), this control can enhance the realism of a matte (**Figures 6.26a** and **b**).

A more drastic approach, when softening and blurring cannot reach larger chunks in the footage, is using the Despot cleanup tools. Crank these up, and you'll definitely notice undesirable blobbiness in your matte. For this reason, I don't trust these controls and usually leave them alone.

A better approach, particularly with miniDV and HDV footage (which, by the way, are both guaranteed to add undesirable noise and are typically not recommended for blue-screen and green-screen shoots), is to

1. Convert the footage to YUV using Channel Combiner (the From pull-down). This will make your clip look very strange, because your monitor displays images as RGB. Do not be alarmed (**Figure 6.27**).

2. Apply Channel Blur to the green and blue channels only, at modest amounts (to gauge this, examine each channel as you work—press **Alt+2/Option+2** or **Alt+3/**

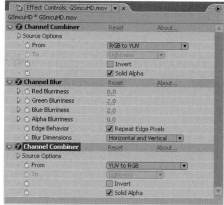

Figures 6.27 This is how an image converted to YUV should look; the monitor was not partially unplugged. Your monitor displays RGB, but those three channels can be set to YUV, just as your alphabet can create other languages. The round-trip around a Channel Blur appears in the Effect controls (but the second Channel Combiner effect is temporarily disabled, hence the strange look).

Option+3 while zoomed in on a noisy area). Make sure Repeat Edge Pixels is checked.

3. Round-trip back from YUV to RGB, using a second instance of Channel Combiner.

4. Apply Keylight, and breathe a sigh of relief.

Fringing and Choking

Sometimes, despite all best efforts, your extracted matte contains extra, unwanted edge pixels (fringing), or the keyed subject lacks subtle edge detail because the matte is choked too far.

Keylight does offer the Screen Grow/Shrink control for such situations. On the other hand, if you find yourself having to shrink or expand your matte, it may be a symptom of other problems. Faced with the need to choke or spread a matte (another way of saying shrink or grow), you might first go back and try the initial key again, possibly breaking it down further into more component parts (say, separating the hair) using holdout masks. More information on choking and spreading follows below.

NOTES

YUV is the digital version of the broadcast video color space. It is used in component PAL television and is functionally similar to YIQ, the NTSC variant. In After Effects YUV, the red channel displays the luminance value (Y) of the shot, while the green and blue channels display blue and red weighed against green (U and V).

235

Spill Suppression

Keylight suppresses *color spill* (foreground pixels contaminated by reflected color from the background) when the matte is initially pulled, as part of the keying operation. Thus spill-kill can be practically automatic if you pull a good initial key.

When is this not what you want? First of all, when it's an unwanted by-product. There are situations when parts of the foreground that you want to keep are close enough in color range to the background that their color is suppressed. **Figure 6.28** shows a scene shot with a green screen out the window in which the interior of the set is also meant to be of a greenish cast, all of which was carefully decided and lit on set.

Adjustments to the matte can also expose areas of the clip that aren't spill suppressed. These areas are indicated by the green pixels in the Status view (as in Figure 6.21); spill suppression of these pixels may now be off. In such cases, you specify a Replace Method setting; Soft Colour set to medium gray is a good choice if the only affected pixels are at the edge. It is a cheat, but it may make your key look better by gently desaturating pixels that might otherwise pop.

Figure 6.28 A green-lit set with a green screen out the window: Things like this happen all the time. Applying the matte to the plate with spill suppression limited to areas (such as the top of the monitor) that are reflecting the green screen solves this problem.

Finally, spill suppression can lead to other undesirable effects on plate footage. In **Figure 6.29**, notice how the whole shape of the girl's face seems to change due to the removal of highlights via spill suppression. Even worse, as mentioned earlier, something about the spill suppression operation in Keylight also seems to enhance the graininess of footage in many cases.

Should Keylight's spill suppression become unwieldy or otherwise useless for any of the above reasons, there is an easy out. Create a nice matte without worrying about spill, precompose the result, and apply it as an alpha matte to the foreground source. Color spill can be removed on a separate pass without adversely affecting the plate footage.

Keylight itself also includes additional spill suppression tools, under the Edge Colour Correction heading (as well as the overall Foreground Colour Correction). Beneath each is a check box to enable it, but nothing changes until you adjust Saturation, Contrast, or Brightness below the check box (or, alternatively, the Colour Suppression and Colour Balancing tools). If necessary, soften or grow the edge to increase the area of influence.

TIP

You can use Keylight for spill suppression only. Follow the same steps as you would to key the footage, but do not adjust any controls below Despill Bias. Change the View setting to Corrected Source; the footage is keyed but the alpha channel remains unaffected.

Figures 6.29 Her face doesn't even look the same without the highlights reflected with the green. Even worse, at this magnification it's easy to see that the amount of grain noise has increased significantly. This is a definite case for pulling the matte on one pass and applying spill suppression separately.

Fixing Typical Problems

As you must know by now, because I've seized every opportunity thus far to drill it into your head, the number one solution to most matte problems is to break the image being matted into multiple sections rather than trying to get one matte in one pass. You can divide the matte as follows:

▶ Core and edge matte (hard and soft matte)

▶ Holdout masks for particular areas of the frame (useful if lighting varies greatly within the frame, or if one area contains a particularly challenging element, such as hair or motion blur)

▶ Temporal split (if light conditions change as the shot progresses)

All other tricks fall short if you're not willing to take the trouble to do this. And now for some more bad news.

On Set

No matter how advanced and well paid you may be, your time is likely to be far cheaper than that of a full crew on set. That means—shocking, I know—you'll have the opportunity to fix things in post that should have been handled differently on set. You could call it job security (but that sounds so cynical); however you think of it, it's bound to be part of your job.

If you're fortunate enough to be supervising the effects shoot (I recommend it for the craft services alone), you can do all sorts of things to ensure that the footage will key successfully later on.

A hard *cyclorama*, or *cyc* (pronounced like "psych"), painted a uniform key color is far preferable to a temp cloth background. If you can't rent a stage that has one, the next best thing might be to invest in a roll of floor covering and paint it, to get the smooth transition from floor to wall, as in **Figure 6.30** (assuming the floor is in shot). Regarding the floor, don't let anyone walk across it in street shoes, which will quickly contaminate it with very visible dust.

The Right Color

The digital age lets shooters play fast and loose with what they consider a keyable background. You may be asked (or try on your own) to pull mattes from a blue sky, from a blue swimming pool, or from other monochrome backgrounds.

If you have the opportunity to create your own keyable background, however, there is one brand to look for when purchasing your paint, fabric backdrop, or adhesive tape: Rosco. Rosco's Digicomp products are of a color designed specifically to allow for the most effective keying, with a purity and intensity of saturation unavailable at your local paint store. They are available in three colors—you guessed it—blue, green, and red.

How different must the background color be from the foreground? The answer is "not very." Red is worth avoiding simply because human skin tones contain a lot of it, but a girl in a light blue dress or a soldier in a dress blue uniform often keys just fine from a blue screen (although spill suppression will require special attention).

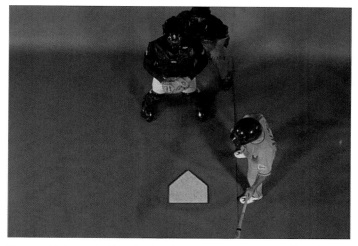

Figure 6.30 On a set with no hard cyclorama, you can create the effect of one—the curve where the wall meets the floor—using blue-screen cloth instead. It doesn't behave as well (note the hotspot on the curve), but it will certainly do in a pinch and is much preferable to removing the seam caused by the corner between the wall and floor. (Image courtesy Tim Fink Events and Media.)

Assuming you begin with a correct-colored, footprint-free background with as few seams and other variations as possible, the most important concerns are to light it correctly, balancing the foreground and background lighting.

This job is, of course, best left to a professional, and any kind of recommendations for a physical lighting setup are beyond the scope of this book. But, hey, you're going to spend more time examining this footage than anyone else, so here are a few things you can keep in mind as the on-set effects supervisor:

▶ Ideally, the light levels on the foreground and background should match. A spot light meter tells you if they do.

▶ Diffuse lights are great for the background (often a set of large 1 K, 2 K, or 5 K lights with a silk sock covering them), but fluorescent lights will do in a pinch. With fluorescents you just need more instruments to light the same space. In correspondence about the previous edition of this book, VFX Supervisor Scott Squires noted that Kino Flo lights are a popular option (**Figure 6.31**).

Figure 6.31 Diffuse white lighting that causes no hotspots in the background is ideal.

▶ It is helpful to keep a good deal of space between the foreground and background. Ten feet is ideal.

▶ Avoid dark unwanted shadows like Indiana Jones avoids snakes, but by all means light for shadows if it looks like you can get some clean ones on the floor. Note that this only works if the terrain in the final shot is as flat as the floor of the studio.

▶ If your scene is set outdoors, definitely consider shooting outside (almost certainly using portable backgrounds such as solid color cloths and carpets). You may require fill lights to avoid hard shadows on the background, but remember that daylight is a difficult—almost impossible—light quality to re-create on a stage, especially for a shot any larger than a close-up.

▶ Record on the highest-quality, least-compressed component video format you can afford. Even if the rest of your project will be shot on HDV, it might be worth shooting the effects a less compressed format and converting them later if you can.

If the setup permits, bring along a laptop with After Effects on it and with some representation of the scene into which the footage you're taking is going to be keyed. This can be enormously helpful not only to you but to the gaffer and director of photography, to give them an idea of where to focus their efforts. You will have to work with the camera operator to get a live signal (and figure out a PCI transfer setup if you're working with HD), and a film camera may require the addition of a video tap, but it is even possible to test shots on set.

Finally, once the lighting has been finalized and before action is called on the shot, ask the camera operator to shoot a few frames of clean plate—the background with no foreground characters or objects to be keyed out later. There are all sorts of ways to make use of this, and it's easy to forget; if you do, try to get it at the end of the setup, or the end of the day.

Matte Problems

It's an ugly fact of life that there will be times that you have to cheat and manipulate the matte that Keylight (or another method) produces. Make sure you're at least using the right tool for the job, with the lightest possible touch.

For whatever reason, Minimax is sometimes employed by artists who would enjoy greater success with either of the tools in the Matte category: Matte Choker or Simple Choker. Minimax is old school: It works in whole pixel increments to choke and spread pixel values. It has some interesting uses—but not for subtle matte edits. It is a quick way to spread or choke pixel data, particularly without alpha channel information.

In many cases, Simple Choker is the tool to use. It allows you to choke or spread alpha channel data (via a positive or negative number, respectively) at the sub-pixel level (use decimal values). That's all it does. It's really no different from its counterpart in Keylight, but you can use it anywhere.

Matte Choker adds tools to introduce extra softness to the choke. Its default settings are an effective starting point for many mattes. Unfortunately, softness controls tend merely to add error to the process and can be the symptom of a bad key. It's also simply not possible to push Matte Choker as far as Simple Choker. Don't be afraid to "settle" for Simple Choker: It's no monkey wrench.

Many computer graphics artists will also shoot environment reference of a set, either using a camera capable of taking ultra-wide angle photos (using a circular fisheye lens), or by aiming the camera at a reflective silver ball (known in garden shops as a gazing ball). Not only does this provide reference for the lighting setup, but it can be used to recreate HDRI lighting in 3D software.

A useful third-party alternative to Minimax is Erodilation from ObviousFX (www.obviousfx.com). It can help do heavy choking (eroding) and hole-filling (dilating) in situations where the Simple Choker, well, chokes, and its controls are simple and intuitive (choose Erode or Dilate from the Operation menu and the channel—typically Alpha).

Edge Selection

If you have the Red Giant Software Key Correct Pro plug-ins (or their predecessor, Composite Wizard), Edge Finder can create a grayscale map outlining only the edges of the alpha channel, which can be applied as a luma matte to an adjustment layer. That adjustment layer's effects—blurs, color correction, or a holdout—apply only to the edge.

If you lack these third-party filters, no worries; with a few extra steps you can make your own. The simplest method is to

▶ Apply Shift Channels. Set Take Alpha From to Full On and all three color channels to Alpha.

▶ Apply Find Edges (often mistaken for a useless psychedelic effect because, as with Photoshop, it appears in the Stylize menu). Check the Invert box (**Figure 6.32**).

Minimax can help choke or spread this edge matte. The default setting under Operation in this effect is Maximum, which spreads the white edge pixels by the amount specified in the Radius setting. Minimum chokes the edge in the same manner. If the result appears a little crude, an additional Fast Blur will soften it (**Figure 6.33**).

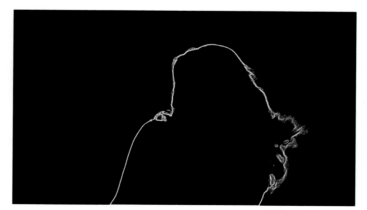

Figure 6.32 A typical use for an edge matte such as this is to blur the edge slightly using this selection, in which case you want to blur the background and foreground together via an adjustment layer. These effects settings are on your disc as edgeMatte.ffx. Beware that the bottom edge is included in the matte; don't let this bite you if your frame has no *padding* (non-visible area at the edge of frame).

Figure 6.33 Need thicker, softer edges? A quick Minimax set to the default Maximum allows you to specify a Radius by which the white area will grow. If the result looks a little chunky, a quick Fast Blur will soften it back. This is very useful, for example, when there is motion blur on the object that needs to be controlled in the edges.

▶ Apply the result via a luma matte to an adjustment layer. You should not need to precompose before doing so.

Now what? Apply Fast Blur to soften the blend area between the foreground and background, yet another way around a chewy matte. Or add a Levels adjustment to the composited edge to darken or brighten it. A de-saturation operation (using Hue/Saturation) has a similar effect to using a gray edge replacement color in Keylight.

Matte Holes

With a good key, there should be no noise or holes in the foreground; a heavily choked core matte will close them.

However, if the background on the set had fundamental problems—uneven lighting, seams, dirt on the floor—you may discover noise and holes in the matte background. A software solution to close these without affecting edges exists, but only as a third-party tool: Alpha Cleaner, which is also a part of the Key Correct set (formerly Miracle Alpha Cleaner in Composite Wizard).

Because it is an automated solution, it will occasionally fill holes that should remain unfilled, such as the little triangular gap that can open up under outstretched arms (**Figure 6.34**). Thus matte holes present a situation in which you

Figure 6.34 An automated solution, such as Alpha Cleaner (part of the Key Correct Pro pack), fills holes in the foreground matte but will also often close holes that you want to keep, such as this tiny gap under the arm. For that reason, veteran effects compositors tend to avoid these solutions, although they present a tempting alternative to rotoscoping.

may have to rotoscope. It's usually not as bad as you think to work this way; the painstaking part of keying is defining the edge. Holes can often be fixed using crude masks or by tracking in paint strokes (each covered in the next two chapters, respectively).

Matte Fringing

Visible fringing around the edge of a feathered matte is often the result of an alpha having been applied via a track matte. For example, it could occur if, in attempting to process color spill outside of Keylight, you applied the Keylight matte as a track matte.

Don't panic and choke all that detail out of your edge! There is a better solution, but it is hidden away in the Channel menu. Remove Color Matting (sometimes vainly sought as "Unmultiply") is designed specifically to suck color out of edges that are behaving as if they should be premultiplied, not straight (if the distinction eludes you, you are encouraged to review Chapter 3).

Premultiplied images are typically matted against black, leaving a dark fringe around the edges. Remove Color Matting uses black as the default Background Color, and this is the only user-adjustable parameter in this effect. You can instead use the eyedropper to sample a background color. If the fringing is bright colored, premultiplication a white or gray background may have been premultiplied.

Color Spill

Color spill need not be a big deal. If you're not happy with the spill suppression in Keylight (or another keyer), you can apply the matte as an alpha track matte to the source footage and pursue alternative options.

Sometimes the Spill Suppressor tool that is included with After Effects will do the trick. It uses a simple channel multiplication formula to pull the background color out of the foreground pixels. All you need to do is select a sample from the background color (you can even copy your original choice of screen color from Keylight, but it really only matters whether you choose blue or green) and leave the setting at 100%.

TIP

The DVD includes the Unmult plug-in from Red Giant Software. John Knoll developed this plug-in specifically for use with Knoll Light Factory, which generates flares that have no alpha channel. Unmult differs from Remove Color Matting in that it always assumes the background is black, and it adds transparency to pixels based on how much black they contain.

If even Spill Suppressor has undesirable side effects, then it may be advisable to open up Hue/Saturation and target the specific hue that is causing you problems, either desaturating or shifting it.

This may sound positively Neanderthal in its lack of subtlety, but it works a surprising amount of the time, provided you can identify the range of color that needs to be removed. Open Hue/Saturation, and select the channel in Channel Control that needs attention—say, Blues.

Look closely at Channel Range. You might not have noticed the little controls beneath the upper color spectrum (**Figure 6.35**). These allow you to set the color range as precisely as you like. The inner hash marks control the range affected by the controls below; the region between those and the outer, triangular markers is the feather area.

In most cases you'll select a channel, refine the selection, and lower Saturation, alter the Hue, or both, to reduce spill. To understand clearly which pixels are affected, crank Saturation up to 100. The pixels in the affected range are easy to spot; if not, you have chosen a range that is unused by any pixels.

Conclusion

Keylight is a powerful tool that should offer the results you're after. It's not the only option, of course. Primatte Keyer is just as powerful, with a completely different methodology (updated with 7.0). (The book's DVD-ROM includes a demo if you want to check it out.)

The next chapter offers hands-on advice for situations where keying can't help, or can't do everything, and rotoscoping is necessary.

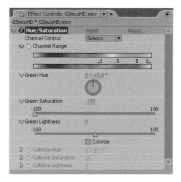

Figure 6.35 The little hash marks and triangles under the upper gradient of the Channel Range control specify a region to desaturate; the amount of desaturation is reflected in the lower gradient. It's quick and dirty but in many cases effective for knocking a particular color out of your scene.

Rotoscoping and Paint

It's a small world, but I wouldn't want to paint it.

—Steven Wright

Rotoscoping and Paint

So, you've gritted your teeth, girded your loins, and opened up the rotoscoping chapter. There's no way to paint an utterly pretty picture, so to speak, of the task you face: Rotoscoping and paint tools are generally a last resort, employed when there is no other way to fix your matte. Rotoscoping is the art (although some would be loath to call it that) of fixing a shot frame by frame, generally using masks. Cloning and filling using paint tools are variations on this task.

To compound matters, After Effects did not gain its fame as a rotoscoping tool. You *can* get good results with the program, but its interface and tools aren't set up expecting rotoscoping to be your main task, as they are in such dedicated programs as Silhouette Roto or the defunct Pinnacle Commotion.

Although sometimes you just can't get around having to clean up footage by hand in After Effects, it's often not as bad as you think if you follow a few basic guidelines:

▶ **Ascertain that rotoscoping is necessary.** Novices and pros alike bite the bullet too quickly, assuming it's time for frame-by-frame work without looking at other ways to break down the problem at hand. Specifically, make sure that these other approaches won't help at least part of your problem:

  ▶ **Keying.** See Chapter 6, "Color Keying," for more on using luma mattes (including matting footage with itself), color keys, and difference mattes.

  ▶ **Tracking.** See Chapter 8, "Effective Motion Tracking," for more on the many ways to track in selections. Paint, by the way, is fully trackable.

▶ **Keep it simple.** This is the number-one piece of advice. If you're articulating a mask, do so with as few points as possible. When keyframing that mask, use as few keyframes as possible.

▶ **Paint is a last resort.** It is very hard to re-create realism of any substantial scale via paint tools, and it will always be slower than working with masks. Assume that paint is an option only when you can't achieve a similar result with a mask. There are, of course, exceptions, such as cases in which you can easily track a paint stroke, or when rapidly filling holes in an alpha channel with paint.

▶ **Review constantly at full speed.** Don't waste time heading down the wrong road. Carefully assess your footage via a RAM Preview every few frames, and determine if your approach is working. If it's not, be prepared to switch tactics.

▶ **Combine strategies.** Effective rotoscoping may employ a mixture of keying (whether color keying or a *hi-con matte*), tracking, animated masks, and paint. Start with the one that protects the most crucial edges, and work your way down to the cruder stuff.

With these guidelines in mind and a solid grasp of the fundamentals of creating selections (explored in Chapter 3, "Selections: The Key to Compositing"), you're ready to consider some rotoscoping specifics.

Articulated Mattes

I've said it before, and I'm saying it again: When animating, or *articulating*, mattes, keep it simple. All of the strategies offered here are for setting up and animating your mattes with as few steps as possible. Not only will this save you time in setup, you'll have fewer elements to fix if something goes wrong. Each new edit you keyframe introduces the possibility for more error, and each new point you add to a mask has to be accounted for on every other frame.

The first question to decide when starting a roto job is whether you prefer to mask in the Composition panel or in the Layer panel. The advantages of the Composition panel

"Keyframing" is so-called because originally (at Disney, in the 1930s) it was the practice of drawing in the key frames—the top of a leap in the air, the moment of impact, the kiss—that would be done by the top animators, leaving lower-level artists to add the in-between frames thereafter. This is the right way to think of keyframing animated masks: Look for the pivotal moments and try to let the computer in-between the others as much as possible.

A *hi-con*, or *high-contrast matte*, is created by taking luminance data from an image—typically one or all of its color channels—and raising the contrast to create a luminance matte, typically to hold out areas of the same image. Chapter 6 explores this process in greater depth.

are that you can see the layer in the composition and that it updates live as you work. This approach, however, does have several potential pitfalls:

▶ On a large scene you may have to wait for all elements to render and the screen to redraw each time you draw a point.

▶ If the layer you are masking has been transformed (and particularly, rotated in 3D, scaled down, or made transparent), you may find it difficult to edit a mask cleanly.

▶ You may need to select and lock other layers to be certain that you're editing the correct layer, particularly if you're creating more than one mask.

▶ The mask you draw in the composition viewer is live by default, causing masked areas to disappear as you work. This can make it impossible to draw complex shapes.

▶ You lose the use of selection tools that exist only in the Layer panel.

You may have guessed by now that the Layer panel is generally a preferable place to create masks. Tweaking mask points in the context of the entire comp is often useful, but I recommend this only as a secondary approach. If you start to create a mask in the Composition panel and realize you're in trouble, double-click the layer in the Timeline; your mask remains live in the Layer panel, ready for you to continue drawing and editing wherever you left off.

The Layer panel includes a couple of important pull-down menus you should be aware of: View and Target. You select your display mode from the View menu (**Figure 7.1**), choosing Masks, Anchor Point Path, or any effect you might have applied to this layer. Keep it set to Masks (the default) to edit masks in this panel. If Anchor Point Path is selected, you may be unable to edit your masks. If you choose None or any effect, masks will not be displayed.

Beside the View menu is a Render check box; toggle it to see the full frame source of your footage and any masks.

The Target menu resides along the bottom bar of the Layer panel (**Figure 7.2**) for one specific purpose. It enables you to select a target mask that is completely replaced if you draw (or paste in) a new mask. This would seem to

Figure 7.1 The View menu specifies what is active in the Layer panel; the Render check box determines whether that particular step is displayed, or the source.

Figure 7.2 Choose a mask from the Target menu and draw a new mask (or paste in a mask shape). The target mask shape will be replaced; this is predominantly useful with a keyframed Mask Shape.

be a boon for rotoscoping, allowing you to draw in a new mask at any time, but there's a gotcha: The First Vertex of the mask shape (which you can control) and the direction in which its points are numbered (which you can't) must match those of the target (see the "First Vertex" section).

RotoBeziers

An invention unique to After Effects among Adobe applications, RotoBezier shapes are effective for creating a mask that changes over time because they have fewer adjustable points than Bezier shapes (discussed in Chapter 3). Fewer controls, theoretically at least, mean less ability to inadvertently create the pops and bubbles (also known as matte *boiling*) that can send your rotoscoping job in the wrong direction (**Figure 7.3**).

NOTES

The first vertex of the mask is identifiable as slightly larger than the others. If you're having trouble matching an animation between shapes and need to edit it, context-click a desired vertex and select Set First Vertex from the resulting menu. More on First Vertex in the "Morphing" section of this chapter.

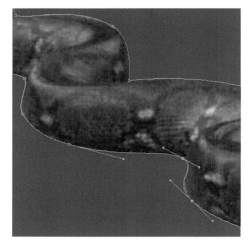

Figure 7.3 Bezier handles are a bad mix with animation; for each point, three points must be managed for each vertex, and crimping inevitably results when handles cross.

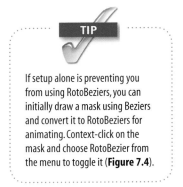

TIP

If setup alone is preventing you from using RotoBeziers, you can initially draw a mask using Beziers and convert it to RotoBeziers for animating. Context-click on the mask and choose RotoBezier from the menu to toggle it (**Figure 7.4**).

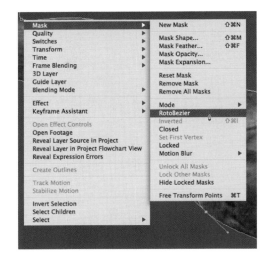

Figure 7.4 Many useful options are tucked away in the Mask context menu: Not only can you convert a Bezier shape to RotoBezier, you can lock and hide masks, close a shape, and set the first vertex for use with such features as Smart Mask Interpolation and the Reshape tool.

There's only one problem: RotoBeziers are never accurate during initial setup. To draw a RotoBezier, choose the Pen tool (**G** key) and check the RotoBezier box in the Tools menu. Pressing **G** repeatedly cycles through the other three mask editing tools; these do not include the Roto-Bezier check box, as they are for editing an existing mask, not drawing a new one.

In RotoBezier mode, try drawing a basic mask around the bus in ext_busPassbyUncorrected_HD. For now, don't worry about how well the mask conforms to the edge, just try following this one instruction: Place a point at the center of any curve and on any corner you can perceive (**Figure 7.5**). As using Beziers probably did when you first used them, this takes practice, so don't sweat the result just yet. The mask won't look right until you adjust tension on the points.

The literal key to your success when editing a RotoBezier shape is the Alt/Option key. After you've drawn your final point and closed the mask, with the Pen tool and all mask points still selected, hold down **Alt/Option**. A double-ended arrow icon appears. This is the Adjust Tension pointer. Dragging it to the left increases tension (counterintuitive if you ask me, but you get used to it). Do so with all mask

Figure 7.5 Your first pass with RotoBeziers should just hit the key transitions quickly and won't look right when you're done. Place a point at the apex of each curve you find, as well as at each corner. The next step is to tighten or loosen individual points.

points active, and they all become corners (**Figure 7.6a** and **b**), just as if you collapsed handles at a Bezier vertex. Now drag in the opposite direction, and all of the points act as if their (imaginary) Bezier handles are extended to the limits.

Although it does help dispel the myth that only Beziers are suitable for shapes with corners, dragging the Adjust Tension pointer with all points selected is not the typical method to edit RotoBeziers. Instead, after laying down the initial points of a RotoBezier mask, deselect it (**Control+Shift+A/Cmd+Shift+A**) and then Alt-drag (Option-drag) the Pen tool (temporarily enabling Adjust Tension) on each point that requires a tension adjustment.

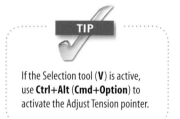

TIP

If the Selection tool (**V**) is active, use **Ctrl+Alt** (**Cmd+Option**) to activate the Adjust Tension pointer.

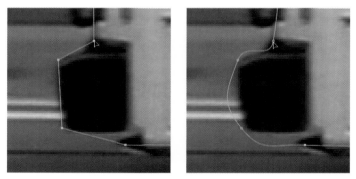

Figures 7.6a and b Contrast all RotoBezier points at full tension (a) and no tension (b) to get an idea of the possible range, and how to drag and adjust. Generally you will adjust points one or two at a time, however, not all at once.

You can freely add or subtract points as needed by toggling the Pen tool (**G** key; look for the cursor to change, adding a plus or minus sign beside it). With the Pen tool in Add mode you can also select a point simply by clicking on it, and deselect a point by Shift-clicking on it. This means that you don't have to continually switch tools (**Figure 7.7**).

The hardest thing to accept about RotoBeziers is that the shape is inevitably so wrong when you first lay in your points, and each point you add changes the shape around adjacent points. Now that you're used to the basics of how RotoBeziers work, try drawing a new mask (say, around one window of the bus) this way: When you place a point on a corner, before moving on to the next point, Alt/Option-drag to the left on the vertex. Voila: It's already a corner, and your shape is much closer to final on the first pass (**Figure 7.8**).

The real advantages of RotoBeziers become evident when you animate them, allowing you to resolve transitions with fewer variables than with Beziers.

Working Quickly

Here is a summary of tips for working efficiently with masks:

▶ The **G** key activates the Pen tool and cycles through its four modes to add and subtract mask points and collapse Bezier handles.

▶ **Alt/Option** activates the Adjust Tension slider, if the Pen tool is active.

▶ **Ctrl+Shift+A** deselects any active mask; **Ctrl+A** (with the layer selected and the viewer active) activates all masks.

▶ The **V** key activates the Selection pointer. To switch a mask to Translate mode, double-click it with this tool. Your mask will transition to Free Transfer mode and be outlined by a gray box with a center that you can offset for rotation and scaling.

▶ With the Selection tool active, context-click on a mask for quick access to most of its editable properties.

▶ If your mouse has a scroll wheel, scrolling with the Layer panel active zooms in and out of frame; holding the **Alt/Option** key as you do this zooms around your cursor. Holding down the **spacebar** activates the Hand tool for fast panning around the frame.

▶ To replace a Mask shape, select the shape from the Layer panel's Target menu and start drawing a new one; whatever you draw replaces the previous shape, creating a Mask Shape keyframe if the stopwatch is enabled. Beware: The first vertex point of the two shapes may not match, creating strange in-between frames. To set the first vertex point, context-click on the mask.

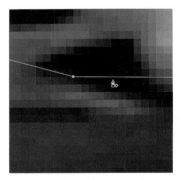

Figure 7.7 The Add Vertex tool (one of the Pen tool's modes) will also select an existing point, without creating a new one. Thus the Pen tool lets you keep working without clicking outside the viewer; the G key cycles through its variations.

Figure 7.8 Once you develop some facility with RotoBeziers, you can adjust point tension on the fly. Alt-drag (Option-drag) to the left to tighten a corner point; other points are unaffected.

Strategies for Complex Shapes

Whether you've been won over to RotoBeziers for creating animated masks or not, the strategies for masking a complex moving shape are largely the same. Here are the main points:

1. Begin by creating whatever matte you can to preserve as much of the existing edge detail as you can. If no color key is possible, carefully examine all three channels of the footage for the one with the greatest contrast and create a hi-con matte.

2. Narrow down the work area to just the section you need for your shot. Try not to rotoscope even one frame more than you need.

3. Use multiple overlapping masks instead of a single mask on a complex, moving shape (**Figure 7.9**). Even a hard-bodied object, such as the bus driving by, benefits from being rotoscoped with several masks instead of one.

4. Go through the clip, and block in the major keyframes for a given shape. This will be the point at which a change of direction, speed, or shape begins or ends.

5. Begin with the frame in which a mask outline can be drawn using the fewest points, and add points (or masks) as needed to progressively more complex frames. Be prepared to break down the shot as much as necessary so that each of your masks describes only one part of the shape, and *each shape stays simple*. Stay under a dozen points if you can.

Block in and refine the first shape, then refine as necessary. Check the result at full speed against a contrasting background, just as you do with color keys. Then move on to the next shape.

In some cases, you can finish the matte this way. In other cases, you'll be left with a few stray holes in your matte here and there that you can go back and clean up with paint strokes. The process for working with paint is detailed in the next section; first, take a look at some of the other strategies at your disposal for masking, to evaluate their relative effectiveness.

Figure 7.9 One key to working quickly is to intentionally create overlapping, separate mask shapes for different parts of your masked area that you know will move independently, or be revealed and concealed (in this case, because of a simple perspective shift). A shape with 20 or more points will be difficult to manage over time.

Although each new mask by default retains the color of its predecessor, your life will be made easier with overlapping mattes if each one has its own color, and the colors are easy to see against the source. As mentioned earlier, you can enable Cycle Mask Colors in Preferences > User Interface Colors to generate a unique mask color with each new mask. Also in the Timeline panel, select the masked layer and press **M** to reveal masks, then click on the colored square beside each mask to edit its color.

Preferences > General includes a preference, on by default, to preserve a constant vertex count when editing masks. Leaving it on prevents inadvertent popping of added vertices or awkward tweening around deleted vertices. But in cases where in-betweening is not an issue (presumably because you're creating a mask on every frame), you can consider turning this off.

Figure 7.10 All of the motion blur on the truck is left to right, so the ideal mask for the hood would employ heavy feathering on the right edge and none on top; this mask is not feathered and does not match. After Effects lacks per-vertex mask feather settings, so you can either combine multiple masks or animate the mask to match the motion of the truck and enable motion blur, creating the feathering effect automatically (Figure 7.13).

Working Around Limitations

At the opening of the chapter I came right out and identified that After Effects is not most artists' first choice as a dedicated rotoscoping tool. This is not a generalized complaint or simply a matter of taste: Other programs' masking tools perform useful functions that are impossible to do with After Effects 7.0. This section will identify some of those holes and focus on the strategies that can help you make the best of the situation. For example

▶ There is no way to apply a tracker directly to an After Effects mask, let alone track individual mask points. That doesn't mean there's no way to track in a mask selection, however.

▶ You can't translate a mask the way you would a layer, by selecting all of the keyframes you want to translate and performing the move; After Effects applies the move to the current frame only. The workarounds are similar to those for tracking.

▶ After Effects lacks the ability to specify whether a feather is applied to the inside or outside of a mask, nor can you vary feather settings on a per-vertex basis (**Figure 7.10**).

▶ Adding points to an animated mask has no adverse effect on other keyframes applying to that mask; the mask retains its shape. Deleting points, however, deforms the other keyframed versions of the mask. Avoid deleting points on a mask animation at all costs. Always start by keyframing the simplest shape, with the fewest points, and work your way up to the most complex.

▶ There is no dedicated morphing tool in After Effects. The elements to do a morph, however, exist in the program.

The following sections elaborate upon the above points in depth.

Tracking and Translating

If you cannot apply a tracker directly to a mask, even using expressions, what are your alternatives? The next chapter will concentrate on successful tracking, so here I'll focus on simply getting set up.

One workaround (effective in limited cases) is to stabilize the layer, precompose it, and mask the stabilized element (which is now held in place); the motion is reapplied by linking Position keyframes to the stabilized anchor point (either via expressions or a simple copy and paste). This may simplify matters when the element being rotoscoped is itself relatively static but the camera is moving; however, it will not work so well if the element is moving around enough to generate substantial motion blur or shape changes, or if it doesn't stabilize properly.

More likely, you will have luck tracking a mask when articulating it isn't so important; for example, an element with a solid surface that doesn't change shape. The workaround in this case is to use the masked layer as a track matte and track the transforms of the track matte layer, which carries the mask with it (**Figure 7.11**).

This same not-very-pretty workaround can also get you out of a tight spot. Suppose you have dozens of mask keyframes that simply need to be offset, scaled, or rotated. Duplicate the masked layer and set it as an alpha track matte, translating the entire track matte layer instead of each individual mask keyframe. If, however, only one (or some subset) of the points of your mask needs to be offset, there is simply no way to ripple that edit through all instances of that mask point. Features for future versions, perhaps.

Figure 7.11 The green holdout area is a corner-pinned mask to which a track can be applied (and a corner-pin track can even track the deformation as it moves across frame). The same idea works in any case where a simple mask shape can be tracked without need to deform drastically over the course of the shot.

Auto-trace

Wouldn't it be great if there was a tool in After Effects that would track masks for you? The good news is there is. The even better news is that it has been further optimized for version 7.0. The bad news (you knew this was coming) is the cases in which it is useful are cases in which you should be creating high-contrast luminance mattes instead. The even worse news is that the process is much slower and more cumbersome than using the techniques from Chapter 6 to create that hi-con matte.

Here's the problem: Auto-trace is a threshold tool that looks either at overall luminance or a specific color channel. You set the threshold (which you can guess reasonably intelligently by sampling pixels using your cursor and the Info palette) in Percent 0-100 mode. Next, add a pixel tolerance setting (whole values only), and then let Layer > Auto-trace work its magic (**Figure 7.12**). The result is an arbitrary number of masks, each describing a single area that meets the criteria. Over the course of the shot, some of these masks will reshape, some will disappear, and some new ones will appear.

Figure 7.12 Auto-trace is applied to the alpha channel of a matte created for the previous chapter. Over two dozen masks appear to outline and hold out areas of detail, but clearly this amount of detail presents a challenge; more useful results can be attained using simpler, higher-contrast source images.

It ends up being a rather unwieldy result for precise work, albeit cool for the motion graphics designers who want to play with those masks. For effects work, however, it's largely pointless compared to trackable mask points, which would be fabulous if only After Effects had them.

Masking Motion Blur

Motion blur happens. That's a good thing; it's a natural artifact of seeing an object in motion captured over a short period of time, and on moving footage it reinforces the persistence of vision required to make a series of still frames look like a moving image (when in fact, a "moving image" is always just an illusion created by a series of still images). Masking motion blur would seem to be something of a nightmare, as its edges defy careful observation.

True, it's not easy by any means, particularly if the mask is also articulated—a rotoscope of a bird flying through frame, for example. Remember to carefully evaluate whether you can pull any kind of key or hi-con matte on a blurred element to get all of those lovely edges before you get out the masking tools.

You can even evaluate whether the blurred element is really enhancing your scene. (Hopefully, we're not talking about the starring element of your shot, but that happens all the time, too.) Consider whether you'd be better off eliminating the element from your scene.

Otherwise, there is one thing to think about. Masks respect the motion blur settings of the composition; a masked element in motion will have motion blurred edges. That means you have a chance of matching the motion blur with a mask whose contours would fit the shape of the object if it were stationary (**Figure 7.13**). To make the mask work with the moving element is a matter of getting the composition's Shutter Angle and Shutter Phase settings to match. (For details, see Chapter 2, "The Timeline.")

This will probably leave you with edge problems that you must work to cleverly conceal, whether by choking, further blurring the edges, forcing them to the background color, and so on.

Figure 7.13 Putting a rotoscope mask in motion via keyframes allows motion blur to come along for the ride, simplifying the seemingly challenging masking situation shown in Figure 7.10.

Figure 7.14 Me and my evil twin, and that awkward adolescent phase in between.

Morphing

Let's talk about morphing—that's right, that crazy craze of the early '90s. Where are you now, Michael Jackson?

Thing is, morphing can come in handy, without being so blatant and obvious, if you think of it as a concealing tool. It's useful when you don't want anyone to notice a transition between two objects or even a transition between one object and itself at a different point in time. Or heck, go crazy morphing together members of your extended family to see if you look anything like the result.

What exactly is a morph? It is, quite simply, a combination of two warps and a dissolve. Given two images, each with a corresponding shape (say, the features of the face), you warp the source image's face shape to the face shape of the target, warp the target from something that matches the source to its face shape, fading the target in over the source.

After Effects has no tool called "Morph," and for a long time, the program offered no good way to pull off this effect. After Effects Professional includes Reshape, a warping tool that lays the groundwork for simple morphs. You can build these up into more complex morphs, with separate individual transitions occurring to create an overall transition.

Using Reshape to Morph

Unfortunately, creating a morph with Reshape is nowhere near a one-button process. This book generally steers away from step-by-step recipes in favor of helping you solve larger problems creatively, but in this case, it's easy to get confused. So here is a step-by-step, using a demonstration of my own resemblance transitioning to that of my evil twin (**Figure 7.14**):

1. Start with two elements that have some basic similarities in their relative position of features. The subtler the distortion required, the more you can get away with.

2. Isolate the two elements you will be morphing from their backgrounds to prevent contamination. If you're working with elements shot against a blue screen, key them out first. Otherwise, mask them. In my example, I have created masks for each layer.

3. Ascertain that the two layers are the same size in the X and Y dimensions and as closely aligned as possible. If they are not, precompose one layer to match the other. *This step is important because it will make matching the source and target masks much, much simpler.* Name the two layers Source and Target (as they are in the example) if it helps you follow along.

4. Choose matching sections from your two clips for the duration of your transition (say, 24 frames). If you have still elements, no worries. The closer your moving elements are to still, the more likely you'll get a clean result.

5. Draw a mask around the boundary that is going to morph in both layers. Be as precise as possible, erring to the inside if at all (**Figure 7.15**). This could be the masks created in step 2, if you created masks there. It need not be active; if you don't need it to mask out the background, set it to None. Rename each mask something descriptive like outer (the name used in my example).

6. Create a mask around the area of the Source layer that is the focus of the morph. In my example, the focus is facial features: the eyes, nose, and mouth (**Figure 7.16**). Make this mask as simple as you can; use RotoBeziers and as few points as will work to outline the features in question.

7. Set the mask mode to None; this mask is your first shape, you don't need it to influence the layer at all; you will use it for the Reshape effect only. Give it a name (mine is called "me").

8. Copy this mask shape and paste it in the Target layer. If the two layers are the same dimensions, it should be an identical size and position as it was in the Source layer.

Figures 7.15 The outline of each head is carefully masked. These two masks need not correspond to one another; they are defining the boundary for the Reshape effect and can have differing numbers and orders of points. This mask prevents Reshape from pulling bits of background into the morph region.

Figure 7.16 The full setup along with the top layer enabled at 100% and color corrected. It begins the final animation at 0% Opacity, reaching 100% at the end of the transition.

9. Duplicate the mask. Give it a different color and re-name it. In my case, I called the mask "it."

10. First scale and rotate, then if necessary move individual points (as little as possible!) so that the it mask surrounds the equivalent area of the Target layer that me does of the source: in my example, the eyes, nose, and mouth.

11. Copy the resulting it mask shape, and paste it to the Source layer to create a new, third mask.

12. You now have three masks for each of the Source and Target layers. Now apply the Reshape effect to each layer.

13. Starting with the Source layer, set the Source Mask (me), the Destination Mask (it), and the Boundary Mask (outer). Set Elasticity to Liquid (you can experiment with other settings later if need be). Set Interpolation to Smooth.

14. At the first frame of the morph transition, still in Source, set a keyframe for Percent (at the default, 0.0%, meaning no reshaping is occurring). At the last frame, set Percent to, you guessed it, 100.0%. Now sit back and wait for the gruesome transformation. Don't worry about how it looks yet.

15. Repeat steps 12 and 13 for the Target layer, with the following changes: Set Source Mask to it and Destination Mask to me. The Percent keyframes should be set to 0.0 at the *last* frame of the transition (where it is keyframed to 100.0 on the Source layer) and, you guessed it, 100.0 at the first frame.

16. You've created the warps, now you just need the cross dissolve. Set an Opacity keyframe for Target at the last frame of the transition (leaving it at the default 100.0%), and then add a 0.0% Opacity keyframe at the first frame.

You should now be ready to preview. The preview may take a long time to build the first frame; subsequent frames render much more quickly, so be patient. The main question to resolve is whether the features line up properly; if not, you must adjust the source and destination mask shapes accordingly, watching the median frame to see whether the changes are improving matters.

At this point my example may be looking good in terms of the face transition (**Figure 7.16**), but, of course, I've made life hard on myself by transitioning from a head of one size to a larger one, and the edges just kind of fade in. Therefore—and this is where it can get really complicated—I add a second morph, using the same steps as before, but all new masks.

Why complicated? Why new masks? These two questions are interrelated. If you set a second Reshape effect, the

TIP

The Correspondence Points in Reshape can be raised from the default of 1 to make the distortion more precise (and in some cases, less twisted). The downside is that this slow effect thus becomes even slower. Better to simplify what you're attempting to do with your masks and fix things there; raise this value only as a last resort.

TIP

If at any point during setup it becomes difficult to interact with the UI because After Effects is taking so long updating a frame, enable Caps Lock on your keyboard to prevent any further frame rendering until you're done.

key is to avoid influencing the result of the first Reshape effect at all. Therefore, on the second instance the Boundary mask should be the boundary of the object *minus the area occupied by the original source and destination masks.* My second set of shapes covers the ears and top of the head, but avoids the area of the previous masks completely (**Figure 7.17**).

Now, a quick look at a detail I left out (by having you duplicate the Source and Destination masks in step 9, for example, rather than draw them from scratch).

Because I know this is complicated, I've included the source project and the final result as projects on the book's DVD-ROM. Please do not use the result as the centerpiece of your horror feature.

Figure 7.17 The full setup to do more than one morph on a single image quickly becomes pretty gnarly. Here are two non-overlapping holdout areas containing two sets of transition curves. This setup also takes exponentially longer to render.

First Vertex

The Reshape tool relies on a concept that was touched upon already, but now looms more significant: that of the First Vertex that exists on every mask. Look closely at a mask, and you will notice one vertex that is larger than the rest; that's the First Vertex.

Reshape relies on the First Vertex to determine which point on the source mask corresponds to which on the destination mask. Above, it was easiest to duplicate the source mask to create the destination mask, because this automatically satisfies the two criteria that are essential for a smooth Reshape effect:

▶ Placement of the First Vertex corresponds on both masks

▶ Each mask has the same number of points

If either of these criteria is not fulfilled, Reshape will execute some not-so-nice compensatory measures, probably deforming the in-between frames in undesirable ways. The easiest solution is usually to duplicate the source mask and edit it, keeping the same number of points. The next easiest method would be to draw a new mask with the same number of points, in the same direction (clockwise or counterclockwise), and to set the First Vertex where you need it (by context-clicking on the mask and choosing Select First Vertex from the menu).

Paint and Cloning

Paint is generally a last resort, and for a simple reason: Paint work is typically painstaking, and more likely to show flaws than approaches involving masks. Of course, there are exceptions. The ability to track clone brushes offers a huge advantage over masks, which are not so easy to track, and painting in the alpha channel is akin to masking with paint.

Paint tasks such as plate restoration and *dust busting* constitute entry-level jobs at larger effects facilities; there's no way to get around them on shows whose shooting conditions and standards demand them.

For effects work, paint controls in After Effects have two predominant uses:

▶ Clean up an alpha channel mask by painting directly to it in black and white

▶ Clone Stamp to overwrite part of the frame with alternate source

Assuming you're using the Professional version, you're lucky. Prior to version 6.0, paint was a convoluted, tacked-on afterthought, available only via a licensed effect that was so counterintuitive that most users had to re-read the manual each (infrequent) time they used it. Now the brush tools are more robust and fully integrated with the application.

Paint Fundamentals

Two panels, Paint and Brush Tips, are essential to the three brush-based tools in the Tools palette—Brush, Clone Stamp, or Eraser. These can be revealed by choosing the Paint Workspace (**Figures 7.18a, b,** and **c**).

The After Effects tools include a user interface functionality patterned after the brushes in Photoshop, but there are

NOTES

With version 7.0, paint and cloning support 32 bit per channel compositing (explored further in Chapter 11, "Film, HDR, and 32 Bit Compositing").

Figures 7.18a, b, and c Use the keyboard shortcut **Ctrl+B** (**Cmd+B**) to cycle through the three basic brush tools (a); to their right is a toggle that reveals (or hides) the Paint and Brush Tips panels (b and c).

a couple of fundamental differences. After Effects offers fewer customizable options for its brushes (you can't, for example, design your own brush tips). More significantly, Photoshop's brushes are raster based, while After Effects brushes are vector based, allowing them to be edited and animated at any stage.

Suppose that you have an alpha channel in need of a touch-up; for example, the matte shown in **Figure 7.19** is from GScombatHD.mov, a difficult matte to key without the need for matte cleanup, due to tracking markers and shadows. With the Brush tool active, go to the Paint palette and set Channels to Alpha (this palette remembers the last mode you used); the foreground and background color swatches in the palette will become grayscale, and you can make them black and white by clicking the tiny black-over-white squares just below the swatches. To see what you are painting, switch the view to the Alpha Channel (**Alt+4/Option+4**); switch back to RGB to check the final result.

When using the paint tools:

▶ Brush-based tools operate only in the Layer panel

▶ Brushes include a Mode setting (analogous to Transfer Modes)

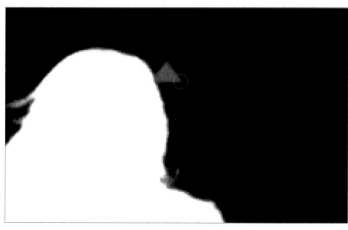

Figure 7.19 To touch up an alpha channel matte (in this case, to remove a tracking marker that intersects with the foreground action): In the Paint palette, select Alpha in the Channels menu, then display the alpha channel (**Alt/Option+4**).

> **TIP**
>
> That the paint tools operate in the Layer panel only is sometimes inconvenient. The older Vector Paint effect (Pro only) remains useful for painting in the context of a comp viewer, but it won't clone, and you may find that you need online help to get it to work correctly.

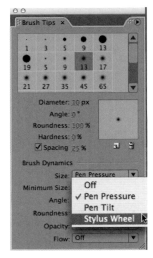

Figure 7.20 Under Brush Dynamics in the Brush Tips panel are several options that apply to tablet users only.

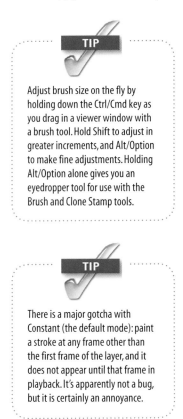

TIP

Adjust brush size on the fly by holding down the Ctrl/Cmd key as you drag in a viewer window with a brush tool. Hold Shift to adjust in greater increments, and Alt/Option to make fine adjustments. Holding Alt/Option alone gives you an eyedropper tool for use with the Brush and Clone Stamp tools.

TIP

There is a major gotcha with Constant (the default mode): paint a stroke at any frame other than the first frame of the layer, and it does not appear until that frame in playback. It's apparently not a bug, but it is certainly an annoyance.

▶ With a tablet, you can use the Brush Dynamics settings, at the bottom of the Brush Tips palette, to set how the pressure, angle, and stylus wheel of your pen affect strokes (**Figure 7.20**)

▶ Brushes are adjusted in the Brush Tips palette, where you can select a preset brush or customize your own by inputting numerical settings for diameter, hardness (which affects the amount of feather on the edge), and so on

▶ The Duration setting and the frame where you begin painting are crucial

By default, the Duration setting in the Paint menu is set to Constant, which means that any paint stroke you create on this frame continues to the end of the layer. For cleaning up an alpha channel, this is typically not a desirable setting because you're presumably painting stray holes in your matte here and there, on single (or just a few) frames. The Single Frame setting confines your stroke to just the current frame on which you're painting, and the Custom setting allows you to enter the number of frames that the stroke will persist.

The other option, Write On, records your stroke in real time, re-creating the motion (including timing) when you replay the layer; this stylized option is for such motion graphics tricks as handwritten script.

The Brush Tips panel menu includes various display options (**Figure 7.21**) and allows features you might not know: You can add, rename, or delete brushes, as well. You can also name a brush by double-clicking it. Brush names do not appear in the default thumbnail view except via tooltips when you move your cursor above each brush.

For an alpha channel, you will typically work in Single Frame mode (under Duration in the Paint panel), looking only at the alpha channel (**Alt+4**/**Option+4**) and progressing frame by frame through the shot (pressing **Page Down**). If you want some practice, this is an effective way to eliminate the tracking markers from GScombatHD.mov.

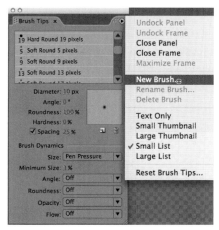

Figure 7.21 Heavy brush users may prefer the List views, which allow you to see and assign your own brush names.

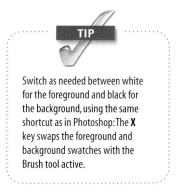

After working for a little while, your Timeline may contain dozens of strokes, each of which in turn contains numerous properties of its own (**Figure 7.22**). New strokes are added to the top of the stack and given numerically ordered names; to select one to edit or delete, you may more easily find it using the Selection tool (**V**) to directly select it in a viewer panel.

Figure 7.22 Without exerting yourself strenuously, it's easy to quickly build up quite a few paint strokes, each with its own properties; in fact, it is generally more work to keep the number of individual strokes to a minimum.

Cloning Fundamentals

Cloning moving footage preserves grain and other natural features that still images lack. Not only can you clone pixels from a different region of the same frame, you can clone from a different frame of a different clip at a different point in time (**Figures 7.23a, b,** and **c**), as follows:

▶ **To clone an offset area of the same frame:** This works just as in Photoshop. Choose a brush, Alt/Option-click on the area of the frame to sample, and begin painting. Remember that by default, Duration is set to Constant, so any stroke created begins at the current frame and extends through the rest of the composition.

▶ **To clone from the same clip, at a different time:** The offset is displayed (and can be edited) in the Clone Options, and you enter the offset value in frames. Note that there is also an option for setting spatial offset, so if you want to clone from the exact same position at a different point in time, set the Offset to 0, 0 and change the Source Time.

> **NOTES**
>
> Cloning has become much more useful in 7.0 with the addition of a single feature: the Aligned toggle in the Paint panel (on by default). Previously, cloned source would be blurry due to anti-aliasing; it was almost impossible to clone directly from pixel to pixel. Deselecting Align causes the same source point to be used for each new stroke, unless you hold the Shift key—rarely useful.

Figures 7.23a, b, and c Clone source overlay is checked (a) with difference mode active, making it possible to line up precisely two shots (b and c) taken with an identical camera setup. Difference mode is on, causing all identical areas of the frame to turn black when the two layers are perfectly aligned.

▶ **To clone from a separate clip:** The source from which you're cloning must be present in the same composition (although it need not be visible and can be a guide layer). Simply open the layer to be used as source, and go to the current time where you want to begin; Source and Source Time Shift are listed in the Paint panel and can also be edited there.

▶ **To mix several clone sources without having to reselect each one:** There are five Preset icons in the Paint panel; these allow you to switch sources on the fly and then switch back to a previous source. Just click on a Preset icon before selecting your clone source and that source remains associated with that preset (including Aligned and Lock Source Time settings).

That all seems straightforward enough, but of course it can't always be that easy.

Tricks and Gotchas

Suppose the clone source time is offset, or comes from a different layer, and the last frame of the layer has been reached—what happens? After Effects helpfully loops back to the first frame of the clip and keeps going. This is dangerous because you may keep painting without knowing it has occurred; it is an automatic, default setting. Similarly, you can use a source with a different frame rate without getting any warning from After Effects.

You can take control of this process by editing the source clip. Time remapping is one potential way to solve these problems, allowing you to stretch a source clip or loop it intentionally.

What if you need to scale the source to match the target? Although temporal edits, including time remapping, are passed through, other types of edits—even simple translations or effects—are not. As always, the solution is to precompose; any scaling, rotation, motion tracking, or effects to be cloned belong in the subcomposition.

Finally, remember: Paint is an effect. Take a peek in your Effects Control panel after applying a stroke or two; you'll see an effect called Paint with a single check box, Paint on Transparent, which effectively solos the paint strokes.

TIP

To clone from a single frame only to multiple frames, toggle on Lock Source Time in the Paint panel.

Figure 7.24 Paint strokes and effects are interleaved; touch-up of the plate occurs after compression artifacts related to 4:2:2 sampling are removed (see previous chapter) but before Keylight is applied.

TIP

New in version 7.0, if you paint, then apply an effect, and then paint again, a new instance of the Paint effect appears after the effect by default.

Because paint is an effect, you can change the render order of paint strokes relative to other effects. By, say, touching up a green-screen plate, then applying a keyer, you could then touch up the resulting alpha channel, all on one layer without precomposing (**Figure 7.24**).

Finally, to help you take control of where paint strokes belong in your effects pipeline, note the View pull-down menu in the Layer panel (**Figure 7.25**). It lists, in order, the paint and effects edits you've added to the layer. To see only the layer with no edits applied, toggle Render off; to see a particular stage of the edit—after the first paint strokes, but before the effects, say—select it in the View menu, effectively disabling the steps below it. These settings are for previewing only; they will not enable or disable the rendering of these items. It's a feature included in most node-based compositing applications by default (like highlighting a single node in the middle of the tree).

Tracking Strokes

As mentioned before, paint strokes include their own editable properties. Not only can you edit or transform their shapes, which isn't so often necessary, you can connect the motion tracker directly to a paint stroke.

Cases come up all the time where artists can save themselves a ton of work by attaching paint strokes to motion-tracked objects. However, to do so requires use not only of the tracker, which is covered in the next chapter, but also of basic expressions. Thus this topic is fully covered in Chapter 10, "Expressions," as an excellent example of a simple use of expressions and offsets.

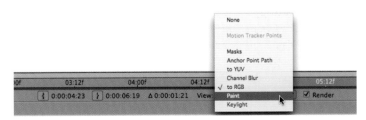

Figure 7.25 The Layer panel's View pull-down menu is a useful method for soloing paint strokes in the overall effects pipeline.

Wire Removal

"Wire removal" and "rig removal" are two terms regularly bandied about in the visual effects industry. Generally speaking, *wire removal* means painting out a wire on a blue-screen shot, a wire usually used to suspend an actor in mid-air. *Rig removal*, meanwhile, is even less glamorous: It's just garbage masking any equipment that showed up in frame.

Some rotoscoping applications have dedicated wire-removal tools, but in After Effects, you're on your own. However, wire removal need not be a painstaking process in After Effects simply because there's no dedicated tool for it. There are several approaches that could conceivably work; if the ends of the wire are trackable, you can track position and rotation and apply these to a null, which would be the parent of a masked element to replace the wire. This specific instance, with an example, is demonstrated in the following chapter.

Rig removal is often aided by tracking motion, because rigs themselves don't move, the camera does. The key is to make a shape that mattes out the rig, then apply that as a track matte to the foreground footage and track the whole matte. See Chapter 8, "Effective Motion Tracking."

Plate Restoration via Cloning

This is as nitty-gritty as rotoscoping gets. For various reasons, even on the highest budget visual effects film, the shooting and transfer process introduces flaws visible on a frame-by-frame basis: Dust and scratches make their way onto the pristine master.

Most of these flaws, alas, will be corrected only via frame-by-frame cloning, sometimes known as "dust busting." Large visual effects houses have teams dedicated to this work, a motley crew of mostly entry-level folks who listen to a lot of audio books. I mention it separately not because it requires a different approach than is outlined here, but because you might not be aware that such a job exists, let alone that it could be an entry-level job at a major facility. If you're in one of the main visual effects hubs (Los

Angeles, San Francisco, London, and so on) this of course is the type of work that increasingly is being "off-shored" to cheaper markets.

One final note about this work: Despite its apparent tedium, it's not all done via a monolithic approach; there really is some art to it. In some cases, cloning with an offset will work. In other cases, you're better off masking out a part of the source to reveal the footage you want to replace by placing that clean version behind it. Never check out completely, because you never know when you might devise a better way to approach a problem, and the problem-solvers are the ones who get the promotions.

Conclusion

And so, like rain, into every effects artist's life a little roto-scoping must fall. The tools outlined here are mostly sufficient for the type of rotoscoping work that compositors will have to do. Dedicated rotoscope artists would likely choose software other than After Effects to ply their trade, or perhaps employ Silhouette as an After Effects plug-in. As long as rotoscoping isn't your stock in trade, however, the After Effects tools will usually allow you to complete the shot without having to look for other software.

The next chapter completes the picture by adding motion tracking to your areas of expertise. As mentioned, motion tracking plus rotoscoping can equal a shortcut around tedious tasks.

Effective Motion Tracking

Even if you're on the right track, you'll get run over if you just sit there.

—Will Rogers

Effective Motion Tracking

The After Effects tracker is a semi-automated solution for two-dimensional match moving and stabilization; it helps you match the motion in source footage and apply it to target layers or remove camera motion from a shot. Set up correctly, it allows you to click a button and derive matched motion more precise than anything you could ever animate by hand.

It can save you piles of time, too, such as the several months I spent hand-matchmoving several dozen shots for Rebel Assault II using After Effects 2.0, which had no motion tracker whatsoever. The feature wasn't added until version 4.0, allowing me to learn everything I know about keyframe animating. But, having the tracker doesn't mean you get to click a button and put your feet up on the desk, George Jetson style.

First, you need to make sure you're using the tracker to best effect. Some of the most common ways to go wrong would be to

- Fail to choose good track points
- Misunderstand how the tracker does its job, and never change the default settings
- Give up on tracks that seem to have gone astray (although abandoning them may be the right idea once you understand what may have gone wrong)
- Forget about motion blur
- Fail to realize all the different ways tracking data can be applied

This chapter will help you with the above and much more.

Once you've nailed down these essential techniques, you can move on to some elegant uses of the tracker; you can

▶ Use the After Effects 3D camera as if it were a physical camera, matching objects you insert in the scene to the scene motion automatically

▶ Procedurally smooth a camera move (beyond simply stabilizing a static shot)

▶ Use a simple expression to continue tracking an object that becomes occluded (the track area moves offscreen or otherwise disappears)

▶ Bring three-dimensional depth to effects even though After Effects does not import 3D meshes

Don't forget, the tracker's uses go beyond those clearly spelled out in the Tracker Controls panel (which can always be revealed by choosing it in the Window menu, although it appears automatically upon applying a track).

The Essentials

There's no point in learning about all the cool tricks you can perform with the tracker if you're still fighting it for a good basic track. If you still find your tracks going astray after reviewing the After Effects documentation (if you haven't read it, at least skim Motion Tracking in the Adobe Help Center, **F1**), read on and don't despair. Just because it is automated doesn't mean that it's automatic; you sometimes have to come to a certain "understanding" with this feature set.

Tracking is a two-step process: First, you set up and run the tracker, then you apply the tracking data thus created. Each step contains unique pitfalls. Once you learn to recognize these and take action, however, they can be avoided easily enough.

Choosing a Good Reference Point

There are trackers that don't require you to choose track points (predominantly dedicated third-party 3D and planar trackers, discussed later in this chapter). After Effects,

> **NOTES**
>
> The tracker is available only in After Effects Professional. If you are using After Effects Standard, skip ahead to the final section of this chapter, which focuses on importing 3D match moves from third-party software.

Figure 8.1 You set After Effects tracking points in the Layer panel, via the Tracker Controls panel.

TIP

As you choose search and feature regions, keep in mind: They don't have to be square! If the feature you want to track is wide and short, widen the feature region to match. Or, if the shot motion is unidirectional—say, a left-to-right pan—the search region should not only be wider (and barely taller) than the feature region, but offset to the right.

however, relies on you to choose a reference point that will track effectively, and it is the most important choice you will make (**Figure 8.1**).

Make sure the feature you plan to track

▶ Contrasts in color, luminance, or saturation from the surrounding area

▶ Has defined edges entirely within the feature region

▶ Is identifiable throughout the shot

▶ Does not have to compete with similar distinct features within the search region at any point during the track

▶ Is close to the area where the tracked object or objects will be added

To find a good candidate for tracking, look for "corners" in your image—places where two or more edges meet (**Figures 8.2a, b,** and **c**).

Figures 8.2a, b, and c Here are shown excellent (a), fair (b), and poor (c) track point candidates. A high-contrast, clearly defined corner, such as that of the painted flag (a) is optimal. The sun glint off the back of the spare tire (b) has clearly defined edges, but as light conditions in the shot change, the track may fail. Although the region in the trees has contrast (c), there is insufficient distinction between the patterns inside the feature region (the small center box) and the search region (the larger outer box); the wind will deform this target over time.

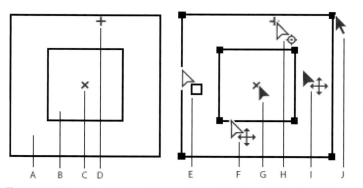

Figure 8.3 Many interactive controls are clustered close together in the tracker. Identified here are: A. Search region, B. Feature region, C. Keyframe marker, D. Attach point, E. Moves search region, F. Moves both regions, G. Moves entire track point, H. Moves attach point, I. Moves entire track point, J. Resizes region. Zoom in to assure you're clicking the right one.

> **TIP**
>
> Be forewarned: The track point is perhaps the most-difficult-to-manipulate user interface item in all of After Effects because of the number of draggable items adjacent to one another; you can easily drag the wrong thing (**Figure 8.3**). Even worse, completed tracks include a point for each tracked frame, more targets to accidentally click and drag, with no undo. Watch carefully for the compass arrow icon before clicking and dragging the feature region (the control you will adjust most of the time).

The search region needs to include only the area where you think the feature region is likely to appear on the very next frame—no more, and certainly no less. Be generous when setting this region, but don't give the tracker any reason to search where there is no helpful detail (**Figure 8.4**).

> **NOTES**
>
> Tracking points in After Effects slow down (requiring more processor cycles) in direct proportion to their size. Although systems are relatively fast and capable these days, the smaller the track region, the faster the track.

Figure 8.4 Knowing that the bus is moving from screen right to left, I offset the search region (the outer box) to the left of the feature region (inner box). Customizing the track regions in this manner speeds up the track and reduces the margin of error considerably.

No Good Reference Point in Sight

Sometimes you get lucky, and you discover a trackable feature right where the target layer belongs. A successful track here is almost like returning to the shoot and placing the object directly on set.

If the best target feature changes or even disappears as the shot progresses, look for strategies later in the chapter for dealing with this.

At other times, however, you may not find very many suitable features in a shot, or a feature may exit frame at an inconvenient moment (one potential solution to this is described in "Continuing a Track with Expressions"). In such cases, you can edit the attach point, that little x in **Figure 8.5**. The attach point defaults to the center of the feature region, but you can offset it anywhere in the frame.

This chapter will show you how to more or less ignore the attach point by using nulls and parenting instead, which let you offset this point and do all sorts of other useful things when tracking. This isn't how the documentation would have you do it, but it tends to solve more problems.

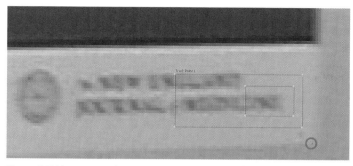

Figure 8.5 You may need to zoom way in to see controls such as the attach point, which has been offset in this case to the low contrast corner. This solves a common problem: a more trackable feature is nearby, but not exactly where the track point needs to be.

Optimizing Tracker Options

Prior to version 6, the After Effects tracker was rather notorious. With default settings geared toward slow systems rather than optimal results, it was practically guaranteed not to produce a good track. Simply pressing Play after setting tracking regions now often yields an effective result.

Nevertheless, defaults will take you only so far. The tracker is packed with plenty of powerful options designed for specific scenarios that, sooner or later, you are bound to encounter.

Typology

It's easy enough to get an idea of the types of tracks available in After Effects: Just have a look at the Track Type menu (**Figure 8.6**). But what exactly are the differences?

Stabilize and *Transform tracking* are virtually identical except for how they are applied. Pressing Edit Target shows the singular difference between them: Stabilize tracks are always applied to the *anchor point of the tracked layer*. Transform tracks are applied to the *position of a layer other than the tracked layer*.

Using Stabilize, the animated anchor point (located at the center of the image by default) moves the layer in opposition to Position. Increasing the anchor point's X value (assuming Position remains the same, which it does when

Figure 8.6 The various available track types are set in the Tracker Controls panel.

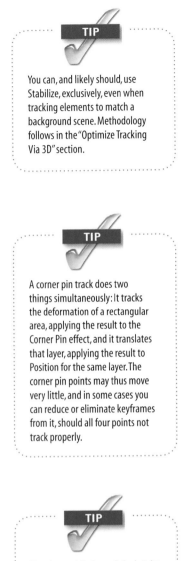

TIP

You can, and likely should, use Stabilize, exclusively, even when tracking elements to match a background scene. Methodology follows in the "Optimize Tracking Via 3D" section.

TIP

A corner pin track does two things simultaneously: It tracks the deformation of a rectangular area, applying the result to the Corner Pin effect, and it translates that layer, applying the result to Position for the same layer. The corner pin points may thus move very little, and in some cases you can reduce or eliminate keyframes from it, should all four points not track properly.

TIP

Rotation and Scale rarely look right when applied directly to a target layer because the relationship between the tracker and the layer is arbitrary. After Effects has no reference for the target layer's proper scale and rotation; it can only make all the frames internally consistent. See the section "Using Nulls to Solve Transform Problems."

you adjust the Anchor Point value directly in the Timeline) moves the layer to the left, just as decreasing the Position value does.

Animating only the anchor point lends Stabilize certain advantages. Any scale or rotation applied to the layer occurs from the corrected (and now consistent) center of the layer. You can freely edit or even animate the position of the layer without inadvertently disrupting the tracking data.

Corner Pin tracking is something else altogether—essentially a cheat to skew a rectangular source so that its four corners appear to translate in 3D space. This is not true 3D tracking in any sense. Instead, Corner Pin tracking applies data to a 2D layer via the Corner Pin plug-in, animating its 2D corner values. Imagine replacing a sign on the side of a moving bus (something you can attempt later in the chapter), and you get the idea. Corner pins are classically for adding a plane (monitor screen content, billboard, and so on) to a framed area of a source shot.

There are two types of Corner Pin tracking. Both generate four points of data, one for each corner of the target layer, but Parallel Corner Pin does so with only three track points. This works as long your target is perfectly rectangular and remains so throughout the shot—a shot of a door, head-on, with the camera at a perpendicular angle, for example. In most cases, you will employ Perspective Corner Pin (**Figures 8.7**).

Finally, *Raw tracks* generate track data only, graying out the Edit Target button. What good is track data that isn't applied anywhere? It can be used to drive expressions or saved to be applied later. It's no different than simply never clicking Edit Target; the raw track data is stored within the source layer (**Figure 8.8**).

Rotation and Scale

Stabilize and Transform tracks can also include rotation and scale data. This method is straightforward enough, employing two track points instead of one, which should

Figure 8.7 The basic corner pin setup. Corner pin tracking is normally applied to a target layer with the same rough dimensions as the source. The results are applied to the Corner Pin effect on that layer. Offsetting a corner like this (lower right) typically does not work with a corner pin, as it cannot properly account for shifts in perspective.

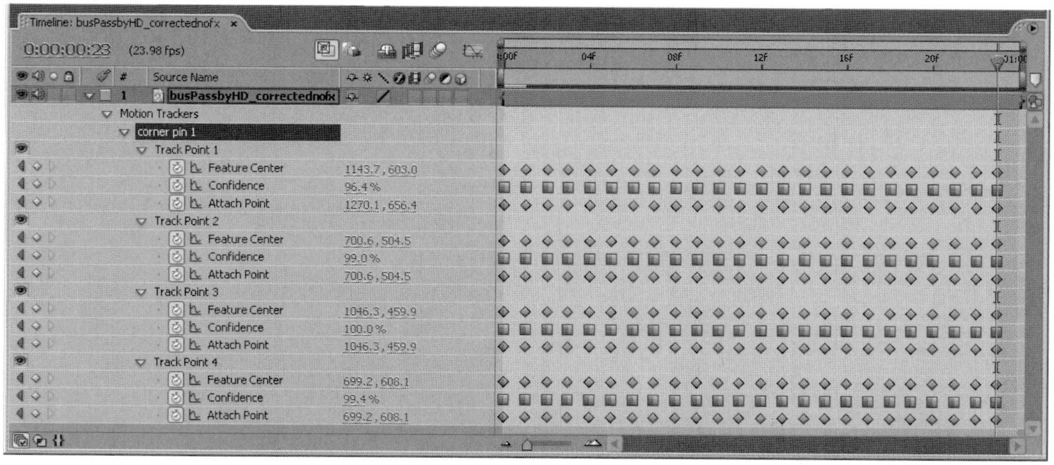

Figure 8.8 Each motion track generates raw data, whether or not it is specified as a Raw track. The data is found here, under Motion Trackers. As shown, the track and its points can be named for future reference, useful on a difficult track requiring multiple attempts.

be roughly co-planar to one another and the object being tracked because of the phenomenon of parallax. Imagine where in Z space the object belongs and track points that are both at that relative depth. Otherwise no bag of tricks—not offsets, not 3D extrapolation—is likely to help.

When tracking rotation and scale, features being tracked typically change from frame to frame (they rotate and scale). In Motion Tracker Options you'll find the Adapt Feature on Every Frame setting, which is like restarting the track on each and every frame. This is not a good default because, theoretically at least, it adds a greater margin of error per frame, but it can solve tracks of features whose appearance changes over the course of the shot. If you know that a feature being tracked is going to change its orientation, or size, or color, or the like over the course of the shot, consider enabling it; for example, try it using the tracker on one of the dolly or zoom shots included with this chapter's project.

If a track keeps slipping going forward, try starting at the end of the clip and tracking in reverse (note that the "play" icons in Tracker Controls go both directions (**Figure 8.9**).

TIP

Tracking in reverse is particularly useful when tracking an object moving away from the camera, whose features and track region otherwise diminish to the point of being untrackable. Adapt Feature on Every Frame is an effective option in this case as well.

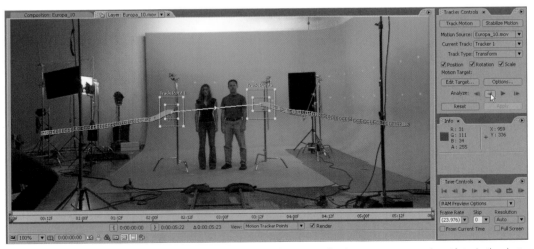

Figure 8.9 When tracking items that become more prominent later in the shot (as do the C stands in this camera dolly), try tracking in reverse. The tracker does a much more effective job of tracking a large pattern as it gets smaller, than the opposite.

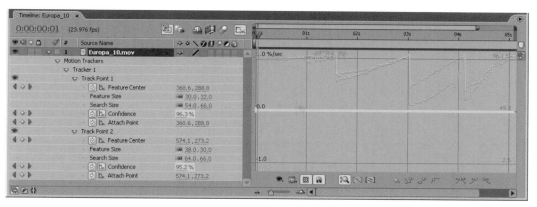

Figure 8.10 Revealing Confidence graphs in the Graph Editor clearly shows where the tracker's confidence has been shaken, so to speak. Just because a frame has low confidence doesn't mean there's a problem, although in this case it is clear that specific frames seem to have slipped, where the graph drops drastically.

Confidence

Below the Adapt Feature check box you'll find a pull-down menu that defines After Effects' mysterious Confidence settings. Take a closer look at the properties listed under a track point (**Figure 8.10**); twirling open Confidence displays a graph of how effective After Effects believes this track point was at a given frame.

What does the Confidence figure mean? It's an algorithm used to extrapolate the relative accuracy of a given track point according to pre-established criteria—which still doesn't explain much, without some frame of reference (so to speak). My experience is that good tracks tend to stay in the 80% to 90% region, and as soon as there is a major problem, confidence drops way off to 30% or less.

After Effects can take specific actions as the track is created, depending on the Confidence settings at the bottom of Motion Tracker Options (**Figure 8.11**). You can assign the track to continue no matter what or to simply stop tracking if confidence drops so that you can manually reset the track at that frame. The Extrapolate Motion option is there for tracked features that disappear for a few frames, retaining more or less steady motion while out of view.

The default setting Adapt Feature If Confidence Is Below 80% is effective in many cases; this is the setting with which you're most likely to get lucky and have the track solved without much extra managing.

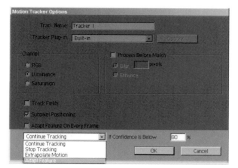

Figure 8.11 The menu at the bottom of Motion Tracker Options (accessible via the Tracker palette) specifies what to do should the Confidence rating drop below a certain threshold during the track.

Other Options

The rest of the Motion Tracker Options (**Figure 8.12**) have to do with methods of examining and analyzing footage. Instead of tracking a clip's luminance, you can use RGB (for unique cases where you have contrasting colors of a similar luminance) or Saturation (should the feature have extraordinarily high and low color saturation but flat color and contrast, which would be unusual). Luminance is preferable most of the time, provided you can locate the aforementioned "corners" with strong bright/dark contrast.

The Track Fields option is more like a reminder to separate them on import (maybe better to just change the Footage Settings—either way, make sure you're working with individual fields if they exist). Likewise, you set Process Before Match to pre-blur or pre-sharpen (Enhance) a clip, but honestly, it may indicate that your footage needs de-graining or, conversely, is too blurry to track effectively in After Effects.

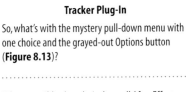

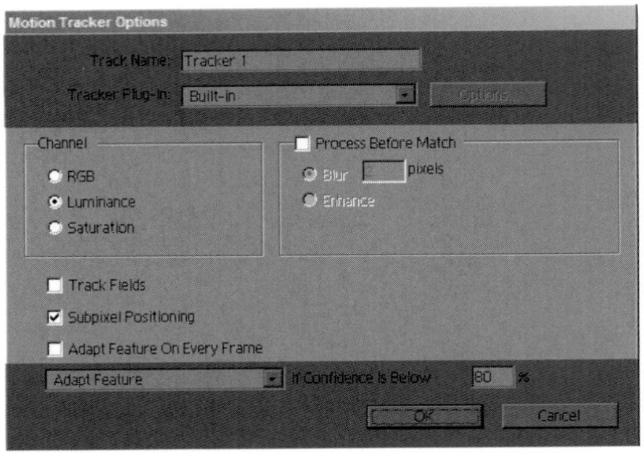

Tracker Plug-In

So, what's with the mystery pull-down menu with one choice and the grayed-out Options button (**Figure 8.13**)?

Where possible, the relatively small After Effects developer team leaves specialized features to third-party developers. Hence, the professional keying tools do not come from Adobe (including Keylight, which is licensed from The Foundry).

A lot of effort went into refining the built-in tracker, but the idea was to open the API for tracking so that one of the many tracking-software specialists could offer one of its own. Thus far, however, no developer seems to have stepped up.

Figure 8.12 These tracker options pertain to options for analyzing pixel data.

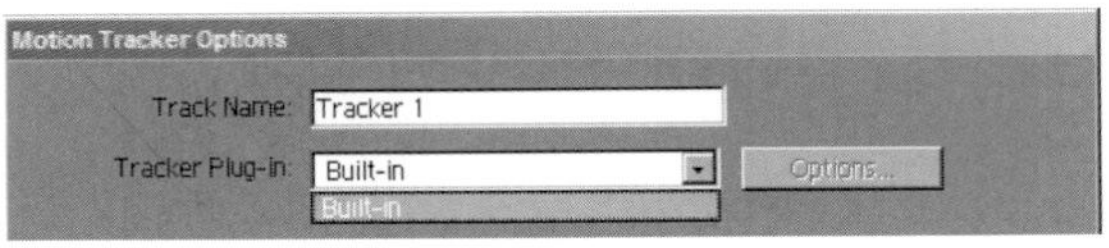

Figure 8.13 What exactly does that mean, "options?" The tantalizing Tracker Plug-in pull-down yields but one choice, and the Options button is in a permanent state of gray. Evidently no third party has, as yet, seen a market for a custom After Effects tracking plug-in.

Fixing Tracks That Go Wrong

The feature you're tracking changes as the shot progresses, and the tracker suddenly jumps to a different, similar feature within the search region. You didn't set Stop Tracking if Confidence drops—or maybe it didn't drop. You pounce on the Stop button in the tracker controls (**Figure 8.14**). Now what? The tracker has created a few frames' worth of bad data.

It's no big deal! Just drag the Current Time Indicator (in the Layer panel) back to the last correctly tracked frame and click Play. In so doing, you have reset the Feature Region contents, so there is a higher likelihood that the tracker will succeed without changing anything. If not, and the tracker continues to drift, the next line of defense is Adapt Feature on Every Frame, followed by altering the Confidence options:

▶ If the problem was caused by some other object briefly passing in front of the object you're tracking, try the Extrapolate Motion option when Confidence is below 80% (or whatever threshold at which your track went wrong, which you can check in the Timeline).

Figure 8.14 All was well, then the left tracker suddenly lost its way for a few frames. You only need to move current time back to the last good frame, and restart the track; in many cases, depending on the Confidence options (Figure 8.10), this will solve whatever problem occurred on the previous pass.

Subpixel Motion

The key feature of the After Effects tracker is subpixel positioning. You could never achieve this degree of accuracy manually; most supposedly "locked off" scenes require stabilization despite that the range of motion is less than a full pixel. Your eye's ability to detect motion is that good. Zoom in on the motion of a scene that is supposedly locked off, and you can actually spot motion occurring below the single-pixel level.

Although it is on by default, you can disable subpixel positioning in Motion Tracker Options if for some reason your shot requires motion in integer values. In most cases, this will make the track look strange and crude.

Do not be fooled as you watch a track in progress, however; the tracker icons preview in whole pixel values, bouncing around as if deriving a very crude track. Only after you've seen the result, or checked the tracked values to see that they go down to 1/10,000 of a pixel (that's right, four places below the decimal point) do you discover that the tracker is, in fact, properly doing its job (**Figure 8.15**).

Figure 8.15 Highlight a tracked keyframe value to reveal its accuracy extending to four decimal places below the whole-pixel level. This level of precision is essential to a realistic-looking track.

NOTES

Any track that you set for a layer remains a property of that layer until you twirl down the layer's properties and then delete it.

If the problem was caused by a feature that has changed its shape, color, or luminance, try Adapt Feature in the pull-down menu (as shown back in Figure 8.11) on the chance that the tracker can understand the change automatically.

If there is truly a problem for which neither of these helps, then Stop Tracking is probably your best option. Sometimes manually resetting the track point at certain key moments of failure is worth the trouble.

Remain flexible, be creative about your choice of points, and be ready to bail and start over if things aren't working too well, and a good track will result with the minimum of hassle.

Using the Timeline

It seems as though the Tracker Controls panel is where all the tracking happens, but the decisions you make there end up in the Timeline, and that's where you can edit and recover tracks.

For example, let's say you explore the various Track Type options and discover that Corner Pin tracks four points. You don't want four points, so you switch back to a simple Transform, but four track points remain in the layer, where you can't delete them. The Timeline panel is the place to find and destroy unneeded track points.

Matching Motion Blur

Don't neglect the possibility of motion blur! It can be your friend until it appears unwanted, and then it's like a malingering houseguest—impossible to ignore. There are a couple of situations in which you must carefully consider motion blur when tracking:

When foreground layers need motion blur to match the appearance of the background plate; for example, you don't have motion blur and you want it

When motion blur already exists in a shot you're trying to stabilize; for example, you have motion blur and you don't want it

The solution to the former problem is relatively simple, and the methodology is similar to that of color matching (as in Chapter 5, "Color Correction"). Zoom into an area of the image that would have well-defined contours were there no motion blur—a solid object with well-defined, high-contrast edges, if possible. Enable motion blur for tracked foreground layers, and see if the length of the blur matches at the default settings. If not, adjust accordingly, via the Composition Settings panel (**Ctrl+K/Cmd+K**), Advanced tab (**Figure 8.17**). You may have to revisit this panel multiple times to nail the adjustment, as there is no interactivity with this setting.

The latter problem is more formidable, that of removing existing blur. Even if you could easily do this in After Effects, footage that is heavily blurred will probably exhibit other problems when stabilized, such as a visible gutter area around the tracked image (**Figure 8.18**). The best solution is probably to forgo a completely locked stabilization in favor of smoothing the camera motion, but leaving some of the movement. This is explained more thoroughly in the "Smoothing a Moving Camera" section.

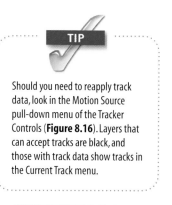

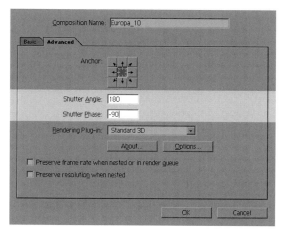

Figure 8.17 In case you missed the discussion of motion blur in Chapter 2, "The Timeline," this is the one and only place you can adjust motion blur settings for layers that have keyframed motion.

Figure 8.16 Easily overlooked, the Motion Source pull-down menu is a one-stop location for all layers in the timeline containing motion tracks.

Figure 8.18 The perils of stabilization: gaps around the repositioned layer, which can be fixed only by scaling and repositioning the shot; that strategy won't work in this case anyhow because of the heavy motion blur on the source plate.

TIP

Applying tracking data to a null is a universally good idea—you might consider making a habit of it. Why? In addition to the benefit described here, you can lock a null, preventing you from inadvertently transforming one of its keyframes.

Use Nulls to Solve Transform Problems

Having difficulty placing your track correctly? Nulls are often the solution. It can be disconcerting to apply a track to a layer and see it repositioned, rotated, or scaled from its correct placement. There's a relatively easy (and easily overlooked) fix: Apply the track to a null, then parent the target layer to the null, and its transform data doesn't change.

Figures 8.19a through **d** shows a particularly fiendish rig removal that was aided by the use of tracked nulls. One section of the moving rope that was not over the set had to be replaced and matched to the movement of the rest of the rope. The problem area was isolated and the movement of the rope along its edges tracked, then a substitute rope section was created using Stroke. By parenting this to the null containing the motion, motion blur was created procedurally as well, selling the final shot.

As you'll see in the next section, and again in the next chapter, nulls are particularly useful to animate a 3D camera, given that it has no anchor point and cannot be the target of a motion track. Parenting a camera to a null is the most sensible and straightforward method to apply tracker data to it.

If you prefer not to add a null object layer, if only because it's just one more layer to manage, there is, of course, an alternative: Apply an expression to offset the tracked transform data. If that sounds tempting, check out Chapter 10, "Expressions." Most users will find the use of nulls simpler and more convenient.

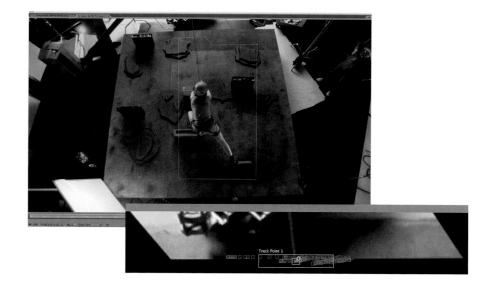

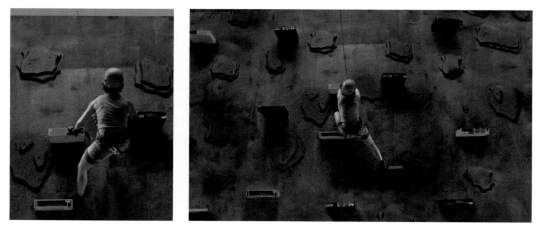

Figures 8.19a, b, c, and d Obviously it is essential that the rope reach the edge of frame, yet the set does not (a). The point where the rope meets the edge of the set can be tracked however (b) and a two-point mask with a Stroke effect added to replace it (c). The final image has motion blur applied, offsets to the shape of the added rope animated as needed, and the colors carefully matched, selling the effect (d).

Optimizing Tracking Using 3D

So you have a good idea how to set and apply a tracker successfully. Is that all there is to know about tracking in After Effects? Not by a long shot—you've only laid the groundwork for the good stuff. Say you want to track an arbitrary number of overlaid elements into a scene, matching the movement of a camera. You might think that you would have to track each layer individually or parent one to another (if that would even work, given that parenting changes the center of a rotation or scale transform).

Wrong. There is a way to set up tracking so that adding in tracked elements, including motion blur, rotation, and even scaling of elements, requires no extra or individual steps. You drop new elements into the scene and they track in as easily as if you added them when the shot was taken, and they look just as natural. That's right, you can approximate the look of 3D tracking on many shots without a 3D tracker.

The key is to stabilize the background layer (which will not appear stabilized in the final shot, unless you want it to, or perhaps you want to smooth it) and then parent a camera to that stabilization. You now have the motion of the scene captured in the movement of a camera, just as it was when shot, so that any elements you add to the scene pick up on that motion. It's quite cool.

The 3D Camera: The One-Stop Solution

The clip used for these steps, as well as a completed project, appears on the book's DVD as 08_tracking.aep.

Suppose you need to add an arbitrary number (more than one, or more as you go along, and so on) of foreground layers to a motion-tracked background plate: CG objects, color corrections, effects with hold-out masks, you name it. Applying track data to each of those layers individually would be a time-consuming headache.

Skip it. Don't apply a tracker at all. Instead, create whatever type of track your shot needs: Position only or with the addition of Rotation or even Scale. Now try this:

1. In the Tracker Controls, change the Track Type from Transform (the default) to Stabilize. (This method is not meant for corner pinning.)

2. Apply Stabilize, which by default goes to the track that generated the track. You actually have no other choice; try choosing a different layer than the source track layer by clicking Edit Target, and you'll find the other layers grayed out.

3. The layer is stabilized and will probably slip and slide around in the frame (**Figure 8.20**). Don't worry; it's one step from looking normal again.

Figure 8.20 A handheld shot creates wobble, even when shooting the world's most obnoxious stretch Humvee. The Graph Editor shows the extent to which the tracker has had to stabilize the shot.

4. Return to the first frame of the track (quite possibly frame 0 of the comp). Turn on the stabilized layer's 3D switch. Add a 3D camera (context-click in an empty area of the Timeline) and parent it to the stabilized layer (**Figure 8.21**).

Everything now seems back to normal, but any new item that you add to the scene joins the motion track as soon as you toggle its 3D switch. Any layer that shouldn't follow the track, such as an adjustment layer, can remain 2D (**Figure 8.22**).

Figure 8.21 A 3D camera is parented to the stabilized background layer, whose 3D is switched on; some orange triangular pylons are added as reference. The shot looks just as it did, except for the pylons, which follow the motion of the shot.

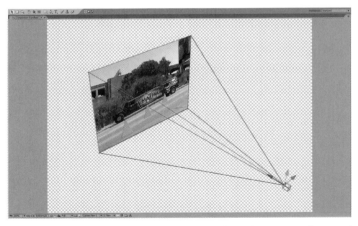

Figure 8.22 The camera is locked to the borders of the plate on every frame, and those orange markers now hold their position on the roadway throughout the shot. This look at the perspective view shows that all layers are essentially 2D, but only the camera and background move (in sync).

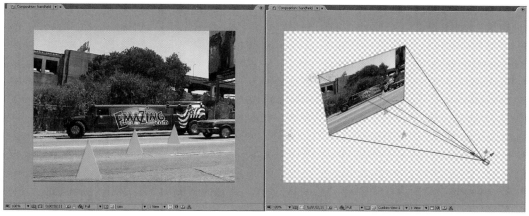

Figure 8.23 Rather than fake perspective of elements in 2D, they can be repositioned in 3D space. View angle and relative distance of the camera and objects must be correct, or they will start to slip and slide in the shot.

The Z-depth value of all layers will typically be 0, so the pylons in Figure 8.22 have been scaled and repositioned, rather than moved in 3D space. It also works to reposition them in 3D space, although it's more work to get the relative Z depth values proportioned so that each object sits where it is supposed to, in perspective; there is no reference or grid (**Figure 8.23**).

Relocating added layers in Z space might be worth the trouble in extreme cases. On *The Day After Tomorrow,* The Orphanage had to create several shots of a helicopter pilot inside a moving cockpit, with a blue screen outside the window to be replaced with a matte painting of the distant horizon. By moving it back several thousand pixels on the Z axis to approximate extreme depth, we added parallax for free. Of course, we didn't have to worry about anything looking as if it was sitting right on the ground plane, as in the Humvee example.

Fake 3D Tracking

If you really enjoying hacking composites, you can even derive something like 3D tracking from a zoom shot. **Figure 8.24** shows a tracked shot in which the camera zooms in. Track Type is set to Stabilize with Rotation and Scale on, resulting in an end frame like the one in **Figure 8.25**. Not right, but it's an interim step.

A 50 mm camera lens in After Effects offers a neutral perspective; a set of 3D layers with a Z Position of 0 will appear the same as they would as 2D layers. Generally, that's a good thing. It is conceivable, of course, that your scene was shot with a wider (or longer) lens, changing relative perspective. If so and you're positioning items in Z space, you may want to try to match it. See Chapter 9, "Virtual Cinematography" for details.

Figure 8.24 This zoom shot tracks easily in reverse. Most of the movement is straight in (Scale), but there is also some wobble (Position and Rotation)—note that all three are enabled.

Figure 8.25 By the end of a scale/rotation/position stabilization (the point at which the shot is most zoomed in) it looks as though the original framing in Figure 8.24 was cropped; as before, a 3D camera will be parented to reestablish the framing and capture the changes in the camera.

Next, add a 3D camera, parent it to this plate layer, then enable the plate layer's 3D toggle. The scaled-down shot pops back to 100% size. As before, the magic begins when you drop objects into the scene, but in this case, enabling their 3D toggles adds changes to their proportions as you zoom in (**Figures 8.26a, b,** and **c**).

Now before you get too excited, let me remind you that this works only in limited cases and that true 3D trackers generate true 3D data (distinguishing between a camera zoom and a push, which this one decidedly does not). Scaling a camera is not something you could do in the real world, but it is akin to zooming its lens in the virtual world.

Smooth a Moving Camera

But wait, there's more.

What about smoothing shaky camera movement? There's no "Smooth" track type, and simply choosing Stabilize obviously locks the shot in place. Is there any way to reduce the jitter or rotation in a shot without removing the camera movement altogether?

Naturally there is, or should I say, there is a natural way to do this. By re-creating the physical camera as an After Effects camera, you generate animation that can be smoothed. Barring extreme jolts that cause sufficient motion blur to blow the gag, it just works.

Figure 8.27 features a very rough hand-held pan across the face of the "defenestration" building in San Francisco, a public art piece where the furniture appears to be leaping out the windows. This example appears in the 08_tracking. aep composition on your disc.

There is one small problem: The camera has no data of its own to smooth; its motion is derived only from being parented to the stabilized layer. You don't want to apply a smooth to that source layer either, as the smoothing effect will be derived from the difference between that layer's motion and that of the camera. Ideally, you would like to be able to adjust the amount of smoothing after applying it, too.

Figures 8.26a, b, and c The result at the beginning (a), middle (b), and end (c) of the shot, with Depth of Field on to blur the nearest pylon as we zoom in. The pylons are fairly well locked to the pavement, but the quality of the result mostly comes down to how good the track was in the first place, because any slight bump ripples out to all of the objects (see the example on your disc).

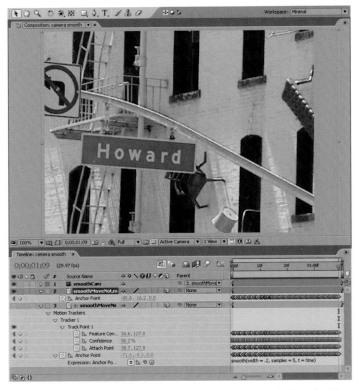

Figure 8.27 The basic steps for smoothing a camera move are in place for this shaky pan shot. The camera is parented to a duplicate of the stabilized layer and a smooth operation is applied to that layer; its visibility is off. The original smoothed layer, with no stabilization, is visible and has been scaled up to provide padding for the smooth operation.

Therefore, duplicate the tracked layer and turn off its visibility. Rename it "stabilizer," or something like that. Just to be on the safe side, make it a guide or adjustment layer as well; that way, there's no possibility of it rendering should its visibility inadvertently be enabled. Figure 8.27 shows this preparation on the example shot; remember that 3D should be enabled for this added layer.

There are a couple of ways to apply smoothing to the motion data of the camera:

▶ Use The Smoother (**Figure 8.28**)

▶ Use a smooth expression (**Figure 8.29**)

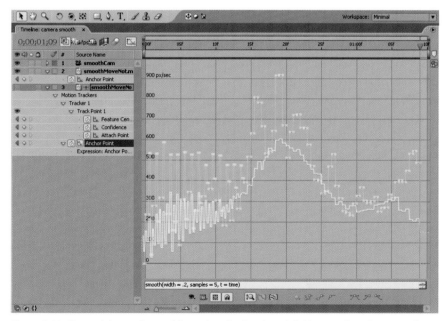

Figure 8.28 Avoid The Smoother! It is a relic from the pre-expressions days of After Effects. Behold its lack of adjustments! Original keyframes are destroyed, replaced by a hodgepodge of (fewer) new ones.

Figure 8.29 Ah, much better: Source (ghosted vertices) and result (white curve) motion are easily compared and adjusted after the fact, by changing those little numbers in between the parentheses, which are known as arguments (Chapter 10 tells more about working with these).

I advise the latter option. The main problem with The Smoother is that it's a one-shot deal: Once you've applied it, you can undo or delete it, but you cannot adjust it. The Smoother is a destructive edit: It changes the keyframe data to which it is applied. Even if you want to adjust it, there is only one setting, for Tolerance; only by trial and error can you know how that setting will influence the track. Expressions are completely nondestructive and offer several adjustable properties.

To apply a `smooth` expression

1. Alt/Option-click on the Anchor Point stopwatch of the layer to which the camera is parented.

2. With the default expression (`anchorPoint`) still highlighted, go to the Expressions menu (**Figure 8.30**) and under Property choose the smooth default: `smooth(width = .2, samples = 5, t = time)`.

In many cases, this default setting will do the trick. If it doesn't, try changing the width value from the default of 0.2, which is the width of time sampled (raising it will use a larger sampled area but take longer), or increase samples from 5 (increase the number of samples within the specified time) for more smoothing. The final argument, `t = time`, is not applicable unless you need to offset the smoothing function in time for some reason.

NOTES

If the very idea of expressions and arguments appears to be sheer gobbledygook, take a look at Chapter 10, then revisit this section.

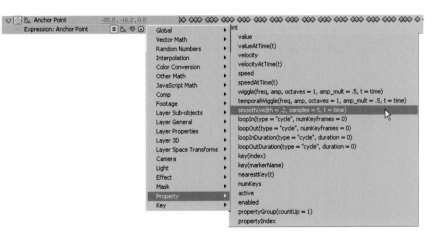

Figure 8.30 No need to type—not much, anyhow—because the expression you need is waiting for you in this menu, and the default arguments are fine in this case.

What about rotation? In the example, the amount of rotation is negligible, but with a shot containing unwanted rotation, you can stabilize it, then either smooth it or eliminate it altogether by deleting keyframes from the Rotation property of the invisible parent layer (leaving them in the visible layer).

To composite other layers into this now smoother scene, and have them share the smooth motion: Toggle their 3D switches and parent them to the smoothed layer. You're golden, as we like to say in the Golden State.

Extending a Track with Expressions

Has your track point disappeared in the middle of the shot? Perhaps it is part of an object that moves off-screen. Or it's possible that your track point was completely obscured for several frames, during which the tracker was unable to extrapolate motion.

Other effects software might include a built-in option for continuing the track, but in After Effects, a simple expression will do it. This works properly only when the tracked item travels more or less steadily in more or less a linear direction. A classic example is a character or object crossing frame: Any point you track may exit (or enter) frame early (or late) compared to the target (**Figure 8.31**). This shot appears in the 08_tracking.aep composition on your disc.

TIP

The same basic approach can destabilize, rather than smooth, a camera motion. Because the expression involved requires a bit of tweaking, discussion is punted to Chapter 10.

Figure 8.31 The door handle of the taxi is an effective track target, but to replace the sign on top of the cab, the track must extend beyond this frame (after which the door handle exits frame) Note that the track points are fairly evenly spaced, making this a good candidate for continuing the track.

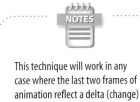

Following is the simple trick to extend a Position track; for a more thorough explanation of what's going on, and variations on the theme (looping incoming frames, repeating a movement pattern, or looping in *and* looping out) visit Chapter 10.

First make certain there are no unwanted extra tracking keyframes beyond the point where the point was still correctly tracked; this expression uses the difference between the final two keyframes to estimate what will happen next.

Reveal the property that needs extending (Position in this case), and Alt/Option-click on its stopwatch. In the text field that is revealed, replace the text (`position`), typing in `loopOut("continue")`. Yes, that's right, typing; don't worry, you're not less of an artist for doing it (**Figure 8.32**).

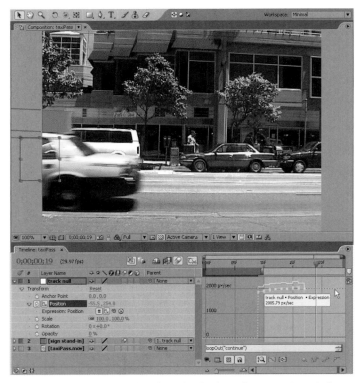

Figure 8.32 The raspberry-colored stand-in for the replacement sign exits frame with the tracking null below it. In the Graph Editor, the dotted line shows that the expression is maintaining a steady Position change of around 2000 pixels per second.

Tracking for Rotoscoping

Other compositing programs, such as Apple's Shake, allow you to track mask vertices, something that is not directly possible in After Effects. So you should give up on the idea of trying to make rotoscoping easier using the tracker, right?

Wrong, of course. I feel a little sheepish writing something so obvious amongst more advanced After Effects tips, but the number of times I've seen fellow artists overlook situations where the tracker would help compels me to bring this up.

Although you cannot track individual mask points to animate an articulated mask, you'll encounter numerous cases where precise tracking is required but the matte retains a more or less constant shape. For example, you might want to add a traveling garbage matte for a green-screen shot with a moving camera, and one of its edges should be tightly tracked to a boundary on the set.

The figures in this section feature a shot in which exactly this was the case. If the front boundary of the garbage matte were not precisely tracked, distracting chatter would result.

Although it's true that there's no way to apply track data (or any transform data) directly to masks, you can work around the problem, as long as you're not actually attempting to articulate the masks using the tracker. Here's how:

Silhouette FX (www.silhouettefx.com) offers a plug-in with an integrated motion tracker for applying motion data to mask points.

1. Line up a solid (with or without a mask) to mask out the layer (**Figures 8.33a** and **b**).

2. Track the background plate and apply the track to the solid. Reposition it (either selecting all Position keys or using the anchor point values) as needed.

3. Apply this masked solid as an alpha track matte to the layer you're masking (**Figure 8.34**).

Once you get it working, you may actually enjoy creating garbage mattes, thanks to this extra boost of automation.

Figures 8.33a and b This plate requires garbage mattes on all sides (a), but the precision of the front edge is essential as the shot dollies in (down the rails). The first step is just to add a solid where the front edge of the action area should be (b). (Baseball images courtesy Tim Fink Events & Media.)

Figure 8.34 The tracking keyframes applied to the alpha matte layer can be seen moving vertically, holding it in place as the shot dollies in.

Paint, of course, is a different story and a much simpler situation once you're comfortable with the basics of expressions. Each paint stroke contains its own transform properties, including a Position property, separate from the layer's Position property. Using the pickwhip, you can link this property directly to tracking data. (For more details, see "Tracking Brushes and Effects" in Chapter 10.)

Using 3D Tracking Data

2D tracking is, of course, only the beginning of the story. After Effects added tracking prior to supporting 3D, but as of yet it does not include a dedicated 3D tracker, in which the result of the track is a virtual 3D camera, rather than 2D tracking data. Fortunately, you can easily work with 3D tracking data created in a separate application, such as 2D3's Boujou or RealViz MatchMover Pro.

After Effects does not work with 3D mesh objects, of course (as one Adobe developer says, it's "postcards in space"), so the workflow with true 3D tracking usually goes like this:

1. Track the scene with a 3D tracking application. This generates 3D camera data, typically exportable in various 3D formats. It should also generate such helpful elements as nulls corresponding to the track points and an axis centered on the "floor," the ground plane of the shot.

2. Import the camera data into a 3D animation program and render 3D elements (assuming there are computer-generated animations to add; you may, instead, only need to composite in 3D, in After Effects).

3. Import the camera data into After Effects, and finish the scene, integrating the plate, rendered 3D elements, and any 2D elements or final touches (adjustment layers tracked in 3D, separate passes of lights and shadows, whatever you need), all matched to the 3D camera in After Effects.

Figure 8.35 shows the final result from the baseball plate; the camera follows the pitch all the way to the plate, where the batter hits it out of the park (of course). This shot is a complete mishmash of 2D and 3D elements. The ball, field, and front of the stands are computer generated, but the crowd was lifted from footage of an actual game.

Figure 8.36 shows a completely different type of shot that also began with a 3D track in Boujou. The fires that you see in the after shot are actually dozens of individual 2D fire and smoke layers, staggered and angled in 3D space as the camera flies over to give the sense of perspective. You'll find more on this shot and how it was set up in Chapter 14, "Pyrotechnics: Fire, Explosions, and Energy Phenomena."

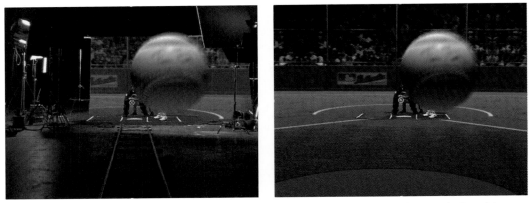

Figure 8.35 True 3D tracking (done in 2D3's Boujou for this shot) is essential to this composite because the feet of the characters must be locked to the computer-generated ground, and a camera on dolly tracks wobbles and bounces. The full shot follows the ball to the plate.

Figure 8.36 Just because you're placing elements in a supposedly "2D" program such as After Effects doesn't mean you can't stagger them all over 3D space to give the illusion of depth, as with this fly-by shot. Tracking nulls from Boujou helped get the relative scale of the scene, important because the depth of the elements had to be to exact scale for the parallax illusion to work. (Final fire image courtesy ABC-TV.)

Working with 3D Tracking Data

Many people don't realize that After Effects can import Maya scenes (.ma files). The only elements that are imported are the rendering cameras, including all translation and lens data (even animated zooms) and nulls that are in the scene. The camera data should be "baked," which is Maya parlance meaning that it should have a keyframe at every frame (search on "baking Maya camera data" in the online help for specifics on this).

3D trackers operate a bit differently than the After Effects tracker. Generally you do not begin by setting tracking points with these; instead, the software creates a swarm of hundreds of points that come and go throughout the shot, and it "solves" the camera using a subset of them. These points correspond to details in the scene and are saved as nulls; there may be hundreds of them. Some of these are useful in After Effects, because they show the position of a recognizable feature.

Besides Position and Rotation, the Camera may also contain Zoom keyframes. Unless Sergio Leone has started making spaghetti westerns again when you read this, zoom shots are the exception rather than the norm and any zoom animation should be checked against a camera report (or any available anecdotal data) and eliminated if bogus. Most 3D trackers allow you to specify whether the shot was taken with a prime lens, in which case zoom is automatically locked.

Importing a Maya Scene

You import a .ma scene the same way you would any element; make sure it has the .ma extension to be recognized properly. After Effects will import either one or two compositions: one for a Maya project with a square pixel aspect ratio, and two for nonsquare (a square pixel version is nested in the nonsquare one).

Your camera may be *single-node* (in which case the camera holds all of the animation data) or *targeted*, in which case the transformation data resides in a parent node to which the camera is attached.

Depending on your tracker and your scene, you may import so many nulls with the scene that it becomes cumbersome. A composition with 500 layers, even nulls, quickly becomes unwieldy, so if possible, weed out the useless nulls, paring it down to a couple dozen of them (descriptively named) in the tracking software or 3D program. It's usually easy to make out what the nulls correspond to in the scene if you watch them over the background plate; they tend to cluster around certain objects.

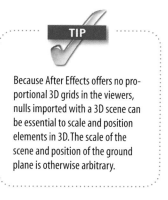

Because After Effects offers no proportional 3D grids in the viewers, nulls imported with a 3D scene can be essential to scale and position elements in 3D. The scale of the scene and position of the ground plane is otherwise arbitrary.

Do you use Maxon's Cinema 4D? Instead of exporting a .ma scene, this software offers its own support for After Effects integration via a plug-in available from Maxon (www.maxon.net).

Need to deal with all of those nulls in After Effects? Once you find the dozen or two that are useful to you in the scene, select those in the Timeline along with the camera and its parent null (if any). Context-click on the selected layers and choose Invert Selection to select the potentially hundreds of other unused nulls. Delete them.

Try It Out for Yourself

If you'd like to try out a 3D tracker, look no further than the book's DVD-ROM. It includes a demo of SynthEyes, a reasonably priced 3D tracker from Andersson Technologies that has been used on feature films (**Figure 8.37**). For about the cost of a typical After Effects plug-in set, you can own your own 3D tracking software (Mac or Windows). The demo is the full version but with a time limit, and projects cannot be saved, so you must execute and export your track start to finish before quitting. The output data, however, is fully usable.

There are also sample files to try out before you create a scene of your own. You may have luck simply importing your shot into SynthEyes, clicking Full Automatic, and exporting the result as AfterEffects via .ma. If there's more involved in getting a good track, however, you will need to learn a bit more about how the software works, and it's beyond the scope of this chapter to document it. SynthEyes is the type of application that yields much better results if you carefully read the online documentation, which is available from the Help menu.

TIP

To learn more about the complex art of match moving, check out *Matchmoving: The Invisible Art of Camera Tracking* (Sybex Inc.) by Tim Dobbert, a colleague from The Orphanage.

Figure 8.37 This tracking data (including nulls) began as a Maya (.ma) scene file created by SynthEyes 3D tracker. The square nulls serve as references for layer placement. This scene is available for download from www.ssontech.com if you want to try it yourself.

Conclusion

Despite all attempts to make it standardized and automatic, tracking remains as much art as it is science, which is probably why most large effects facilities retain a staff of match movers. Even if you've understood everything in this chapter and followed along closely, working on your own shots will open a process of trial and error.

The next chapter will delve further into the ways in which After Effects can replicate what a physical camera can do, expanding on some of the concepts touched on earlier in the "Optimizing Tracking via 3D" section.

Virtual Cinematography

A film is never really good unless the camera is an eye in the head of a poet.

—Orson Welles

Virtual Cinematography

As visual effects artists, we strive not only to re-create the natural world realistically, but also the camera's view of the world. These goals are by no means the same. The camera sees only a limited piece of the world, and from a specific perspective.

Capturing a scene from this perspective requires a host of decisions that constitute a full-blown storytelling art known as cinematography. After Effects offers compositors the opportunity to re-create and even change some of these decisions, long after the crew has struck the set and called it a wrap. The title of the chapter may seem grandiose, given how many fundamental cinematographic choices are out of reach to compositors, but thinking like a director of photography and understanding the workings of the camera are the goals if you're going to fool the viewer into believing your effects shot.

This far-reaching chapter deals with several aspects of replicating a physical camera in After Effects and matching, influencing, or changing the camera's perspective; you can

- ▶ Take control of the After Effects 3D Camera to replicate the settings of a physical real-world camera
- ▶ Interpret, manage, and re-create other effects of using a film or video camera, including grain and lens distortion
- ▶ Make 2D source appear three dimensional
- ▶ Re-create both the look of camera blur and the effects of depth of field in the camera
- ▶ Explore the looks of different cameras, including the fundamental distinctions between film and video

These seemingly disparate points all involve understanding how the camera sees the world and how film and video record what the camera sees. All of them transcend mere aesthetics, influencing how the viewer perceives the story itself.

2.5D: Pick Up the Camera

What if you could pick up a camera and move it around a world of objects that were flat and two dimensional, yet were related to one another and to a virtual camera in 3D space? As was touched upon near the end of the previous chapter, that's pretty much the dimensional model After Effects offers you. You might call it a "2.5D" world, comprised of objects that can exist anywhere but have no depth of their own.

There are a lot of fun, stylized ways to play around with 3D in After Effects, but there are also ways in which you can get the After Effects 3D camera to match the behavior of a real camera, if you understand how they are similar and how they differ. Therefore it's worth taking a closer look at how 3D works in After Effects, and how its various features—the camera, lights, and shading options—correspond to their real world counterparts.

Understand the After Effects Camera

You can begin using 3D in After Effects without setting a camera—just toggle a layer to 3D and *voila*, its properties contain three axes instead of two—but it's a little bit like driving a race track using a car with an automatic transmission: You can't maneuver properly, and before long you'll probably run into something hard.

Furthermore, when you set a camera, you encounter an area of the After Effects user interface that includes a physical diagram: the Camera Settings dialog (**Figure 9.1**). If you understand it, the diagram and its settings tell you virtually everything you need to know about how the After Effects camera views the 3D world.

One confusing point about After Effects' virtual camera is its use of lens settings that correspond to those of still SLR (single lens reflex) cameras, which really aren't used a whole lot in film and video production.

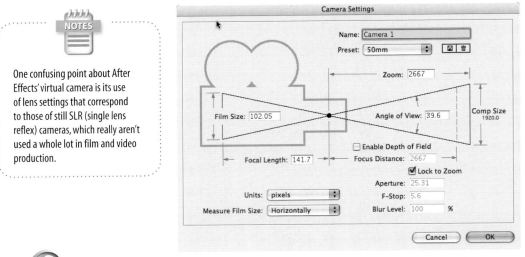

Figure 9.1 Visual artists love visual user interfaces, and the Camera Settings dialog is one of the few to include a diagram. That's a good thing because it also contains a lot of settings that most users find a bit abstract. Here are the default settings for a 50 mm preset, which happens to be the setting that introduces no change of lens angle from a flat 2D view.

7.0 View Options

Version 7.0 makes working in 3D easier than previous versions. At the bottom of the Composition viewer is a View Layout pull-down menu allowing you to select multiple views in a single viewer. These can be used for 2D compositions, but their real use is to allow you to see several 3D angles simultaneously. Click in each viewer and you'll see the 3D View pop-up change its context to that view; small yellow triangles in the corners show you which view is active.

At the bottom of the View Layout options is a Share View Options toggle; this causes all viewers to use the same Fast Previews settings (for OpenGL and so on).

In Grid and Guide options you can choose to display 3D Reference Axes; although After Effects does not display full 3D grids, these can help orient you.

Finally, if you're having difficulty seeing wireframes for cameras and lights, check the settings for Camera Wireframes and Spotlight Wireframes in the Composition panel menu's View Options.

Lens Settings

The default After Effects camera employs the 50 mm preset (listed in the Preset pull-down menu in the Camera Settings dialog; you see this when you create a new camera, or when you choose Layer > Camera Settings). Switching all of your layers to 3D, then adding this camera does not change the appearance of the scene whatsoever, whereas all other lengths do.

Unfortunately, "50 mm" is a "virtually meaningless" term because virtual space doesn't contain millimeters any more than it contains kilograms, parsecs, or bunny rabbits. Virtual space, as you know, is typically measured in pixels.

Any physical camera has a corresponding lens length that would be considered neither long nor wide; its size varies with the size of the image gathering medium or device. Such a lens will capture a scene without shifts in perspective and distortion, features—not all of them displeasing—associated with lenses that are wider or longer, tending respectively more toward the fisheye or telephoto perspective (**Figures 9.2** through **9.4**).

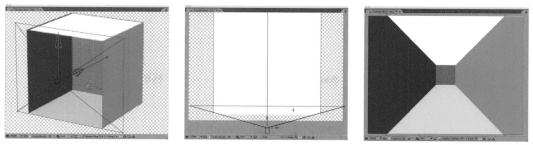

Figure 9.2 The extreme wide or *fisheye* lens pointed inside an evenly proportioned 3D box. Note that the "long" look of the box is created by this "wide" lens, which tends to create very strange proportions at this extreme. A physical lens with anything like this angle would include extremely distorted lens curvature.

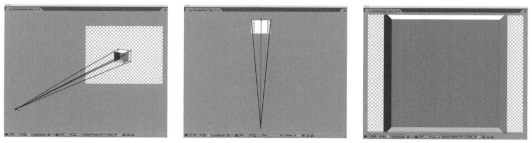

Figure 9.3 A telephoto lens (using the 200 mm setting) pushes items together in depth space, shortening the distance between the front and back of the box dramatically.

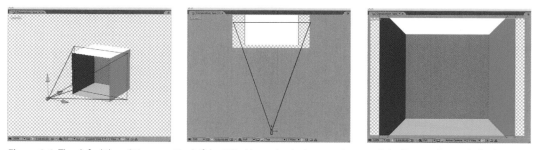

Figure 9.4 The default lens (50 mm setting). If the Z Position value is the exact inverse of the Zoom value, and all other settings are at the default, this is the view you get, and it matches the appearance of setting no After Effects camera whatsoever.

50 millimeters is the median lens length of a 35 mm SLR still camera, as has been used for professional photography for decades. SLR cameras are familiar to a wider audience (including After Effects developers, evidently) than professional film or video cameras.

On a feature film, your source would much more likely have been shot with a 35 mm motion picture camera shooting Academy ratio, a completely different beast that just so

How many movies have been shot predominantly using an SLR camera? Not many; *La Jetée*, a 1962 science fiction film by Chris Marker was the inspiration for Terry Gilliam's movie *12 Monkeys*, and consists entirely of still shots that were presumably taken with a 35 mm camera.

There is an optional fifth numerical field in the Camera Settings diagram, indirectly related to the other four: Focus Distance, which is enabled by checking Enable Depth of Field. This corresponds to a camera's aperture setting; I'll touch on it separately later.

happens to employ a 35 mm default lens length. Had your footage been shot with a miniDV camera, however, the tiny CCD would employ an equally tiny default lens length of around 4 millimeters. The appearance of different lens lengths is directly related to the size of the backplate or video pickup, the area where the image is projected inside the camera. The smaller the film size (or CCD size), the shorter the default lens.

My point is that millimeters don't mean a whole lot unless they're measuring the actual physical lens of an actual physical camera. The only setting in the Camera Settings that truly, universally applies, whether images were shot in IMAX or HDV or created in a 3D animation package, is the Angle of View.

Real-World Camera Settings

The most important question is: How do the After Effects camera's settings correspond to those of a camera in the physical world? In other words, suppose you know a camera's settings, how do you put them to use in your shot?

Look again at the diagram in Camera Settings (Figure 9.1). Four numerical fields—Film Size, Focal Length, Zoom, and Angle of View—are oriented around two triangles sharing a common hypotenuse. Using a physical camera with a prime lens, these values are all fixed. With a zoom lens, the Film Size is of course fixed, but Zoom and Focal Length can be adjusted, resulting in a change in the Angle of View. These four settings, then, are interrelated and interdependent, as the diagram implies.

The After Effects camera simulates this setup: Change one of Angle of View, Zoom, or Focal Length, and the other two values change proportionally, while Film Size remains fixed. Film Size is useful only to emulate a specific camera (more about that in a moment).

Lengthen the lens, and Focal Length increases as Angle of View decreases. A physical telephoto lens really is longer from lens to back plate, and adjusting its zoom does make the lens longer or shorter. The only feature that would make this diagram any clearer would be for it to articulate, visually displaying the changing Angle of View settings as clearly as can be seen (particularly in the top views) in Figures 9.2 through 9.4.

Make Your Adjustments

The only two settings that must hold your focus (pun only slightly intended) are Zoom (for animation) and Angle of View (to match source where that measurement is available). The others, Film Size and Focal Length, make sense only relative to those two.

Angle of View is the actual radius, in degrees, that the camera sees. The setting corresponds directly to real-world cameras, and Angle of View is a setting you will see in other computer graphics programs, so it can be matched precisely in 3D animation software.

The Zoom value is the distance of the camera lens, in pixels, from the plane of focus (generally, the subject being photographed). By default, a new camera employs a Z Position value equivalent to the negative of its Zoom value. This retains framing of all layers at the default Z position of 0.0 (the appearance doesn't change switching from 2D to 3D). The plane of focus icon represents an area the size of the composition (**Figure 9.5**) so it can be used to frame a shot.

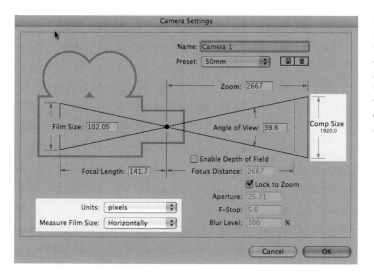

Figure 9.5 It's easy to overlook the highlighted settings. Comp Size (at the right) is the horizontal size, in pixels; it changes according to how Units and Measure Film Size settings are set (left). Comp Size appears to display a vertical measurement (the diagram does not change according to the Measure Film Size setting).

There are several cases in which it is ideal that the Zoom value is in pixels. It makes for easy reference when measuring depth of field effects, and it makes it possible to link the position of the camera and the zoom together via expressions for depth of field and related effects (discussed later).

Emulate a Real Camera

And how do you put all of this knowledge to work? You probably have one of two goals: Either you're matching the camera settings of source footage so that your elements appear to have been taken with that camera, or you're creating a shot from scratch but want it to appear as if shot with a particular camera and lens. Here are some of the things you have to consider:

- ▶ **Depth of Field:** Is everything in the shot in focus, or does the shot require a narrow depth of field with elements in the foreground and background drifting out of focus?

- ▶ **Zoom or push:** If you are moving in or out on the shot, which type of camera move is it (discussed further in the section called "Move the Camera")?

- ▶ **Motion blur and shutter angle:** These settings are not controlled via the 3D camera. (They're composition settings—for more, review Chapter 2, "The Timeline.")

- ▶ **Lens angle and distortion:** The perspective and parallax of layers in 3D space change according to the angle of the lens used to view them. Real lenses introduce *lens distortion*, curvature that can be especially apparent with wide angle lenses (hence the term "fisheye lens"). The After Effects camera does not employ a lens and so, does not generate lens distortion, but it can be recreated (see "Optics Compensation").

- ▶ **Exposure:** New to After Effects 7.0 is the Exposure control, which appears in the Composition viewers of a 32 bpc project. Exposure in After Effects is similar, yet completely different from that of a real camera. Suffice it to say that exposure is not related to the 3D camera, and you should see Chapter 11, "Film, HDR, and 32 Bit Per Channel Composition," for theoretical understanding, and Chapter 12, "Working with Light," for practical examples.

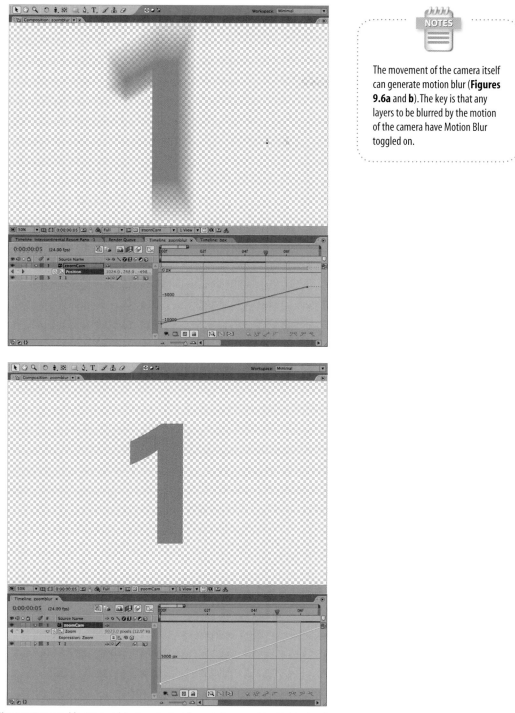

Figures 9.6a and b Motion blur is activated for a stationary object (a), but only the camera moves. Zooming the camera instead generates no motion blur (b).

One specific piece of information that can help you match existing footage is a camera report, a record of the settings used when the footage was taken. If the crew included a camera assistant (or equivalent), this information was probably logged at the shoot.

Make Use of a Camera Report

If you know the type of camera and the focal length used for your shots, you have enough information to match the lens of that camera with your After Effects camera.

Table 9.1 details the sizes of some typical film formats. If your camera is on the list, and you know the focal length, use these to match the camera via Camera Settings. The steps are

1. Set Measure Film Size to Horizontally.

2. Set Units to Inches.

3. Enter the number from the Horizontal column of the chart that corresponds to the source film format.

4. Set Units to Millimeters.

5. Enter the desired Focal Length.

Once the Angle of View matches the footage, any objects that you track in (perhaps using techniques described in Chapter 8, "Effective Motion Tracking") will maintain position in the scene as the shot progresses. It's vital to get this right if your camera is going to move during the shot, and especially if a wide or long lens was used.

Lens Distortion

If a virtual camera is set with a wide lens angle, the software simply samples a wider (and taller) area of the scene, as in Figure 9.2. This dramatically changes the perspective of 3D space, but it does not actually distort objects the way a real camera lens does because a digital camera uses no lens. A virtual camera can widen the view area and scan it in a linear fashion.

A lens curves light to project it properly on the camera backplate. A real camera cannot simply widen its view area,

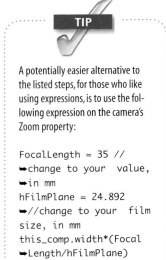

TIP

A potentially easier alternative to the listed steps, for those who like using expressions, is to use the following expression on the camera's Zoom property:

```
FocalLength = 35 //
➥change to your  value,
➥in mm
hFilmPlane = 24.892
➥//change to your  film
size, in mm
this_comp.width*(Focal
➥Length/hFilmPlane)
```

TABLE 9.1 Typical Film Format Sizes

Format	Horizontal	Vertical
Full Aperture Camera Aperture	0.980	0.735
Scope Camera Aperture	0.864	0.732
Scope Scan	0.825	0.735
2:1 Scope Projector Aperture	0.838	0.700
Academy Camera Aperture	0.864	0.630
Academy Projector Aperture	0.825	0.602
1.66 Projector Aperture	0.825	0.497
1.85 Projector Aperture	0.825	0.446
VistaVision Aperture	0.991	1.485
VistaVision Scan	0.980	1.470
16 mm Camera Aperture	0.404	0.295
Super-16 Camera Aperture	0.493	0.292
HD Full 1.78	0.378	0.212 (Full Aperture in HD 1.78)
HD 90% 1.78	0.340	0.191 (90% Safe Area used in HD 1.78)
HD Full 1.85	0.378	0.204 (Full Aperture in HD 1.85)
HD 90% 1.85	0.340	0.184 (90% Safe Area used in HD 1.85)
HD Full 2.39	0.3775	0.158 (Full Aperture in HD 2.39)
HD 90% 2.39	0.340	0.142 (90% Safe Area used in HD 2.39)

Courtesy Stu Maschwitz/The Orphanage

which is essentially fixed. It can only "see" what is perpendicular to the surface of the lens glass, so it combines a convex lens and a short lens length to pull a more disparate (wider) range of view.

At the extremes, this causes lens distortion that is easily visible; items in the scene known to contain straight lines don't appear straight at all, but bent in a curve (**Figure 9.7**). In a fisheye lens shot, it's as if the screen has been inflated like a balloon. It's rare, but not unprecedented, for a shot in a movie to look like this (for example, the droid's point of view in a certain well-known science fiction film).

Figure 9.7 The almost psychedelic look of lens distortion at its most extreme; even the flare caused by the front lens element is extremely aberrated. An equivalently wide lens using the After Effects 3D camera would not cause straight lines (the ground plane, the building outline) to appear curved.

Figures 9.8a and b In a close-up area of a shot (a), an attempt to corner-pin a yellow solid to the side of the building fails; it is not possible to make all four corners and edges line up properly. Grid lines over footage of the bus clearly show that it is distorted—note the bowed appearance of straight lines on the pavement, and the background building (b). (Building examples courtesy Stu Maschwitz; bus footage courtesy Pixel Corps.)

As you gain experience evaluating shots, you may notice that many shots that aren't as extreme as a fisheye perspective contain a degree of lens distortion. You might notice that motion tracks from one side of the frame don't seem to apply equally well at the other side of the frame, proportions go out of whack, and things don't quite line up as they should (**Figures 9.8a** and **b**).

There's no way to introduce lens distortion directly to a 3D camera, but the Optics Compensation effect (Professional version only) is designed to add or remove it in 2D. **Figure 9.9** shows this effect in action. Increasing the Field of View makes the affected layer more fisheyed in appearance; to correct a shot coming in with lens distortion, check Reverse Lens Distortion and raise the Field of View (FOV) value.

This process is not exactly scientific because the Field of View settings don't correspond to measurable phenomena, such as the Lens Angle. You must locate what should be a straight line in the scene and adjust the setting until you're happy with the match. The specific workflow is

1. Having identified that there is lens distortion on a background plate to which you must add foreground elements (as in Figure 9.8a), drop the background into

a new composition that is at least 20% larger than the plate to accommodate stretching the corners.

2. Add an adjustment layer above the plate layer, and apply Optics Compensation to that layer. Check Reverse Lens Distortion and raise the Field of View (FOV) setting until lines that should appear straight in your image look straight.

3. Add a Beam effect below the Optics Compensation effect (so that it is unaffected by Optics Compensation). Make its Inside Color and Outside Color settings match (using any color you'll be able to see easily), and align the Starting Point and Ending Point along an apparently straight line near the edge of frame. Fine-tune the Field of View setting a little more until the line is plumb (**Figures 9.9a** and **b**).

Figures 9.9a and b Distortion removal takes place in a composition larger than the source; the padding allows space for the corners of the image. In the building image, the Beam effect serves as a virtual plumb line (a); with the bus, it is clear from the grid that distortion has been corrected (b).

4. Precompose all of these layers and set this new composition as a guide layer. In **Figure 9.10**, you can see that the corner pin is now successful. You must now match the distortion of the source shot.

5. Create a new master composition containing the background plate and the laid-out foreground elements. Copy Optics Compensation from the adjustment layer where you undistorted the background and paste it to the foreground element but turn off Reverse Lens Distortion. The exact distortion of your background is applied to your foreground elements, which now match up (**Figure 9.11**).

You have tricked After Effects into compositing in distort-o-vision. Here is an original Stu Maschwitz haiku to sum up the process:

> undistort, derive
>
> reunite distorted things
>
> with an untouched plate

Mixing 2D and 3D

Use of a 3D camera in an effects situation typically entails mixing 3D elements and a 2D plate background. This is no big deal, as After Effects doesn't demand an exclusively 2D

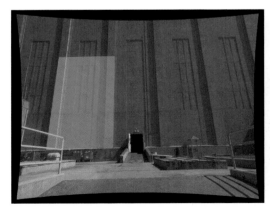

Figure 9.10 Over the undistorted background plate, you can freely position, animate, and composite elements as if everything were normal. Note that the perspective is still that of a very wide angle lens, but without the curvature.

Figure 9.11 The Optics Compensation effect with Reverse Lens Distortion unchecked restores the original look of the frame; the foreground distorts to match the background, and features now line up properly.

or a 3D world; elements of both can be layered together. This is a huge advantage as long as you're clear about how it works:

▶ A 2D background remains in place no matter how you move the camera (as in the motion tracking examples using a 3D camera in the previous chapter).

▶ 2D adjustment layers set to comp size and default position affect the whole composition, including 3D layers.

▶ Foreground layers from 3D programs imported with 3D camera tracking data can be manipulated in 3D while remaining rendered 2D elements.

Everybody wins.

Where are the gotchas of this approach? They are all special cases:

▶ A 2D layer can use a 3D track matte, and vice versa. Beware of combining a 3D track matte and a 3D layer: It's rarely (if ever) what you want, and maintaining the positional relationship relative to the camera is usually tricky. At least one layer typically should be unaffected by camera motion.

▶ Certain effects emulate 3D perspective by making use of the After Effects camera. Typically (and paradoxically) these operate on 2D layers only. Examples include Trapcode's Particular and 3D Stroke (**Figure 9.12**).

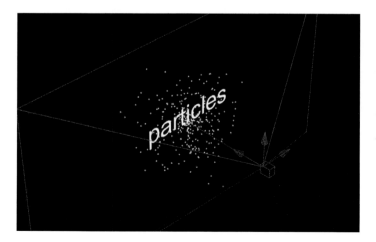

Figure 9.12 Incredibly, particles generated by Trapcode Particular occupy true 3D space, as is evident in a perspective view. Paradoxically, the effect is applied to a 2D layer. It calculates 3D data internally using the After Effects camera as a reference, an elegant workaround for the fact that 3D layers in After Effects are always flat planes.

▶ Precomposing a set of 3D layers effectively causes them to collectively behave like a single 2D layer. They no longer interact in 3D space unless you enable Collapse Transformations for the precomp layer. Doing so bypasses the camera in the embedded composition, and uses the 3D position of the precomposed layers. (More on this in Chapter 4, "Optimizing Your Projects.")

So go ahead, freely mix 2D and 3D layers—just remember these tips if things start to seem funky.

Storytelling and the Camera

A decision as simple as creeping the camera slowly forward can change the whole dramatic feel of a shot. The main limitation you face is the two-dimensionality of After Effects layers, but that's a huge step forward from the bad old days of optical compositing, when it was scarcely possible to move the camera at all.

Nowadays, most directors aren't satisfied with a locked-off camera for effects shots, yet sometimes the decision to move the camera won't be made until the post-production phase. That's no big deal, as long as you don't completely break the rules for what you can get away with.

Specifically, don't worry about planes of motion and parallax for elements that are lost in the background, that are at the edges of the frame, that appear for a few frames only, or that otherwise won't ever be noticed. The "Sky Replacement" section in Chapter 13, "Climate Control: Air, Water, Smoke, and Clouds," contains just such an example, in which a flat card stands in for a fully dimensional skyline; people aren't watching the skyline for shifts in perspective, they're watching the lead character walk through the lobby and wondering what he's got in his briefcase (**Figure 9.13**).

Moving the Camera

You may have worked with a 3D camera in other applications, but the After Effects implementation is unique. For example, the After Effects camera contains Transform options that are unique from all other types of layers (**Figure 9.14**), as well as a couple of hidden features.

TIP

Always keep in mind where the audience's attention is focused—you can employ the magician's technique, misdirection, to get away with something you shouldn't. Robert Rodríguez was only able to make his debut film, *El Mariachi*, with meager funds by knowing that if the audience were to notice its many continuity errors, the story would have been considered a failure.

Figure 9.13 Prominent though it may appear in this still image, the audience is only subliminally aware of what is going on with that skyline outside the window. As the camera pans and tracks to the right, the pyramid building should creep out from behind the foreground skyscraper. It doesn't, because the background skyline is a still image; no one notices because the focus is on the foreground character. (Image courtesy The Orphanage.)

Camera Orientation

The most common confusion about the After Effects camera stems from the fact that by default, it includes a *point of interest*, a point in 3D space at which the camera always points, for auto-orientation. To clarify:

▶ Auto-orientation via a point of interest is *fully optional*. You can turn it off (making the camera a *free* camera) or change it to orient automatically along the path of camera motion. To do so, context-click on the camera, then choose Transform > Auto-Orient or use **Ctrl+Alt+O** (**Cmd+Option+O**) to access the menu of settings (**Figure 9.15**).

▶ To move the camera and its point of interest in sync, don't attempt to match keyframes for the two properties—this is sheer madness! You can parent the camera to a null and translate that instead.

▶ Orientation works differently depending on whether auto-orientation is on (causing it to revolve around the point of interest) or not (in which case it rotates around its center).

▶ The auto-oriented camera flips to remain upright when crossing the X/Y plane while orbiting the center; the free camera does not. The auto-oriented behavior is helpful for beginners positioning a camera, but not for camera animation—don't let it surprise and frustrate you.

Thus the default camera in After Effects includes a point of interest that often must be disabled to maintain or control the direction of the camera as it is translated. This will not come up all the time given that the camera is often put to more modest uses, such as a simple camera push.

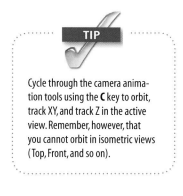

Figure 9.14 Just in case you've never taken a close look, a camera layer contains no Anchor Point, but includes two sets of rotation data: the Orientation (its basic angle), as well as separate X, Y, and Z rotation values (to avoid problems with complex 3D rotations). The point of interest appears only when the default Orient Towards Point of Interest option is active (Figure 9.15).

TIP

Cycle through the camera animation tools using the **C** key to orbit, track XY, and track Z in the active view. Remember, however, that you cannot orbit in isometric views (Top, Front, and so on).

NOTES

The Y axis is upside down in After Effects 3D, just as in 2D; increasing the Y value moves a layer downward. The 0,0 point in After Effects space was placed at the upper-left corner of the frame when it was 2D only, and it was left this way with the addition of 3D for consistency's sake.

Figure 9.15 So many 3D camera tragedies could have been avoided if more users knew about this dialog box (**Ctrl+Alt+O** or **Cmd+Option+O**). By disabling auto-orientation, you are free to move the camera anywhere without changing its direction.

Push versus Zoom

Knowledgeable effects artists understand the huge distinction between a camera push, in which the camera moves closer to the subject, and a zoom, in which the camera stays in place and the lens lengthens.

Figures 9.16a and **b** demonstrate the difference between pushing and zooming a real camera. Zooming changes the actual lens angle, and has more of an effect on the immediate foreground and faraway background framing than a push.

Is the zoom merely out of fashion, or is it truly inferior to the camera push? Keep in mind that a push mimics the human perspective as we move through space; the naked eye has no means to zoom in on anything, so that effect makes us aware we're looking through a camera. You decide.

Figures 9.16a and b The difference between a push in (a) with a wide angle lens and a zoom (b) from a distance is evident particularly by what happens to the placement of the orange ball in the background. Zooming makes its apparent scale much greater; it looms larger in this shot than in an image shot with a wider lens, but close-up.

Most of the time, you will animate a push; zooming in, generally speaking, had its heyday in the era of Sergio Leone. That's a good thing for you, because it is easier to work with a static lens angle. The relationship and perspective of objects close-up do not change with a push the way they do with a zoom.

Push It Good

Suppose a shot calls for a push in on a 2D composition. Is it worth adding a 3D camera, or can you simply scale the 2D layers?

Animation > Keyframe Assistant > Exponential Scale is the old-school, pre-3D way to fake the illusion of a camera move in on a 2D layer. There is no good reason to employ this feature when you can instead animate a 3D camera.

A scale is too linear to achieve the illusion of moving in Z space with anything but the smallest move; as you draw closer to an object, its rate of scaling must increase logarithmically. Moreover, a 3D camera lets you add eases, stops and starts, a little bit of destabilization—whatever works for the shot.

Camera motion will appear more natural with keyframe eases (Chapter 2), which can add the impression that there was a human camera operator behind the lens. You may choose to augment the default eases with a little extra hesitation or irregularity to lend that feeling of a camera operator's individual personality (**Figure 9.17**).

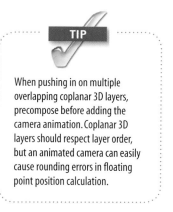

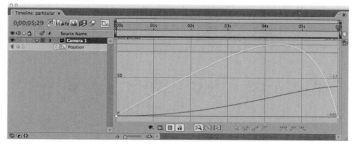

Figure 9.17 A simple camera animation can be finessed simply by applying Easy Ease (highlight keyframes and press **F9**), but why stop there? Lengthening the curve of the first keyframe gives the camera added (realistic) inertia transitioning from a static position.

A move in or out of a 2D shot can easily look wrong due to the lack of parallax, unless it's subtle or contains few depth cues. Tracking and panning shots, crane-ups, and other more elaborate camera moves will blow the 2.5D gag unless they remain rather minute. When in doubt, rough it in and ask a neutral observer (or supervisor) if it looks believable.

You can get away with more layering soft, translucent organic shapes, such as clouds, fog, smoke, and the like. Staggering these in 3D space, you can fool the eye into seeing 3D volume where there are only planes (more on this in Chapter 13).

Camera Projection

Camera projection (or *camera mapping*) is the process of taking a still photo, projecting it onto 3D objects that match the dimensions and placement of objects in the photo, and then moving the camera—typically only along the Z axis—providing the illusion that the photo is fully dimensional (right up until the camera move goes too far, revealing some area of the image that wasn't part of the photograph).

Figures 9.18a, **b**, and **c** show a camera projection that ambitiously features two parked military vehicles in the foreground. A dozen separate white solids with masks were created to form a crude 3D model, ready to receive a projected image (**Figure 9.19**). This example shows both the magic of this technique—deriving perspective shifts from a flat, still image—and the associated problems of image tearing when an area of the frame is revealed that had previously been obscured in the source photo.

The key to this effect is the setup: How is it that the one "texture" of the image (the photo) sticks to the 3D objects? The fundamental concept is actually relatively simple; getting it right is a question of managing details, and that part is fairly advanced and not for the faint of heart (which is why mention of a third-party option follows this

Figures 9.18a, b, and c The progression from the source image (a) through the camera move. By the final frame(c), image warping and tearing are evident, but the perspective of the image is essentially correct for the new camera position. The tearing occurs simply because as the camera moves it reveals areas of the image that don't exist in the source.

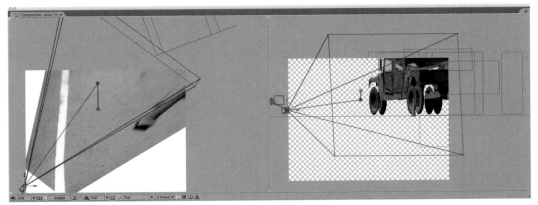

Figure 9.19 The rather complicated setup for this effect: from the top and side views you can see the planes that stand in for the vehicles and orange cone, which appears stretched along the ground plane.

description). The steps to projecting any still image into 3D space (an example of which , 09_cameraProjection.aep) can be found on the disc) are as follows:

1. Begin with an image that can be modeled as a series of planes.

2. Create a white solid for each dimensional plane in the image. Enable 3D for each, and under Material Options, change the Accepts Lights option to Off.

3. Add a camera named Projection Cam; if you know the Angle of View of your source image, add that value.

4. Add a Point light called Projector Light. Set its position to that of Projection Cam, then parent it to Projection Cam. Set Casts Shadows to On.

5. Duplicate the source image, naming this layer Slide. Enable 3D, and in Material Options, change Casts Shadows to Only and Light Transmission to 100%.

6. Slide not located properly? Add a null object called Slide Repo; set its position to that of Projection Cam, and parent it to Projection Cam. Now parent Slide to it, and adjust its scale downward until the image is cast onto the white planes, as if projected.

7. Now comes the painful part: masking, scaling, and repositioning those white solids to build the model, ground plane, and horizon onto which the slide is projected. Toggle on the reference layer and build your model to match that, checking it with the slide every so often.

8. If planes that you know to be at perpendicular 90 degree angles don't line up, you need to adjust the Zoom value of the Projection Cam, scaling the model and slide as needed to match the new Zoom value. The example file includes an expression applied to the Scale value of the slide layer so that the slide scales up or down to match however you adjust the Zoom of the camera, which is not necessary but is helpful.

9. Once everything is lined up, duplicate Projection Cam, and rename the duplicate (the one on the higher layer) Anim Cam. Freely move this camera to take advantage of the new dimensional reality of the scene.

The best way to learn about this is probably to study the example file included on this book's disc; if it seems enticing rather than aggravating, feel free to give it a whirl.

Camera Blur

Real cameras blur images in unique and specific ways when areas of the image fall out of focus. This is not always seen as a flaw; it has practical purposes, such as narrowing the audience's attention. Hence a *rack focus* shot, in which the focus changes from a figure in the background to one in the foreground, or vice versa, is a fully fledged storytelling tool for a cinematographer.

Like the camera, your eye has a limited focal range, so limitations of depth of field are quite natural to vision. Camera lenses additionally contribute their own blur characteristics which many visual artists consider beautiful to behold when shot properly. The Japanese coined a term for the quality of the out-of-focus image, *boke* (also spelled *bokeh*, which is closer to a phonetic spelling).

After Effects 7.0 can help you achieve each of these types of blur, but not both together; new in this version is the addition of the Lens Blur effect from Photoshop, while the 3D camera includes properties that can mimic depth of field with a blurring algorithm that does not re-create lens effects.

Image Planes and Rack Focus

If source footage can easily be divided into planes of depth, you can achieve a rack focus effect that matches the way this effect is achieved in a physical camera. The focal point passes from an object in the foreground to one in the background or vice versa, and the depth of field is narrow enough that only the immediate plane of focus is seen in sharp detail.

With a physical camera, this type of shot requires a narrow depth of field, which is created by lowering the f-stop value. Doing so influences shutter angle and the amount of light passing through the aperture, so the color response and likelihood of motion blur in the shot are affected.

Not so with the After Effects 3D camera, which includes Aperture and F-Stop settings (**Figure 9.20**). These affect only focal depth, not exposure or motion blur. The two settings are tied together, so changing one in the Camera Settings dialog has a nonlinear, inverse effect on the other. F-Stop is the setting more commonly referenced by camera operators, and yet only Aperture appears as a property in the Timeline.

After Effects depth of field settings can be matched to a camera report, provided that it includes the f-stop setting used when the footage was shot. If so, open up the Camera Settings dialog (**Ctrl+Shift+Y/Cmd+Shift+Y**, or click on the Camera in the Timeline panel), check the box labeled Enable Depth of Field, and enter your value for F-Stop.

The key here is to offset at least one layer in Z space so that it falls out of focal range. Now, in the Top view, set the Focus Distance (under Options) to match the layer that will be in focus at the beginning of the shot, add a keyframe, then change the Focus Distance at another frame to match a second layer later in the shot (**Figure 9.21**).

A static focus pull doesn't look quite right; changing focus on a real camera will change the framing of the shot

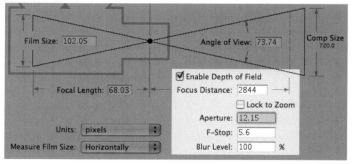

Figure 9.20 Checking Enable Depth of Field in Camera Settings activates Focus Distance (the distance in pixels that is sharply in focus, which can be locked to the Zoom value—note the check box), as well as Aperture and F-Stop, which are two different ways to measure depth of field. A low F-Stop (or high Aperture) with a Blur Level of 100% will create a shallow focal effect.

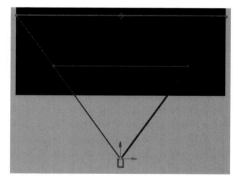

Figure 9.21 With Enable Depth of Field on, the Focus Distance is denoted by a red boundary line, easily viewed and animated in isometric views.

Figure 9.22 The final shot combines a rack focus with a gentle pull-back, using ease keyframes to animate Position and Focus Distance.

slightly. To sell the example shot, which starts on a view of the city and racks focus to reveal a sign in the foreground, I add a slight camera pull-back, which takes advantage of the nice shift in planes of motion from the offset layers (**Figure 9.22**).

Boke Blur

Racking focus in this manner generates camera blur that is accurate relative to the plane of focus, but it does not include the look of a truly defocused lens.

Boke connotes the phenomenon whereby points of light become discs of light (also called *circles of confusion*) that take on the character of the lens itself as they pass through the camera lens and aperture. Like lens flares (covered in Chapter 12) these are a phenomenon of cameras, not human vision; they (subjectively) add beauty and suspense to your shot.

How so? Out of focus elements in a shot are mysterious. We may have a notion of what we are seeing, or we may not (**Figure 9.23**). We remain intrigued as the shot focuses in from a strange wash of color and light (**Figure 9.24**).

What, exactly, causes this phenomenon? A perfect lens passes a defocused point of light to the back of the camera

Figure 9.23 What is that mysterious object? The answer is revealed at the end of this section.

Figure 9.24 Even in the very first, most blurred frame of this pull-back shot, you may have a good idea what you're seeing, yet its appearance is strange and compelling. Note that a few blades of grass in the extreme foreground retain the quality of boke even once most of the shot is in focus.

as a soft, spherical blur. What was a bright point remains bright, but is larger and softer. Simply blurring an image in 8 or 16 bit per channel color mode dims the highlights (**Figures 9.25a**, **b**, and **c**).

Moreover, most camera lenses are not perfect, so you will not see perfect blurred spheres. The digital images in Figure 9.24 show spheres that are brighter toward the edges than in the middle; an anamorphic lens will show squashed spheres, and as with lens flares, the blades of the aperture diaphragm will sometimes be visible in the circles of confusion, making them hexagonal (or pentagonal, and so on, depending on the number of blades in the opening).

Go for Boke

Okay, suppose you have a shot that calls for boke blur. What can be done in After Effects to recreate it?

Chapters 11 and 12 explore ways in which working in 32 bits per channel can help recreate at least one aspect of realistic camera blur—that the hotspots do not dim down as they are blurred, but retain their brightness. This color

Figures 9.25a, b, and c Motion blur generated the standard way (a and b) literally pales in comparison to true motion blur on illuminated elements created by a moving camera (or objects) while the shutter is open (c).

space includes overhead for overbright pixels, and so you can build up and blur super-bright elements in the scene. But this is not all there is to boke.

New to After Effects 7.0 is the Lens Blur effect. This effect does not operate in 32 bpc mode—it is a 16 bpc effect that is designed to fake the effects of boke. Use of the verb "fake" is not meant to imply that there is a preferable "real" method; as with Optics Compensation, this effect recreates phenomena that occur via a physical lens. In other words, on a computer, there is no choice but to fake it.

Lens Blur is a direct port from Photoshop; as such, it has a few flaws when used in After Effects (for example, that it doesn't operate at 32 bpc), and if these become too much, there are third-party options to consider. Its other limitations: You can't blur beyond 100 pixels, and it does not understand non-square pixels (it always creates perfect circles).

Nevertheless, it does include what you need to create some characteristics of Boke blur in 8 and 16 bit per channel projects. **Figure 9.26** shows the effect of Lens Blur on an image with some specular highlights that bloom into hexagonal disks by boosting Specular Brightness and lowering Specular Threshold slightly. If you're working with computer-generated 3D images, you can even specify a depth map, allowing you to choose which areas of the image are in or out of focus.

The most respected third-party tool for lens blurs is Frischluft's Lenscare. The default settings are not reliable, but with adjustments and depth maps (for 3D footage), you can derive some lovely results (www.frischluft.com and on the DVD).

Figure 9.26 Lens Blur doesn't yield a perfect result when cranked up this high, but it does generate the disk shapes around specular highlights characteristic of Boke blur (here, set as hexagons). The result on the larger specular area of the lamp is odd (due to a low threshold of 90%), and there is no repeat edge pixel option, leading to a translucent fringe.

You may not be able to recreate the look of that twenty-dollar bill in Figure 9.23 so easily, but if you pay attention to what happens in these surprising reference images, your camera blur will approach that of a real, defocused camera.

The Role of Grain

Literally beyond lens effects stands another attribute of images shot with a real camera: grain. Grain is essentially high-frequency noise that can be found in each channel of most footage, to varying degrees. Far from being a mere annoyance or problem, grain can be your friend, given its due.

Grain adds texture and life to images and can help to conceal a multitude of small details, enabling compositors to get away with all kinds of stuff (in particular, adding life to a still image source in a moving image composition). Just like depth of field and motion blur, moderate amounts of grain are part of the key to a cinematic look.

For compositors, perhaps the most important role of grain is its role integrating a flat, static layer with moving footage, adding life to an element that otherwise looks oddly suspended out of the time and place of the rest of the scene (**Figure 9.27**).

The day may come when digital cameras can deliver moving footage with no grain whatsoever. Already, high-definition video cameras used to shoot movies pick up clearer detail than film cameras, all other things being equal, and all digital movies that use no footage, such as those by Pixar, also do not employ grain.

Figure 9.27 Solid areas of color without fine detail such as this section of blue screen (zoomed to 800%, blue channel displayed) are the best to sample and evaluate grain. At right of frame is a color-matched solid that evidently fails to blend with the background.

Proper grain is not simply switched on or off, however; it needs to be carefully adjusted. You can become quite theoretical about all this, but really you need to concern yourself with only two basic factors:

- Size of the grain, per channel
- Amount of grain, or amount of contrast in the grain, per channel

The emphasis here is that these factors typically vary from channel to channel. Blue is almost universally the channel likeliest to have the most noise; happily the human eye is less sensitive to blue than red or green, but this can be bad news for blue-screen shoots.

How much grain is enough? As with color in Chapter 5, "Color and Light: Adjusting and Matching," the goal is typically to match what's there already. If your shot has a background plate with the proper amount of grain in it, you match your foreground elements to that. In the case of a fully computer-generated scene, you might have to match surrounding shots that have plate reference, which you would match in the same manner.

Excessive grain is often triggered by a low amount of scene light combined with a low-quality image-gathering medium, such as miniDV, whose CCD has poor light-gathering abilities.

Grain Management Strategies

After Effects Professional includes a suite of three tools for automated grain sampling, grain reduction, and grain generation: Add Grain, Match Grain, and Remove Grain. Add Grain you adjust entirely manually, but Match Grain and Remove Grain sample a noise source layer to give you an initial result that you can then adjust.

If you've been reading closely up to this point, you know I'm not a fan of using the automated solutions. Not so in this case. The Match Grain effect does not seem to be appreciably slower due to grain sampling than Add Grain, which does not perform any sampling and includes all of the same controls. Therefore, I recommend you see what Match Grain can come up with as a starting point, and then work from there. In either case, the steps are the same:

1. Look for a section of your source footage that contains a solid color area and little or no motion for 10 to 20 frames. Most clips include an area satisfying these

criteria, and those that don't tend to let you get away with less precision anyhow.

2. Zoom to 200% to 400% on the solid color area, and create a Region of Interest around it. Set the Work Area to the 10 or 20 frames with little or no motion.

3. Add a solid that is small enough to occupy part of the Region of Interest. Apply a Ramp effect to the solid, and use the eyedropper tools to select the darkest and lightest pixels in the solid color area of the clip. The lack of grain detail in the foreground gradient should be clearly apparent (**Figure 9.28**).

4. Apply the Match Grain effect to the foreground solid. Choose the source footage layer in the Noise Source Layer pull-down. As soon as the effect finishes rendering a sample frame, you have a basis from which to begin fine-tuning. You can RAM Preview at this point to see how close a match you have. In most cases, you're not done yet.

5. Twirl down the Tweaking controls for Match Grain, and then twirl down Channel Intensities and Channel Size. You can save yourself a lot of time by doing most of your work here, channel by channel.

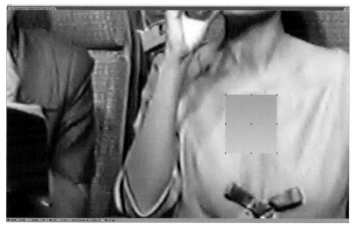

Figure 9.28 Insert a small solid and add a Ramp effect, then use the eyedropper tools in Ramp to sample the brightest and darkest areas of the background. This offers a clear evaluation of a grain match once Match Grain or Add Grain is applied.

CLOSE-UP

Using Noise to Add Grain

Prior to the addition of Add Grain and Match Grain to version 6.5 Professional, the typical way to generate grain was to use the Noise effect. The main advantage of the Noise effect over Match Grain is that it renders about 20x faster. However, After Effects doesn't make it easy for you to separate the effect channel by channel, and scaling it requires a separate effect (or precomposing).

You can employ three solid layers, with three effects applied to each layer: Shift Channels, Noise, and Transform. You use Shift Channels to set each solid to red, green, or blue, respectively, set Blending Modes to Add, and set their Opacity very low (well below 10%, adjusting as needed). Next, set the amount of noise and scale it via the Transform effect.

If the grain is meant to affect a set of foreground layers only, hold them out from the background plate either via precomposing or track mattes. If this sounds complicated, it is, which is why Match Grain is preferable unless the rendering time is going to kill you.

6. Activate the red channel only in the Composition window (**Alt+1**/**Option+1**) and adjust the Red Intensity and Red Size values to match the foreground and background (**Figure 9.29**). Repeat this process for the green and blue channels (**Alt+2**/**Option+2** and **Alt+3**/**Option+3**). RAM Preview the result.

7. Adjust Intensity, Size, or Softness controls under Tweaking according to what you see in the RAM Preview. You may also find it necessary to reduce Saturation under Color, particularly if your source is film rather than video.

In most cases, these steps yield a workable result; the example project (09_grainMatch.aep, located on the disc) used for these figures is included on your disc. The effect can then be copied and pasted to any foreground layers that need grain. If the foreground layer already contains noise or grain, you may need to adjust the Compensate for Existing Noise percentage for that layer.

Obviously, whole categories of controls are untouched with this method (**Figure 9.30**); the Application category, for example, contains controls for how the grain is blended and how it affects shadows, midtones, and highlights individually. Typically these are overkill, as are the Sampling and

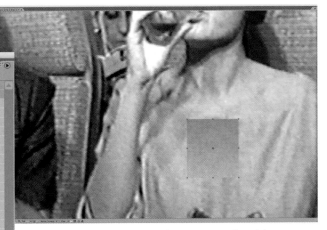

Figure 9.29 As with color matching, grain matching is best performed channel by channel. Match Grain is the best type of automated plug-in because it is really only semi-automated, enabling you to control and improve upon the initial result easily.

Animation controls, but how far you go in matching grain before your eye is satisfied is, of course, up to you and your team. This is one more case in which slamming the result can help ascertain its effectiveness (**Figure 9.31**).

Grain Removal

Removing grain, or sharpening an image in general, is an entirely different process from adding grain. On a well-shot production, you'll rarely have a reason to reach for the Remove Grain tool.

If you do, the reason for doing so may be unique to your particular footage. In such cases, you may very well find that Remove Grain at the default settings gives you a satisfactory result. If not, check into the Fine Tuning and Unsharp Mask settings to adjust it.

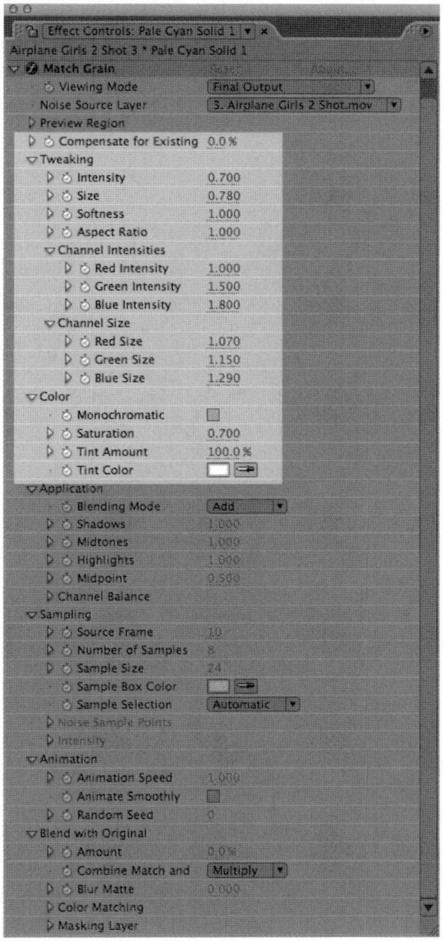

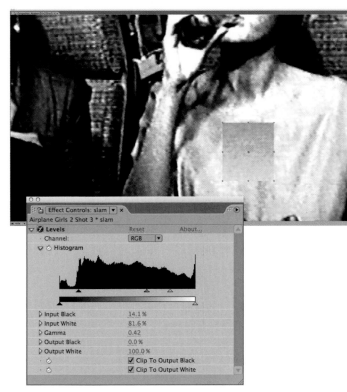

Figure 9.31 Slamming the result—with an adjustment layer containing a Levels effect, in this case with Gamma and Input levels adjusted—reveals the effectiveness of the match (and the full gnarliness of the grain).

Figure 9.30 Highlighted are the essential controls in Match Grain, which contains a lot of properties. It is best to procede top to bottom through these, first adjusting overall Intensity, Size, and Softness, then refining the individual Channel Intensities and Channel Size (as in Figure 9.28).

341

Figure 9.32 It may suit a still figure in a book (applied at the right side of this image), but Remove Grain on an entire shot with the default settings is rarely desirable. In full motion the grain-reduced shot looks a bit strange and retains a certain soft lumpiness.

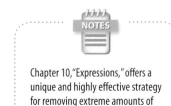

TIP

If you're using Remove Grain to improve the likelihood of a clean blue-screen or green-screen key, apply the resulting matte back to your source footage as an alpha track matte. This offers the best of both worlds: a clean matte channel and realistic grain on the source color layer.

NOTES

Chapter 10, "Expressions," offers a unique and highly effective strategy for removing extreme amounts of grain from a locked-off shot.

Remove Grain is often best employed "behind the scenes"—not across the entire frame (**Figure 9.32**), or intermediately in combination with other effects.

When to Employ Grain Strategies

The most obvious candidates for grain addition are computer-generated or still image layers, because they lack any of the moving grain found in film or video footage. As soon as your shot has to match anything that came from a camera, and particularly in a large format such as HD or film, you must manage grain.

Blurred elements may also need grain addition, even if they employ matching source footage. Blurry source shots contain as much grain as focused ones because the grain is an artifact of the medium recording the image, not the subject itself. Elements that have been scaled down in After Effects contain scaled-down grain, which may require restoration. Color keying can also suppress grain in the channel that has been keyed out.

Other compositing operations will instead enhance grain. Sharpening, unless performed via Remove Grain, can strongly emphasize grain contrast in an element, typically in a not-so-desirable manner. Sharpening also brings out any nasty compression artifacts that come with footage that uses JPEG-type compression, such as miniDV video.

Lack of grain, however, is one of the big dead giveaways of a poorly composited shot. It is worth the effort to match the correct amount of grain into your shot even if the result isn't apparent as you preview it on your monitor.

Film and Video Looks

Grain is one of several properties commonly associated with a "film look." People tend to mean different things when they speak about a film or video look, perhaps because they have different purposes in mind for these looks. For example, perhaps:

▶ The story calls for a sequence to appear as if it was shot on old home movie stock, such as Super 8 (a popular format from the '60s and '70s)

▶ The filmmaker wishes to shoot as cheaply as possible, yet achieve the look of an expensive feature film

The first situation is relatively simple and straightforward. In the same way that you match the color and grain of foreground elements to the background, you can match a whole shot to the look of an old film stock using those same grain and color tools, along with details such as a *vignette* effect, which makes footage brighter in the center and fading to black at the edges as with an old projector (**Figure 9.33**). Good reference will help.

The second situation is plenty broad enough to constitute a whole other book, one that is currently being written by the author of Chapter 15 (see Note). I almost hesitate to broach the topic here, but enough student or low-budget filmmakers have clearly gone for a filmic look and missed in elementary ways that it seems helpful to offer a few pointers.

Figure 9.33 Clichés of aged film, recognizable even with an otherwise blank frame, include heavy grain, a vignette, and a lack of saturated reds and yellows.

Look for *The DV Rebel's Guide: An All-Digital Approach to Making Killer Action Movies on the Cheap* by Stu Maschwitz late in 2006, from Peachpit Press.

Here are three important film/video distinctions that novices overlook:

▶ **Garbage in, garbage out.** It sounds obvious, but if you're shooting your own footage (on, say, miniDV tape), simple decisions on the shoot have profound consequences in After Effects. Too often, artists learn too late what they will try (and fail) to fix in postproduction.

▶ **Frame rate and format matter.** Frame rate and aspect ratio might seem to be inconsequential or a matter of personal preference, but I would argue that when low-budget video producers are trying to make shots look filmic, frame rate, at least, is significant.

▶ **Color affects story.** Changes to color and contrast can change the overall mood of a shot.

The following sections offer a few simple pointers for anyone with an effects shoot on a tight budget and the goal of producing a shot that will stand up against feature film footage.

Garbage In, Garbage Out

Garbage in, garbage out isn't a new principle. But what does it mean in this context? Here are some specifics (with details following):

▶ If you, the After Effects compositor, are on the set, you are the "bad cop" who must continually look for flaws that will be difficult to fix in post.

▶ Don't underlight a scene, but for God's sake don't overlight it. Maintain a low level of overall contrast when shooting digitally, as contrast can be enhanced later.

▶ If directing your own project, plan carefully: Storyboard, scout, and eliminate variables.

The most radical decision you can make on set to ensure a good result when shooting miniDV or HDV video is to aim for a low-contrast master. This is "radical" because it is bound to look horrible to the director of photography, but it carefully preserves highlight detail that, once blown out, is impossible to recover (**Figure 9.34**).

NOTES

No prejudice is intended against the look of video, other than recognizing it as the medium of news reports, reality television, and home movies. Many amazing shots have convincingly made it appear as if a computer-generated element was shot with a Handycam.

Figure 9.34 Sunsets and other light flares present a problem for digital cameras; once the highlight areas are blown out, they're not coming back unless you're working with a medium like film that can handle them. This problem is a center-piece of Chapter 11.

Most camera operators are inclined to deliver an image on set that is as close as possible to final, which is often an appropriate strategy with film. A low-contrast digital video source leaves ample room to enhance dynamic range using tools such as Levels and Curves in After Effects, even working with super-bright pixels in 32 bits per channel.

Frame Rate Matters

Others would argue this point, but if you want your footage to look filmic, the frame rate should be 24 fps.

A compelling demonstration of the difference between 24 fps film and 59.94 *fields* per second NTSC video dates back to the Golden Age of television and is available on DVD. In 1960, when the original *Twilight Zone* was in production, video cameras were briefly tried instead of film during the second season as a cost-cutting measure.

The experiment lasted six episodes, then was abandoned. The difference in how the drama "reads" on video versus film is simply incredible. The video versions play almost

NOTES

To see the *Twilight Zone* episodes mentioned, look for DVD's from Season 2 including "Static," "Night of the Meek," "The Lateness of the Hour," "The Whole Truth," "Twenty-Two," or "Long Distance Call" as well as the other filmed episodes.

like a soap opera; the film versions retain the spare, noir ironic distance and mystique that made the series famous. In short, the videotaped versions have immediacy, but the filmed versions appear timeless.

If you're with me on this, but you're still faced with shooting NTSC video, consider carefully if there's any way to capture your footage using the slower frame rate. Many contemporary video cameras include a 24 fps mode; prior to that, digital filmmakers would use 25 fps PAL format cameras and slow the footage down to 24 fps.

If the immediacy of reality television is what you're after, by all means, go for it: Shoot source with a video camera and maintain a 30 fps (29.97 fps) frame rate throughout the process.

Format Matters

As the world transitions from standard definition to high-definition broadcast television, formats are undergoing the same transition that they made in film half a century ago. The nearly square 4:3 aspect ratio yields to the wider 16:9 format, but also 1.85 Academy aperture, 2.35 Cinema-scope, and who knows what else.

Big-budget films are often created for multiple formats, and yours can, too. For a film destined both for theatrical release and video markets such as airplanes, all shots are typically created at a 4:3 aspect ratio and then masked off for the wider theatrical version.

The Day After Tomorrow employed a theatrical mask positioned near the top of frame, where all essential action had to appear. This took on the nickname Ueli-mask, after the film's cinematographer, Ueli Steiger.

Color Affects Story

The influence of color decisions on the final shot, and by extension on the story being told in the shot, is an immense topic, hashed over by cinematographers and colorists the world over. Any attempt to distill this into a few pithy paragraphs would be a disservice.

NOTES

The numbers "1.85" and "2.35" give the width, relative to a height of 1, so it's like saying 1.85:1 or 2.35:1. The 16:9 format, which has become popular with digital video and HD, is equivalent to a 1.77:1 ratio, slightly narrower than Academy, but wide compared to the standard television format of 4:3 (which translates to 1.33:1).

Figure 9.35 Radical color transformation is undertaken to give this no-budget action movie parody the feel of the kind of big budget action films it satirizes. Techniques such as using a color solid to transform the lighting and color of footage are explored throughout Chapter 12. (Images courtesy markandmatty.com.)

Thus, if you're new to the idea of developing a color look for a film or sequence, look at reference. Study other people's work for the effect of color on the mood and story in a shot, sequence, or entire film. **Figure 9.35** is taken from an independent short film series shot on DV but intended to parody the look and attitude of big budget action movies, of which color is an essential component.

Conclusion

And really, you've just scratched the surface of what's possible. The inventive compositor can and should always look for new methods to replicate the way that the camera sees the world, going beyond realism to present the realism we've become so accustomed to seeing—realism through the lens.

Third-party After Effects plug-ins exist specifically to add a film look to video. The Magic Bullet Suite (a set of plug-ins for After Effects and Apple's Final Cut Pro) was created so that The Orphanage could help filmmakers shoot cheaply using digital cameras and achieve the look of film in post (demo version on the disc).

Expressions

Music is math.

— Michael Sandison and Marcus Eoin
(Boards of Canada)

Expressions

Expressions extend the functionality in After Effects by enabling you to link elements of your project together and apply logical and mathematical relationships.

Did your eyes just glaze over? Here is where the standard disclaimer is usually added about how artists don't like logic and bits of math and where I promise to shield you from it as much as possible.

I don't buy it: As an After Effects artist, you already deal with this stuff all the time. If you're not making full use of expressions, you're missing out on a more elegant approach that can eliminate tedium.

Eliminate tedium? But, you reply, expressions require the use of code. What could be more tedious to a visual artist than managing code?

This chapter makes the case that it's worth dealing with a little code—often just one line in these examples, all or part of which can be entered automatically—to attain the flexibility and power of expressions. The examples given here relate directly to other techniques explored in this book. They are practical, not theoretical.

To give you a taste of what is possible with expressions, here are some of the case studies explored in this chapter:

▶ Create an automatic one-to-one relationship between data from two animation channels (whether from the same layer, separate layers, or even separate compositions)

▶ Scale and offset property values

▶ Link values to a slider control for easy access

- ▶ "Mute" keyframe values by replacing them with a constant value
- ▶ Loop, with several different options how you do it
- ▶ Destabilize or smooth camera moves or any animation data (without affecting or destroying the data)
- ▶ Use time and index values to progress animation data
- ▶ Create a conditional statement that causes something to happen when specified criteria are met
- ▶ Trigger actions to occur automatically under specific circumstances
- ▶ Emulate 3-D tracking in a forward-moving shot

Overall, the goal, as always, is to provide a guidebook rather than a recipe book, enabling you to build on the understanding you gain here by moving from simple to complex examples.

Logic and Grammar

There are two keys to an understanding of expressions:

- ▶ You must understand the solution you are pursuing in a methodical, step-by-step fashion.
- ▶ You must translate this ordinary language methodology to the logic and syntax of expressions, to lines of code.

Expressions do only one thing: translate data values. Granted, that's a little bit like saying your computer's hard drive only has ones and zeros on it, but fundamentally, there are three types of data on which expressions do their work:

- ▶ Numbers
- ▶ Booleans (True/False or Yes/No)
- ▶ Text strings (and text hardly comes into play; After Effects is mostly about numbers)

Expressions can either

- ▶ Link to existing values found among data in After Effects
- ▶ Fabricate new data using criteria that you, the user, specify

Numerical and logic data can come from almost anywhere in the world of After Effects. They can derive from

▶ Basic transform data of a layer

▶ Current time in the composition

▶ The index number of a layer (its order in the composition)

▶ Dimensions and duration of the source composition or footage

▶ Either/or conditions about the layer, such as whether it has a parent

Essentially every piece of numerical or Boolean data that exists in your After Effects project is accessible to expressions and can be used to create animations.

What *Can't* Expressions Do?

Expressions cannot natively evaluate certain types of data:

▶ Pixel values

▶ Audio waveforms

▶ Mask data

Nor can they handle certain complex effects data, such as effects channels that can be keyframed but whose keyframe values are not made up of four or fewer numerical values. For example, expressions work with RGBA data—red, green, blue, and alpha channel values normalized between 0 and 1—but they can't handle the Channel Range color control in Hue/Saturation.

Therefore although you can change the pixel values and audio levels of a layer using expressions, you can't sample a given pixel's RGB values, the decibel level of a soundtrack, or the position of a mask point.

Expressions are also only ever aware of conditions at the current point in time. You can create expressions that create a progression over time, but every frame up to the current one has to be recalculated from scratch on each frame, causing the expression to run more and more slowly over time. This can make physical simulations (such as the motion of a spring or the progression of a pattern) impractical.

NOTES

The After Effects expressions language is based on JavaScript (or, more precisely, ECMAscript, the standardized version), a scripting language that was originally devised for Web browsers at Netscape. Many functions that are fundamental to JavaScript, such as the ability to perform mathematical operations, work identically in After Effects. Of course, many other functions from JavaScript are specific to the Web and interactivity. Likewise, After Effects adds its own keywords, functions, and attributes; these use the same basic syntax and rules of JavaScript but would not be recognized by it.

Muting Keyframes

You may have wished for the ability to temporarily disable keyframes in After Effects. Your wish is granted via the simplest possible expression: a static value.

Where would you use this? Let's say that you have an element whose Opacity is keyframed to 0% at its starting frame of an animation. Or perhaps you want to adjust an element to match the rest of a scene at a time when it is out of frame. The idea is to temporarily change the property value without touching the keyframes.

The expressions solution for this is trivially easy, and it doesn't require an understanding of JavaScript. It might even help you understand something basic about expressions: They hold a value that can be the result of calculating various properties or can simply be typed in.

Open 10_basicExpression.aep and look at the composition called bouncing ball for expression. A Tint effect has been added that turns the ball red each time it hits the floor. Suppose that you wish to disable this effect temporarily without deleting its keyframes altogether.

Begin by revealing Tint (with the layer highlighted, press **E** to reveal effects or **U** for all keyframed properties) and set an expression for the Amount to Tint property. To do this, you can use Animation > Add Expression or its keyboard shortcut (**Alt+Shift+=/Option+Shift+=**), but the most direct method is to Alt-click (Option-click) the stopwatch of the property that requires the expression.

A few changes occur as the result of setting an expression (**Figure 10.1**). A new line is revealed below the Amount to Tint property that reads Expression: Amount to Tint. A button whose icon looks like an equals sign appears to the right, highlighted; this Enable Expression toggle activates and deactivates the expression. The other icons come into play a little later. Over in the main area of the Timeline (Graph Editor off for now), the text `effect("Tint")(3)` is automatically highlighted, and a cursor blinks to the right of this text, indicating that you can edit it by typing.

Creative Accounting

There are, of course, workarounds to the limitations of expressions. The commonly used Levels effect, for example, has an Individual Controls version that was created expressly (pun intended) for use with expressions.

For sampling sound, Trapcode (www.trapcode.com) offers Sound Keys, which can translate waveforms into numerical data suitable for expressions.

As for such unreachable data as mask vertices, scripting, not expressions, is capable of interacting with their values. Although scripting and expressions use the same language, there is at present no way to call a script with an expression.

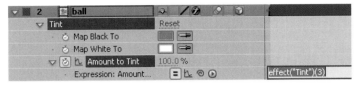

Figure 10.1 The expression is activated by Alt-clicking on the stopwatch. The value for Amount to Tint is now displayed in red, and a second line appears containing the Expression controls; the expression text itself appears in the main area of the Timeline and is highlighted until you click elsewhere.

The default expression `effect("Tint")(3)` tells After Effects to look at the layer's effects for the one called Tint and to use the value of its third property (Amount to Tint). Simply applying an expression changes nothing about where the value comes from.

This example is admittedly a bit esoteric for the sake of simplicity; situations in which I've found this technique useful include removing transforms from an element I want to color correct, and holding opacity at 100% for an element that is blinking or animating at a nearly invisible level in the scene.

Now write your own expression by typing a number. Replace `effect("Tint")(3)` with `100` and either press Enter (not Return) or just click outside the text area. Amount to Tint now uses this one value, 100, on every frame of the composition (**Figure 10.2**). The keyframes have effectively been "frozen" or "muted" (whichever term you prefer), replaced with a constant value.

Toggling the Expressions button (that equals sign in the expression controls) enables and disables the keyframes. What could possibly go wrong here? Why, you could forget to disable or delete (Alt/Option-click on the stopwatch) the expression when you're done and want the animated values to render. That's about it.

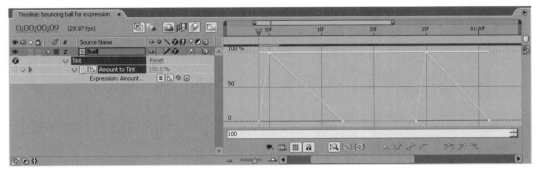

Figure 10.2 If a numerical property contains keyframes, entering a number in the expressions field overrides those keyframes with the specified value. The flat white line along the top of the Graph Editor demonstrates what's going on, relative to the gray lines below showing the previous animated values.

Things do get a little more complex with properties that contain more than one value, such as Position. These are called *arrays* and are detailed in the next section.

Linking Animation Data

The bread-and-butter role of expressions is to link individual animation properties. Other linking methods all have their place, but have their limitations as well:

▶ **Parenting** links translation data between layers, but you can't pick and choose which properties are linked: You always get Position, Rotation, and Scale (plus any offset between the layers). You can't even using parenting to link translation data to other properties, such as brushes and effects positions.

▶ **Precomposing** allows you to group layers and animate them as a group, but that's about it.

▶ **Copying and pasting** keyframes allows you to copy data from one property over to a completely different property or to create a loop by hand, but this brute force method does not maintain any link should the source data change. Futhermore, you cannot easily scale or offset the result, nor copy from a one-channel to a multiple-channel property or vice versa.

None of these methods allows for more complex relationships, such as a nonlinear relationship between two sets of values (changing existing keyframe values by doubling or scaling them).

The key to easy linking of individual properties is the pickwhip, a nifty tool for grabbing bits of data and turning them effortlessly into useful bits of code (**Figure 10.3**).

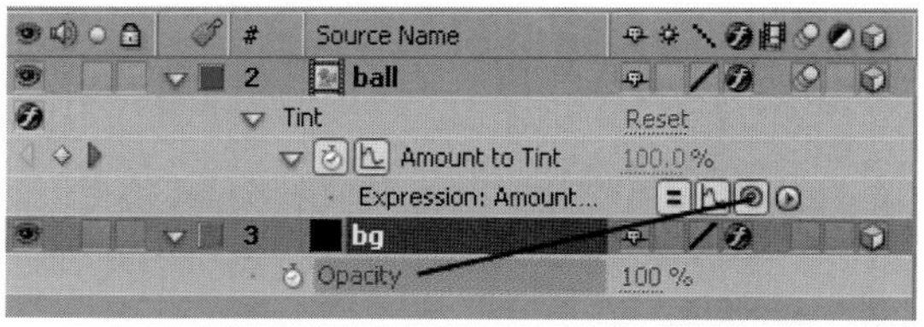

Figure 10.3 The pickwhip in action: Set it by dragging from the pickwhip icon to the target property.

Tracking Brushes and Effects

Chapters 7, "Rotoscoping and Paint," and 8, "Effective Motion Tracking," alluded to a method for combining paint tools and the tracker. The simplest, most flexible solution for attaching a tracker to a paint stroke is to use the pickwhip. To set up a one-to-one relationship between two properties, the pickwhip and some knowledge how to use it are all you need.

Figure 10.4 shows the passing bus that has appeared in a couple of examples already; suppose that the Muni logos on the side of the bus need to be removed so that the shot isn't clearly taken in San Francisco. The reason to use the clone tool in this case is that the appearance of the side of the bus changes, due to changing light, as it progresses through the shot, and you want to avoid having to match it by hand if at all possible.

Begin by tracking one of the logos. Create a new composition with just the footage in it. Now track the logo; for simplicity's sake, move the attach point over to the area being used as source for the clone (say, that empty area to the right of the logo as in Figure 10.4).

Having tracked the logo, return to the first frame (still in the Layer panel) and use the Clone Stamp tool to eliminate the logo. Choose a reasonably large (50 pixel) and

To try this, import the busPassbyHD footage into After Effects, or open 10_cloning.aep to see a composition with the following steps already completed.

Figure 10.4 A raw track of the logo is generated with the attach point (admittedly, difficult to see in a figure) offset to the right.

hard (75%) brush, then Alt/Option-click in the same place where you see the attach point, to the right, and paint at the center of the track area. Best in this case is to clone out the unwanted object in one stroke, so that you only have to join the tracker to that one Clone brush, but you can repeat this step as needed.

With the layer highlighted in the Timeline, press **UU** to expose the tracker and brush data. Set an expression on the Position of the brush, then drag the pickwhip—the swirl icon—to the words "Feature Center." Now set an expression for Clone Position, and pickwhip "Attach Point."

Done. The resulting expressions look something like

```
motionTracker("Tracker 1")("Track Point 1").
➡attachPoint
```

and

```
motionTracker("Tracker 1")( "Track Point 1").
➡featureCenter
```

But why sweat the syntax? You've just set up an automatic link between properties without having to type, and with the pickwhip, you can always grab available data in this manner.

Offsetting an Element

In the real world (and quite likely in your attempt at the above example), it is difficult to get tracking data to line up perfectly; you often need to offset tracking data. You could apply the tracker to a null and parent the repositioned element to that, moving the null as needed with all Position keyframes selected, but it's simpler to add a numerical offset to the expression.

Offsets are quite intuitive even to people who don't understand JavaScript very well. Perhaps you want to offset a value by –100. What would you add at the end of the default expression text? That's right, –100. Try it on a Position value and it works—kind of. The object moves 100 pixels, but on the X axis only.

Geek Alert: Unpacking Syntax

If you're the type who's not satisfied until you understand that little piece of code you get for free via the pickwhip, good for you. Take a closer look at the syntax of that brush stroke:

```
motionTracker("Tracker 1")
➡("Track Point 1").attachPoint
```

The basic structure is similar to pathnames in Unix or Windows: Starting at the left, motionTracker contains Tracker 1, which has a Track Point 1, which in turn contains the property you're after, the attach point.

What's up with the parentheses, the quotations, and the dot? Parentheses in JavaScript contain *arguments*, which are specifics needed to clarify settings, in this case, telling After Effects which point, in which tracker, you're after. The motionTracker property is unusual in that it needs two sets of arguments, each in its own set of parentheses, one for the tracker and one for the specific point. The dot works the same way a forward slash would in Unix (or a back slash in Windows): It identifies the next level down in the hierarchy, like opening a folder. The quotations are there to say that they contain a text string, which should be read as a label rather than a command.

Keywords in expressions use inter-caps, so that a keyword is made of two words with no spaces. For example, motion tracker and attach point, end up as motionTracker and attachPoint, respectively.

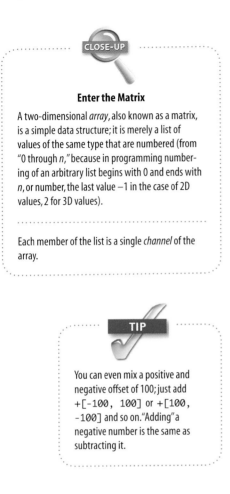

CLOSE-UP

Enter the Matrix

A two-dimensional *array*, also known as a matrix, is a simple data structure; it is merely a list of values of the same type that are numbered (from "0 through *n*," because in programming numbering of an arbitrary list begins with 0 and ends with *n*, or number, the last value −1 in the case of 2D values, 2 for 3D values).

Each member of the list is a single *channel* of the array.

TIP

You can even mix a positive and negative offset of 100; just add +[-100, 100] or +[100, -100] and so on. "Adding" a negative number is the same as subtracting it.

NOTES

When you apply a motion track, you are given the option to apply it to the X or Y axis only, but most of us wish this option and dialog would disappear, given how simple it is to restrict motion to a single axis yourself.

Position is an array, a property with multiple values. A 2D Position property has two values, X and Y, and a 3D layer's Position property adds a third (as do Anchor Point and Rotation, which change from one to three values in 3D). So although offsetting and scaling values is simple—you use the basic math operators (+, -, *, /)—things get slightly less straightforward with arrays—but only slightly.

An array value is written in expressions as [x, y] for a 2D value or [x, y, z] for 3D. So to mute a Position keyframe at the center of a 720, 540 frame, enter [360, 270] (half each value), and to offset each value by negative one hundred (-100), add -[100, 100] after the pickwhip data to add the offset (**Figure 10.5**).

Admittedly, this is quick and dirty; the goal here is to expose the low-hanging fruit, the things you do all the time with expressions that are easy to pick up. A more elegant way of setting a constant position at the center of the frame would be

```
[thisComp.width/2, thisComp.height/2]
```

as this expression would adjust itself to any composition size. There are typically many ways to write any expression; the simplest approach (with the fewest lines or operations) that applies to the greatest number of variables (such as changes in the comp size) is typically optimal.

One Channel Only

Suppose you wish to link a property on one axis only, keeping the value of one axis in a static position, and applying your track to the other axis. This offers opportunity to learn a useful new bit of syntax. You know how to create an array, but how do you identify one portion of it only? Each component is identified like this

```
[position[0], position[1]]
```

Figure 10.5 The Position value of a paint stroke is a two-dimensional array; the highlighted text adds a simple offset of such an array.

Don't freak out; it's just more brackets. Position is expressed as two values separated by a comma in brackets, and the values themselves are identified by trailing numbers, also in brackets. The numerical order starts at 0, not 1; it's just how programming languages generally work. One of the lead developers of After Effects, Dan Wilk, is even in the habit of emailing numbered steps starting with 0, so stubborn a computer scientist is he.

So, to maintain the existing value on the X axis and pickwhip the Y axis, you would enter `position[0]` and a comma, then pickwhip the Y value to the Y value of the attach point. Drag the pickwhip to a single value of the target property—the second one, in this case—and it copies the code for that value alone (**Figure 10.6**). Once again, the pickwhip has saved you from typing in some gnarly code.

To do the same on the other axis, just reverse the steps, pickwhipping before the comma and entering `position[1]` following it.

Building Your Own Controls

Here's another cool yet simple thing you can do with expressions: link effects controls to properties that are not part of an existing effect, allowing you to control them in the Effect Control panel.

The effects found within the Expression Controls subcategory don't do anything until you attach an expression to them. That's why they exist, to offer you a user interface for adjusting your expressions values interactively. The one you'll most often use is Slider Control, but look carefully at the other five, as each corresponds to a different type of property (**Figure 10.7**).

Figure 10.6 You can pickwhip from a single channel of an array (a property with multiple values) to the corresponding single channel of a separate array.

TIP

A typical method for hosting expression controls is to apply them to a null or adjustment layer named Zoom Control or something equally intuitive.

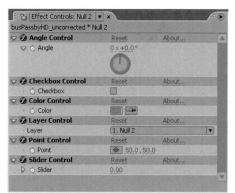

Figure 10.7 The full array of available expression controls, all applied to a single layer. Each generates a unique type of data: Angle generates radians and degrees, Checkbox is a Boolean, Color three values between 0 and 255, Layer a layer in the current comp, and Point an array of two values. Only Slider generates a single floating-point number, and it is most used by far.

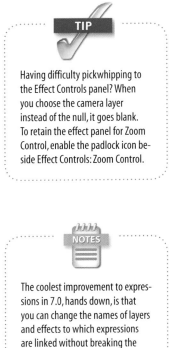

TIP

Having difficulty pickwhipping to the Effect Controls panel? When you choose the camera layer instead of the null, it goes blank. To retain the effect panel for Zoom Control, enable the padlock icon beside Effect Controls: Zoom Control.

NOTES

The coolest improvement to expressions in 7.0, hands down, is that you can change the names of layers and effects to which expressions are linked without breaking the expression.

NOTES

What's up with spaces? Typing "x * x" or "x*x" in an expression has the same result. In fact, you can put as many spaces as you want between the operator (*) and its operands (x). It's purely a matter of what you prefer to look at. Where you get into trouble is in adding spaces where they don't belong, such as in the middle of a name; valueX is not the same as value X. If there are spaces in a name you pickwhip, the name appears in parentheses, for example: `motionTracker ("Tracker 1") ("Track Point 1")`.

Suppose you want a zoom control slider for a 3D camera; to try this, open the 09_rackFocus project from the previous chapter. Open the "no expressions" composition. You can't apply any effect directly to a camera, so you must apply the slider to a different layer; it hardly matters which one, because the slider will have no direct effect on the layer hosting it until an expression is linked to it.

Create a new null object called Zoom Control (editing the layer name after creating it) and apply Slider Control. Now apply an expression to the Zoom property of the camera, insert a plus sign with spaces around it after the default expression, and pickwhip to the Slider Control property. You can even pickwhip up to the Effects Controls panel instead of revealing it in the Timeline, provided you lock it first.

Rename Slider Control Zoomer after setting the pickwhip and behold, the connection is maintained. Anyone who has worked with expressions in a previous version of After Effects, or in a competing application such as Shake, is now jumping for joy.

You can raise the slider to zoom in, but the 0 to 100 range is not sufficient for Zoom values, which can range much higher. Context-click on the property, choosing Edit Value, and change the Slider Range values (**Figure 10.8**).

Alternatively, you can make this slider do more within a narrower range; the Zoom values can increase logarithmically, by the square of the Zoomer value. How do you square a value? You multiply it by itself. Take the existing pickwhip path, copy it, add a * symbol directly after the original version, and then paste the copied text. Voila, the zoom control operates more like a real zoom.

Figure 10.8 You can set Slider Range values anywhere between the specified maximum and minimum values, not only for the Expression Slider but any effect.

Looping Animations

Perhaps the most useful feature unique to expressions (one that users who won't touch expressions beg for) is the ability to loop a set of keyframes. It's so easy to learn and powerful, however, that once expressions-phobes understand it, even they start to like it.

In some cases, all you need to do to create a loop is to replace your source expression text with a default loop expression. These are found in the Property submenu of the Expressions menu (**Figure 10.9**).

The loop effects have two *arguments*, the settings found in parentheses after the command. The first one is mandatory; you must specify the type of loop you're requesting by choosing one of the three loop types—and here is the major flaw, as only one of them appears as an option in the menu, and it's not the most useful one of the three. The second argument, specifying how far the loop extends, is optional (and in some cases, unavailable).

An example in which you can use the default expression is a blinking light, animated via keyframes in its Opacity property. To blink, these keyframes animate from 100% to 0% and back, then repeat. 10_loop.aep contains a light layer set to blink.

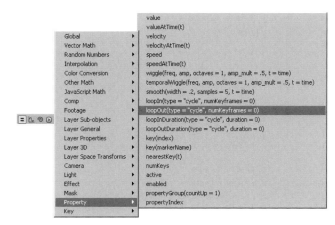

Figure 10.9 Try not to be overwhelmed—the expressions menu is a well-organized cheat sheet of After Effects keywords. Once you understand its basic organization and most useful items, you can browse with confidence. The Property submenu, shown here, contains several essential functions.

Saving Useful Expressions

Version 7.0 has made saving expressions for reuse easier than in the past via a very simple change; for cases in which the expression uses no keyframe data, you can now save an Animation Preset that contains only the expression, not the static value of the property.

All you have to do to take advantage of this feature is to choose Animation > Save Animation Preset for a property with no keyframes. Only the expression is saved.

Expressions Menu and Hierarchy

The Expressions menu is a bit overwhelming to the uninitiated—nearly two dozen submenus with several entries each. How do you know where to find anything?

Two significant observations can make this menu less daunting:

▶ Most of the entries don't do anything, technically speaking, other than point to a value that you can sample.

▶ The menus are organized hierarchically, from most global to most local. So at the top is the Global submenu, which has shortcuts to areas of After Effects that are available on the broadest or most global level. At the other end of the menu are Property and Key, which work on an individual property of an individual effect applied to an individual layer in an individual comp. In other words, these are the most nested expressions.

So don't worry, it's not as gnarly as it first appears.

Figure 10.10 A light is set to blink on the mixing panel, but only one cycle of on to off and back to on has been keyframed (with an offset and an ease to give it character). The rest will be done with expressions.

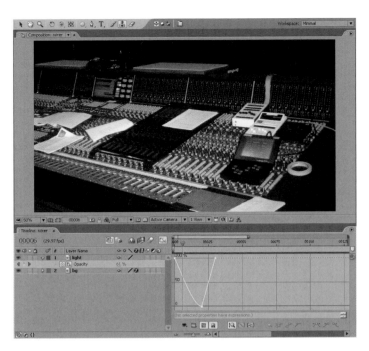

NOTES

For loopOut("cycle",0) to work properly, the last keyframe value must match that of the first keyframe, or the loop will be missing its first frame. This can be frustrating if you don't know the secret, and it only seems to be a problem with the "cycle" version of loopOut().

To begin, create one cycle of this animation, start to finish. You might start with a keyframe of 0%, then 100% a couple of frames later, and 0% again about a second after that (**Figure 10.10**).

Now set an expression for Opacity, and with the default expression still highlighted, choose

```
loopOut(type = "cycle", numKeyframes = 0)
```

Press the Enter key or click outside the text area. The keyframes now loop, as can be seen in the Graph Editor (**Figure 10.11**).

Before moving on to other looping options, check out the other arguments you can set for this expression. For example, numKeyframes specifies how many keyframes before the final one are used in the loop; set to the default of 0, it uses all keyframes. You can get rid of this argument altogether in such a case (see the sidebar, "Extraneous Verbiage"), leaving loopOut("cycle") to yield the same result. Set numKeyframes to a value of 1 and it uses the last two keyframes only (**Figure 10.12**).

Figure 10.11 A simple loop expression is applied. The pattern repeats in the dotted lines, where the expression has taken over. The default expression (chosen from the menu per the instructions) would work, but unnecessary arguments have been removed here to shorten it (see the sidebar, "Extraneous Verbiage").

Extraneous Verbiage

How can two expressions

```
loopOut(type = "cycle",
➥numKeyframes = 0)
loopOut("cycle")
```

achieve the exact same result? Here's a quick explanation: Expressions don't do a lot of hand-holding in terms of telling you what to enter and where, but the default settings sometimes come with extra keywords that are totally optional; their only purpose is to remind you what the values are for. In the case of this example, not only are the keywords "type =" and "numKeyframes =" optional, but the whole second argument will default to 0 if it's missing.

Now how the heck would you know this? After a while, you start to anticipate it because it's somewhat standard. As you begin, however, the only way to know it is to read it in a book like this one. Sad, but true.

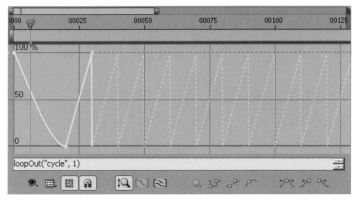

Figure 10.12 Giving the second argument (numKeyframes) a value of 1 actually causes loopOut to use the last two keyframes only (because a one-frame loop is impossible, I suppose). This makes looping only a portion of a more complex animation possible.

Now, back to that fundamental flaw. There are, in fact, three types of loops, not just one, but the other two cannot be found in the expressions menus (they are hidden in the help documentation):

```
loopOut("cycle")
loopOut("pingpong")
loopOut("continue")
```

Of these three, continue is the one you are likely to use the most; in fact, continue loops are among the most useful expressions period, so they get special treatment in the next section. Meanwhile, the pingpong option is like cycle except that it alternates looping backward and forward (**Figure 10.13**).

As for the other loop types available, loopIn("cycle") provides a method to create a loop that precedes the existing keyframes, rather than following them in time (**Figure 10.14**). Both loopOutDuration() and loopInDuration() enable you to specify an interval, in seconds, between loops. For example, loopOutDuration("cycle", 2) cycles a loop every two seconds.

Continue Loops

Although a cycle is intuitively a "loop" in the strictest sense of the word—a repeat of what came before—the continue loop is hands-down the most useful. Chapter 8 contained one use of a continue loop, to extend a motion track beyond the edges of the frame (where the tracker cannot go). Let's draw some clear boundaries around what is possible with continue loops.

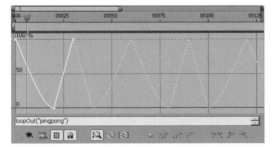

Figure 10.13 The useful pingpong loop is applied here, causing the same pattern to loop backward and forward, alternately.

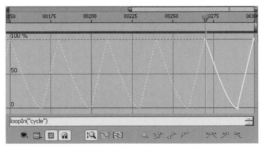

Figure 10.14 A loopIn() expression works just like a loopOut with the simple difference that the loop precedes the keyframes.

There are essentially only two options with continue loops: loopIn("continue") or loopOut("continue"); the second argument is not accepted because continue is looking for two things only: the vector (direction) and velocity of the animation at the first (loopIn) or last (loopOut) keyframe. It causes the animation to proceed linearly along that vector at that velocity, and that's it. It has no understanding of Bezier handle influence, so any curve in the motion is not looped.

Nonetheless, it is useful in any case where you have the basic direction and rate of animation correct and wish to replicate those qualities. And what about a case in which you have the middle keyframes of an animation, but want to continue in and out of them? That situation is covered later in the "Conditionals" section.

Smoothing and Destabilizing

Chapter 8 alluded to methods for smoothing and destabilizing a camera that are preferable to the Smoother and the Wiggler, After Effects' built-in solutions that predate expressions. It's time to take a closer look at these expression-based methods; they're fairly easy to learn and will expand your capabilities quite a bit.

Steadicam and Camera Shake

Some applications offer specific effects for smoothing or destabilizing the camera, and I've seen at least one other author claim that After Effects has no tools for camera stabilization and destabilization. Let's see about that.

If you followed the steps in Chapter 8 for using a 3D camera to motion track a scene in such a way that the track is applied only to the layer and camera, you're ready to proceed. If not, please review that section briefly if you want an idea of how the setup can be applied to a motion-tracked camera. You can destabilize a camera using wiggle without tracking data (**Figure 10.15**).

Figure 10.15 The camera in this shot is parented to a null with a `wiggle` expression applied to its Position value to automatically destabilize the camera, making it feel handheld.

Once again, application of the expression is easy. Given a set of keyframes, you can smooth them—averaging them against the closest adjacent keyframes (you control how many)—or add noise and jitter, respectively applying one of the following expressions:

```
smooth()
wiggle(freq, amp)
```

The default text is more verbose, but I'm hoping that presenting them in their minimal form makes them appear easier to use than they do with the menu defaults (explained below).

You can apply `smooth()` as is, and see the result in the Graph Editor. This graph constitutes an additional advantage to applying smoothing with an expression, because you can see the amount of change without even previewing the animation (**Figure 10.16**).

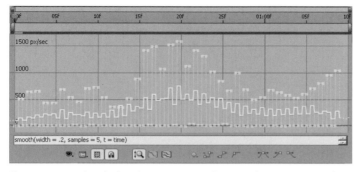

Figure 10.16 A close look at the operation used to smooth a camera move from Chapter 8 shows how effective this method is, even with the default expression in place. If this was not smooth enough, you could raise the "width" or number of samples, described here.

You can of course tweak the amount of smoothing with the help the verbose parameters shown in the default expression:

```
smooth(width = .2, samples = 5, t = time)
```

These are the default settings; `width`, `samples`, and `t` are there to offer you a clue what each argument does, and they are designed not to break the expression if left in. The = sign followed by a value tells you that they have default values if you leave them out. Here's what each specifically does:

▶ **width** specifies the amount of time, in seconds, to either side of the current frame that is averaged into the smoothing calculation

▶ **samples** specifies how many increments to examine within that keyframe range (choose an odd number to include the current frame in the calculation)

▶ **time** allows you to offset the smoothing in time, something you'll rarely, if ever, need to do

The `wiggle` expression requires two arguments by default, and has the option for as many as five. At a minimum, you must enter values for `freq` (frequency, the number of wiggles per second), and `amplitude` (the maximum amount the wiggle will change a value—in this case, the number of pixels). The full default expression reads

```
wiggle(freq, amp, octaves = 1, ampMult = 5, t = time)
```

TIP

Although it wasn't possible in earlier versions of After Effects, in 6.5 you can apply `wiggle()` to a property that has no keyframe data whatsoever, useful for adding the jitter of a handheld camera to a static setup.

Geek Alert: Wiggle versus Random

The `wiggle()` function adds random data to an animation channel. How does it differ from the functions in the Random Numbers submenu?

Random numbers are truly random; any number generated has no relationship to the number preceding it. They can be constrained to a particular range, and Gaussian random numbers will tend toward the center of that range (following a Gaussian distribution pattern that weights random numbers toward the median), but the effect is one of values that pop around completely randomly.

With `wiggle()`, the seeming randomness is generated by adding an organic noise function to existing data. The randomness is not quite so random: It takes existing data and deviates from it, within a set range (`amplitude`) and at a set number of times per second (`freq`). The `wiggle()` function, then, not only has the advantage of using animation data to determine its range, but of generating an effect that does not feel so chaotic as random data.

Wondering what value an expression generates? You can check it by applying the Numbers effect to a solid and setting an expression for Value/Offset/Random Max. For example, try entering `thisComp.frameDuration` and you'll see the value returned by that expression.

For the most part, `freq` and `amplitude` are all you need, but to give a complete picture, `octaves` controls how many noise samples are averaged together, and won't usually need to be more than 1. A higher value for `octaves` doesn't mean more noise, it just means more samples, and `ampMult` multiplies the result—all to provide variety. If you want more noise, raise frequency and amplitude. Time, once again, is an offset.

To apply `smooth()` and `wiggle()` expressions to a 3D camera that has been tracked to match the background, try opening the example from Chapter 8, 08_tracking.aep, and look again at the smoothCam composition.

Alternatively, to generate random numbers within a given range (rather than wiggling keyframe values), you can use the various random, Gaussian random, and noise functions found in the Random Numbers submenu (see the sidebar, "Wiggle versus Random"). Or, to wiggle the temporal position of keyframes themselves (to offset them randomly in time), try

```
temporalWiggle(freq, amp)
```

It's not the most commonly used, but it is useful if you need the animation values to stay in exactly the same range (to follow a path, for example) but to move back and forth semi-randomly on that path.

Offsetting Layers and Time

Some of the coolest things you can do with expressions involve increments of layer index numbers (the number of the layer to the left of the source name) or time itself. The following example makes use of both.

Time in expressions is measured in whole seconds. Frames and fields are calculated as decimal fractions of seconds. Of course, if you're ever worried about calculating this, you can use fractions instead: in 24 fps footage, frame 65 would be `time = 65/24` (or 2.7083 seconds). See how easy?

You can also use `thisComp.frameDuration` to calculate time based on frames. It returns the fraction of one second that each frame lasts.

A frame's index and time become especially useful when using conditionals. In the example, index and time serve to average grain between several frames of a sequence, for situations in which regular grain removal methods aren't cutting it with a locked-off shot. Now, get ready to move beyond one-liner expressions.

Grain Averaging

There are cases (which don't come up all the time, but which do come up) in which the normal methods of dealing with grain—tools as powerful as the Remove Grain effect (detailed in Chapter 9, "Virtual Cinematography")—just don't do the trick. The noise simply obscures too much of the source. There is an interesting alternative, one that came in handy when I was working on *The Day After Tomorrow*.

This effects plate was taken on a huge blue-screen stage: actors trudged across a snowy plain. It was meant to be snowing fairly hard in the shot, and unfortunately, it was decided to use practical snow on set. I understand that typically, as in **Figure 10.17**, this is done with little bits of plastic confetti or, the old school way, cornflakes painted white. We were already successfully adding computer-generated

Figure 10.17 Ah, the fall of fresh artificial snow on a blue-screen stage.

snow to all kinds of exterior shots. Worse, the lighting grid appeared in frame; the garbage mask to remove it left a big hole in the falling snow. I needed to get rid of the plate snow altogether and start over. Happily it was a locked-off shot and the following trick worked with the addition of a gentle camera push.

I determined that the frames I wanted to average were the ones at the end of the shot, where I could easily eliminate the only moving element in the shot, actors crossing the snowy plain. I did not really know how many frames I would need to average (5? 20?), but I knew that if I took a series of different frames and set their Opacity correctly I could average them together to create an opaque image.

This technique would remove the huge flakes of snow (or any large grainy noise) as follows: on a given frame, a given snowflake would appear at a given place in the frame, but not in adjacent frames. My technique would therefore average out the flakes. If I needed to average ten frames, then the opacity would have to decrease 10% from bottom to top.

Without expressions, this process would be a real pain, because I need to experiment interactively with how many layers to combine. Each added layer would require adjusting the opacity of all of the layers. Instead, I was able to apply two expressions to one layer and simply duplicate that layer until I had enough iterations to accomplish the effect of averaging.

This same trick works with any type of noise in footage, so long as the camera is locked off. Included on the disc is 10_degrain.aep, which was cobbled together from a short sequence—just a few frames—shot in sequence in a downpour using a still camera. The fact that this technique basically works with such crude source should serve as an endorsement.

Drop the sequence (or noisy footage of your own) into a new composition and reveal the layer's Opacity setting. Apply an expression to Opacity and replace the default expression by typing:

```
Index*100/thisComp.numLayers
```

NOTES

If you composite ten frames each with an Opacity of 10%, the result will not be completely opaque. This is not an error on the part of After Effects, although it is not how things work in similar applications such as Shake. Imagine holding up two pieces of paper that are 50% opaque up against a light. Would two sheets of semi-transparent paper, held together, completely block it out? No.

This expression simply says, "Multiply 100 (full opacity) by the index number of this layer, and divide this amount by the number of layers total in this composition." The keywords thisComp and numLayers can be found in the expressions menus, in case you're wondering where they came from.

Next, to average together the last few frames of the composition, counting backwards for each additional layer, apply Time Remapping and add the expression

```
thisComp.duration-(index / (1/thisComp.
➥frameDuration))
```

The duration of a composition is measured in seconds; from that, we're subtracting the current index number divided by the frame rate, which is derived by dividing the frameDuration into 1. Instead of (1/thisComp.frameDuration) you could enter 24 for 24 fps, or 29.97 for 29.97, and so on. Now each successive layer in the Timeline becomes a still frame, incremented backward one frame.

Now you get to use your artist's eye. Duplicate (**Ctrl+D/Cmd+D**) the layer until you no longer see noise being reduced in the shot; or delete excess layers if you've overshot the mark. In this example, we are unfortunately limited to 7 frames because that's all we have, but you can still see that the "noise" caused by the falling rain is greatly reduced (**Figures 10.18a** and **b**).

Figures 10.18a and b In case the dramatically lower amount of rain in 10.18a isn't apparent when compared with one frame of the source (b), it should be obvious that the passing car has also been removed procedurally.

Conditionals and Triggers

Also called *If/Then statements, conditionals* open up extra possibilities by allowing you to use any circumstance that expressions can recognize—pretty much any numerical or Boolean state anywhere in the Timeline—as a condition for an event or a series of events to occur.

Triggers often use conditional statements; they wait for a specific event to occur and use this to trigger another event. The possible uses for triggers are seemingly endless.

Trigger a Dissolve

Here's a simple trigger that needs no conditonal statement: A composition marker triggers a one-second filmic dissolve (this will work equally well with layer markers). This expression could just as easily be set up to trigger a different operation, such as a simple opacity fade to black or white, but once you understand the basics, you can adapt it however you like.

A layer marker can be set by highlighting a layer and pressing * at the frame where the marker should appear. You can use this shortcut to set a marker interactively while looping a RAM Preview.

Add the Levels (Individual Controls) effect to the layer. Reveal controls for Input Black and Output White; you'll apply the same expression to each, with the variation that they will animate in opposition. The expression for Input Black is

```
mark = marker.key(1).time;
linear(time, mark, mark+1, 1, 0)
```

The inversion for Output White is

```
mark = marker.key(1).time;
linear(time, mark, mark+1, 0, 1)
```

Here's what's happening. This is the first example in this chapter of a *variable*. This one is called mark, named for the fact that it identifies a marker (and in expression of

the author's vanity). How do you know it's a marker and which one it is? The variable's argument tells you; the `marker` portion signifies a layer marker, `key(1)` specifies the first one, and `time` specifies the time at which that marker occurs.

The `linear(t, tMin, tMax, value1, value2)` command is so compact and efficient that it's easy to forget it even exists. It has five (count 'em) arguments, all required, that identify, in order, the

▶ Time that the effect evaluates

▶ Time to start a linear transition

▶ Time to end a linear transition

▶ Value at the start

▶ Value at the end

Each expression first evaluates the current time (`time`). When that time reaches `mark` (marker 1), After Effects performs a linear transition from `0` (0%) to `1` (100%), and the transition lasts one second (until `mark + 1`, or one second past marker 1). The result is visible in the Graph Editor and the composition itself (**Figures 10.19a** and **b**).

Now, why go to all that trouble to do an effect that would only require a few keyframes? There are a couple of good reasons. You can set composition and layer markers as you preview footage, interactively, like an editor would, and see immediate feedback. You can also save this effect and expression as an Animation Preset and re-use it; no keyframes ever required.

This still seems like a lot to remember, but most of the components of this expression are available via the Expressions menu. Look in the Comp category for `marker`; you need to add the dot separation between them and the semi-colon at the end yourself. With all of its arguments, `linear()` interpolates and is found in the Interpolation category. (Two versions live there, one of which uses fewer arguments.)

You can apply an expression directly from the Effect Controls panel by Alt/Option-clicking on the stopwatch, the same way you would in the Timeline panel. This can be convenient because the property with the expression is revealed in the Timeline as well, where you can edit the expression.

Any time you use a unique name followed by an equals sign, you are telling After Effects to save you the trouble of having to repeatedly type whatever comes after that equals sign. That's all. Variables = no big deal.

Figures 10.19a and b Expressions are set for Input Black and Output White (a). Note how the look differs from a simple fade to black (b). Although it's difficult to spot in a printed figure, the highlights become richer while the blacks deepen, as opposed to the entire image turning gray.

Conditionals

As mentioned in the discussion of continue loops, setting up a set of keyframes to both loop in *and* loop out poses something of a challenge; it cannot be done without the use of a conditional statement (or a split layer). Splitting a layer is inelegant, and the conditional is simple.

Suppose that you have an accurate track of an element's motion in the middle of its animation, but it needs to start from the beginning of the composition and extend to the end. The example of a sign attached to a passing vehicle from Chapter 8 contains just such a situation; the element is moving at just the right speed for the frames on which it's animated, and needs extending at the beginning and end (**Figure 10.20**).

Figure 10.20 The addition of a conditional statement to the loop expression used to track the sign on top of the taxi (from Chapter 8) allows the motion to be continued both in and out, extending right off the edge of the frame in both directions.

Here is the expression to apply in such a case:

```
t1 = key(1).time;
t2 = key(numKeys).time;
if (time < t1) loopIn("continue") else if (time >
➥t2)loopOut("continue") else value
```

There are actually several different ways you could write this expression; this happens to be among the most compact. The first two lines set variables, and the third line contains the full conditional statement. Here's how it works.

The first variable corresponds to the time at which the first keyframe appears; key(1).time is how you say "the first keyframe's time" in expressions language.

Similarly, because there could be an arbitrary number of total keyframes, the final keyframe's number will be the same as the total number of keyframes, hence key(numKeys).time provides the point in time at which the expression must loop out.

The conditional itself can be written in a few different ways; the method shown uses the least amount of extra punctuation and no line breaks. The first condition is set by the word if; the condition itself, (time < t1), must appear in parentheses, followed by the action loopIn("continue"), which occurs under that condition. In other words, "If we haven't reached the first keyframe, loop in, continuing the vector—direction and speed—of the first two keyframes."

There are two more conditions, the first of which is set by else if, setting the inverse condition from the first case; "Otherwise, if we've passed the final keyframe, loop out, continuing the vector of the final two keyframes."

You can add additional else if statements as needed, but in this case we now move to the final condition, set by else, which simply returns value. "Between the first and final keyframes, proceed normally, using the current value of each keyframe."

NOTES

There are other methods for writing conditional statements that are more suitable to complex, multi-step expressions that don't fit nicely on a few lines. See the end of this chapter for suggestions on how to learn more about scripting structure.

Conditional Triggers

By combining these two concepts, of triggers and conditionals, you can set up events that occur at layer markers. The project 10_triggers.aep file was created by Dan Ebberts, whose Web site motionscript.com is mentioned as a resource for learning more about expressions at the end of this chapter. It contains four compositions, each of which uses an expression in the top layer to trigger an event at each layer marker.

These compositions contain comments to help elucidate what is going on, and I encourage you to try and deconstruct them; this is the very best way to learn to create expressions. Three of them contain a small subroutine that yields the number of the previous layer marker, or 0 if one hasn't yet been encountered, moving through time. Here it is with comments added to each line (after the // marks, which make it safe to type any text you want on the line):

```
n = 0; // by default, the variable n is zero, until
➡the first marker
if (marker.numKeys > 0){ // if any markers exist
 n = marker.nearestKey(time).index; //n set to
➡nearest marker number
if (marker.key(n).time > time){ //if that marker
➡hasn't been reached
 n--; //subtract one from n (so that it's always the
➡previous one)
}
}
```

The final line of the composition is then a simple conditional statement based on the result.

```
if (n > 0) time - marker.key(n).time else 0 //restart
➡time at last marker
```

At the frame where a marker is encountered, the trigger occurs, and it continues either until it's done or until the next keyframe is encountered.

Tell Me More

So there you have some broad applications for expressions in visual effects work. Maybe you still want more—a more thorough understanding of the basics, if you're a beginner, or more advice on developing your own expressions, if you're an expert.

Unfortunately, expressions is one area where the official After Effects documentation falls short. Plenty of information is there, but it's organized in such a way that you already need to know quite a bit about expressions before you can understand it.

Happily, a couple of Web sites take up the slack.

▶ **www.motionscript.com:** This site is the work of Dan Ebberts, a prolific contributor of expressions information in various online forums. One section of the site, Mastering Expressions, thoroughly explains how JavaScript works as is implemented in After Effects. The Expressions Lab contains more hands-on examples for you to dissect.

▶ **www.aenhancers.com:** This is a forum-based site filled with sample expressions and scripts created for specific purposes, as well as areas for discussion about how they work. These sites also contain information on scripting, automation, and UI customization, a feature set in After Effects that, alas, makes creating expressions look like child's play (and I should know, having documented this feature on Adobe's behalf for version 6.0 and 6.5). Someday, perhaps the development team will be able to add recordable Actions as are found in Photoshop, and scripting will be unlocked for the masses. For now, however, the scripting controls are double-black-diamond expert features for most After Effects artists, typically requiring full-fledged programming skills to accomplish anything truly significant.

The book's disc also includes a couple of scripts (located in the Redefinery folder) that were created just for this book by Jeff Almasol, whose site, www.redefinery.com, contains many useful After Effects scripts. These are

▶ **rd_MergeProjects.jsx:** Suppose that you followed the advice given back in Chapters 1 and 4 and created a comp template with a custom file hierarchy for your project. The problem is that if you need to combine two such projects (by importing one into the other), you end up with two hierarchies, one nested inside the other. This script automatically merges the contents of folders in the imported project into folders with the same names in the master project (**Figure 10.21**).

▶ **rd_Duplink.jsx:** One very cool feature that competing programs such as Fusion 5 contain is instance objects, whereby you can duplicate an object and all properties of the duplicates (sometimes known as slave objects) update when the master is updated. This script recreates some of this functionality; when you use it to create duplicates of a layer, it adds expressions to the types of properties that you specify (including masks, material options, and effects) linking them to the source layer, so that as you edit it, the instanced layers change (**Figure 10.22**).

And hold on to your hats, because the complicated stuff isn't over with yet. The next chapter deals with issues specific not only to film but to a high dynamic range pipeline, which is now part of After Effects thanks to the addition of 32-bit-per-channel compositing.

Figure 10.21 Scripts can launch floating palettes such as this one, for rd_MergeProjects.jsx, which allows you to specify whether to consolidate redundant folders and footage, remove them, or both. (Script courtesy Jeff Almasol.)

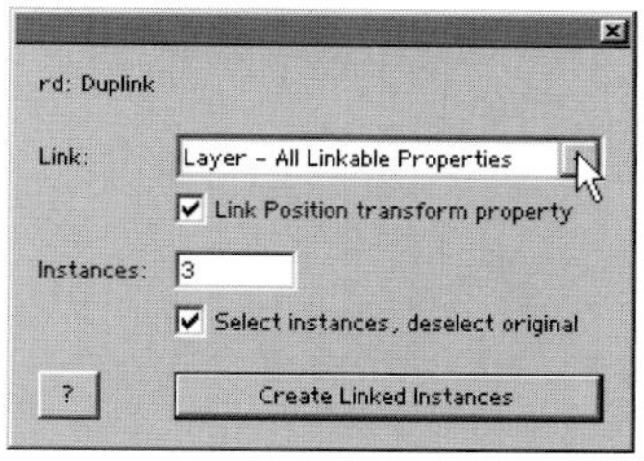

Figure 10.22 The palette, for rd_Duplink.jsx, contains options to create instances of the selected layer that remain linked to it via expressions. (Script courtesy Jeff Almasol.)

11

Film, HDR, and 32 Bit Compositing

True realism consists in revealing the surprising things which habit keeps covered and prevents us from seeing.

—Jean Cocteau (French director, painter, playwright, and poet)

Film, HDR, and 32 Bit Compositing

The most revolutionary and far-reaching change to After Effects 7.0 is also one that initially resonates with few artists, but in many ways it represents a paradigm shift in compositing. If 32 bit per channel floating point color mode, which allows high dynamic range (HDR) color adjustments, generates fear, uncertainty, or doubt, it's simply because we've trained ourselves to live without HDR, although it is in line with fundamental phenomena of the world around us.

The previous edition of this book contained a guest chapter written by Brendan Bolles, who helped create eLin, a third-party tool that allowed for *linear floating point* compositing in After Effects (if the meaning of this term eludes you, hold on—it is drawn out thoroughly in the discussion ahead). That chapter forms the foundation of this discussion of HDR compositing with the new features in After Effects 7.0.

Destined to be a marginal tool, ignored by over 99% of After Effects artists, eLin made the After Effects workflow more complicated for the sake of benefits that seemed applicable only to the highest end projects. Although it's not true that the benefits would only be seen by feature film compositors, only they seemed to welcome the cumbersome addition to the pipeline.

HDR compositing in After Effects, as made possible by 32 bit per channel mode, may seem to begin its life in a similarly marginalized role; it changes the inner (and outer) workings of After Effects in ways that are not immediately obvious. Yet its benefits are within immediate reach of anyone, on virtually any kind of project. These benefits include

▶ Goodbye to clipping: If illuminations extend outside of the range of your monitor, their appearance remains as natural as in real life; highlights and shadows are not inadvertently crushed.

▶ There is no good reason to use the Glow filter, or a bunch of other imitations of natural light phenomena, ever again. Fewer Blending modes can do more of the work, more naturally, with an HDR pipeline.

▶ The world inside After Effects can represent the real world of additive color and light. Illuminate elements in the same way that you adjust a light or lens aperture, without having to compensate for strange results.

▶ Once you start combining light levels naturally, new techniques that would previously have been off-limits emerge as natural solutions to various lighting situations.

▶ Many benefits can be enjoyed immediately, without the need to convert to *Linear Blending* mode (explained further on) or to restrict effects use to 32 bpc compatible plug-ins (of which there are currently only a handful). You don't even need to begin with HDR source.

Of course, it would not be honest to tout the benefits without also acknowledging some limitations and challenges:

▶ 32 bits per channel requires more processor power than 8 or 16. It's twice as many bits, but 2 to the sixteenth power or 65,536x more numerical data per pixel. Multiplied by the previous capacity of 16 bit per channel values, we are talking trillions of colors per channel.

▶ A complete HDR pipeline is not possible. Presently there are very few digital HDR input devices (cameras) or monitors (the ones available now are extraordinarily expensive and could not simply be plugged into your PC). Of course, the analog medium of film has always been, and remains, an "HDR" format.

▶ The benefits of HDR are not difficult to grasp or use, but the other piece of the puzzle that truly completes the picture—compositing using linear values—is a challenge to learn and understand, so unfamiliar are the underlying issues to most digital artists.

▶ Along with linear compositing comes the need to work between multiple *color spaces*—an issue to which print digital artists have been accustomed for years, but which is virtual terra incognita, and for many, an unwelcome development, in video.

▶ No model yet exists to extend custom color spaces to other parts of the pipeline—image gathering (the camera) or output (conversion to the playback medium), so the benefits that print artists receive from color management seem elusive at this stage for their film and video counterparts. In some ways, Adobe's role is similar to what it was a decade ago with print—to lead artists in a helpful new direction that nonetheless seems confusing at first.

But these points include concepts and terms that won't even be defined or discussed until later in this chapter. First, let's revisit Brendan's excellent primer to try to nail down why any of this is even worth the trouble in the first place.

Details

The difference between jaw-dropping movie effects and the motion graphics made by a budding artist comes down to one thing: details. The real world is full of detail we take for granted and rarely articulate, but it is the job of visual effects artists and supervisors to recognize where real-world detail is missing in a shot and then know how to add it.

The basic principle behind visual effects is that we are trying to replicate how each shot would look if it had simply been a real-world event captured on film. For example, when shooting a cruise ship seen from the air, a camera will shake as the helicopter it is mounted to hits turbulence and wind blows against the lens. Nature can sometimes be a nuisance, but it is unavoidable. So in creating a

NOTES

The discussion first moves to issues associated with film, before covering the 32 bit compositing environment; film in many ways represents the analog standard against which digital HDR technologies are measured, which Brendan explains well.

computer-generated boat, these motions also need to be added to the virtual camera to achieve movie-like realism. Such "imperfections" won't hurt your beautiful computer graphics, they will sell them.

Another unavoidable fact about movies is that they are always made with cameras—cameras that capture light, light that exposes film. So we need an understanding of light and film to perform our job of creating images that could have come from the real world. Because this is a matter of physics, the details can get pretty technical and the points they make may seem trivial, but grasping them will help turn a shot that looks great into one mistaken for real.

This is a chapter about details.

Film 101

The first step to understanding film is simply knowing the basic format it comes in. Thomas Edison created 35 mm film in 1889, and it remained the standard for decades. In response to the growing popularity of television in the 1950s, Hollywood conjured up a number of different widescreen formats through experiments with anamorphic lenses and film stocks as wide as 70 mm. These systems— CinemaScope, VistaVision, Panavision, and so on—haven't completely faded away, but their presence in the modern era is mostly felt in the way that films are displayed, not how they are shot. 35 mm is once again the most popular shooting format, specifically the full-aperture version known as Super 35 mm.

Standard 35 mm film has an aspect ratio of 4:3, which is not coincidentally the same as a television. Almost all current movies are filmed in this format as if originally intended for the small screen. When shown in a theater using a widescreen aspect of 1.85:1 (also known as 16:9, the HDTV standard) or 2.35:1 (CinemaScope/Panavision), the full 4:3 negative is cropped (**Figure 11.1**). Theater patrons actually pay $10 to see *less* than if they waited for the movie to get broadcast full screen on cable! You may be surprised that movies are shot with TV in mind, until you consider

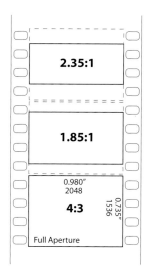

Figure 11.1 Super 35 mm film format is always 4:3 at full aperture; the typical ratios at which Super 35 is projected are crops of the full aperture, still occupying four perforations of the negative.

that home video sales have surpassed theater revenues recently. But rest assured, directors still compose their films with the theatrical aspect ratio in mind. As television transitions to HDTV, meanwhile, the 16:9 format becomes more and more common.

After a movie has been filmed, the negative is developed, and then shots destined for digital effects work are scanned frame by frame, usually at a rate of about 1 frame per second. During scanning, the Telecine process (pronounced Tell-eh-sin-ee), some initial color decisions are made before the frames are output as a numbered sequence of *Cineon* files, named after Kodak's now-defunct film compositing system. Both Cineon files and the related format, DPX, store pixels uncompressed at 10 bits per channel. Scanners are usually capable of scanning 4 K plates, although most elect to scan at half resolution, creating 2 K frames around 2048 by 1536 pixels and weighing in at almost 13 MB. Cineon files used to be transported to visual effects companies using computer tape formats, but now portable FireWire hard drives are the method of choice.

Working with Cineon Files

Because the process of shooting and scanning film is pretty expensive, almost all Cineon files ever created are the property of some Hollywood studio and unavailable to the general public. The only known free Cineon file is Kodak's original test image, affectionately referred to as Marcie (**Figure 11.2**) and available from Kodak's Web site (www.kodak.com/US/en/motion/-support/dlad/) or the book's disc. To get a feel for working with film, drop the file called dlad_2048X1556.cin into After Effects, which imports Cineon files just fine.

The first thing you'll notice about Marcie is that she looks funny, and not just because this photo dates back to the '80s. Cineon files are encoded in something called *log color space*, which is explained shortly. To make Marcie look more natural, apply After Effects' Cineon Converter, found

Figure 11.2 For a sample of working with film source, use this image, found on the book's disc.

under Channels in the Effects menu. The Cineon Converter follows equations described by Kodak for converting log space images to the video space of your monitor.

In working with film, the goal is to add whatever magic on top of the original image and then return it to the studio. Because the Cineon Converter can also convert video images back to log space, it would seem natural to convert everything to your monitor's color space, work as you always have, and then convert the end result back to log. But upon further examination of what happens in After Effects when you convert from log to linear (as After Effects calls it) and then back to log, you see a problem: With an 8 bpc (or even 16 bpc) project, the bright details in Marcie's hair don't survive the trip (**Figures 11.3a, b**, and **c**).

The obvious alternative is to leave Marcie unconverted in log space, and use the Cineon Converter for preview only. Although this is a workable plan, there are many pitfalls with this method because none of the tools in After Effects were designed with log images in mind.

What's going on with this mystical Cineon file and its log color space that makes it so hard to deal with? And more importantly, why? Well, it turns out that the engineers at Kodak know a thing or two about film and have made no decisions lightly. But to properly answer the question, it's necessary to discuss some basic principles of photography and light.

NOTES

After Effects 7.0 includes a whole new Color Profile workflow, which potentially supersedes the use of Cineon Converter when a color Working Space is active. Usage is further described later in the chapter.

NOTES

As will become evident later in the chapter, the choice of "linear" to describe the alternative to "log" space for Cineon Converter is unfortunate, because "linear" now has a specific meaning that is not appropriate in this case; what Cineon Converter calls "linear" is in fact gamma encoded.

Figures 11.3a, b, and c When you convert an image from log space (a) to linear (b) and then back to log (c), the bright details are lost.

Figure 11.4 Different exposures of the same camera view produce widely varying results.

Dynamic Range

The pictures shown in **Figure 11.4** were taken within a minute of each other from a roof on a winter morning. Anyone who has ever tried to photograph a sunrise or sunset with a digital camera should immediately recognize the problem at hand. With a standard exposure, the sky comes in beautifully, but foreground houses are nearly black. Using longer exposures you can bring the houses up, but by the time they are looking good the sky is completely blown out.

The limiting factor here is the digital camera's small *dynamic range*, which is the difference between the brightest and darkest things that can be captured in the same image. An outdoor scene has a wide array of brightnesses, but any device will be able to read only a slice of them. You can change exposure to capture different ranges, but the size of the slice is fixed.

Our eyes have a much larger dynamic range and our brains have a wide array of perceptual tricks, so in real life the houses and sky are both seen easily. But even eyes have limits, such as when you try to see someone behind a bright spotlight or use a laptop computer in the sun. The spotlight has not made the person behind any darker, but when eyes adjust to bright lights (as they must to avoid injury), dark things fall out of range and simply appear black.

White on a monitor just isn't very bright, which is why our studios are in dim rooms with the blinds pulled down. When you try to represent the bright sky on a dim monitor, everything else in the image has to scale down in proportion. Even if a digital camera could capture extra dynamic range, you still couldn't display it on a monitor. And how would that extra range be stored in an image?

A standard 8-bit computer image uses values 0 to 255 to represent RGB pixels. If you could record a value above 255—say 285 or 310—that would represent a pixel beyond the monitor's dynamic range, brighter than white or *overbright*. Because 8-bit pixels can't actually go above 255, overbright information is stored as floating point decimals where 0.0 is black and 1.0 is white. Because floating point numbers are virtually unbounded, 0.75, 7.5, or 750.0 are all acceptable values, even though everything above 1.0 will clip to white on the monitor (**Figure 11.5**).

In recent years, techniques have emerged for taking a series of exposures (such as the sunrise shots) and creating *high dynamic range* (*HDR*) images—floating point files that contain all light information from a scene (**Figure 11.6**). The best-known paper on the subject was published by Malik and Debevec at SIGGRAPH '97 (go to www.debevec. org for more details). In successive exposures, values that remain within range can be compared to describe how the camera is responding to different levels of light. That information allows a computer to connect bright areas in the scene to the darker ones and calculate accurate floating point pixel values that combine detail from each exposure.

But with all the excitement surrounding HDR imaging, many forget that for decades there has been another medium available for capturing dynamic range far beyond what a computer monitor can display.

That medium is film.

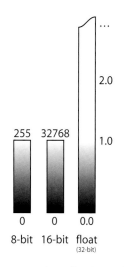

Figure 11.5 8-bit and 16-bit pixels stop at white, while floating point can go beyond. Floating point also extends below absolute black, 0.0, values that are theoretical and not part of the world you see (unless you find yourself near a black hole in space).

Darker Sky: 1.9

Bright Sky: 7.5

Dark Tree: 0.03

Houses: 0.8

Figure 11.6 Consider the floating point pixel values for this HDR image.

Cineon Log Space

A film negative gets its name because areas exposed to light ultimately become dark and opaque, and areas unexposed are made transparent during developing. Light makes dark. Hence, negative.

Dark is a relative term here. A white piece of paper makes a nice dark splotch on the negative, but a lightbulb darkens the film even more, and a photograph of the sun causes the negative to turn out darker still. By not completely exposing to even bright lights, the negative is able to capture the differences between bright highlights and *really* bright highlights. Film, the original image capture medium, has always been high dynamic range.

If you were to graph the increase in film "density" as increasing amounts of light expose it, you'd get something like **Figure 11.7**. In math, this is referred to as a logarithmic curve. I'll get back to this in a moment.

Digital Film

Because all the computer film work is essentially the processing of Cineon files and then sending a new set back to the client to be printed on film, some further examination of the Cineon log color space and its properties will serve you well.

I'll tell you now that if a monitor's maximum brightness is considered to be 1.0, the brightest value film can represent

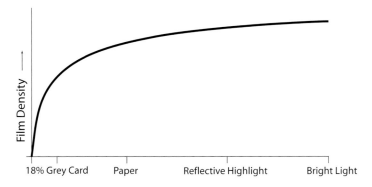

Figure 11.7 Graphing the darkening of film as increasing amounts of light expose it results in a logarithmic curve.

is officially considered by Kodak to be 13.53 (although using the more efficient ICC color conversion, outlined later in the chapter, reveals brightness values above 70). Note this only applies to a film negative that is exposed by light in the world as opposed to a film *positive*, which is limited by the brightness of a projector bulb and is therefore not really considered high dynamic range. A Telecine captures the entire range of each frame and stores the frames as a sequence of 10-bit Cineon files. Those extra two bits mean that Cineon pixel values can range from 0 to 1023 instead of the 0 to 255 in 8-bit files.

Having four times as many values to work with in a Cineon file helps, but considering you have 13.53 times the range to record, care must be taken in encoding those values. The most obvious way to store all that light would simply be to evenly squeeze 0.0 to 13.53 into the 0 to 1023 range. The problem with this solution is that it would only leave 75 code values for the all-important 0.0 to 1.0 range, the same as allocated to the range 10.0 to 11.0, which you are far less interested in representing with much accuracy. Your eye can barely tell the difference between two highlights that bright—it certainly doesn't need 75 brightness variations between them.

A proper way to encode light on film would quickly fill up the useable values with the most important 0.0 to 1.0 light and then leave space left over for the rest of the negative's range. Fortunately, the film negative itself with its logarithmic response behaves just this way.

Cineon files are often said to be stored in log color space. Actually it is the negative that uses a log response curve and the file is simply storing the negative's density at each pixel. In any case, the graph in **Figure 11.8** describes how light exposes a negative and gets encoded into Cineon color values according to Kodak, creators of the format.

One strange feature in this graph is that black is mapped to code value 95 instead of 0. Not only does the Cineon file store whiter-than-white (overbright) values, it also has some blacker-than-black information. This is mirrored in the film lab when a negative is printed brighter than usual

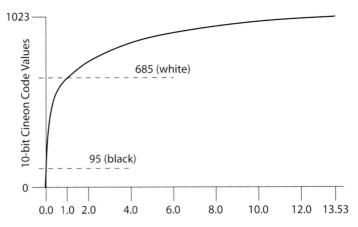

Figure 11.8 Kodak's Cineon log encoding is expressed as a logarithmic curve, with labels for the visible black and white points that correspond to 0 and 255 in normal 8-bit pixel values.

All About Log

You may first have heard of logarithmic curves in high school physics class, if you ever learned about the decay of radioactive isotopes.

If a radioactive material has a half-life of one year, half of it will have decayed after that time. The next year, half of what remains will decay, leaving a quarter, and so on. To calculate how much time has elapsed based on how much material remains, a logarithmic function is used.

Light, another type of radiation, has a similar effect on film. At the molecular level, light causes silver halide crystals to react. If film exposed for some short period of time causes half the crystals to react, repeating the exposure will cause half of the remaining to react, and so on. This is how film gets its response curve and the ability to capture even very bright light sources. No amount of exposure can be expected to affect every single crystal.

and the blacker-than-black information can reveal itself. Likewise, negatives can be printed darker and take advantage of overbright detail. The standard value mapped to monitor white is 685, and everything above is considered overbright.

Although the Kodak formulas are commonly used to transform log images for compositing, other methods are emerging. The idea of having light values below 0.0 is dubious at best, and many take issue with the idea that a single curve can describe all film stocks, cameras, and shooting environments. As a different approach, some visual effects facilities take care to photograph well-defined photographic charts and use the resultant film to build custom curves that differ subtly from the standard Kodak one.

As much as Cineon log is a great way to encode light captured by film, it should not be used for compositing or other image transformations. This point is so important that it just has to be emphasized again:

Encoding color spaces are not compositing color spaces.

To illustrate this point, imagine you had a black pixel with Cineon value 95 next to an extremely bright pixel with Cineon's highest code value, 1023. If these two pixels were blended together (say, if the image was being blurred), the result would be 559, which is somewhere around middle gray (0.37 to be precise). But when you consider that the extremely bright pixel has a relative brightness of 13.5, that black pixel should only have been able to bring it down to 6.75, which is still overbright white! Log space's extra emphasis on darker values causes standard image processing operations to give them extra weight, leading to an overall unpleasant and inaccurate darkening of the image. So, final warning: If you're working with a log source, don't do image processing in log space!

Video Gamma Space

Because log space certainly doesn't look natural, it probably comes as no surprise that it is a bad color space to work in. But there is another encoding color space that you have been intimately familiar with for your entire computer-using life and no doubt have worked in directly at some point: the video space of your monitor.

You may have always assumed that 8-bit monitor code value 128, halfway between black and white, makes a gray that is half as bright as white. If so, you may be shocked to hear that this is not the case. In fact, 128 is much darker—not even a *quarter* of white's brightness on most monitors.

A system where half the input gives you half the output is described as linear, but monitors (like many things in the real world) are nonlinear. When a system is nonlinear, you can usually describe its behavior using the gamma function, shown in **Figure 11.9** and the equation

$$\text{Output} = \text{input}^{\text{gamma}} \qquad 0 <= \text{input} <= 1$$

In this function, the darkest and brightest values (0.0 and 1.0) are always fixed, and the gamma value determines how the transition between them behaves. Successive applications of gamma can be concatenated by multiplying them together. Applying gamma and then 1/gamma has the net result of doing nothing. Gamma 1.0 is linear.

Mac monitors usually have a gamma of 1.8, and the gamma value for PCs is 2.2. What this really says is that the electronics in your screen are slow to react from lower levels of input voltage and everything is darkened as a result.

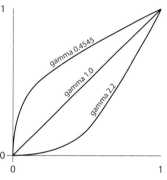

Figure 11.9 Graph of monitor gamma (2.2) with file gamma (0.4545) and linear (1.0). These are the color curves in question, with 0.4545 and 2.2 each acting as the direct inverse of the other.

The description of gamma in video is oversimplified here somewhat because the subject is complex enough for a book of its own. An excellent one is Charles Poynton's *Digital Video and HDTV Algorithms and Interfaces* (Morgan Kaufmann Publishers).

Gamma-rama

In case all this gamma talk hasn't already blown your mind, allow me to mention two other related points.

First, you may be familiar with the standard photographic gray card, known as the 18% gray card. But why not the 50% gray card?

Second, although I've mentioned that a monitor darkens everything on it using a 2.2 gamma, you may wonder why a grayscale ramp doesn't look skewed toward darkness. 50% gray on a monitor looks like 50% gray.

The answer is that *your eyes are nonlinear too!* They have a gamma that is just about the inverse of a monitor's, in fact. Eyes are very sensitive to small amounts of light and get less sensitive as brightness increases. The lightening in our eyeballs offsets the darkening of 50% gray by the monitor. If you were to paint a true gradient on a wall, it would look bright. Objects in the world are darker than they appear.

Getting back to the 18% card, try applying that formula to our gamma 0.4 eyes:

$$0.18^{0.4} = 0.504$$

Yep, middle gray.

The reason digital images do not appear dark, however, is that they have all been created with the inverse gamma function baked in to pre-brighten pixels before they are displayed (**Figure 11.10**). Yes, *all* of them.

Because encoding spaces are not compositing spaces, working directly with images that appear on your monitor can pose problems. Similar to log encoding, video gamma encoding allocates more values to dark pixels, so they have extra weight. Video images need converting just as log Cineon files do.

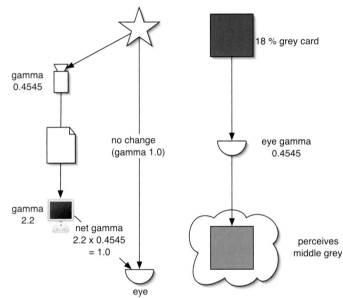

Figure 11.10 Offsetting gammas in the file and monitor result in faithful image reproduction.

Battle of the Color Spaces

Right about now, many of you are looking around to see which window to throw this book out of. You have done perfectly fine working with unconverted video, thank you very much.

Truly, much great work has already been created by artists working in nonlinear color spaces, some even in log space. But the color space you work in is going to affect the final image, so you must pick the one that helps you accomplish what you've set out to do, which is to simulate how the world is photographed by a camera. When you brighten a scene, you want to mimic the addition of another on-set floodlight or an expanding camera aperture. An image is blurred to imitate light from out-of-focus objects spreading out across the film gate. To do this properly, you need the compositing math to mimic light in the real world.

In the real world, light behaves linearly. The nonlinear encoding in video and film is introduced *after* all the light has been added linearly. Turn on two lightbulbs of equivalent wattage where you previously had one and your entire scene will become exactly twice as bright. By working in a linear color space, you can perfectly simulate this effect simply by doubling your pixel values. You are getting back to the color space of the original scene. For this reason, linear pixels are often referred to as *scene-referred values*.

The examples in **Table 11.1** show the difference between making adjustments to digital camera photos in their native video space and performing those same operations in linear space. In all cases, an unaltered photograph featuring the real in-camera effect is shown for comparison.

The table's first example brightens the image by one stop. A stop refers to clicks on a camera's aperture—the iris that controls how much light coming through the lens will expose the film within. Widening the aperture by one stop allows twice as much light to enter, and each additional stop redoubles the exposure again. An increase of three stops brightens the image by a factor of eight ($2 \times 2 \times 2$, or 2^3).

Doubling the pixels in video space causes bright areas in the image to blow out very quickly. Video pixels are already encoded with extra brightness and can't take much more. Notice how the curtain and computer screen have lost detail in video space, while the same operation performed in linear space has retained detail. Also notice how the linear image is nearly indistinguishable from the actual photo for which camera exposure time was doubled (another practical way to brighten by one stop).

The second example simulates an out-of-focus scene using Fast Blur, one of the most common operations performed in After Effects. You may be surprised to see that it actually causes an overall darkening with bright highlights fading into the background—at least when applied in video space. In linear, the highlights pop much better. See how the little man in the Walk sign stays bright in linear but almost fades away in video because of the extra emphasis given to dark pixels in video space.

Try squinting your eyes as you look at these images to see how only the video image has darkened overall. Because a

TABLE 11.1 Comparison of Adjustments in Native Video Space and in Linear Space

	BRIGHTEN ONE STOP	LENS DEFOCUS	MOTION BLUR
Original Image			
Filtered in Video Space			
Filtered in Linear Space			
Real-World Photo			

defocused lens doesn't cause any less light to enter it, the video blur is not behaving like a true defocus. Comparison with the real-world defocus drives the point home even more, although this simple linear example doesn't mimic the camera's aperture shape or the scene's overbright information, so it isn't completely identical to the real photograph either, but it's close.

The table's third example uses After Effects' built-in motion blur to simulate the streaking caused by quick panning as the photo was taken. Pay particular attention to the highlight on the lamp; notice how it leaves a long, bright streak in the linear and in-camera examples. Artificial dulling of highlights is the most obvious giveaway of nonlinear image processing.

Artists have dealt with the problems of working directly in video space for years without even knowing. A perfect example is the Screen transfer mode, which is additive in nature but whose calculations are clearly convoluted when compared with the pure Add transfer mode. Screen uses a multiply-toward-white function with the advantage of avoiding the clipping associated with Add. But Add's reputation comes from its application in bright video-space images. Screen was invented only to help people be productive when working in video space, without overbrights; Screen *darkens* overbrights (**Figures 11.11a**, **b**, and **c**). Real light doesn't Screen, it Adds. Add is the new Screen, Multiply is the new Hard Light, and many other Blending modes become evident as mere kludges in linear floating point.

Figures 11.11a, b, and c Adding in video space blows out (a), but Screen in video looks better (b). Adding in linear is best (c).

Floating Point

A common misconception is that if you work solely in the domain of video you have no need for floating point. But just because your output will ultimately be restricted to the 0.0 to 1.0 range doesn't mean that overbright values above 1.0 won't figure into the images you create.

In the **Figures 11.12a**, **b**, and **c**, each of the bright Christmas tree lights is severely clipped when shown in video space, which is not a problem so long as the image is only displayed, not adjusted. 11.12b is the result of following the rules by converting the image to linear before applying a synthetic motion blur. Indeed, the lights are creating pleasant streaks, but their brightness has disappeared. In 11.12c the HDR image is blurred in 32 bit per channel mode, and the lights have a realistic impact on the image as they streak across. Even stretched out across the image, the streaks are still brighter than 1.0. Considering this printed page is not high dynamic range, this example shows that HDR floating point pixels are a crucial part of making images that simulate the real world through a camera, no matter what the output medium.

Floating point's benefits aren't restricted to blurs, however; they just happen to be an easy place to clearly see the stark difference. Every operation in a compositing pipeline gains extra realism from the presence of floating point pixels. The simple act of combining one layer with another via a Blending mode benefits hugely; this may be the area above all where the old ways will start to look like cheap tricks compared with the brave new world of HDR.

Figures 11.12a, b, and c An HDR image is blurred without floating point (a) and with floating point (b), before being shown as low dynamic range (c). (HDR image courtesy Stu Maschwitz.)

Figures 11.13a, **b**, and **c** feature an HDR image on which a simple composite is performed, once in video space and once using linear floating point. In the floating point version, the dark translucent layer acts like sunglasses on the bright window, revealing extra detail exactly as a filter on a camera lens would. The soft edges of a motion-blurred object also behave realistically as bright highlights push through. Without floating point there is no extra information to reveal, so the window looks clipped and dull and motion blur doesn't interact with the scene properly.

And now, a two-part news flash for anyone wondering what this has to do with your own work:

1. After Effects 7.0 supports floating point compositing natively; all that needs to be done is to toggle a project to 32 bpc mode.

2. After Effects 7.0 also supports true linear compositing. Unfortunately, this requires a bit more than flipping a switch: You must learn how to manage color spaces, which raises questions whose answers are not easily guessed. The rest of this chapter will attempt to address those questions and answers in depth.

Just to be perfectly clear, you can have number 1 without bothering with number 2 in After Effects. It's a nifty way to pull off some cool lighting effects, such as the look of the lightsaber in Chapter 14, "Pyrotechnics: Fire, Explosions, Energy Phenomena," simply by creating some threshold values that, when boosted above monitor range, exhibit the glowing effects of high-intensity light.

Even more surprising, After Effects allows number 2 without number 1 as a prerequisite; linear blending is maintained even when a project is switched to 8 bpc or 16 bpc mode, unless you choose specifically to disable it.

But to composite naturally in an HDR world means to work with radiometrically linear, or scene-referred, color data. For the purposes of this discussion, this is perhaps best called "linear light compositing," or "linear floating point," or just simply, "linear." The alternative mode to which you are accustomed is "gamma-encoded," or "monitor color space," or simply, "video."

Figures 11.13a, b, and c A source image (a) is composited without floating point (b) and with floating point (c). (HDR image courtesy Stu Maschwitz.)

32 Bits per Channel

Imagine that you had the use of a digital video camera that was capable of recording all of the detail in a scene, no matter how dark and underlit or completely blown out with light (or, as is often the case, both in the same scene). Now imagine that you could transfer all of that data to your computer with a monitor that could precisely display that tremendous range of color as you worked it into a final result, and that any changes you made worked with light as naturally and dynamically as light functions in nature itself. Finally, imagine that you could retain that dynamism and precision on whatever device (monitor, projector, film printer) was used to display the result.

This is the dream for HDR, but a dream that may not be quite as impossible (or far into the future) as it seems. For now, there are several hurdles:

▶ Most digital video cameras record compressed 8-bit data that is limited to the same range as your monitor; a camera such as the Viper Filmstream is the rare exception that can match the 4:4:4 10-bit log output of Cineon-converted film. Although still well short of the almost incomprehensible range of HDR, this is a vast improvement over what a normal DV camera delivers: 8 bit per channel gamma encoded signal with no more dynamic range than a JPEG you download off of the Web or the monitor that displays it.

▶ Few displays exist offering output range that extends beyond the 8 bits per channel to which we're all accustomed; those that do, such as the Sunnybrook HDR display (with a contrast ratio of 60,000:1), are currently astonishingly expensive, not to mention that you cannot simply plug it into your current display outputs.

▶ No standard exists to maintain color as it is transferred from one media/device to another, and thus from one color working space to another. The video industry has barely begun to standardize color the way the print industry did beginning a decade ago.

So, not only is After Effects 7.0 also After Effects HDR 1.0 (so to speak), but it must currently exist in a less-than-perfect world for HDR. Adobe's point right now is to improve the way color is handled right in After Effects (along with Photoshop), regardless of what happens with the other pieces of the puzzle (**Figure 11.14**). With version 7.0, the essentials have been put in place.

Welcome to the World of HDR

Although it is not necessary to use HDR source to take advantage of an HDR pipeline, it offers an effective way to get a glimpse of this brave new world. Open 11_treeHDR_lin.aep; it contains a comp made up of a single image in 32 bit EXR format (used to create Figures 11.12a, b, and c). With the Info panel clearly visible, move your cursor around the frame.

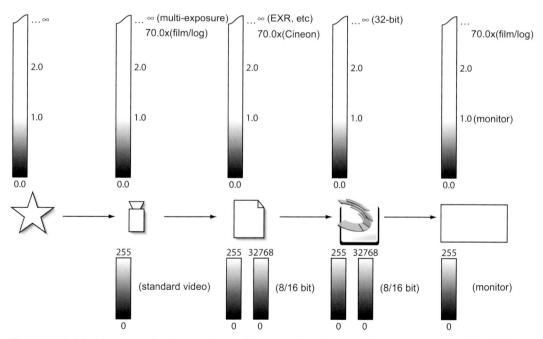

Figure 11.14 As is shown in this flowchart, each step of the process has the potential to accommodate HDR pixels; it is also possible to use the HDR range only at one or two steps of the process and still benefit. At this writing, there are no common digital HDR capture (camera) or display (monitor) formats, although HDR stills can be created from multiple exposures. To say that 32-bit formats have "infinite" range is admittedly not mathematically accurate, but as far as human vision goes, it is effectively true.

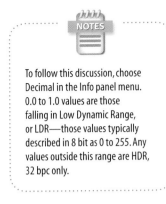

As your cursor crosses highlights—the lights on the tree, specular highlights on the wall and chair, and most especially, in the window—the values are seen to be well above 1.0, the maximum value you will ever see doing the same in 8 bpc or 16 bpc mode. Remember that you can quickly toggle between color spaces by Alt/Option-clicking the project color depth identifier at the bottom of the Project panel.

Any experienced digital artist would assume that there is no detail in that window—it is blown out to solid white forevermore in LDR. However, you may have noticed an extra icon and accompanying numerical value that appears at the bottom of the composition panel in a 32 bpc project (**Figure 11.15**). This is the Exposure control; its icon looks like a camera aperture and it performs an analogous function—controlling the exposure (total amount of light) of a scene the way you would stop a camera up or down (by adjusting its aperture).

Figure 11.15 Exposure is an HDR preview control that appears in the Composition panel in 32 bpc mode.

Drag to the left on the numerical text and something amazing happens. Not only does the lighting in the scene decrease naturally, as if the light itself were being brought down, but at somewhere around -10.0, a gentle blue gradient appears in the window (**Figure 11.16a**).

Drag the other direction, into positive Exposure range, and the scene begins to look like an overexposed photo; the light proportions remain and the highlights bloom outward (**Figure 11.16b**).

Figures 11.16a and b At -10 Exposure (a), the room is dark other than the tree lights and detail becomes visible out the window. At +3, the effect is exactly that of a camera that was open 3 stops brighter than the unadjusted image (b).

The Exposure control in the Composition panel is a preview-only control (there is an effect by the same name that renders); scan with your cursor and Info panel values do not vary according to its setting. This control offers a quick way to check what is happening in the out-of-range areas of a composition. With a linear light project, each integer increment represents the equivalent of one photographic stop, or a doubling (or halving) of linear light value. And (perhaps unbeknownst to you) this particular project is not only 32 bpc, but linear.

Linear Blending

Before getting into the nitty gritty of how a linear color project is set up in After Effects, it's worth exploring first-hand how things work differently in linear HDR.

First of all, apply a Levels effect and lower Output White to 0.5; the bright pixels go gray and blah-looking in exactly the manner to which you're accustomed in LDR. But lo and behold, Levels has a couple of new check boxes that, alas, are enabled by default even in a 32 bpc project; Clip to Output Black and Clip to Output White. Uncheck these (although only the latter matters in this case) and overbright values are restored to the scene, although it is darker overall. How much darker? Exactly one half, or one stop darker.

Take a snapshot of this setting (**Shift+F5**) and turn off Levels. Now apply an Exposure effect (a new addition to the Color Correction section) and set Exposure to –1.0. Press **F5** to compare, and note that the result is the same—it's one stop darker (remember, that's what one integer Exposure value represents).

Now create a middle gray solid the size of the composition; go to the Hue/Saturation/Brightness settings and make Saturation 0% and Brightness 50%. Set the solid's Blending mode to Multiply. Again, press **F5** to compare, and again, note that the result is to stop down the image one stop. Duplicating the source image layer and setting Blending to Add would be exactly like raising exposure one stop. One benefit of working in linear floating point is that these photographic terms (and concepts) can be employed faithfully and logically.

Keep in mind that for each 1.0 adjustment upward or downward of Exposure you double (or halve) the light levels in the scene. Echoing the earlier discussion, a +3.0 Exposure setting sets the light levels 8x (or 2^3) brighter.

Output Black and White are clipped by default in Levels for backward compatibility. It's such a pain to remember to uncheck them for HDR compositing that you're better off getting in the habit of using an Animation Preset that has them already unchecked, such as Levels_Unclipped.ffx (on the disc).

These and other applied examples of HDR usage (re-creating those described in the Floating Point section earlier in this chapter) can be found in 11_linearHDR.aep, with comments as to what is happening in each. These are among the basic benefits of linear floating point composit-ing. Now it's time to look at how to set up a linear project of your own, and the price you must pay for being an early adopter.

Color Management

With 11_linearHDR.aep open, choose File > Project Set-tings (**Figure 11.17**); anyone familiar with this dialog box from previous versions will notice the addition of the Color Settings portion.

Although Linear Blending is unchecked by default, in this project, you will find it activated, meaning that all blending operations (such as the medium gray solid multiplied over the image) occur as linear operations. Import/Output 32 bpc Formats as Linear Light is checked by default; we'll revisit that one in the "Project Setup" section later.

The Linear Blending toggle is applicable only to apply linear blending behind the scenes within a standard gamma encoded work-ing space. This example project uses a linear color project working space (as described below) so this toggle makes no difference in this case; the blending is linear whether or not it is activated.

Figure 11.17 The new Color Settings area is command central for color management in After Effects. It includes Working Spaces with confusingly long names and a rather intimidating amount of fine print, but it is also the key to simplifying a linear floating point workflow.

And that brings us to the area of this dialog that may really make you wince—the Working Space drop-down menu, where you will find a list of specified ICC color profiles. This includes a laundry list of video formats, as well as profiles of any other output devices that may have been added to your system (such as monitors or printers). The Working Space included with this project (which is not installed with After Effects) has the catchy name "Linear sRGB IEC6 1966-2.1 (D65)." You're getting ready to throw this book out the window again, aren't you?

Earlier the "Battle of the Color Spaces" section outlined two basic types of color space: nonlinear and linear. But from the "Cineon Log Space" section, you also know that there are at least two radically different color spaces within the "nonlinear" category: monitor gamma and Cineon log. In truth, there is a potentially unlimited number color spaces, some subtly different from one another, others profoundly so. What the heck are they doing in After Effects?

The Project Working Space offers a couple of specific and forward-looking benefits. The end goal for Adobe is to resolve the battle of the color spaces, as follows

- ▶ To control how After Effects interprets colors internally, so that linear, log, and video input can be used together in the appropriate Project Working Space without the need to keep track and transfer them back and forth manually (although you can do so using the Color Profile Converter, as is detailed below)

- ▶ To accurately preview the appearance of the image on a specified output device or media (which can be done independently of the Project Working Space using the Proof Colors feature)

Let's look at a couple of practical situations where this actually makes life easier, not more complicated.

The Project Working Space

Suppose you are working on a project whose output should look right on a broadcast television monitor, and you don't have a Sony BVM preview monitor attached to your rig for easy previewing. Switching the Project Working Space to

CLOSE-UP

Linear Color ICC Profiles

In order to set up your own color-managed linear floating point project, you must select a linear color profile as your Project Working Space, and After Effects does not ship with any because Adobe was concerned about the can of worms that would be opened for anyone who didn't know what they were doing. Courtesy of The Orphanage are two such profiles, which can be found in the Profiles folder on this book's disc. They should be installed with the system's other ICC profiles. For Mac users, the location is

~/Library/ColorSync/Profiles

and on Windows, it is

C:\Program Files\Common Files\Adobe\Color\Profiles

Restart After Effects and these are listed in Project Settings.

SMPTE-C (**Figure 11.18**) should accurately represent the look of that broadcast monitor, provided your own monitor has been calibrated (either using a system calibrator such as the Apple Display Calibrator Assistant, or even better, with a monitor calibration tool and associated software).

Project Working Space uses an ICC profile to recreate the primary colors and *gamut* of a broadcast video monitor on your RGB display. Gamut is simply the range of colors that can be displayed, and as you may have noticed, it varies from device to device. The same shot may look blue on your monitor, neutral on film, and magenta/purple on a broadcast monitor. It turns out these variations are largely measurable and predictable, just as with print.

If setting a SMPTE-C profile helps you to live without a broadcast monitor as you work in After Effects, great. For

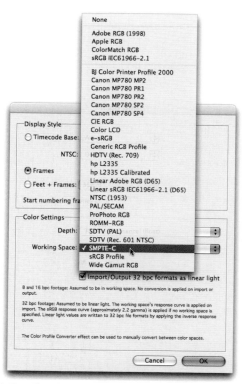

Figure 11.18 Even if you're not working on a linear floating point project, you can benefit from Working Spaces; the SMPTE-C setting re-creates the display gamut of a pro broadcast monitor on your calibrated display.

this system to really operate correctly, each image that you import or export should also contain its own ICC profile, but After Effects does not offer a method to attach a profile to a render, nor does it detect one on import (you must set it manually using the Color Profile Converter, as is explained in the "Project Setup" section). If all of this is making color profiles seem, well, not that cool, let's look at one unique situation where the full pipeline has been implemented—for Cineon film compositing.

Theater Preview

Remember setting the Cineon Converter to see the Marcie image look correct earlier in the chapter? That method is officially old-school now that After Effects 7.0 includes a Color Working Space, which allows you to work with log files without having to apply an effect to see them look correct. Here's how to set up a film project using 10-bit Cineon source now (making sure that you have first installed the ICC Profiles as detailed in the "Linear Color ICC Profiles" sidebar):

1. Create a new project.

2. In File > Project Settings, set Depth to 32 bits per channel (float), and Working Space to Linear Adobe RGB (D65), although any chosen Working Space will allow these steps to be completed; what you cannot do is leave Working Space unspecified.

3. Import the Marcie image (dlad_2048X1556.cin)

4. With the image selected, choose Interpret Footage (**Ctrl/Cmd+F**) and click More Options.

5. Choose Kodak 5218 ICC Profile and click OK twice.

6. Create a new comp containing Marcie.

7. With the comp or Timeline active, choose View > Proof Setup > Kodak 2383 Theater.

8. Select View > Proof Colors.

To see a project set up this way, open 11_cinemaPreview. aep. Whatever work you do on this composition is now accurately previewed as it will appear on Kodak Vision film

Figure 11.19 With Proof Colors activated and set to emulate Kodak Vision film stock, Marcie takes on a deeper, richer look that accurately reflects the color response of the film.

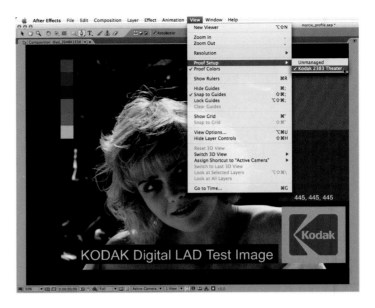

You are probably aware that there is more than one type of film stock in the world. Kodak Vision is a widely popular but not universal standard, and for the debut of this feature, it was evidently decided that one managed Proof Setup is better than none.

stock (provided, of course, that the monitor itself has been calibrated). I know of at least one effects artist who pipes this output via HDMI to his LCD projector so that his director can plunk down on an eight-foot beanbag chair and preview how his effects will appear on film (**Figure 11.19**).

Meanwhile, Back in the Real World...

There are more ways in which 32 bpc linear compositing is ideal, but now that we've explored a few of the features, we need to discuss what is really required to incorporate your work into this pipeline and where you are likely to face some challenges. Clearly, the ideal world in which all source is HDR is not a current reality, nor are more than a handful of effects in After Effects compatible with 32 bpc color. Finally, there is the crucial question of getting the material out of After Effects looking as it should in LDR formats, given that desired final output isn't likely to be 32 bits per channel.

Project Setup: Color Profile Converter

Most of the footage and files you import into After Effects are likely to be LDR with no attached ICC profile. Try importing normal 8 bpc footage (such as one of the Artbeats clips on the disc, located in the Artbeats\Clips_QuickTime folder), set the Project Working Space to Linear Adobe RGB, and you'll notice the image becomes brighter. It contains the boosted gamma of a standard video image and must be linearized to look right.

Apply a Color Profile Converter effect (found in Effect > Utility, **Figure 11.20**). All you must do in this case is choose an RGB profile appropriate to your image; in my experience and on my system, ColorMatch RGB returns the image to its prior appearance, but you might prefer one of the other top four: Adobe RGB, Apple RGB, or sRGB. Output remains set to Project Working Space. The gamma of the image has now been assimilated into the linear light project.

And what if the source actually has an embedded RGB profile (most likely created in Photoshop or Illustrator)? It will seem strange that After Effects includes no method either to assign this on import or even to parse it from the source file. If you know what it is, enter it as the Input Profile. If not, you can use the application that created the file (in Photoshop, choose Edit > Assign Profile).

Most HDR source images these days are output from a computer graphics application (perhaps a 3D animation renderer such as Mental Ray or Brazil). These images should be created as linear floating point, meaning they require no Color Profile Converter effect to operate in a linear 32 bpc After Effects project. However, creating linear renders requires some understanding of linear floating point on the part of the artist or technical director who creates them. If EXR images or other 32 bpc source images appear too bright, you can uncheck Import/Output 32 bpc Formats as Linear Light in File > Project Settings (which changes the content of the copious fine print below the toggle).

Included on the disc are two images from The Orphanage, sanityCheck.exr and sanityCheckEXR.tif (**Figure 11.21**). The 32 bpc EXR file is linearized, but the 8 bpc TIFF file is not. Two corresponding projects are also included, one using no color profile, the other employing a linear profile. These should help illustrate the different appearances of a linear and a gamma-encoded image.

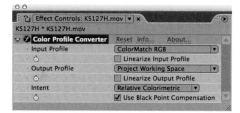

Figure 11.20 Color Profile Converter is set to convert normal gamma encoded source (the Input Profile) to the Project Working Space (the Output Profile). This is how you bring non-HDR footage into a linear floating point project.

NOTES

Clearly, the failure to parse embedded color profiles in After Effects is not ideal, but for most users it is certainly preferable to an After Effects equivalent of the "Missing Profile" and "Embedded Profile Mismatch" warnings that are legion in Photoshop CS.

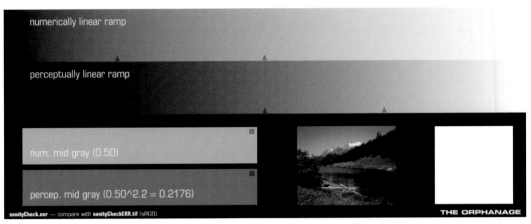

Figure 11.21 Two "sanity check" files included on the disk are identical except for their respective color spaces, making it easy to reference the difference between, say, perceptual and numerical middle gray (marked in blue and red, respectively) in linear and gamma-encoded space.

Incompatible effects

Okay, so the source is imported. How many effects can be safely applied in an HDR project? The answer is 31—that is, if you're counting only the 32 bit per channel effects that ship with After Effects (which you can preview by selecting Show 32 bpc Effects Only in the Effects & Presets panel menu). Some truly essential color correction and blur effects, along with Keylight and a number of utilities specifically for HDR, are included, along with effects such as the Expressions Controls that don't handle pixels at all.

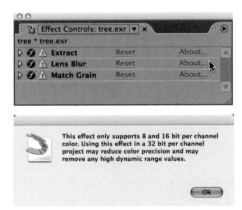

Figure 11.22 After Effects warns you in various ways that applied effects do not support 32 bpc mode.

But try and apply a 16 bpc or (shudder) 8 bpc effect to tree. exr and notice that, although the image may appear no different, the overbrights are gone—all clipped to 1.0. Any effect will reduce the image being piped through it to its own color space limitations. A small warning sign appears next to the effect to remind you that it does not support the current bit depth. You may even see a warning explaining the dangers of applying this effect (**Figure 11.22**).

Of course, this doesn't mean you need to avoid these effects to work in 32 bpc. It means you have to cheat, and After Effects includes a preset allowing you to do just that: Compress-Expand Dynamic Range (contained in Effects & Presets > Animation Presets > Image – Utilities; make certain Show Animation Presets is checked in the panel menu).

This preset actually consists of two instances of the HDR Compander effect, which was specifically designed to bring floating point values back into LDR range. The first instance is automatically renamed Compress, and the second, Expand, which is how the corresponding Modes are set. The way it works is like this: you set the Gain of Compress to whatever is the brightest overbright value you wish to preserve, up to 100. The values are then compressed into LDR range, allowing you to apply your LDR effect. The Gain (as well as Gamma) of Expand is linked via an expression to Compress, so that the values round-trip back to HDR. The approach is similar to that of eLin in After Effects 6.5 (**Figure 11.23**).

If banding appears as a result of Compress-Expand, Gamma can be adjusted to weight the compressed image more toward the region of the image (probably the shadows) where the banding occurs. You are sacrificing image fidelity in order to preserve a compressed version of the HDR pipeline. We can all hope that in some subsequent version of After Effects, most essential effects will operate in 32 bits per channel, obviating the need for this workaround, but for now it's one cost of living on the bleeding edge.

CLOSE-UP

Floating Point Files

As you've already seen, there is one class of files that does not need to be converted to linear space: floating point files. These files are already storing scene-referred values, complete with overbright information. Common formats supported by After Effects are Radiance (.hdr) and floating point TIFF, but the newest and best is Industrial Light + Magic's OpenEXR format. OpenEXR uses efficient 16-bit floating point pixels, can store any number of image channels, supports lossless compression, and is already supported by most 3D programs thanks to being an open source format.

If the knowledge that Industrial Light + Magic created a format to base its entire workflow around linear doesn't give it credence, it's hard to say what will.

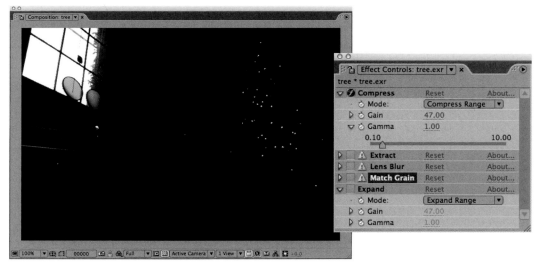

Figure 11.23 The Compress-Expand Dynamic Range preset round-trips HDR values in and out of LDR range; the Gain and Gamma settings of Compress are automatically passed to Expand via preset expressions. Turn off Expand and an image full of overbright values will appear much darker, the result of pushing all values downward starting at the Gain value.

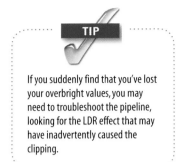

If you suddenly find that you've lost your overbright values, you may need to troubleshoot the pipeline, looking for the LDR effect that may have inadvertently caused the clipping.

Additionally, there are smart ways to set up a project to ensure that Compander plays the minimal possible role. As much as possible, you should group all of your LDR effects together, and if you can, keep them away from the layers that use Blending modes, where float values are most essential. For example, apply an LDR effect via a separate adjustment layer instead of directly on a layer with a Blending mode. Also, if possible, apply the LDR effects first, then boost the result into HDR range to apply any additional 32 bpc effects and Blending modes.

Output

Finally, what good is it working in linear floating point if the output bears no resemblance to what you see in the composition viewer? Or, suppose you want to render the appearance with Proof Colors on for review in dailies?

If you are simply working in 32 bits per channel without a Project Working Space assigned, you don't need to do anything; just render to your preferred format and the output looks exactly as it does in the viewer.

Otherwise, with a linear profile assigned, Color Profile Converter is once again the key. Depending on which workflow you prefer, you can either add an adjustment layer containing this effect to the top of the master Timeline or to a separate Output composition (as was recommended way back in Chapter 4, "Optimizing Your Projects"). Input should be set to Project Working Space, and Output should be set to your preferred RGB setting (again, mine is ColorMatch RGB; you may prefer Adobe RGB or sRGB).

The image appears too bright after assigning a gamma correction in this manner because the project is still set up overall to expect only linear pixel data (**Figure 11.24**). Here's where View > Proof Colors once again comes in handy, but this time, choosing View > Proof Setup > Unmanaged provides the correction. What's going on here? The underlying Project Working Space is still linear, but the Unmanaged setting actually returns display output to what you might consider its normal state (before there was such a thing as a working space in After Effects). The Project Working Space is not passed through to the display.

Figure 11.24 The viewer displays an image that appears too bright because the project expects it to be linear but the effect converts it to video space. It appears to have been gamma encoded twice, although the output will in fact appear correct.

The result of this conversion is that the HDR values are still present, but the composition has a video gamma applied. Any LDR effects you apply will clip the highlights, but the presumption is that, at this stage, you are done with them. And that is one of the most difficult things for artists new to the HDR workflow to comprehend; when it's time for final output, you can essentially throw away most of the data that was available, because it was mostly there to help you along the way. Even going to film, the billions of colors of 10-bit Cineon log represent no perceptible compromise when compared to the trillions of colors of HDR; they are able to capture the contrast range of film. If linear floating point ever becomes truly standard, it may become normal to use 32 bpc files as output, but only when there are devices commonly available that are actually capable of displaying all that range of contrast.

Therefore, to output 10-bit Cineon log, you follow the same steps to apply Color Profile Converter as with video output, with two changes: Output Profile must be set to DPX Scene – Standard Camera Film, and Intent must be switched to Absolute Colorimetric. This clips overbrights

Proof Colors is set on a per-composition basis, which is why a comp or its Timeline must be selected when setting it. In a linear project, linear comps need it off, and gamma-corrected (video) comps need it on.

To review the setups described here, check out 11_HDRworkflow.aep on the disc.

that are outside 10-bit log range (above 70.0 or so), which is appropriate, given that film cannot store or display values that bright without clipping them (nor can the eye easily distinguish them, making it no great loss for output).

Finally, to render a gamma-encoded video clip that includes the appearance of the Theatre Preview created back in Figure 11.19 (so that the video that is played in dailies looks like Kodak Vision film), add a second Color Profile Converter effect. Set the Input Profile to DPX Theater Preview – Standard Print Film and the Output Profile to SMPTE-C.

Conclusion

And to think that all of that constitutes just an overview of linear floating point compositing in After Effects 7.0. Applied of examples working in 32 bpc mode follow in the next chapter, and throughout Section III.

This chapter concludes Section II, which focused on the most fundamental techniques of effects compositing. In the next and final section, you'll apply those techniques. You'll also learn about the importance of observation, as well as some specialized tips and tricks for specific effects compositing situations that re-create particular environments, settings, conditions, and natural phenomena.

SECTION III

III

Creative Explorations

Chapter 12 Working with Light   417

Chapter 13 Climate: Air, Water, Smoke, Clouds   455

Chapter 14 Pyrotechnics: Fire, Explosions, Energy
              Phenomena   483

Chapter 15 Learning to See   507

Working with Light

There are two kinds of light: the glow that illuminates and the glare that obscures.

—James Thurber

Working with Light

Light is the most complex phenomenon a compositor must understand, and in much the same way a painter or cinematographer understands it. In other areas of digital production, elaborate models are derived to simulate the way light works in the physical world. Accurate modeling of the physics of light is crucial to realistic 3D renders, and the science of light phenomena, such as radiosity, caustics, the inverse square law, environment mapping, and many more, have transitioned from theoretical papers delivered at SIGGRAPH to features readily available in high-end 3D software.

The world of the compositor is less pure and scientific, which if anything makes an understanding of light phenomena in a scene that much more significant. Like a painter, you must observe the workings of light in the three-dimensional world so that you can re-create them in a two-dimensional frame, using your software toolbox. Like a cinematographer, you must have a feeling for how lighting and color decisions affect the beauty and drama of a scene.

Several chapters in this book have already touched upon principles of the behavior of light. Chapter 5, "Color Correction," focused on the most fundamental work of the compositor: matching the brightness and color of a foreground layer to a background source. Chapter 11, "Film, HDR, and 32 Bit Compositing," explored the complex issue of working with light values that extend beyond the range that your monitor can display.

This chapter is dedicated to situations in which you as a compositor must create or emulate specific lighting conditions in your scene. You'll explore the actual behavior of

NOTES

Chapter 11 introduced the radical idea that there are alternative color models to the ones with which you're already familiar and that one of these in particular, linear floating point, represents the direction in which digital imaging is headed. Linear floating point is supported natively in After Effects 7.0; the basic workflow was described in that previous chapter, and hands-on examples follow toward the end of this chapter.

light, its direction, intensity, color, position, reflection, diffusion, occlusion, and volume, and methods of re-creating these in realistic and dramatic ways, including such special situations as backlighting, flares, glints, blurs, and defocused lenses. I'll distinguish between lighting conditions you can easily emulate and those that are essentially out of bounds—although, for a compositor with a good eye and patience, the seemingly "impossible" can be met as a welcome challenge.

Light Source and Direction

Often, when you need to match elements to a source, the steps outlined in Chapter 5 to match brightness, contrast, and hue are sufficient. In many scenes, however, there is clearly more involved with light than brightness and contrast. In some cases, the direction of the light plays a role, especially where the quality of the light is *hard* (direct) rather than *soft* (diffuse).

Such a huge variety of light situations is possible in a shot, and in an infinite array of combinations, that it becomes difficult to make any broad statements stand up about lighting. This section, however, tries to pin down some general guidelines and workflows for manipulating the light situation of your scene.

Location and Quality

You may have specific information about the lighting conditions that existed when your plate footage was shot. On a set, you can easily enough identify the placement and type of each light; this information is contained to some extent in a camera report also. If the source shot was taken only with natural lighting, you're seeking the position of the sun relative to the camera (**Figure 12.1**). This information can help you puzzle out highlights and shadows when it's not clear how to match the lighting of the plate.

Sometimes the location and direction of light is readily apparent, but surprisingly often, it's not. As I write this, I'm looking out the window on an overcast day. The sunlight is coming from the south (on my left), but as I look at

Figure 12.1 Three shots lit only by the sun; in each case shadows tell you the light is coming from behind and to the right of camera, but as the sky becomes more overcast, the light becomes more diffuse and its direction more difficult to discern.

objects in my backyard, it seems to have no direction at all, because it's not direct, it's diffuse. Furthermore, it keeps changing.

The quality of light in a scene is the most subjective and elusive of criteria. Hard, direct light casts clear shadows and raises contrast, and soft, diffuse light lowers contrast and casts soft shadows (if visible at all). That much seems clear enough. But these are broad stereotypes, which do not always hold as expected. For example, hard light aimed directly at a subject from the camera's point of view flattens out features, effectively decreasing contrast. And when multiple lights combine to light a subject, hard shadows can be diffused, a typical result of artificial lighting (**Figure 12.2**).

Figure 12.2 It's typical on a larger stage to use multidirectional lighting, causing light and shadow areas to overlap and cancel one another out to some degree. (Image courtesy Pixel Corps.)

Heightening Drama with Light

Although the color and contrast of the scene can be nailed down precisely, light direction and quality can be slippery, surprising, changeable, and difficult to re-create. All true, but there's still plenty you can re-create—or get away with—by following a few basic guidelines:

▶ **Use elements with similar source lighting.** This is the most obvious point. Matching hard- and soft-lit elements is generally difficult, if not impossible. Sometimes contrast of soft shadows can be raised, or existing shadows can be softened, but there's always a limit. If possible, use elements that were shot, rendered, or painted with a similar quality of light to the plate.

▶ **Changing apparent light direction is just about impossible, particularly in a hard-lit scene (Figure 12.3).** Incorrect light direction, in cases where it's evident, is one of the big giveaways of bad compositing, although for whatever reason it isn't always noticed by the audience the way matte lines and other such basic compositing mistakes are noticed.

Figure 12.3 It sounds good in theory to keep lighting even and diffuse in order to be able to change it later, but most dramatic shots—and in particular, those which include faces—demand the opposite, strong lighting choices that enhance expressions. (Image courtesy Kenwood Media Group.)

▶ **Shadows are often broken up by indirect or reflected (bounced) light.** This phenomenon has given rise to global illumination in 3D rendering programs. Study the world around you, and you start to notice interesting things that light does as the result of reflected light mixing with direct light. A clear, black cast shadow is rarely as interesting as one contaminated by secondary light. This knowledge can free you from the need to faithfully play it straight with cast shadows.

▶ **Natural light can change rapidly over time.** Clouds overhead, trees rustling, an open flame, the sunlight reflected off of a shimmering pool—all of these create dramatic interactive lighting in a scene, helping bring it to life (and distracting the viewer if there's too much of it). If they're part of the story, you want these elements, but there are only limited ways to add them in 2D **(Figure 12.4).** Some are explored in this chapter.

▶ **Foreground elements that you add can change the lighting situation.** Be aware that if an element is highly reflective (and even more so, if self-illuminating), you must account for its interaction with the rest of the scene.

TIP

If you minimize its effects, mismatched light direction seems to be one category where you can get away with something.

Figure 12.4 Trying to re-create the effect of dappled natural light caused by an overhanging canopy of trees blowing in the breeze? Good luck—better to get this lighting set, perhaps using an old trick such as a bicycle wheel with pieces of paper woven through its spokes slowly moving in front of the key light.

Mastering the use of light in a scene is no simple matter. For centuries, painters defined themselves as much by their observation and use of light as anything; a new school of thought would develop, typically driven by a "master" who had observed something novel and revolutionary about how light works, and the course of art history would change. So instead of looking for the lazy quick fix, keep studying reference for details you can steal.

Neutralizing Light Direction

If your source was shot with a light direction that is incorrect for the composited shot, that's a pretty big problem, depending on how hard and directional the light actually is. The solution is generally to neutralize—that is, isolate and then minimize—rather than to attempt to actually fix the discrepancy.

Because every camera setup in the world has unique light characteristics, it's hard to offer a "fix" that will apply to a majority of shots; it depends on the lighting you have (the source) and the lighting you want (the result). For the purposes of discussion, consider a situation in which shadows and highlights clearly indicate the key light position. Also assume that a simple quick fix, such as flopping the shot, is not possible (which it usually isn't). Then you can

▶ Isolate and remove directional clues from the element, such as cast shadows (probably via matting and rotoscoping).

▶ Isolate and reduce contrast of highlights and shadows; this may use a combination of a luma key (to isolate highlights or shadows) and a Levels or Curves adjustment. Color Finesse is also often a sophisticated tool for these types of overall image corrections.

You can also flatten out uneven lighting, especially on a background that is meant to be relatively uniform, using the following technique.

Leveling Uneven Light and Hotspots

There is a simple trick that can be used to even out lighting in cases where it should appear uniform and does not. The basic idea is simple: Create a counter gradient that weights an image adjustment by bringing up the shadows, bringing down the highlights, or both. What's surprising is how powerful the technique is—and to how many situations it applies.

You can create the gradient to do this by eye. In some cases, such as scenes with low contrast, you can use the inverted, blurred source itself to create the matte. But as a compositor used to looking at light, you should be able to discern where the hotspot is, and how far it reaches (**Figure 12.5**). You might even find this kind of fun.

Figure 12.5 This scene is lit by a single key light aimed at the center of the scene, causing a distracting hotspot on the torso of the second bunny from the left.

Figure 12.6 A simple gradient created to match the offensive area of the hotspot. The center and edge of the radial gradient, created with the Ramp effect, have been positioned by eye to match Figure 12.7.

The next step is to create a white-to-black gradient using the Ramp effect that matches your perception of the hotspot in the scene (**Figure 12.6**). You could apply the result directly to the scene with a Blending mode, but you'll have more control if you apply it as a luma track matte to an adjustment layer containing a Levels or Curves effect. This allows you to select whether you're adjusting highlights and shadows or gamma.

The result won't necessarily obliterate all evidence that there was hot lighting anywhere in the scene (**Figure 12.7**), but as always, the goal is not only aesthetic beauty but also the viewer's focus. If there seems to be a distracting spotlight on the middle of some part of the scene, there's a problem.

Figure 12.7 It's not as though all traces of the single hard key light have been eliminated, but that was not the aim of this adjustment. Instead, the effect of the light has been reduced so that it no longer puts the viewer's focus in the wrong place.

TIP

The examples depicted here are included on the disk using still images, as if shot with a static camera. However, should the camera move during the shot, the gradient start or end points can be joined to a tracker, via either expressions or parenting. (See Chapter 8, "Effective Motion Tracking," as well as Chapter 10, "Expressions," for details.)

Conversely, you can also add a *vignette* or *eye light* effect using a radial gradient at the center of the frame, with the corners slipping away to darkness. This is often associated with projected or heavily treated film and with handheld low-light shooting. The easiest way to do this is not with Ramp but with a heavily feathered and inverted elliptical mask applied to a black solid, which is easier to move and scale (**Figure 12.8**).

Figure 12.8 Reference of film footage that was shot and processed with a vignette, and addition of the equivalent vignette effect in After Effects. Double-click the Elliptical Mask tool to fill the frame, then open the mask controls (MM), check Invert, and set a high Mask Feather (500 for this 2K resolution source).

Figure 12.9 The same gradient as in Figure 12.6, but duplicated with a Multiply Blending mode, creating the inverse-square fall-off. Ordinary incandescent lights such as the one depicted exhibit this phenomenon.

CLOSE-UP

Geek Alert: Inverse Square Law

3D artists and lighting directors out there will be aware that a linear gradient is not the perfect model for light falloff and that light's intensity diminishes proportionally to its distance from the source squared. So if I'm twice as far from a single light source as you are, I will be illuminated by one-quarter the amount of light.

So I suppose you want a gradient that behaves this way? Simple. Duplicate your layer with the radial gradient, and set the upper of the two layers to a Multiply Blending mode. There you have it: inverse square dissipation of intensity (**Figure 12.9**). Instead of using a gradient layer directly as a luma matte, put the two combined gradients into a single precomposition, and you're good to go.

Who knows, maybe you'll even find a situation where you notice the difference; the number of shots taken with a single light source is not high, but the same adjustment would work with any single light that is too hot. If nothing else, you've just avoided paying money for one more third-party plug-in that offers one more capability you can easily create for yourself.

To see what I mean, compare the behind-the-scenes footage on *The Matrix* DVD with the look of the film itself.

Creating a Look with Color

Study a movie that you consider to be visually compelling. Particularly if it was created in the last few decades, chances are that the use of color in that film is bold and deliberate. If you've ever seen behind-the-scenes video taken on the set of a film, you might have been startled at how flat and boring all the action looks.

Some of that movie magic process is the direct result of photochemical processes applied to the film. For example, much of the strange, detached, futuristic appearance of the film *Minority Report* was derived from the use of the "bleach bypass" method used to process the film. To some degree, it is possible to re-create these kinds of looks purely in After Effects, particularly with good reference.

Using a Solid

Suppose a client or supervisor requests that the shot be "warmer" or "cooler." What tool does this? Levels, Hue/Saturation, Tint, Color Balance—all of these effects and more are capable of satisfactorily altering the color look of your shot.

Before even going there, however, try a more direct and interactive method. The result looks a bit like a colored filter added to the imaginary lens of your virtual camera, because that's effectively what it is.

Add a colored solid with its Blending mode set to Color. Choose a color that is pleasing to your eye, has brightness and saturation well above 50%, and fits your color criteria: blue or green for a cooler look, red or yellow for a warmer one (**Figure 12.10**).

At 100%, this is the equivalent of a full-color tint of the image, which is not typically the goal. Instead, dial Opacity back to somewhere between 10% and 50%, to the threshold where the source colors remain discernable, although filtered by the color added; you're dialing in the look. What I find powerful about this approach is that, assuming you've gotten the color right, you need only adjust it with that Opacity slider. With this approach, you are only ever

Figure 12.10 The source shot and a blue, yellow, and blue-green (or "Matrix") filter, each added via solids of those colors and the Color Blending mode.

Figures 12.11a, b, and c The distinction between color detail using a color solid (a) and a Hue/Saturation adjustment (b) may be too subtle for print (if so, check out 12_tintcomparison.aep) but even on the page of this book, the Tint effect (c) makes the source look drowned in pea soup.

two adjustments away from transforming the look of your shot. Furthermore, the effect is more natural and subtle, allowing more of the source color through than the alternatives of adding a Tint or an HSB effect (**Figures 12.11a, b, and c**).

Day for Night

Go further with this filter idea and you emulate camera optical effects such as making a daytime scene appear as if it were shot on a moonlit night.

NOTES

Because it involves blending color values, this technique does benefit, subtly, from being performed as a linear operation (as described in the previous chapter). Projects with both setups are included on the disc: 12_colorlook_8bpc.aep and 12_colorlook_32bpc.aep.

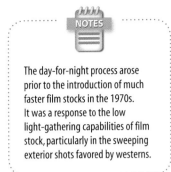

The day-for-night process arose prior to the introduction of much faster film stocks in the 1970s. It was a response to the low light-gathering capabilities of film stock, particularly in the sweeping exterior shots favored by westerns.

It's such a classic old Hollywood effect that it became the title of French "new wave" filmmaker Francois Truffaut's ode to filmmaking: the day-for-night effect, or as it is known in French, *la nuit américaine.* The trick is a simple one: Shoot a normally lit scene using a dark blue filter on the lens, creating the appearance of night—sort of. Ideally, the source would be shot under diffuse, cloudy conditions, but circumstances didn't always cooperate, so the "moon" would sometimes cast hard shadows. It was amazing how bright a specular highlight the moon could cause, kicking off the barrel of the hero's drawn gun.

Lighting techniques and film itself have improved at the high end, but it is still handy (and a good exercise) to completely change the lighting conditions of a shot. Digital cameras are notoriously poor at getting anything but grain out of low-lit scenes; witness the popularity of the cheesy Sony Handicam Nightshot feature, which is destined to go down as a hallmark look of this era (similar to how Super 8 film says 1960s and '70s).

Figure 12.12 shows a demonstration of a day-for-night effect achieved primarily with a dark, desaturated blue solid over a desaturated and darkened background image. This is another good example of where the methodology differs depending on whether you work in 8 bpc or linear floating point; the latter option yields more subtleties and flexibility (which you can check out for yourself by opening 12_dayfornight.aep and 12_dayfornight_32bpc.aep).

Figure 12.12 Sunset becomes moonlight. Most of the color subtleties of this operation are lost to print and best seen on screen.

The basic idea is to add a dark blue filter. In LDR color, this is best done via Overlay mode, but in linear floating point, this becomes a Multiply operation. Not only is the white point of the underlying image brought down significantly, the image is desaturated using the Tint effect at the default settings. The art in this case is to let a little of the yellow of the sun remain as the yellow glow of moonlight, so Tint is lowered from 100% to more like 60% (**Figure 12.13**). The next section explains why Tint, and not Hue/Saturation, is used to desaturate the color.

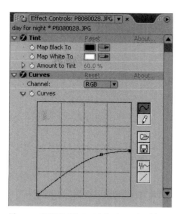

Figure 12.13 Tint at black and white and 60% partially desaturates the image, and Curves lowers the white point while maintaining some overall brightness with a gamma boost.

Using Effects

Solids, then, can be an effective filter for an entire image, but what about cases that demand the colorization or desaturation of a single element? In these cases, effects such as Hue/Saturation or Tint may be more useful because of how they can be applied individually.

To remove color entirely, rendering an element grayscale, there is a significant difference between these two effects. Tint maintains the human distinction of the relative brightness of red and green and blue. Hue/Saturation does not, but instead maintains numerical proportions. This distinction deserves explication, offered in **Figures 12.14a** through **d** using the Mars flag and as follows.

Figures 12.14a through d Ladies and gentlemen, the Flag of Mars (a): three fields of pure red, green, and blue—a perfect candidate to demonstrate that Tint (b), and a monochrome (white, gray, or black) solid with Color Blending mode (c) re-create (and thereby maintain) perceptual differences in the brightness of red, green, and blue, while Hue/Saturation (d) does not. Hue/Saturation is mathematically correct; the perceptual differences are a subjective phenomenon of human vision.

NOTES

The flag of Mars is a red, green, and blue tricolor selected by the Mars Society and flown into orbit by the Space Shuttle Discovery. Seriously. It bears no apparent resemblance to the one Marvin the Martian used to claim Planet X.

TIP

Hue/Saturation is fine when used lightly to desaturate footage (or less often, to boost saturation). What is not so obvious to a novice artist is when to use it. If you find yourself fighting a color correction and you're focused only on brightness and contrast (using Levels), notice whether overall saturation is a little hot—this is often the case in heavy color corrections.

Each color of the flag is fully saturated in one channel. Mathematically, the correct thing to do is to average the luminance of each channel for each color, turning them all an equivalent gray; this is what Hue/Saturation does. It causes all of the apparent contrast between the colors to vanish because it ignores the way the eye sees color.

As mentioned in Chapter 6, "Color Keying," there is a standard weighting used in digital imaging to replicate and maintain the relative proportions at which the eye perceives the brightness of the primary colors. This weighting is employed by the Tint effect, and in most situations where After Effects internally converts color to luminance. For example, a solid with a 0% Saturation value set with the Color Blending mode has a similar result to a black-and-white Tint at 100%.

Therefore, Hue/Saturation is ill advised as a grayscale conversation tool. It is, however, very useful and convenient for quickly colorizing an element. On *The Day After Tomorrow* all of us on the compositing team at The Orphanage came to memorize the exact Hue value that the supervisor tended to love (my recollection is that it was $237°$) and applied it to various snow and fog overlay elements that had been created as grayscale mattes.

Three-Way Color Correction

For those of you keeping score, After Effects offers no three-way color corrector, although considering that such a tool recently debuted in Adobe Premiere Pro 2.0 (**Figures 12.15a and b**), you might expect it to appear in a future version of After Effects.

This tool, for those unfamiliar with the term, separates color controls into three basic regions—highlights, midtones, and shadows—and enables you to adjust each separately. After Effects actually has a seldom-used effect that does just the same: Color Balance (HLS). The problem with this tool is its user interface, which consists only of a bunch of sliders. A typical three-way color corrector, such as the one in Premiere Pro, orients its user interface around three color wheels that allow a target color to be set for each of the three tonal regions.

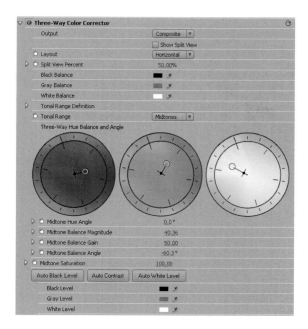

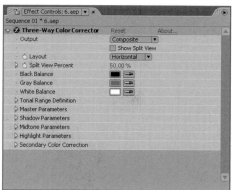

Figures 12.15a and b The Adobe Three-Way Color Corrector is part of Premiere Pro (a), not After Effects, where it is a hidden effect that appears only when included as part of an imported Premiere Pro project (b).

Figure 12.16 The image is again tinted predominantly blue via the Master color picker, but warmer tones are introduced to the shadow, midtone, and highlight areas. All of the actual work is done by the Color Balance effect, which is not adjusted directly but via expressions linked to the five controls preceding it. (3-Way Color Balance courtesy Stu Maschwitz.)

Undeterred by these usability limitations, the author of Chapter 15 decided to design a custom interface for Color Balance (HLS) using expressions. It is included on the disc as 3WayCB_01.ffx; **Figure 12.16** shows it in action. The result can be as strong as filtering with a solid, but is designed to allow you to experiment with adding extra subtleties.

"Kiss of love" is not a technical term. It is attributed to Stu Maschwitz from when he supervised *Star Wars, Episode One: The Phantom Menace* at Industrial Light + Magic. "I still use that term today," he says. "It's a great way to get an artist to think of a shot as theirs. Examples of kisses of love are reflections in things that might not strictly need it, aperture flares for lights leaving the frame (carefully matched to reference), or animating a starfighter pilot's head to turn as he banks."

As you may know, light wrap plug-in effects do exist for After Effects. This is a case where "roll your own" works just as well, if not better.

Backlighting, Flares, Light Volume

Situations in which light sources appear prominently in a scene are something of a gift to a compositor: They offer a clear target. Nail them, and you will sell your scene in ways that the viewer can hardly perceive. This is the *kiss of love*, that something extra that isn't necessary to get the shot finaled but that adds to the shot.

The early days of computer graphics were littered with bad light artifacts. In one particular sci-fi series, any shot in outer space that included a sun or a star (which seemed to be most of them) got a big, prominent lens flare. This was based not on visual reference, but stereotyped ideas and tricks based on cool new tools. It was years before NewTek's LightWave 3D, which actually can render beautiful images, lost its reputation as "the lens flare software."

Ironically, big, bold, daring choices about light can and should become almost invisible if they are appropriate to a scene. Generally, the rule about strong lighting choices is this: If the choice is going to stand out, it should do something to place the viewer's attention where it needs to be to serve the story. If a strong choice doesn't serve the story, maybe it had better not hog the focus of the shot.

Backlighting and Light Wrap

The conditions of a backlit scene are a classic example where the compositor often does not go far enough to match what actually happens in the real world. This is the general subject of Chapter 15, "Learning to See," which alludes specifically to light wrap. Here, then, is the methodology for creating your own light wrap.

This technique is designed for scenes that contain backlighting conditions and a foreground that, although it may be lit to match those conditions, lacks light wrapping around the edges (**Figure 12.17**).

You set up the light wrap effect as follows:

1. Create a new composition that contains the background and foreground layers, exactly as they are positioned and animated in the master composition. You

can do this simply by duplicating the master comp and renaming it something intuitive, such as Light Wrap. If the foreground or background consists of several layers, it will probably be simpler to prcompose them into two layers, one each for the foreground and background.

2. Set Silhouette Alpha Blending mode for the foreground layer, punching a hole in the background (**Figure 12.18**).

3. Add an adjustment layer at the top, and apply Fast Blur.

Figure 12.17 The silhouetted figure has been color corrected to match the scene, but lacks any of the light wrap clearly visible around the figures seated on the beach.

Figure 12.18 Using the alpha of the layer to which it's applied, Silhouette Alpha punches a hole through that layer and all underlying layers.

4. In Fast Blur, check the Repeat Edge Pixels toggle on and crank up the blurriness (**Figure 12.19**).

5. Duplicate the foreground layer, move the copy to the top, and set its Blending mode to Stencil Alpha, leaving a halo of background color that matches the shape of the foreground (**Figure 12.20**).

6. Place the resulting comp in the master comp and adjust opacity (and optionally switch the Blending mode to Add, Screen, or Lighten) until you have what you're after. You may need to go back to the Light Wrap comp to further adjust the blur (**Figure 12.21**).

Figure 12.19 Heavy Fast Blur causes the background image color to bleed into the area of the underlying alpha channel.

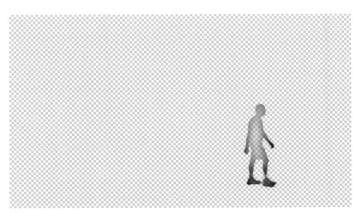

Figure 12.20 Stencil Alpha provides the inverse effect, preserving only the areas of the composition inside the alpha of the top layer to which it is applied. You have your light wrap.

Figure 12.21 The addition of light wrap causes the figure to appear as part of the scene.

One final thing to keep in mind as you adjust a scene with backlit conditions: If there is no fill light on the foreground subject whatsoever, most cameras are incapable of picking up as much detail in the foreground as your eye might see. In your reference photo, an unlit foreground subject might appear completely silhouetted. Because the foreground subjects are often the stars of the scene, you might have to compensate, allowing enough light and detail in the foreground that the viewer can see facial expressions and other important dramatic detail.

In other words, this might be a case where your reference conflicts with what is needed for the story. Try to strike a balance, but remember, if the story loses, everyone loses.

Glints and Flares

Just because that big lens flare coming from the sun peeking around the side of that sci-fi moon looks cheesy doesn't mean all lens flares are cheesy. Of course, real lens flares are never cheesy: Our eyes accept them as natural, even beautiful artifacts without necessarily understanding anything about what actually causes them (**Figures 12.22a**, **b**, and **c**).

To get lens flares or even simple glints right, it is vital to look at good reference. This will seem strange if you consider it; probably only a tiny percentage of your viewers can

---

CLOSE-UP

Three-Way Blur

After Effects offers lots of different blur effects, but most artists use one of three. Some automatically reach for Gaussian Blur; others have noticed that Fast Blur, applied to a layer set to best quality, is no different (except that it renders faster); and finally, there is Box Blur, which if used correctly supercedes the other two.

The key is the Iterations setting. At the default (1), the result of a Box Blur can seem crude and, well, boxy, but it also approximates the look of a defocused lens (in some ways obviating the need for Lens Blur, which is not HDR compatible). But you can raise this setting as high as you want, up to 50, which not only amplifies but also refines the blur kernel.

Box Blur has a couple of other advantages as well. Blur Dimensions can be set to Horizontal or Vertical only, creating a directional blurring effect. Finally, there is a bug with Fast Blur in After Effects 7.0: Applied to a masked layer, with Repeat Edge Pixels activated, it fails to blur beyond the boundaries of the mask (making it virtually unusable in such a case).

Figure 12.22a, b, and c Three situations in which what the camera yielded in reality might not be what you'd expect in theory. Figure 12.22a has no lens flare, when you might expect one; 12.22b has just the barest suggestion of a flare spiking out of the huge light source pouring in through the window, and 12.22c has a lens flare that is more natural but far less apparent than the flares you would get from the Lens Flare effect.

You won't see lens flares in many Hollywood films made prior to the 1970s. Flares were long regarded as errors on the part of the cinematographer, and shots containing them were carefully noted on the camera report and retaken. This all changed with the appearance of such films as *Easy Rider*, which seemed to demand a casual, documentary style, as well as pictures from space that showed the sun emerging brilliantly around the curve of our own planet.

tell the difference between lens flares from a 50 mm prime and a 120 mm zoom lens. Yet somehow, if you get the lens flare wrong, it reads as phony to a majority of viewers. Weird.

As is acknowledged in Chapter 15, it's possible to create a lens flare effect from scratch, potentially using well over a dozen nested compositions, based on reference. This brings up two very cool points:

▶ Lens flares are consistent for a given lens. Their angles vary according to the position of the light, but not the shape or arrangement of the component flares, so nothing need stop you from re-creating your own.

▶ Although a 17-element lens flare makes for a good battle story, some of the most natural-looking lens flares barely grab your attention at first and have only one or two simple components—even just a bright spot in the frame, sometimes.

Moreover, not every bright light source that appears in frame will cause a lens flare—not even the sun. (Look again at Figure 12.22a.)

Most After Effects users will prefer a built-in solution that goes beyond the three settings included with the program's rather useless built-in Lens Flare (useless because everyone knows those three flares; they haven't changed in the better part of a decade). There is more than one option available on the market.

John Knoll is responsible for a great lens flare package called Knoll Light Factory, available from Red Giant Software. A demo is included on the book's disc. Without lapsing into a full-fledged product endorsement, there are two very helpful things about this set: First is that John knows flares, and the presets that are contained in these plug-ins are derived from careful studies of the corresponding lenses. If they're in there, it's probably because Industrial Light + Magic shot a project with that lens, and John took the time to get the preset right. Second, you don't have to rely on presets with this one; it is modular, allowing you to pick and choose various flare effects. In the interest of fairness, I will say that many users like to use the lens flare plug-in offered by The Foundry as part of Tinderbox. You can create a realistic looking flare with that plug-in, but some pretty goofy-looking flares are made with its default settings. No matter which software you use, the key, as always, is to do your visual research.

Glints

Glints are related to lens flares in that they are also the result of bright light found directly in the scene, but glints are unique in that they are a natural effect, commonly seen with the naked eye, not a lens effect. **Figure 12.23** shows an example of a glint in the footage that was used in the Chapter 5 color matching example.

The glints observed on passing cars, then, represent an opportunity to replicate them directly on the computer-generated plane passing through the shot. This is a great example of a detail that is rarely added, which constitutes a kiss of love for the shot.

CLOSE-UP

Geek Alert: What Causes a Lens Flare?

Lens flares are artifacts that are never seen with your naked eye. They are artifacts created within the camera lens itself, caused by secondary reflections bouncing around between the camera elements. Because they are caused within the lens, they will always appear superimposed over the image, even over objects in the foreground that partially block the background light.

Unlike your eye, which has only one very flexible lens, camera lenses are typically made up of a series of inflexible lens elements. These elements are coated to prevent light reflecting off of them under normal circumstances. Extreme amounts of light, however, are reflected somewhat by each element.

Zoom lenses contain many focusing elements and tend to generate a complex-looking flare with lots of individual reflections. Prime lenses generate fewer.

Several other factors besides the lens elements also contribute to the look of a flare. Aperture blades within the lens cause highly reflective corners that often result in streaks, the number of streaks corresponding to the number of blades. The shape of the flares sometimes corresponds to the shape of the aperture (a pentagon for a five-sided aperture, a hexagon for six). Dust and scratches on the lens also reflect light.

Finally, lens flares look very different depending on whether they were shot on film or video, the excess light bleeding out in different directions and patterns.

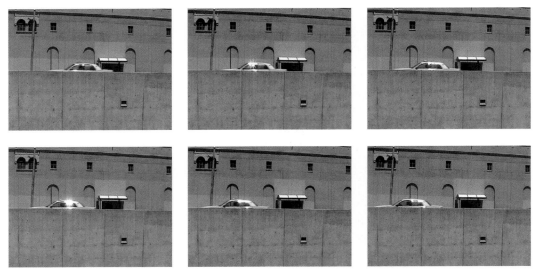

Figure 12.23 This sequence shows the glint that plays off the chrome areas of the taxi as it passes a spot in the frame where the sun is reflected directly into the camera lens.

Figure 12.24 There's not a whole lot to a glint when you look at it closely, especially at video resolution.

The great thing about glints is that they're easily observed (especially if they're already in the shot) and nearly as easily replicated, although in the taxi example shown, getting them right may involve adding unique glints to several frames in a row. The glint is caused when something in the frame (chrome along the taxi's windows in the example) acts like a mirror, reflecting the overhead sun directly toward the camera.

In the shot from Chapter 5, the plane moves rather quickly through frame, and the glints on the taxi seem to occur just to the left of the frame's center, so that's the reference. You're looking for a hotspot on the plane that passes that point in the frame, and you get one on the tail.

By zooming in on your reference, you get the color and shape of a typical isolated glint (**Figure 12.24**). And behold: It's a white blotch with six thin streaks coming off of it (which probably corresponds to a six-sided aperture). Looks like something you can paint rather quickly, no?

This is a perfect case in which it's best not to be a perfectionist. Close-up, the result of my quickly painted glint

Figure 12.25 The plane passes by, hand-painted glints added to its tail.

Figure 12.26 The glows of a full moon on a clear night, of a taillight receding into the distance, of stadium lights at dusk—we get so used to seeing the halo around these we hardly notice it after a while.

looks most unimpressive indeed. But place it into a fast-moving shot that was never meant to be studied frame by frame, and I've just bought myself a good dose of extra realism for a few minutes' extra work (**Figure 12.25**).

Light Scattering and Volume

The phenomena of light scattering and its most dramatic and visible result, volumetric light, are also the result of what happens to rays of light as they encounter particles in the air. The atmosphere does not permit light to travel directly to the camera, uninterrupted. Instead, the light ricochets off tiny particles in the air, revealing its path.

There are other situations in which this phenomenon occurs, closer up and more dramatically. Lights that appear in the scene, casting their beams at the camera, tend to have a glowing halo around them. If the light traveled directly to the camera, the outline of the source light would be clear. Instead, light rays hit particles on their way to the camera and head off in slightly new directions, causing the halo (**Figure 12.26**).

Place more particles in the air (in the form of smoke, fog, or mist), and you get more of a halo, as well as the conditions under which volume light and such related phenomena as *God rays* can occur. These are the result not only of light scattering, but of the fact that light from an omnidirectional source, such as the sun, travels away from the source via a continuous arc of potential angles (**Figure 12.27**).

What does all this mean to you? You ought to re-create these phenomena when they're called for, not only because they look realistic but because they tend to look cool. As a compositor you don't want to miss an opportunity like that. After Effects has no built-in, one-button function for adding these types of effects, and so your method will vary depending on the shot.

A soft feathered mask roughly the shape of the source, applied to a solid that is roughly the color of the intended effect is often all you need. For visible particulate matter, a Fractal Noise effect can be animated (as is detailed in the following chapter).

Although After Effects contains no ability to create and render direct visible lights and their effects (for example, if you place a point light in your scene, you see its result but not the light itself), a plug-in from Trapcode called Lux adds that capability, so it is an option as well. A demo of Lux is included on the book's disc.

On *The Day After Tomorrow*, one of the shots done at The Orphanage required "inverse" God rays (occlusion, really) caused by the Empire State Building blocking the sun in a heavy snowfall. In other words, just as the rays themselves array outward, so do the shadows caused by large objects blocking them. With this phenomenon nailed, the shot was not only more accurate but more interesting to watch.

Figure 12.27 The cathedral of light known to the pious and pagan alike as God rays.

Shadows and Reflected Light

Uh-oh, I guess the time has come for shadows. If lighting is complex, shadows are even more so. At least with lights, their placement in the source scene can be re-created. But you could have the full dimensional information of the scene at your disposal, as well as all the lighting, and only a vague notion of how the shadows should behave. Your sole advantage is that the audience doesn't know, either.

The addition of 3D features, including lights and shadow casting, to After Effects 5.0 improved the fakery potential, if only somewhat. The problem remains that you're still basically stuck using a flat 2D plane (or planes) to project a shadow and a flat plane (or planes) to receive it, and the greater the angle of difference between the camera and a given light, the less possible it is for that shadow to be accurate.

Figure 12.28 illustrates the problem, showing a keyed figure lit from the left side with a spot. Keying to keep the shadow proved difficult. But re-creating it using the silhouette of the character is nearly impossible; clearly, his outline from the side bears almost no resemblance to his outline as seen by the camera. As you saw in Figure 12.6, there's not much possibility of changing his light direction here; it seems pretty evident that all of his lighting is coming from the left.

Figure 12.28 Compare the source shadow taken on set with the type of shadow you can re-create by casting 3D lights onto the 2D keyed figure, and the lack of dimensionality is immediately apparent. Atrocious.

Creating Shadows

Figure 12.29 shows the classic 2D solution for cast shadows, corner-pinning the matte to an angle that is something like that at which the camera sees the object, with a figure whose outline is complex and lit from an angle more than 10 or 15 degrees off axis from the camera. It doesn't work very well here, but it is certainly possible to pull it off with simpler objects.

Figure 12.29 Sigh. Not much better is the corner pin approach, skewing a duplicate of the matte layer as if lying down. This one would need a lot of hand-painting to get it right at all, and the angle in this case is completely wrong. Dismal.

TIP

You can use the shadow matte itself directly, setting its Outpoint White (in Levels) to 0 and then adjusting its Opacity down to soften the shadow. If you instead apply it as a luma track matte to an adjustment layer, then adjust the shadow using a Levels or Curves control, this gives you a bit of extra control over how the shadow interacts with the background, its effect on highlights versus already dark areas, and so on.

Another 2D trick is one borrowed from the games industry; The Orphanage was actually able to use this one extensively for the Level Four sequence of *Spy Kids 3-D* because the story of the movie was characters trapped inside a video game. The cheat is that characters only cast a small pool of shadow beneath their feet or where they're sitting, and so on. The simple way to create this one is to mask off part of the matted character and translate only that into position. By feathering the mask and blurring the matte contained inside it quite a lot, you add some subtle interactivity between the character and the ground plane and basically just hope nobody really thinks about it too much (**Figure 12.30**). Likewise, a contact shadow such as was employed back in Figure 5.38, which is a tighter, less blurred version of the same idea, will help sell a shot such as the one depicted.

Figure 12.30 Almost acceptable only if dialed back to the point of near imperceptibility, a pool of shadow is created by masking the parts of the figure nearest the floor, offsetting and blurring them, then using the result as the alpha channel of an adjustment layer. It's basically a handmade drop shadow. Yeesh.

Using 3D Planes

The addition of virtual lights and 3D compositing to After Effects means that you can aim a light at the matted layer and cast a shadow onto a 3D plane that corresponds to an actual surface in the scene (**Figure 12.31**). This works especially well if a 3D camera match move has been solved for the scene using third-party 3D tracking software. There are still several strong limiting factors, however. Your shadow is still only as good as the matte that casts it, and the surface receiving the shadow is going to be made up of flat planes only (although you can use several of them if you have the patience). As has been demonstrated, this technique has serious limitations if the light angle doesn't match that of the camera that shot the element.

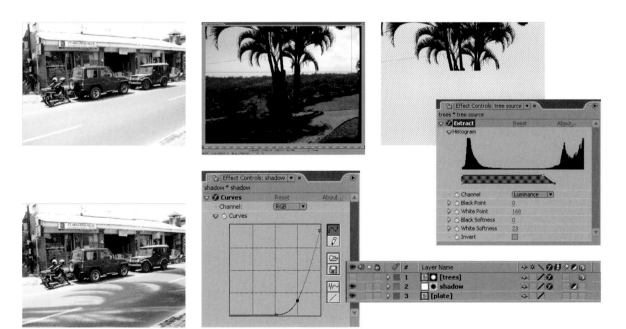

Figure 12.31 With the right source, such as this background and foreground, a 2D shadow will work. The silhouetted trees are luma keyed, then added to the scene as a 3D layer. The final result uses this layer as a track matte for an adjustment layer containing Levels, which creates a more convincing (and better matched) shadow than simply overlaying semi-opaque black. 12_shadow.aep contains the basic setup.

Overall, these examples demonstrate that when there are shadows present on set, it is preferable to do everything possible to recover them—even to rotoscope them for a separate key— than to submit to the humiliation of the desperate approaches outlined here. Or better yet, cheat: Design a background environment—say, a grassy clearing—in which the shadows would be mostly obscured.

Reflected and Interactive Light

It's easy to forget the actual physics of what gives an object a certain color, probably because it's strange and even counterintuitive. The color of the surface is made up of the colors of light that it does not absorb. Most of what we see as light and color is the result of reflected light.

Most surfaces in the natural world are diffuse, and the light that they reflect is sent out softly in all directions. Thus in some subtle way, objects in a shot together light one another, and characters or objects that pass through a scene are relit to some degree as they change position. Two objects composited together are completely missing the light interactions that would be present between them had they been photographed together (**Figure 12.32**).

Computer software is becoming better at re-creating these types of interactions. Global illumination and radiosity features have been added to 3D rendering programs in recent years to re-create the many effects of reflected light, enhancing the realism of completely synthesized scenes. For the compositor, however, lighting remains more art than science, and the subjective evaluation of observed phenomena will in many cases go farther than the application of objective principles. In other words, the 3D artist can be more like a sculptor, letting the light play over the created work, but the compositor is still more like a painter, observing and artistically interpreting the world without the benefit of realistic physics.

Figure 12.32 The color influence of indirect light is not always so evident, yet it is a constant.

Light that interacts directly with objects in a scene presents an opportunity for a compositor. Nail down appropriate interactive lighting, and the scene is infused with life and realism, helping to tell the story.

HDR Lighting

The previous chapter laid out the rules for how linear floating point compositing is implemented in After Effects 7.0. Now it's time to see that workflow in action, with the help of an HDR project.

As was discussed, HDR is a perfect solution that must currently find its place in an imperfect world—one in which the vast majority of source imagery is gamma encoded and does not contain values outside of monitor range. The question is how to put linear floating point to use in such a world. It's worth reviewing that there are two basic benefits resulting from this workflow:

▶ Light blends the way that it does in the natural world—the "linear" benefit

▶ Dynamic range is dramatically increased, not only for greater accuracy but to allow for light values too bright (or even too dark) for your monitor to display—this is the "floating point" benefit.

You can actually have one of these benefits without the other in After Effects (note that Linear Blending in File > Project Settings can be enabled at any bit depth, not just 32 bpc), but together they make for a paradigm shift if you know how to use them. Following is an example that begins with LDR source footage and adds an HDR element to transform the scene.

Dynamic Range

Figure 12.33 shows stills from two HD clips included on the book's disc, courtesy of Artbeats. These are beautifully shot, featuring dramatic lighting (which is simply to say that the lighting has a high dynamic range)—dramatic enough, in fact, that values in each image clip at full 1.0 (a.k.a. 255) luminance.

Because these clips were not supplied as 10-bit Cineon or HDR format, but rather in plain old 8 bits per channel, there is nothing that can be done to recover the detail in those highlights, or to bloom them out further. **Figure 12.34** shows the result of changing the Exposure setting in a 32 bpc After Effects project; it does not supply a natural result.

Figure 12.33 Each of these stills from HD Artbeats footage included on the disc contains values that clip at full white in 8 bits per channel: the areas of light bloom on the girls' heads, the midair water splashes, and the sun and cloud detail in the sunrise sequence.

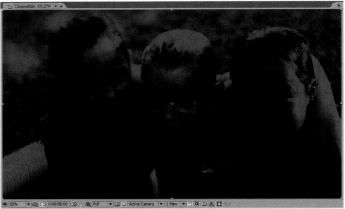

Figure 12.34 Raising Exposure in 32 bpc does not naturally bloom the high-lights, but instead crushes more areas of the image to white rather ungracefully, while lowering it does not increase detail in the areas that were already blown out. The Exposure control at the lower right of the compositing viewer is there for the purpose of letting you check images for out-of-range values in this manner.

What's missing is threshold information: gradations of luminance. You can add these to an LDR image, as in **Figure 12.35**, but you can't recover the gradations that were present in the natural world when the footage was shot, the way it was possible to recover a whole gradient of color outside the window of an EXR shot in the previous chapter (Figure 11.16a). This is what is happening to imaging devices now: they are becoming better and better at reproducing finer gradations within a wider dynamic range, widening the contrast ratio.

Figure 12.35 It's possible to softly bloom out the highlights in linear floating point by adding a blurred version of the image to itself; this brightens its levels one stop and is similar to an LDR approach that uses Hard Light instead of Add mode, like adding a soft filter to an overexposed image.

Meanwhile, even using only LDR source, there are plenty of situations in which you can take advantage of the almost infinitely higher contrast ratio that is available within an After Effects 32 bpc project. Following is a situation in which you would be faking it without HDR.

A New Day

The previous edition of this book featured a detailed step-by-step to relight **Figure 12.36a** using the eLin plug-in for linear floating point compositing for a result like **Figure 12.36b**. A 32 bpc version of that example is included on the disc as 12_afternoon.aep; this time around, I decided to take advantage of the Artbeats HD footage of a sunrise depicted in Figure 12.33 and imagine a scenario in which the director wanted a bigger sunrise that would realistically interact with an object in front of it, yielding a result more like **Figure 12.36c**. You are welcome to check out the final version, 12_sunrise.aep, and to try it yourself from scratch.

Figure 12.36 HDR can heighten not only the dynamic range, but the dynamism of a shot. (Eiffel Tower source photo courtesy of Micah Parker via Creative Commons license.)

The first task is to make a bigger sun with overbright values (above 1.0). To get started

1. Create a new linear floating point project: in File > Project Settings, set Depth to 32 bits per channel (float), enable Linear Blending, and set Working Space to Linear Adobe RGB (D65). If you don't see that option, follow the instructions in the previous chapter to install the profile, or open a project that contains it (such as 12_sunrise.aep).

2. Import SE123H.mov from Chapter 12's Source folder on the disc (copy it to your local drive for better performance).

3. Create a new composition containing this footage.

4. The footage looks brighter than it should because like all 8 bpc files it is gamma encoded. Convert it to linear by applying Effect > Utility > Color Profile Converter and choosing ColorMatch RGB as the Input Profile.

5. Create a bright, medium-yellow solid with width and height of 1000 pixels each.

6. With the toolbar visible (**Ctrl+1/Cmd+1**) toggle to the Elliptical Mask tool (**Q** on your keyboard) and double-click it, creating a circular mask for the solid.

7. Press **MM** to reveal mask properties. Set Mask Expansion to –250.0 (that's a negative setting, chosen to simplify the steps) and Mask Feather to 100.0.

8. Boost the sun into the overbright world: Choose Effect > Color Correction > Exposure and raise the Exposure setting to 2.00.

What was a mono-colored disc is now a fiery gas ball thanks to the feathering in the edges. Without that threshold, it would just appear as a white disc, despite containing overbright values (**Figure 12.37**).

Now to place the sun on the horizon

1. Go to the last frame (for visibility) and move the sun solid down so just its glowing edge is above the horizon.

Figure 12.37 The hard-edged white disc contains values well above full white, but only by softening the edges to add contrast does it seem white hot.

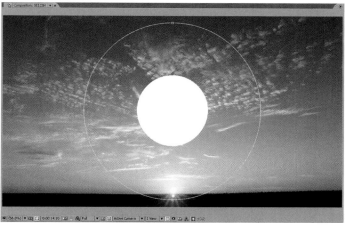

2. Add a black solid the size of the composition called "horizon mask." Turn its visibility off.

3. Create a rectangular mask around the existing horizon. Press **F** to reveal Mask Feather and set it to 5.0. Turn visibility back on.

4. Animate the sun to rise at roughly the same rate as the sun in the plate footage, setting a Position keyframe at the first and last frame.

5. Select the horizon mask and sun layers and precompose them; name the new composition "sunrise."

6. Set an Add Blending mode for sunrise.

Figure 12.38 Sun, sun, sun, here it comes.

Without too much effort, you have yourself a home-grown sunrise (**Figure 12.38**). Now to take further advantage of those overbright pixels:

1. Add Eiffel.jpg to the project, and to the composition. Again, it's too bright, but don't add Color Profile Converter just yet.

2. Instead, apply the Extract effect, and drag the White Point (upper right corner below the histogram) down to remove the sky from the shot. Soften the effect by raising White Softness (lower right corner). I used settings of 115 and 29 for White Point and White Softness, respectively.

3. Move the Eiffel image downward so that its horizon matches that of the plate.

4. Now add Color Profile Converter with Input Profile set to ColorMatch RGB.

5. Make the tower a black silhouette with Levels; lower Output White and raise Input Black.

6. Set a Levels keyframe at 8:00. At the final frame, raise Red Output Black to match the red in the shadows to the plate (**Figure 12.39**), mimicking the effect of the sunrise.

7. Soften the silhouette slightly: Add a Box Blur and set the Blur Radius to 1.0.

That's good, but more is needed where the tower, sun, and horizon overlap.

1. Apply a Fast Blur with a Blurriness of 8.0 to the sunrise layer.

2. Add an Exposure effect, with Exposure raised to around 5.0, to expand the sun further in all directions, including over the horizon.

3. To get more interaction between the sun and the base of the tower, more of a threshold region is required between them. Create an adjustment layer at the top of the layer stack. Call it extra blur.

4. Duplicate the sunrise layer and move it to the top of the stack. Set it as a luma matte for the extra blur layer.

5. Apply a Box Blur to extra blur and set Blur Radius and Iterations both to 2.

There is now some realistic interaction happening in the areas where the base of the tower and the sun overlap (**Figure 12.40**). You can boost the amount of blur to see this happen even more, as a reference for other situations that might call for HDR backlighting.

From here, it's just a question of what else to add in order to complete the shot. The final version on the disc includes a Knoll Light Factory lens flare, as well as a simulated lens

NOTES

Remember that any shot rendered as normal gamma-encoded output from a linear project such as this will appear too bright—"double-gamma'd"—unless a Color Profile Converter is added converting the final shot back to a standard RGB color space. Details about doing this are included in the previous chapter. At The Orphanage there is a traditional penalty for double-gamma: The offending compositor has to bring donuts into dailies the following day.

filter to change the look of the sky; this "lens filter" is actually just a Ramp effect creating a gradient from white to a burnt orange color (although it could be any color you like; see actual filters used by cinematographers for ideas). The great thing about linear compositing is that such a simple element needs only to be layered in via a Multiply Blending effect and it offers the same natural look that its real-world counterpart would (**Figure 12.41**).

Figure 12.40 Extra light and blur at the base of the tower enhance the hot look of the sun; too much more and it would look as if the tower were about to blast off.

Figure 12.41 In standard gamma-encoded compositing, there is no simple way to add this gradient layer to an image and derive a result as subtle and photographic as the one you get by setting it with a Multiply Blending mode in a linear color project.

Conclusion

So there you have it; once you get used to the extra steps required to set up a linear project and import LDR footage, you are rewarded with a simple, powerful workflow.

This exercise only touched upon what is possible with linear floating point compositing, but it should at least make the point that light behaves much more the way it does in the real world. This is light in its purely natural, "additive" state (where the addition suddenly makes simple sense).

Keep in mind that many Blending modes besides Add and Multiply (as well as Lighten and Darken) will not work correctly with linear blending and HDR overbright values. For example, Screen, Overlay, and most of the "Light" Blending modes will yield strange results. The formula for the Screen operation (Chapter 3)

$$newPixel = 1-((1-A) * (1-B))$$

clearly shows that you have a problem if the pixel of the top layer (A) or bottom layer (B) contains a value above 1; subtracting it from 1 yields a negative number. If the value of each pixel is 2.0, the resulting blended pixel is pure black. 12_screenHDR.aep shows this phenomenon in action.

There is no doubt that support for linear floating point compositing will only improve with future versions of After Effects. Clearly, it will help for more effects to be 32 bit compatible, but it would also help if fundamental controls such as Levels and Curves had some way of showing you what is happening outside of monitor range. For example, gamma corrections on individual color channels are tricky in HDR because the gamma curve continues right out of monitor range; a gamma that has been "lowered" in 0.0 to 1.0 space may actually be higher above 1.0 (**Figure 12.42**). For this reason it is advised by those in the know to apply gamma adjustments last, after all other adjustments have been made.

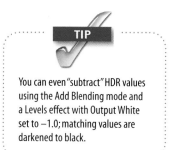

TIP

You can even "subtract" HDR values using the Add Blending mode and a Levels effect with Output White set to −1.0; matching values are darkened to black.

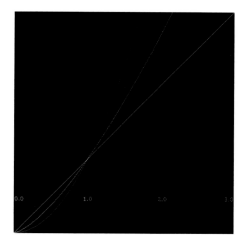

Figure 12.42 Curves only lets you see monitor range, the area inside the gray box, but what happens to gamma adjustments to individual colors beyond that range is counterintuitive, as this graph shows. This need not be cause for concern as long as you leave gamma adjustments until last, so that what you see is what you get.

The greatest advantage of all of those extra color values is that it is virtually impossible to ever lose color detail in your image to the point where it can't be brought back with another operation. You are encouraged to try "normal" compositing in linear floating point projects in cases where you might want to be able to push color values in and out of monitor range, and you may soon become accustomed to working with light the way that light works in nature.

13

Climate: Air, Water, Smoke, Clouds

Conversation about the weather is the last refuge of the unimaginative.

—Oscar Wilde

Yes, yes, let's talk about the weather.
—W. S. Gilbert, *The Pirates of Penzance, or, The Slave of Duty*

Climate: Air, Water, Smoke, Clouds

Even if you're not called upon to re-create extreme weather events such as those depicted in *The Day After Tomorrow*, climate conditions along with natural elements of water and wind are a constant in dramatic storylines. You may need to re-create these effects from scratch, or you may be called upon to subtly tweak what's already in the shot.

This chapter will give you some pointers on creating such natural elements as particulate matter in the air, replacement skies, mist, fog, smoke, the effects of wind, and water in its three states.

Why would you want to do this? Simply because the crew couldn't get the conditions the story required on the day of the shoot? In extreme cases, yes. But actually, any large exterior shot will exhibit some sort of meteorological influence, and everything in the shot (and sequence) is interrelated. This chapter investigates phenomena that you can influence or even replace wholesale, including

▶ **Particulate matter in the air:** The look of particles in the air can offer important clues to a scene. Is it ever complicated to deal with particulate matter? Where does it not apply?

▶ **Sky replacement:** This one comes up regularly. What is the sky, after all, but a big blue screen? What else is involved?

- **Clouds of fog, smoke, or mist:** Motion, color, and even depth inhabit this element. How can these be created in After Effects?

- **Billowing smoke:** What about thick plumes of smoke? Those need to be created with some sort of complex 3D dynamics system, right? Wrong.

- **Wind:** How do you re-create something you can't see? Cheap and easy ways that show its presence via secondary animation can really sell a shot.

- **Water and precipitation:** The presence of water can influence a shot, even if off-screen. How do you handle rain and snow?

It's rare indeed that weather conditions cooperate on location, and even rarer that a shoot can wait for perfect weather. Transforming the appearance of a scene using natural elements is one of the most satisfying things you can do as a compositor. The before and after comparison alone can be stunning, and the result can be worthy of a blockbuster film.

Particulate Matter

Particulate matter in the air influences how objects appear at different depths. What is it? Fundamentally, it is water, and other gas, dust, or visible particulate usually known as pollution. Even an ideal, pristine, pollution-free environment has water in the air—even in the dry desert. The amount of haze in the air offers clues as to

- The distance to the horizon and of objects in relation to it

- The basic type of climate; the aridness or heaviness of the weather

- The time of year and the day's conditions

- The air's stagnancy (think *Blade Runner*)

- The sun's location (when it's not visible in shot)

The color of the particulate matter offers clues to how much pollution is present and what it is, even how it feels: dust, smog, dark smoke from a fire, and so on (**Figure 13.1**).

Figure 13.1 The same location under varied weather conditions. This type of study reveals environmental subtleties, such as how backlighting emphasizes even low levels of haze and reduces overall saturation, or how more diffuse conditions desaturate and obscure the horizon while emphasizing foreground color.

Particulate matter does not occur in outer space, save perhaps when the occasional cloud of interstellar dust drifts through the shot. Look at photos of the moon landscape, and you'll see that the blacks in the distance look just as dark as those in the foreground.

Essentially, particulate matter in the air lowers the apparent contrast of visible objects; secondarily, objects take on the color of the atmosphere around them and become slightly diffuse (**Figure 13.2**). This is a subtle yet omnipresent depth cue: With any particulate matter in the air at all, objects lose contrast further from camera; the apparent color can change quite a bit, and detail is softened. As a compositor, you use this to your advantage, not only to re-create reality, but to provide dramatic information.

As an example, consider Figure 13.2, shot with a long lens. Long (or telephoto) lenses bring background elements more prominently into the frame; and a long lens is sometimes employed when a background element is meant to loom large or seem menacing. Anything far away that appears not only large but crystal clear, however, will simply look wrong. With the right amount of haze for the weather conditions, even a shot highly compressed with a very long lens will be something the viewer simply believes.

Figure 13.2 This shot was taken with a long lens. The structures one block away retain a good deal in the black of their shadows; buildings a mile or two away, far less; and the foothills ten miles away are so desaturated they begin to fade right into the sky—at first you don't even notice them.

Match an Existing Shot

Figure 13.3 features the results of an exercise that is also included on the book's disc (as 13_planePlanes.aep). Imagine the same aircraft flying through the scene as a toy model in the near foreground, a low-flying daredevil in a full size airplane a block or two away, and high in the sky, miles away.

Figure 13.3 The difference between a toy model airplane flying close, a real airplane flying nearby, and the same plane in the distant sky, is conveyed with the use of Scale, but just as importantly, with Levels that show the influence of atmospheric haze.

In this case, each plane of depth has pretty good reference to gauge how much atmospheric haze is in play. The street sign in the foreground has no haze (and as an additional bonus, contains little color) making it a basic reference for black, white, and gray levels. Buildings a block or two away, particularly those in neutral colors, show the black and white levels become muted, but only slightly. Out on the horizon, nothing is even close to pure black; the blacks and whites take on some of the blue color of the sky, as well.

The example file contains a pass at setting Levels for each aircraft layer that is subjective, not definitive; you are encouraged to try resetting them and creating them yourself. For more of a challenge, try replicating the same principles (greater contrast in the foreground, much less in the far distance) with the image shown in **Figure 13.4**, which contains only midground reference.

The technique used here is the same as outlined in Chapter 5, "Color Correction," with the additional twist of understanding how atmospheric haze influences the color of the scene. Knowing how this works from studying a scene like Figure 13.3's helps you create it from scratch without good reference in a scene like Figure 13.4's.

The plane as a foreground element seems to make life easier by containing a full range of monochrome colors.

> **TIP**
>
> If an added object is meant to be further than one object in the plate but closer than another, you can directly match each and average the values.

Figure 13.4 The dome provides a great grayscale reference. But what about placing an item in immediate foreground, or in the background sky, where no reference is visible? The same approach as in Figure 13.3 applies, but you must adjust according to an understanding of the phenomena rather than by checking reference right in the shot.

When matching a more colorful or monochrome element, you can always create a small solid and add the default Ramp effect. With this element, it is simpler to set Levels to add the proper depth cueing, and then apply those levels to the final element (**Figures 13.5a, b,** and **c**).

Creating a New Shot

What about creating a new background from scratch, as with a matte painting or 3D rendered background? In either case there is no longer reference built into the shot, but that doesn't mean you can't still use reference if you need it; a photo containing the necessary conditions will get you started.

To recreate depth cues in a shot, you must somehow separate the shot into planes of distance. If the source imagery is computer-generated, the 3D program that created it can also generate a depth map for you to use (**Figure 13.6**). If not, you can slice the image into planes of distance, or you can make your own depth map to weight the distance of the objects in frame.

Figures 13.5a, b, and c If a foreground element does not contain enough of a range of values to make matching easy (for example, it is monochrome), you can use stand-ins (a) and apply the Levels adjustments to these (b), matching contrast channel by channel (as in Chapter 5). Slam the result to check the accuracy of Levels settings (c).

Figure 13.6 A depth map of a cartoonish 3D city. This map can be applied directly to an adjustment layer as a Luma Inverted Matte (inverted in this example because the most distant objects should be most affected), and then dial in any contrast (via Levels) and softening (via Fast Blur) effects; they are weighted to affect the background more than the foreground, and the contrast of the map itself can be adjusted to change the relative weighting. (Image courtesy Fred Lewis/Moving Media.)

TIP

Getting reference is easy for anyone with an Internet connection these days, thanks to such sites as flickr.com for browsing, not to mention Google image search when you need something specific.

NOTES

A basic 3D render of a scene is often useful with a matte painting, even when most of the detail will be created with Photoshop. Not only are perspective and lens angle included in the render, and adjustable thereafter, but a depth map is also easy to generate which remains valid as the 2D work evolves.

There are several ways in which a depth map can be used, but the simplest is probably to apply it to an adjustment layer as a Luma (or Luma Inverted) Matte, and then add a Levels or other color correction adjustment to the adjustment layer. With the depth matte in Figure 13.6, the heaviest level adjustments for depth cueing would be applied to the furthest elements, so applying this matte as a Luma Inverted Matte and then by *flashing* the blacks (raising the Output Black level in Levels), you would instantly add the effect of atmosphere on the scene.

Depth data may also be rendered and stored in an RPF file, as in **Figure 13.7** (which is taken from an example included on the disc as part of 13_multipass.aep). RPF files are in some ways crude, lacking even thresholding in the edges (let alone higher bit depths), but they can contain several types of 3D data, as are listed in the 3D Channel menu. This data can be used directly by a few effects to simulate 3D, including Particle Playground, which accepts RPF data as an influence map.

More extreme conditions may demand actual particles, and the phenomena that accompany them. These conditions are examined in the following sections of this chapter.

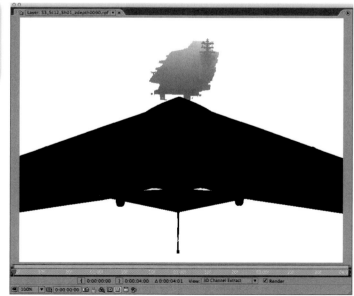

Figure 13.7 Look closely at the edges of RPF data and you will see jagged pixels along the diagonals, but a depth map does not always have to be perfectly pristine. The 3D Channel Extract effect allows After Effects to work with RPF data. (Created by Fred Lewis; used with permission from Inhance Digital, Boeing, and the Navy UCAV program.)

Sky Replacement

Sky replacement is among the cheapest and easiest extensions that can be made to a shot. This opens up various possibilities to shoot faster and more cheaply. Not only do you not have to wait for ideal climate conditions, you can also swap in not only a different sky but even an extended physical skyline.

Skies are, after all, part of the story, often a subliminal one but occasionally a starring element. In *Vanilla Sky*, for example, the surreal-looking sky was the first clue that maybe Tom Cruise's character was no longer inhabiting the real world. An interior with a window could be anywhere, but show a Manhattan or San Francisco skyline outside the window and locals will automatically gauge the exact neighborhood and city block of that location, along with the time of day, time of year, weather, outside temperature, and so on, possibly without ever really paying conscious attention to it.

Why spend extra production money on background conditions for a scene that could be shot cheaper elsewhere? You could spend tens (even hundreds) of thousands of dollars for that view apartment on Central Park East for a scene at golden hour (the beautiful "hour" of sunset that typically lasts about 20 minutes and is missing on an overcast day). The guerilla method would be to use your friend's apartment, light it orange, shoot all day, and add the sunset view in post. In many cases, the real story is elsewhere, and the sky is a subliminal (even if beautiful) backdrop that must serve that story (**Figures 13.8a** through **d**).

There is sometimes no replacement for the real thing. If you want well shot dawn/dusk reference, or just love the look of magic hour, study *Days of Heaven*, which required a couple of years to shoot, often less than one golden hour per clear day at a time.

The Sky Is Not (Quite) a Blue Screen

Only on the clearest, bluest days does the sky become a candidate for blue-screen keying. Look at an actual sky (there may be one nearby as you read this) or even better, study reference images, and you may notice that the blue color desaturates near the horizon, cloudless skies are not always so easy to come by, and even clear blue skies are not as saturated as they might sometimes seem.

Figures 13.8a through d For an independent film with no budget set in San Francisco, the director had the clever idea of shooting it in a building lobby across the bay in lower-rent Oakland (a), pulling a matte from the blue sky (b), and match moving a still shot of the San Francisco skyline (from street level, c) for a result that anyone familiar with that infamous pyramid-shaped building would assume was taken in downtown San Francisco. (Images courtesy The Orphanage.)

Still, some combination of a color keyer, such as Keylight, and a hi-con luminance matte pass or a garbage matte, as needed, can remove the existing sky in your shot, leaving nice edges around the foreground. Chapter 6, "Color Keying," focuses on strategies for employing these, and Chapter 7, "Rotoscoping and Paint," describes supporting strategies when keys and garbage mattes fail.

The first step of sky replacement is to remove the existing "sky" (which may include other items at infinite distance, such as buildings and clouds) by developing a matte for it. As you do this, place the replacement sky in the background; a sky matte typically does not have to be as exacting as a blue-screen key because the replacement sky often bears a resemblance to the source (**Figure 13.9**). The 13_skyReplace1.aep project on the book's disc contains a simple example.

Figure 13.9 This rather poor blue-screen matte is acceptable for this type of shot because the color range and contrast of the target background are not so different from the source. The holes in the matte are the result of reflected sky color in the highlights of the foreground; this looks acceptable in the final shot.

Infinite Depth

A locked-off shot can be completed with the creation of the matte and a color match to the new sky. If, however, there is camera movement in the shot, you might assume that a 3D track is needed to properly add a new sky element.

Typically, that's overkill. Instead, consider:

▶ When matching motion from the original shot, if anything in the source sky can be tracked, by all means track the source.

▶ If only your foreground can be tracked, follow the suggestions in Chapter 8, "Effective Motion Tracking," for applying a track to a 3D camera: move the replacement sky to the distant background (via a Z Position value well into four or five digits, depending on camera settings). Scale up to compensate for the distance; this is all done by eye.

▶ A push or zoom shot (Chapter 9, "Virtual Cinematography," describes the difference), may be more easily re-created using a tracked 3D camera (but look at Chapter 8 for tips on getting away with a 2D track).

The basic phenomenon to re-create is that scenery at infinite distance moves less than objects in the foreground. This is the parallax effect, which is less pronounced with a long, telephoto lens, and much more obvious with a wide angle. For the match in Figure 13.8, a still shot (no perspective) was skewed to match the correct angle and tracked in 2D; the lens angle was long enough and the shot brief enough that they got away with it. A simpler example is included on the disc in 13_skyReplace2.aep.

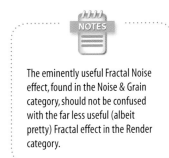

The eminently useful Fractal Noise effect, found in the Noise & Grain category, should not be confused with the far less useful (albeit pretty) Fractal effect in the Render category.

The Fog, Smoke, or Mist Rolls In

An animated layer of translucent clouds is easily enough re-created in After Effects. The basic element can be fabricated by applying the Fractal Noise effect to a solid, and then using a Blending mode such as Add or Screen to layer it in with the appropriate Opacity setting. 13_smokyFlyover. aep contains a simple example of layers of smoke laid out as if on a three-dimensional plane.

Fractal Noise at its default settings already looks smoky (**Figure 13.10**); switching Noise Type setting from the default, Soft Linear, to Spline, improves it. The main thing to add is motion.

An Evolution animation creates internal movement, while Transform animations cause the overall layer to move as if being blown by wind. Offset Turbulence can be used to reposition infinitely without running out of space.

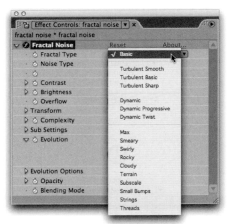

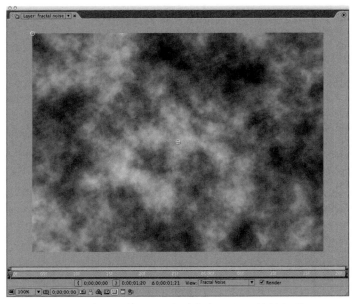

Figure 13.10 Fractal Noise (shown at the default setting, with Noise Type set to Spline) is a decent stand-in for organic-looking fog. You can try varying the Fractal Type or Noise Type to get different looks, and you must animate the Evolution if you want any billowing of the element. Several Fractal Types are available, as seen in the pull-down menu.

Brightness, Contrast, and Scale settings determine the apparent scale and density of the noise layer. Complexity and Sub Settings also affect apparent scale and density, but with all kinds of undesirable side effects that make the smoke look artificial.

The look is greatly improved by layering at least two separate passes via a Blending mode (as in the example project).

Masking and Adjusting

When covering the entire foreground evenly with smoke or mist, a more realistic look is achieved using two or three separate overlapping layers with offset positions (**Figure 13.11**).

The unexpected byproduct of layering 2D particle layers in this manner is that they take on the illusion of depth and volume. The eye perceives changes in parallax between the foreground and background, and automatically assumes these to be a byproduct of full three-dimensionality, yet you save the time and trouble of a 3D volumetric particle render. Of course, you're limited to instances in which particles don't interact with movement from objects in the scene; otherwise, you instantly graduate to some very tricky 3D effects.

TIP

Fractal Noise texture maps can loop seamlessly (allowing re-use on shots of varying length). In Evolution Options, enable Cycle Evolution, and animate Evolution in whole revolutions (say, from 0° 2 x 0.0°). Set the Cycle (in Revolutions) parameter to the number of total revolutions (2). The first and last keyframes now match.

Figure 13.11 The smoke in this shot is made up of one large rendered fractal noise element that is sliced up, staggered (as seen with the layer outlines), and animated in pseudo-3D.

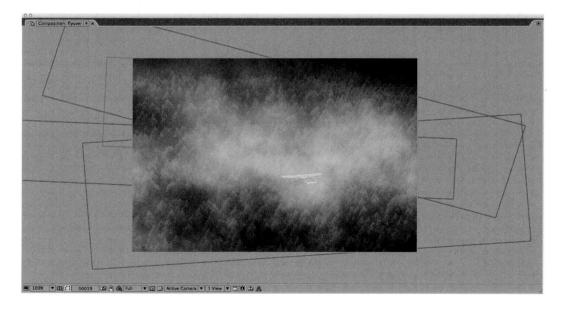

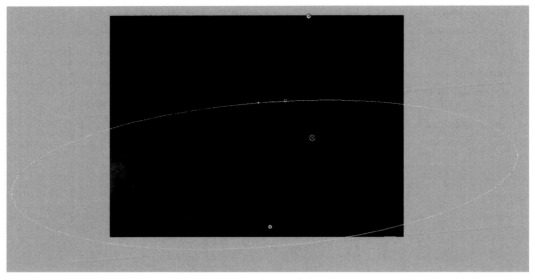

Figure 13.12 This mask of a single smoke element from the shot in Figure 13.10 has a 200-pixel feather, despite that the resolution of the shot is D1 video (720 × 486). The softness of the mask helps to sell the element as smoke and works well overlaid with other, similarly feathered masked elements.

Particle layers can be combined with the background via Blending modes, or they can be applied as a Luma Matte to a colored solid (allowing you to specify the color of the particles without having a Blending mode change it).

To add smoke to a generalized area of the frame, a big elliptical mask with a high feather setting (in the triple digits even for video resolution) will do the trick; if the borders of the smoke area are apparent, increase the mask feather even further (**Figure 13.12**).

Moving Through the Mist

The same effect you get when you layer several instances of Fractal Noise can aid the illusion of moving forward through a misty cloud. That's done simply enough (for an example of flying through a synthetic cloud, see 13_smokyLayers.aep), but how often does your shot consist of just moving through a misty cloud? Most of the time, clouds of smoke or mist are added to an existing shot.

You can use the technique for emulating 3D tracking (see Chapter 10, "Expressions") to make the smoke hold its place in a particular area of the scene as the camera moves through (or above) it. To make this work, keep a few points in mind:

▶ Each instance of Fractal Noise should have a soft elliptical mask around it.

▶ The mask should be large enough to overlap with another masked instance, but small enough that it does not slide its position as the angle of the camera changes.

▶ A small amount of Evolution animation goes a long way, and too much will blow the gag. Let the movement of the camera create the interest of motion.

▶ Depending on the length and distance covered in the shot, be willing to create at least a half-dozen individual masked layers of Fractal Noise.

13_smokyFlyover.aep features just such an effect of moving forward through clouds. It combines the tracking of each shot carefully into place with the phenomenon of parallax, whereby overlapping layers swirl across one another in a believable manner. Mist and smoke seem to be a volume but they actually often behave more like overlapping, translucent planes—individual clouds of mist and smoke.

Billowing Smoke

Fractal Noise works fine to create and animate thin wispy smoke and mist. It will not, however, re-create thick, billowing clouds. When clouds are opaque enough to have their own shape, shading, and topography, built-in After Effects plug-ins will not carry the weight. Luckily, all you need is a good still cloud element and you can animate it in After Effects. And all you need to create the element is a high-resolution reference photo—or a bag of cotton puffs.

That's right, cotton puffs, like you get at the pharmacy. I first heard about this trick on a visit to the digital matte department at Industrial Light + Magic about a decade ago (back when the department was made up of four artists), where visionary matte painter Yusei Uesegi was given credit for devising it. He showed me a jaw-dropping shot of a pirate ship in flames, smoke billowing from the masts.

CLOSE-UP

Selling the Effect with Diffraction

There is more to adding a cloud to a realistic shot than a simple A over B comp; water elements in the air, whether in spray, mist, or clouds, not only occlude light but diffract it. This diffraction effect can be simulated by applying Compound Blur to an adjustment layer between the fog and the background and using a precomposed (or prerendered) version of the fog element as its Blur layer.

You want details, and you'll get them, but you have to make it to the last chapter of the book, where guest author Stu Maschwitz lays it all out in detail.

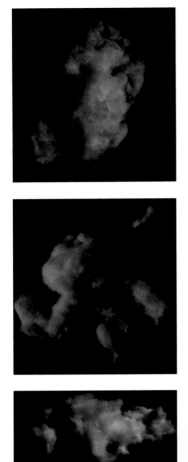

The simplest way to create your basic cloud is to arrange the cotton balls on a large piece of nonreflective black poster board. Take the board outside on a sunny day so you get some nice highlights and shadows. When you photograph it at different angles to the light, the results look like puffy white clouds already (**Figure 13.13**). You can also suspend the cotton (without the backboard) against an incandescent light for the feel of sunlight through the clouds.

To give clouds shape and contour, open the image in Photoshop, and use the Clone Stamp tool to create a cloud with the shape you want. You can do it directly in After Effects, but this is the kind of job for which Photoshop was designed. Clone in contour layers of highlights (using Linear Dodge, Screen, or Lighten blending modes) and shadows (with Blending set to Multiply or Darken) until the cloud has the look you're after (**Figure 13.14**).

So now you have a good-looking cloud, but it's a still. How do you put it in motion? This is where After Effects' excellent distortion tools come into play, in particular Mesh Warp and Liquify. A project containing just such a cloud animation appears on the disc as 13_smokeCloud.aep.

Figure 13.13 You may have noticed how cotton puffs can be arranged to resemble fluffy clouds. But who knew you could get away with sticking them in a movie?

Figure 13.14 The elements from Figure 13.13 are incorporated into this matte painting, with the shot in the background for reference. The cotton is painted in via a dozen overlapping layers. The topmost use Screen mode (to highlight) or Overlay mode (to darken), bringing out the contours. Can you tell which smoke is made up of cotton?

Mesh Warp

Mesh Warp lays a grid of Bézier handles over the frame; you animate distortion by setting a keyframe for the Distortion Mesh property at frame 0, and then moving the points of the grid, and realigning the Bézier handles associated with each point, to bend to the vertices between points. The image to which this effect is applied follows the shape of the grid.

By default, Mesh Warp begins with a seven-by-seven grid. Before you do anything else, make sure that the size of the grid makes sense for your image; you might want to increase its size for a high-resolution project, and you can reduce the number of rows to fit the aspect ratio of your shot, for a grid of squares (**Figure 13.15**).

You can't typically get away with dragging a point more than about halfway toward any other point; watch carefully for artifacts of stretching and tearing as you work, and preview often. If you see stretching, realign adjacent points and handles to compensate. There is no better way to learn about this than to experiment.

Laying cotton on a black card or scanner is not the only way to get a cloud sample, nor is it the easiest in this digital age. Reference images of clouds at high-resolution will obviously work as well. Modeling cotton allows you to be specific and creative: for the effect of light coming through the clouds, the cotton can be suspended over an incandescent light (without the black card).

Mesh Warp, like many distortion tools, renders rather slowly. As you rough in the motion, feel free to work at quarter-resolution. When you've finalized your animation, you can save a lot of time by pre-rendering it (see Chapter 4, "Optimizing Your Projects").

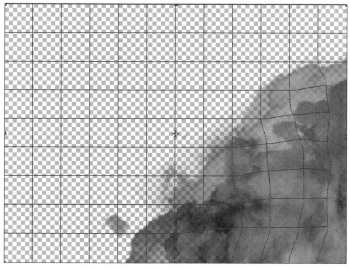

Figure 13.15 The Mesh Warp controls are simple, just a grid of points and vectors. You can preset the number and quality, and animate the position of the grid overall (one keyframe controls all grid points). Points can be multiselected and dragged, and each point contains Bezier handles for warping the adjacent vectors.

Liquify

Mesh warp is appropriate for gross distortions of an entire element. The Liquify effect is a brush-based system for fine distortions. 13_smokeCloud.aep includes a composition that employs Liquify to swirl a cloud. Following is a brief orientation to this toolset, but as with most brush-based painterly tools, there is no substitute for trying it hands-on.

The principle behind Liquify is actually similar to that of Mesh Warp; enable View Mesh under View Options and you'll see that you're still just manipulating a grid, albeit a finer one that would be cumbersome to adjust point by point—hence the brush interface.

Of the brushes included with Liquify, the first two along the top row, Warp and Turbulence, are most often used (**Figure 13.16**). Warp has a similar effect to moving a point in Mesh Warp; it simply pushes pixels in the direction you drag the brush. Turbulence scrambles pixels in the path of the brush.

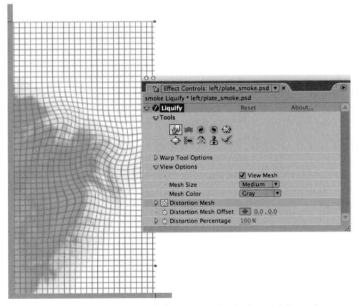

Figure 13.16 Liquify is also a mesh distortion tool, only the mesh is much finer than Mesh Warp's and it is controlled via brushes, allowing more specific distortions.

The Reconstruction brush (rightmost on the bottom row) is like a selective undo, reversing distortions at the default setting; other options for this brush are contained in the Reconstruction Mode menu (which appears only when the brush is selected).

Liquify has the advantage of allowing hold-out areas. Draw a mask around the area you want to leave untouched by Liquify brushes, but set the Mask mode to None, disabling it. Under Warp Tool Options, select the mask name in the Freeze Area Masked menu.

Lest you think the methods described in this section are some crude kludge, inferior to procedural particle dynamic effects created by a technical director in a sophisticated 3D rendering program, here's an anecdote that demonstrates how this generalized approach (refined to a high degree) saved the day on a movie with an eight-figure budget. A few short weeks before the final deadline for all shots to be completed on *The Day After Tomorrow*, the render pipeline at The Orphanage was slammed, but the "super cell" element for the freezing of New York City sequence (that huge cloud bank swirling around on the horizon) had not been approved by the client other than in matte paintings.

It was clear that even if a technical director could re-create the look in 3D—and no one had done so yet—there wasn't going to be time left to render it. By animating the matte paintings using the techniques outlined in this section, the shots were completed and approved within a couple of weeks. As always, the key was breaking the problem down into component parts. The final super cell rig had over a dozen individual component layers and instances of Mesh Warp and Liquify, along with holdouts, overlays, offsets, and Blending modes built up among them to give the effect the appropriate organic complexity and dimension.

Combining Techniques

Because each project varies, the techniques offered are meant to form only the basis of your finished effect. The goal is to provide you with a few keys that you can combine

> **NOTES**
>
> New to version 7.0, the Liquify effect can extend beyond the boundaries of a layer—no need to precompose.

or piece out on your own, rather than nail you down to specific steps that work only in one context.

So, for example, selling a shot of the smoke plume might involve not only warping effects, but also some thinner, faster-moving smoke nearest the flames or in the foreground of the scene, which could be created with Fractal Noise. Or, if the drifting Fractal Noise smoke needed more specific directionality—say, to flow around an object—you could apply a Mesh Warp on top of its animation, or flow it right through the Mesh Warp grid (**Figure 13.17**).

Figure 13.17 You can get pretty creative with your use for Mesh Warp: Here, Fractal Noise is animated to move left to right through a grid that deforms it as it animates.

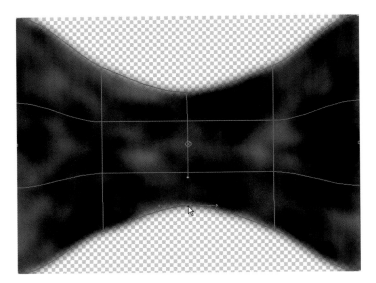

Smoke Trails

Many effects, including smoke trails, don't require particle generation in order to be re-created faithfully. This section is included less because the need comes up often and more to show how, with a little creativity, you can combine techniques in After Effects to create effects that you might think require a dedicated solution. Check out the reference in **Figure 13.18** and you'll notice that smoke trails are essentially just clouds.

Therefore, initial setup of this effect is simply a matter of starting with a clean plate, painting the smoke trails in a separate still layer, and revealing them over time (presumably behind the aircraft that is creating them). The quickest and easiest way to reveal such an element over time is often by animating a mask, or you could use techniques described in Chapter 8 to apply a motion tracker to a brush.

The optional second stage of this effect would be the dissipation of the trail; depending on how much wind is present, the trail might probably drift, spread, and thin out over time. That means that in a wide shot, the back of the trail would be more dissipated than the front.

A simple method to achieve this (which could work with a distant shot, at least) would use a black-to-white gradient (created with Ramp) and Compound Blur. The gradient is white at the dissipated end of the trail and black at the source (**Figures 13.19a** and **b**); each point can be animated or tracked in. Compound Blur uses this gradient as its Blur Layer, creating more blur as the ramp becomes more white.

Wind

What is wind doing in this chapter? You can't see it. How do you composite it into your shot? Although it's invisible, the effects of wind on a shot are certainly integral to its realism. Besides the effect of wind on particles, what other roles does wind play?

As I write this chapter, it is a warm, still, sunny day, but in my backyard leaves and tree branches do sway gently from time to time. If I wanted to re-create the scene from a still or 3D render or if I wanted to add an element to it, the result just wouldn't look right without these subtle bits of motion.

The fact is that most still scenes in the real world contain ambient motion of some kind. Not only objects directly in the scene, but reflected light and shadow might be changing all the time in a scene we perceive to be motionless.

As a compositor, part of your job is to think about these kinds of ambient effects, and to look for opportunities

Figure 13.18 Clearly, this effect could easily be painted with no external source whatsoever.

Figures 13.19a and b Getting creative with a quick-and-dirty effect on Figure 13.18: A gradient is created to match the start and end of the plane's trajectory, masked and pre-composed (a). This is then applied via a Compound Blur to the source layer (b)—a simple example of building up your own effect with the tools at hand.

to add to them in ways that contribute to the realism of the scene without stealing focus. Obviously, the kinds of dynamics involved with making the leaves and branches of a tree sway are mostly beyond the realm of 2D compositing, but there are often other elements that are easily articulated and animated ever so slightly. Successful examples of ambient animation should not be noticeable, and they often will not have been explicitly requested, so it's an exercise in subtlety.

Adding and Articulating Elements

To make it easier on yourself, look for elements that can be readily isolated and articulated; you should be able to mask the element out with a simple roto or a hi-con matte if it's not separated to begin with. Look for the point where the object would bend or pivot, place your anchor point there, then animate a gentle rotation. 13_ambientAnim.aep (on the disc) offers a simple animation of the arm of a streetlight, held out from the background. A little warp on the clouds behind it, and this still image could convincingly be a brief moving shot (**Figure 13.20**).

Figure 13.20 The arm of the streetlight is masked, its anchor point moved to the base, and a simple wiggle to the Rotation gives it ambient motion as would be caused by wind.

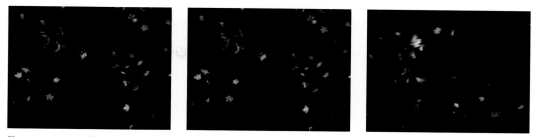

Figure 13.21 An effects element can enhance the ambient feeling a scene. It would be very difficult to create the impression of a windstorm in a shot from scratch, but if the shot is taken in windy conditions (or using large fans on set) an element like this will enhance the impression of a blustery day. (Footage courtesy Artbeats.)

You also have the option of acquiring and adding elements that indicate or add to the effect of wind motion. **Figure 13.21** shows an element of blowing autumn leaves shot against a black background for easy removal and matting; granted, you could add an element this turbulent only to a scene that either already had signs of gusts in it or that contained only elements that would show no secondary motion from wind whatsoever.

Indirect Effects

Another idea is to add the indirect effects of ambient motion generated by wind; moving shadows and the play of light also enliven a static scene, and capturing or synthesizing these elements to interact with objects in the scene will more readily appear realistic than re-creating them directly.

So, for example, adding the swaying branches of a tree to your scene is complicated, but creating a hi-con matte of existing footage of a tree and turning it into a shadow cast on the ground plane might not be as bad, if the ground plane is flat (**Figure 13.22**). The same goes for fire, which might flicker and reflect off the faces of characters in the scene, or water, whose rippling reflections can be more easily synthesized than the look of water itself. The simpler the plane receiving the reflection, the more likely you might get away with this.

CLOSE-UP

Primary and Secondary

When animating physical objects, it is common to delineate between primary and secondary animation. *Primary animation* is the gross movement of the object, the movement of the object as a whole. *Secondary animation* is the movement of individual parts of the object as a result of inertia. So, for example, a helicopter crashes to the ground: That's the primary animation. Its rotors and tail bend and shudder at impact: That's the secondary animation. For the most part, in 2D compositing, your work is isolated to primary animation.

Figure 13.22 Animating your own trees swaying in the breeze just to make a shadow would be a big pain. Why not steal their silhouettes and get the motion for free? The process is detailed in Chapter 12, "Working with Light."

Water

You've already examined the effect of water in its gaseous form (as fog, mist, or steam); what about water in its liquid and solid states? Although it's not possible to re-create *The Perfect Storm* or *The Day After Tomorrow* without elaborate 3D and practical effects, compositing plays a pivotal role in re-creating rain and snow and in enhancing practical and computer-generated scenes.

Realistically, though, it's rare to create elaborate water effects without relying on some even more elaborate practical or computer-generated source. I'll assume that you're trying to complete shots only in After Effects, but I'll focus on techniques that are equally valid even if your particle and water animations are created elsewhere.

Precipitation

One area where After Effects' built-in features fall short is particle generation. The Particle Playground effect, which ships with the program and hasn't changed much since around version 3.0, is slow, crude, and cumbersome. I have yet to work with anyone who had the patience to coax realistic effects out of this plug-in.

If you're called upon to create rainfall or snowfall from scratch, consider the Particular plug-in from Trapcode (a demo is included on the book's disc). Not only does it outdo Particle Playground in features and ease of use, but also, if set up correctly, it obviates the need for creating precipitation in a dedicated 3D program.

Creating the Element

Particular contains all the controls needed to create a great precipitation element, but it also contains a lot of controls, period. Here is a brief attempt to outline a few of the most significant ones, followed by an example of how to use a final element.

A standard particle shape can be used, or customized particles, such as an irregular snowflake shape. There are several choices of particle emitters, but one great option is to use a spotlight, making the light layer's Transform controls available to establish the position and direction of the particles in 3D space (**Figure 13.23**).

The most important settings are found in the Emitter and Physics categories. Emitter settings establish the amount, velocity, and direction of particles, while Physics contains controls pertaining to the environment itself: gravity, air resistance, wind, turbulence, and spin.

The Visibility category contains controls affecting the depth of your particles. You may find that, as with smoke earlier in the chapter, several planes will offer a better result than one big simulation, allowing you to control, say, the foreground separate from everything else.

Particular resides on a 2D layer, but the effect is 3D-aware, so if you add a camera to the composition, the particles will behave as if seen through that camera.

It's nothing against dedicated 3D programs or the artists who use them to recognize that a faster and better-integrated result can often be achieved in After Effects because its workflow and impact on a shot as a whole are more direct. These types of effects contain lots of variables, and often require many iterations—fewer if performed in the context of the whole shot.

Waterfalls

A waterfall remains a challenging element to re-create in software, so here's an old school practical way to shoot this element as a miniature instead: Use sand.

You can adjust and color correct sand coming out of a funnel or trough to look a lot like a waterfall. Depending on how heavy the sand is, you might even get some of the spray at the base (as a cloud of dust). The tricky part is setting up the shoot properly; everything that is not sand must be negative space, so you'll need a miniature stage (which can be all cardboard) in a solid color (Rosco blue, say, or flat black), lighting, and a matched camera perspective. Cue the sand, and roll the camera.

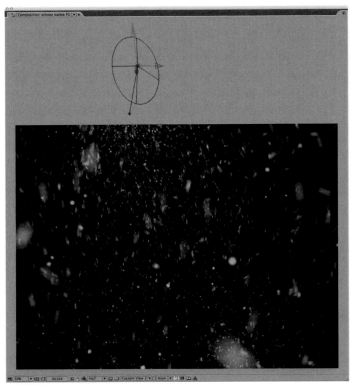

Figure 13.23 The axes belong to a light used as an emitter for Particular. It can be freely translated in 3D space.

Reflected Water Light

The presence of water (outside of the shot area) is implied by the presence of its reflected light in the scene. Light from water has a compelling shape and movement, and if you've set up the scene so that the viewer knows there's a swimming pool or a lake nearby, it may even be expected.

The question is how to get the sample of the play of light, reflected off of the waves. With patient adjustments, you can use Wave World, an effect included when you register your copy of After Effects. The default settings won't do. For one thing, View must be changed to Height Map just to preview the effect, and Grid Resolution must be raised (it's set for a feeble 1990s-era computer) along with optional Pre-roll settings. Reflect Edges can be set to All. Then the trick is to set Position and Amplitude for a natural look. The compositing technique is similar to what is done with shadows (Chapter 12): Position the plane and choose a blending mode, such as Add or Vivid Light, or apply it as a Luma Matte to an adjustment layer containing Levels.

Compositing the Element

When it comes time to integrate falling rain or snow with a background plate, you can do better than a simple A over B comp; in fact, the key is to show the effect of these elements on the scene rather than showing the elements themselves.

Raindrops and snowflakes are translucent, their appearance heavily influenced by the environment. More than that, these individual bits of precipitation behave like tiny lenses that diffract light, defocusing and lowering the contrast of whatever is behind them, but also picking up the ambient light themselves. Therefore, on *The Day After Tomorrow* our crew found success with using the rain or snow element as a track matte for an adjustment layer containing a Fast Blur and a Levels effect.

To allow you to sample the results of a Particular render, included on the DVD are a foreground and background snow animation, which have been applied as follows in 13_snowfall.aep.

Blurriness is set very high (200), so that the area behind each individual raindrop or snowflake becomes a wash of color. Levels is applied with a slightly lowered (90%) Output White value, and a very high (80%) Output Black value. The precipitation is visible by its effect on the scene, lightening dark areas, darkening light ones, and adding diffusion throughout (**Figure 13.24**).

The best thing about this approach is that it works independently of the background appearance. There is no need to decide the color of the element for a given shot, and shots retain source colors, the precipitation having a similar influence on each shot in a sequence.

Figure 13.24 You must look closely to see the added snowfall in a still image with so many bright regions; to see it applied in motion via adjustment layers, open 13_snowfall.aep. (Source image courtesy Eric E. Yang via Creative Commons).

Conclusion

To fully mess with climatic effects may require elaborate 3D simulations, but even then, the compositing approach remains much the same. The chapter's focus has been on how elements behave in the real world, and how best to emulate that reality in After Effects. This approach should serve you well even if an element is needed—frost, say, or hail—that was not covered directly here.

The next chapter heats things up with fire, explosions, and other combustibles.

14

Pyrotechnics: Fire, Explosions, Energy Phenomena

My nature is to be on set, blowing things up.

— Ken Ralston (winner of five
Academy Awards for visual effects)

Pyrotechnics: Fire, Explosions, Energy Phenomena

I have become convinced that a significant number of people first became interested in visual effects work because they qualify as borderline pyromaniacs. Creating fire effects entirely on the computer might not be as much fun as being an on-set pyrotechnician, but hey, keeping these people busy with either job is better than letting them loose on society at large.

This chapter focuses on effects that have traditionally been re-created live on set or via practical elements such as miniatures. The craft of the on-set pyrotechnician is not obsolete by any means, but these days there are many, many cases (particularly the smaller, more common ones) in which compositing can save a lot of time and expense at the shoot, no matter the budget of the production. Blowing stuff up on set is fun, but it involves extensive setup and a not insubstantial amount of danger to the cast and crew, and often you get only one take to get it right.

As a director, I would never subject actors to real gunfire and bullet hits on set unless it was clearly the only way to get the shot. The death of Brandon Lee on the set of *The Crow*, when a gun loaded with blanks shot an empty cartridge (still in the barrel from a previous shot) into his abdomen, was fully preventable—not only by a more attentive arms or prop master, but by never loading the gun in the first place. At the risk of sounding glib, it is indisputable that compositing could save a life in this scenario.

And gunfire is only where this chapter begins. Equally tricky and dangerous on set are explosive bullet hit *squibs*, small explosives that must be rigged and exploded by an on-set special effects technician, lest anyone damage soft body tissue. You'll learn how to create those in After Effects as well. From there, you'll move on to the science-fiction equivalent of gunplay: weapons of pure energy, such as the *Star Wars* blaster and lightsaber or the *Star Trek* photon torpedo. After that, it's heat distortion, fire, and explosions.

Then, perhaps, a nice, warm cup of tea.

I hope it's not disappointing that not everything pyrotechnical can be accomplished start to finish in After Effects. Some effects require extra preparation of physical or fabricated elements, and all will benefit from your familiarity with good reference. There is, alas, no easy way to create realistic fire or explosions completely from scratch in After Effects, but that does not mean that these are off-limits; they're hard to create on computers, period. Compositing may be the key to making these shots work at all.

And of course, sometimes a storyline calls for the destruction of something that cannot, in real life, be destroyed on any budget. The famous shot of the White House being blown to smithereens in *Independence Day* is one example, but this limitation was also very much in place on a little known ABC-TV movie called *Superfire*, whose concept was articulated as "*The Perfect Storm*, but with fire." Infernos consuming acres of forest were central to the plot, and even if the budget had allowed for purchasing and razing hundreds of acres of wilderness, environmental concerns—not to mention horrendous PR—would in all cases mitigate against it. The solution turned out to be varied: in some cases, to composite fire from scratch; in others, to augment what was already there.

To provide examples, this chapter features stills from low-budget independent films that couldn't afford to create the kind of destruction required on screen. *The Last Birthday Card* is a short narrative film that Stu Maschwitz created while still working at Industrial Light + Magic. *Mark and Matty* is a satirical series poking fun at the conventions of action movies with effects (as well as acting), done by Matt Ward, a veteran of Lucasfilm, Industrial Light + Magic, and the late, lamented ESC Entertainment. In both cases, the effects are quick and dirty, not meant even for the level of scrutiny they are afforded via still figures in this book, and intended only to convey the story—which in both cases, incidentally, features hapless victims pursued by unhinged assassins.

Firearms

Re-creating gunplay is relatively straightforward via compositing. The key is that everything happens very quickly—usually over the course of a frame or two, three at most.

Two basic types of shots are outlined here: the firing of the gun itself and the result of bullet hits in the scene. The former can be done entirely with compositing. For the latter, compositing helps, but more active scenes of mayhem typically require practical elements, photographed on set.

Ready, Fire, Aim

It can be difficult for actors to work on set without practical effects. The lack of a kick from a handgun, however, shouldn't pose much of a problem. A prop gun clicks when the trigger is pulled, and the actor need only mime the motion of the recoil, or *kick*. The kick is minor with small handguns, and a much bigger deal with a shotgun (check reference).

So that's how you start, with a shot of an actor pulling the trigger and miming the kick (**Figure 14.1**). From there, you typically add just a few basic elements via compositing:

▶ The muzzle flash

▶ A smoke puff (optional depending on the lighting and type of gun)

▶ Discharge of the cartridge or shell (on a semi-automatic)

▶ Interactive light on the subject firing the gun (depending on the scene lighting and angle)

The actual travel of the bullet out of the barrel is not something you have to worry about; at roughly one kilometer per second, it is generally moving too fast to see amid all the other effects. The bullet is usually evident more by what it causes to happen when it hits something, which is covered in the next section.

TIP

There's undoubtedly a scene in some movie somewhere that contains excellent gunplay reference for any scene imaginable. As you prepare to stage these effects, you are encouraged to carefully study, frame by frame and loop after loop, sequences similar to those you wish to create—be they from cheesy television westerns and cop shows to such high-end shoot-'em-ups as *The Matrix* and *Terminator 2*.

Figure 14.1 Just by virtue of pulling the trigger on the prop handgun, the actor creates enough motion to set the reaction over which the ensuing muzzle flash will be added. (Image courtesy The Orphanage.)

Muzzle Flash and Smoke

The clearest indication that a gun has gone off is the flash of light around the muzzle, at the end of the barrel. This small, bright explosion of gunpowder typically lasts only one frame per shot (a repeating firearm is just a series of disconnected single frame flashes), and it can be painted by hand, cloned in from a practical image, or composited from stock reference (**Figure 14.2**).

Figure 14.3 shows the addition of a single-frame muzzle flash for the firing of a handgun. Because it is in close-up, the flash obscures much of the frame. It is a mixture of flash and smoke matted in from a pyrotechnic reference shot. All that is really required for this single shot is a single-frame overlay; there's no need to carefully dissipate the smoke to make the shot believable.

Contrast that with **Figure 14.4,** which shows a Gatling gun fired from a helicopter. Clearly, this scene has a lot more going on in it than just muzzle flash and smoke. Because it's a repeating gun, the flashes occur on successive frames and the smoke builds up along with debris caused by bullet impacts. The way the shape of the muzzle flash varies over time as well as its relative size and placement are the keys to the shot, picked up from reference.

The shape of the muzzle flash depends on the type of gun being fired. Just as with lens flares and other equipment-specific visual elements, you are encouraged to find

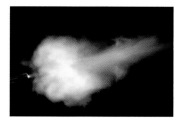

Figure 14.2 The angle of the shot and the type of gun affect the muzzle flash effect. The first image is from an M16 rifle; the other is from a handgun. (Images courtesy Artbeats.)

Figure 14.3 This close-up of a muzzle flash was added to the plate from Figure 14.1, using only a single frame of smoke from a photographed source via Add mode. (Image courtesy The Orphanage.)

Figure 14.4 The fiery muzzle flash of a Gatling gun has a characteristic teardrop profile shape; here it was painted in from fire source. (Image courtesy The Orphanage.)

TIP

Typically, an explosion travels in two directions from the end of the barrel: arrayed outward from the firing point and in a straight line out from the barrel. If you don't have source that makes this shape at the correct angle, it may be simplest to paint it.

Figure 14.5 A shell pops off of the fired handgun. Note that the shell appears only as a blurred, elongated white element in frame with no discernable detail. A blue-screen shot of an automatic weapon shows a much more discernable shell. (Images courtesy The Orphanage and Artbeats.)

a movie that has your gun in it. You can even consult the NRA-ILA Web site (www.nraila.org) to learn details such as the relationship of the color and amount of smoke to the type of gunpowder.

To summarize, you can easily create custom muzzle flashes as follows:

▶ Search for (or create) smoke, explosion, or fire source (a still image is good enough).

▶ Add it as a layer with a blending mode (typically Add).

▶ Automatic weaponry demands that you paint frame by frame (unless you shoot matching effects source), but especially with good reference showing how crude these flashes are, and their basic shape, this can be quick and dirty work, as there is no need for one frame to match the next.

▶ With any budget for stock footage, you can buy muzzle flashes (such as the Artbeats Gun Stock collection, www.artbeats.com); these are shot over blue or black, ready to be matted, blended, or painted into your shot.

Shells and Interactive Light

If the gun in your scene calls for it, that extra little bit of realism can be added with a secondary animation of a shell popping off the top of a semi-automatic. **Figure 14.5** shows just such an element in action. All you need is a four-point mask of a white solid, animated and motion blurred (**Figure 14.6**). You don't have to worry about the color; instead adjust the element's Opacity to blend it into the scene.

Figure 14.6 All that is required to transform a four-point masked white solid to a shell popping off the gun is heavy motion blur and a sufficiently low Opacity setting. (Images courtesy The Orphanage.)

The bright flash of the muzzle may also cause a brief reflected flash on objects near the gun as well as the subject firing it. Chapter 12, "Working with Light," offers the basic methodology: Softly mask a highlight area, then flash it using an adjustment layer containing a Levels effect or a colored solid with a suitable blending mode.

As a general rule, the lower the ambient light and the larger the weapon, the greater the likelihood of interactive lighting. A literal "shot in the dark" would fully illuminate the face of whomever (or whatever) fired it, just for a single frame. It's a great dramatic effect, but one that is very difficult to re-create in post. This is a rare case where firing blanks on set might be called for, unless you can fake it by dropping in a single-frame still of the brightly lit assassin.

Bullet Hits

Bullets that ricochet on set are known as *squib hits* because they typically make use of squibs, small explosives with the approximate power of a firecracker that go off during the take. Sometimes squibs are actual firecrackers. It is possible to add bullet hits without using explosives on set, but frenetic gunplay will typically demand a mixture of on-set action and post-production wizardry.

Figure 14.7 shows a before-and-after shot adding a bullet hit purely in After Effects. In this case, the bullet does not ricochet, but is embedded directly into the solid metal of the truck. In such a case, all you need to do is to add the results of the damage on a separate layer at the frame where the bullet hits; you can paint this, or acquire it from stock footage. The element can then be motion tracked to marry it solidly to the background (**Figure 14.8**).

At the frame of impact, and continuing a frame or two thereafter, a shooting spark and possibly a bit of smoke (if the target is combustible—not in the case of a steel vehicle) will convey the full violence of the bullets. As with the muzzle flash, this can vary from a single frame to a more fireworks-like shower of sparks tracked in over a few frames (**Figure 14.9**).

Figure 14.7 This sequence of frames shows a second bullet hitting the cab of the truck, using two elements: the painted bullet hit and the spark element, whose source was shot on black and added via Screen mode. (Images courtesy markandmatty.com.)

Figure 14.8 The bullet hit is one opportunity to develop your paint skills. The example shows a bullet hole in metal, which has a fairly consistent look. Here, the result is motion tracked to match the source background plate. (Images courtesy markandmatty.com.)

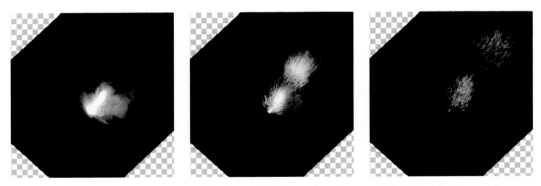

Figure 14.9 A source spark element using Add or Screen blending mode to drop out all of the black background. (Images courtesy markandmatty.com.)

A bullet hit explosion can be created via a little miniature effects shoot, using a fire-retardant black background (a flat, black card might do it) and some firecrackers (assuming you can get them). The resulting flash, sparks, and smoke stand out against the black, allowing the element to be composited via a blending mode (such as Add or Screen), a hi-con matte (Chapter 6, "Color Keying"), or a plug-in such as Knoll UnMult. If dangerous explosives aren't your thing, even in a controlled situation, stock footage is available.

Figure 14.10 shows a before-and-after shot of a scene that demanded a lot of extra flying debris as the character's apartment was strafed by the previously depicted helicopter. Compositing in this debris after the shot was taken would be highly inconvenient, causing an impractical amount of extra work when compared with firing a BB gun at items on the set and enhancing the effect with sparks and smoke in After Effects (the actual method used).

So to recap, a good bullet hit should include

- ▶ Smoke or sparks at the frame of impact, typically lasting between one and five frames
- ▶ The physical result of the bullet damage (if any) painted and tracked into the scene
- ▶ Debris in cases where the target is prone to shattering or scattering

Later in this chapter, you'll see how larger explosions have much in common with bullet hits, which are essentially just miniature explosions. In both cases, a bit of practical debris will often enhance believability.

Figure 14.10 A BB gun was aimed at various breakaway objects on location while assistants hurled other small objects into the scene to add the necessary amount of debris and mayhem on location. Practical debris is very difficult to add after the fact. (Images courtesy The Orphanage.)

Sci-Fi Weaponry

Now we shift into a more imaginary area, albeit one with a few roots in our own world. How do you create the look of pure energy used for the blasters and lightsabers in *Star Wars* or the phasers and photon torpedoes in *Star Trek* (whose distinctions are familiar to me as an ex-Lucas employee). These are now visual clichés, yet they tap into an area of visual effects that seems to come up regularly.

The key seems to be that even these imaginary weapons of pure energy contain recognizable resemblances to phenomena from our own world: high-powered lasers and high-voltage electrical arcs, for example. The other key is that 32 bit per channel compositing makes the play of the superbright forces in a scene more natural, provided you know how to set them up.

The final key is really to take these effects beyond the tried and true, but that involves art direction concerns that are mostly beyond the scope of this book. The basic look is relatively simple: a hot white core surrounded by a luminescent glow.

Full Control

A couple of effects in the Render category of the Effects menu automatically create an element with a core and a surrounding glow. For your basic blaster or lightsaber effect, you might be tempted to reach for Beam. And why not, especially now that you can supercharge the look of Beam by working in 32 bpc?

True, a canned effect such as this surrenders artistic control for convenience, but it lays the groundwork necessary for what this section is all about by providing an element with built-in thresholding (albeit in 8 bit—I'll review why that doesn't particularly matter in a moment). Other than the shape, it's customizable, as follows:

1. Apply the Beam effect to a solid layer above the plate layer. Beam can be applied directly to the plate by checking Composite on Original, but working with the element in HDR requires that it be a separate layer.

NOTES

Disclaimer: Although the author of this book and the guy who shot the footage used in this section both ex-Lucas employees who worked on Star Wars movies (in Matt's case) and related projects (in Mark's case), this bears no relationship to the "official" method for creating a lightsaber at ILM, which will never be publicly divulged by any soul, living or otherwise.

2. Extend the length to 100% and set the Starting and Ending points to the ends of the stick.

3. Add some Thickness: 24 for Starting and 30 for Ending (the non-uniform settings lend an artificial impression of three-dimensionality with 3D Perspective checked on, as it is by default).

4. The basic element is there but it's not looking too cool. Switch the Project to 32 bpc mode and apply the Levels effect. Uncheck Clip to Output White and lower Input White way down (to around 30%), and you'll see the beam get white hot.

5. Finesse the look by manipulating the Softness and Outside Color settings in Beam and Gamma in Levels (**Figure 14.11**).

TIP

With Length in Beam set to less than 100%, you can animate the beam traveling between the Starting and Ending Points using the Time setting: this is designed as a quick way to animate a blaster shot, or power-up of the saber in this case.

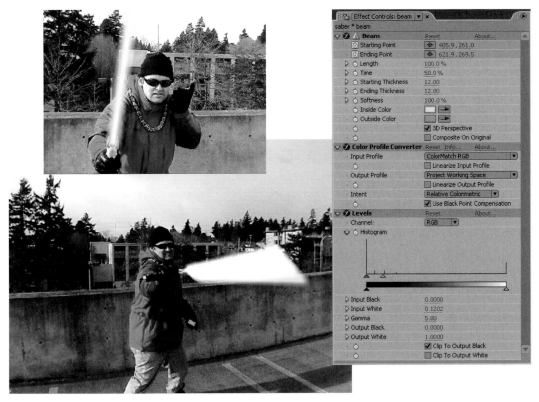

Figure 14.11 If you're still unconvinced about the power of 32 bit per channel HDR mode, check out how good this effect looks even though it's based on a simple (cheesy, really) 8 bit per channel Beam effect, with a Color Profile Converter to make it linear (optional) and, most essentially, Levels set to push the threshold areas into overbright land. (Source footage courtesy markandmatty.com.)

What happens next is what gives it the cool factor, and just offhand there are several available options:

▶ Animate the saber being waved around and enable motion blur

▶ For other types of shots: add interactive lighting where needed, such as the glow on nearby faces and passing objects

▶ Add bullet hits, either like those discussed earlier or your own special version of energy coursing through the target

▶ Create this effect for yourself, without Beam, using the same basic formula: a bright (or white) core layer and a darker-colored, blurred duplicate (or several) to create the basic element, which is then made to glow in 32 bpc using Levels (**Figure 14.12**).

Figure 14.12 All kinds of trippy sci-fi looks can result from blending the type of "high energy" elements described in this section via HDR compositing.

Heat Distortion

Heat distortion, that strange rippling in the air that occurs when hot air is dissipated into cooler air, is another one of those effects compositors love. Like a lens flare, it's a highly visible effect that, if properly motivated and adjusted, lends realism to your scene rather than distracting from its story.

Figures 14.13a and **b** show the fabricated results of heat distortion in a scene. Its rippling effect adds to the dynamism or chaos of the scene. When your eye sees heat

Figures 14.13a and b The effect of heat haze has been added to the general mayhem being issued by the helicopter (a). A comparison with an unaltered shot of the building (b) emphasizes the amount of distortion. (Images courtesy The Orphanage.)

distortion, it understands that the environment is dynamic, containing an abrupt mix of hot air with cold air. This adds to the visceral reality of the shot, whether it's a desert exterior, a day at the racetrack, jet engine exhaust, or all three (which describes the pod race sequence from *Star Wars* pretty well). When the fire itself is in the shot and you can see through it or anywhere above it, you expect the fire to heavily distort whatever is visible behind its heat.

What Is Actually Happening

Stare into a swimming pool, and you can see displacement caused by the bending of light as it travels through the water. Rippled waves in the water cause rippled bending of light. There are cases in which our atmosphere behaves like this as well, when ripples are caused in it by the collision of warmer and cooler air, a medium which is not quite as transparent as it seems.

As you know from basic physics, hot air rises and hot particles move faster than cool ones. Air is not a perfectly clear medium but a translucent gas that can act as a lens. This "lens" is typically static and appears flat, but the application of heat causes an abrupt mixture of fast-moving hot air particles rising into cooler ambient air. This creates ripples that have the effect of displacing and distorting what is behind the moving air, just like ripples in the pool or ripples in the windows of an old house.

NOTES

It can be useful to generate heat distortion particles in 3D animation software, when the distortion needs to be attached to a 3D animated object, such as a jet engine or rocket exhaust.

You might assume, therefore, that a physics model devised in 3D animation software would be more accurate than faking this effect in 2D. However, 3D software generally does not take into account the role of air in a shot. In any case, this effect behaves like an overlaid distortion on top of whatever lays beyond the hot air from the point of view of the camera. Therefore it's a perfectly appropriate compositing effect, useful when there is an object in the scene capable of generating a significant amount of hot air.

How to Re-create It

The basic steps for re-creating heat distortion from an invisible source in After Effects are

1. Create a basic particle animation that simulates the movement and dissipation of hot air particles in the scene.

2. Make two similar but unique passes of this particle animation—one to displace the background vertically, the other to displace it horizontally—and precompose them.

3. Add an adjustment layer containing the Displacement Map effect, which should be set to use the particle animation comp to create the distortion effect, and apply it to the background.

On the book's DVD, 14_heatDisplacement.aep contains the effect applied over a checkerboard background. You can easily see the results even in a still image (**Figure 14.14**). Setting up the particles is potentially the trickiest part, and of course the settings are unique for each scene.

Particle Playground is perfectly adequate for this type of use, and it is included with After Effects Professional. Unfortunately, Particle Playground is generally slow to render and cumbersome, full of not-quite-intuitive properties. The help documents are thorough, but there are dozens of pages of documentation. Thankfully, this effect requires only a few simple adjustments:

▶ Under Cannon, move Position to the source in the frame where the heat haze originates (in this case, the bottom center, but it could even be out of frame).

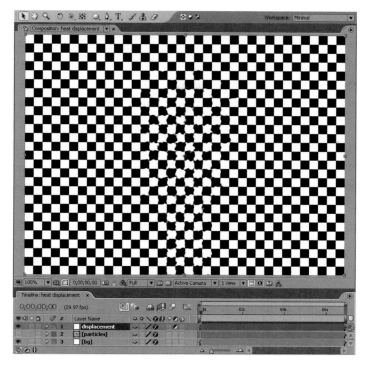

Figure 14.14 A subtle effect, the heat displacement has been laid over a checkerboard where it is clearly visible traveling up the center of the image.

► Open up Barrel Radius from the default of 0.0 to the width, in pixels, of the source. I chose 50, only because 720, the width of the frame, would require many more particles and slow down the example.

► Boost Particles Per Second to 200. The larger the Barrel Radius, the more particles needed.

► Under Gravity, set Force to 0.0 to prevent the default fountain effect.

The default color and scale of the particles is fine for this video resolution example, but you might have to adjust them as well according to your shot. A larger format (in pixels) or a bigger heat source might require bigger, softer particles.

4. Now duplicate the particles layer and set the color of the duplicated layer to pure green. To vary it slightly so that the particles don't overlap, raise Direction Random Spread and Velocity Random Spread from their defaults of 20 to 25.

Figure 14.15 The particles used to create the displacement. By default, Displacement Map uses red for horizontal displacement and green for vertical displacement. A slight amount of blur was added to soften the effect of each individual particle. The effect is exaggerated (to show up in a still figure) at the left of the plane wing.

TIP

Heat displacement often dissipates before it reaches the top of the frame. Making particles behave so that their lifespan ends before they reach the top of the frame is accurate, but painstaking. A simpler solution is to add a solid with a black-to-white gradient (created with the Ramp effect) as a luma matte to hold out the adjustment layer containing the displacement effect.

5. The heat animation is almost complete; it only needs some softening. Add an adjustment layer with a moderate Fast Blur setting of 4.0 (**Figure 14.15**).

Now to put the animation to use: Drag it into the main comp, and turn off its visibility. The actual Displacement Map effect is applied either directly to the background plate or preferably to an adjustment layer sitting above all the layers that should be affected by the heat haze. Displacement Map is set by default to use the red channel for horizontal displacement and the green channel for vertical displacement; all you need to do is select the layer containing the red and green particles under the Displacement Map Layer pull-down.

Fire

Synthesizing fire from scratch remains an advanced topic within the upper reaches of visual effects research and development. I was employed at The Orphanage during its work on *Hellboy*, a story featuring a leading character, Liz, whose preternatural gift is to create lots and lots of fire when upset. There was no way to use photographed fire for those shots because they required too much interaction with the rest of the scene. I was amazed at what the team responsible for these effects was able pull off.

Within After Effects, fire synthesis is way too hot to handle. If fire is at all prominent in a shot, it will require elements that come from somewhere else—most likely, shot with a camera. Take a look at what's involved.

Creating and Using Fire Elements

Figure 14.16 shows fire elements filmed for effects usage. The big challenge when compositing fire is that it doesn't scale very realistically. You might think that any fire that you shoot with a camera will look better than something you create on a computer, but a fireplace fire looks like it came straight from your hearth, no matter how it is scaled or retimed.

The bigger the fire you need to shoot, however, the more expensive it's likely to be because you really need the fire to be shot in negative space—against a black background—so that you can composite it using Blending modes. Fire is obviously capable of illuminating the entire environment around it, so if that environment has specific detail, it can be all but impossible to isolate the fire from the environment.

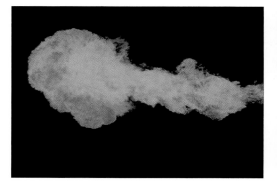

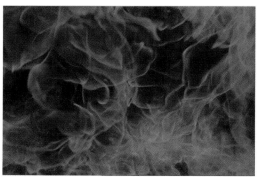

Figure 14.16 Fire elements are typically shot in negative (black) space, or occasionally in a natural setting requiring more careful matting. By adjusting Input Black in Levels, you can control the amount of glow coming off the fire as it is blended via Add mode, lending the scene interactive lighting for free. (Images courtesy Artbeats.)

This, then, is a case where it's worth investing in proper elements. In many cases, stock footage companies, such as Artbeats (represented on the book's CD-ROM), have anticipated your needs. Whether you require burning half-height miniature trees or a flamethrower, you're sure to find solutions for a wide variety of shots in these stock collections. As a result the scale and intensity may be more correct than what you can easily shoot on your own.

Hang Fire

When employing a fire element shot against black (for example, the Artbeats_RF001H_fireExcerpt.mov included on the disc), it is best in 8 bpc mode to employ Screen or Add Blending modes (not a luma matte) to permit the background to be seen behind the fire. The Unmult plug-in from Knoll Light Factory, which is freeware included on the disc, will also effectively transform the black background into transparency. None of these methods by itself, however, is enough for a final composite (**Figures 14.17a** through **d**).

Figures 14.17a through d No way would you ever want to try to luma matte fire (for example, using Extract as in 14.17a); it will never look good. Add mode tends to appear oversaturated in 8 bpc mode (b), while it and Screen (c) both are initially more transparent than they should be. Unmult gets the transparency more correct by removing black pixels, but the result lacks contrast (d). (Fire courtesy Artbeats, included on the disc.)

If you simply lay the fire layer over the background and apply Screen mode, the effect may look rather weak. There are several ways to strengthen it, but this is a case where linear blending and Add mode are ultimately the best combination. To firm up a fire (or flare, or other bright) element you can

▶ Apply Unmult in addition to setting a Blending mode (Screen or Add)

▶ Fine-tune the result with a Levels effect, pushing in on Input White and Black (as well as color matching overall)

▶ Overlap multiple occurrences of the fire element to create a raging inferno

However, the more elegant solution is to switch your project to 32 bpc linear (see Chapter 11, "Film, HDR, and 32 Bit Compositing," for more on this) and use Add; the result is far more natural and less of a kludge (**Figure 14.18a**). Additionally, as with fog elements (Chapter 15, "Learning to See"), the "secret sauce" is a Compound Blur effect on the background, using the Luminance of the fire element (**Figure 14.18b**).

Figures 14.18a, b, and c Add mode behaves more naturally with linear blending via 32 bpc mode (a). To really sell the effect, however, requires the addition of a compound blur effect to the background (b). The combination is immediately more believable (c).

Figures 14.19a and b The background plate was stock footage of a raging fire (a), but it wasn't raging quite enough. Layering extra raging inferno footage helped the opaque look of such intense fires to break through the overlaid extra layers of smoke (b). (Figure 14.19b courtesy ABC-TV.)

A final composition will, of course, often involve multiple fire elements as well as smoke (**Figures 14.19a** and **b**). As always, things go better in linear floating point.

Light Interacts

Provided that your camera is not moving too much, a 2D fire layer should read adequately well as being fully three-dimensional. If it's not looking believable in your scene, the problem is likely a lack of interactive light. As was stated above, fire tends to illuminate everything around it with a warm, flickering glow.

There are a few ways to add this. First of all, as you can see in **Figure 14.20**, your fire element may include a certain amount of glow that you can use. Raising Input Black when adjusting Levels tends to eliminate this glow, so that control is an effective way to dial the glow in and out.

Note, however, that this glow isn't anything particularly unique or special; you can re-create it either via a heavily blurred duplicate of the source fire or using a masked and heavily feathered orange solid, with perhaps a slight amount of wiggle added to the glow opacity to cause a bit of interactive flickering.

TIP

For a shot featuring a character or object that reflects firelight, there's no need to go crazy projecting fire onto the subject. In many cases, it is enough to create some flickering in the character's own luminance values, for example by wiggling the Input White value at a low frequency in Levels (Individual Controls).

Figure 14.20 Depending on the Levels settings applied to the source fire element (specifically Input White and Black on the RGB and Red channels), you can end up with a lot of extra glow or omit the glow entirely.

Figures 14.21a, b, and c Before-and-after sequential stills of a flyover shot. Because of the angle of the aerial camera, the shot required 3D motion tracking, originally done using 2D3's Boujou. (Images courtesy ABC-TV.)

Into the Third Dimension (and Beyond!)

You can pull off the illusion of fully three-dimensional fire, especially if the camera is moving around in 3D space, directly in After Effects. I was frankly surprised at how well this worked in the shot featured in **Figures 14.21a, b,** and **c.**

As shown, the background plate is an aerial flyby of a forest. Because of the change in altitude and perspective, this shot clearly required 3D tracking (touched upon at the end of Chapter 8, "Effective Motion Tracking"). The keys to making this shot look fully dimensional were to break up the source fire elements into discrete chunks and to stagger those in 3D space so that as the plane rose above them, their relationship and parallax changed (**Figure 14.22**).

It is easy to get away with any individual fire element being 2D in this case. Because fire changes its shape constantly, there is nothing to give away its two-dimensionality. Borders of individual fire elements can freely overlap without being distracting, so it doesn't look cut out. The eye sees evidence of parallax between a couple dozen fire elements, and does not think to question that any individual one of them looks too flat. The smoke elements were handled in a similar way, organized along overlapping planes. As I mentioned in the previous chapter, smoke's translucency aids the illusion that overlapping smoke layers have dimensional depth.

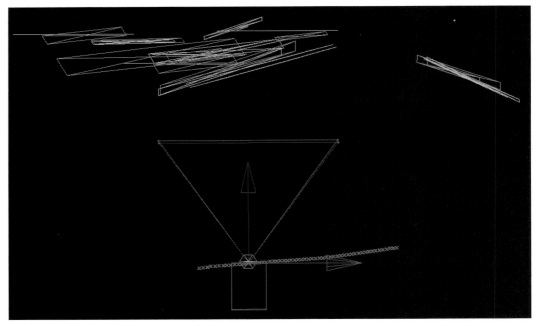

Figure 14.22 A top view of the 3D motion-tracked camera from Figure 14.21b panning past one set of fires (of which the final composition had half a dozen). The pink layers contain fire elements, the gray layers smoke.

Explosions

The example forest fire shot also contained a large explosion in a clearing. There is not a huge fundamental difference between how you composite an explosion and how you composite fire, except that an explosion is far more likely to require a mixture of strategies. It is largely a question of what is exploding.

All explosions are caused by rapidly expanding combustible gases; implosions are caused by rapid contraction. Just by looking at an explosion, viewers can gauge its size and get an idea of what blew up, however, so you need to design the right explosion for your situation, or your result will be too cheesy even for 1980s television sci-fi. How do you do it?

Light and Chunky

Each explosion you will see is a little bit unique, but to narrow the discussion I'll organize all explosions into two basic categories. The easier one to deal with is the *gaseous explosion*, one made up only of gas and heat. These behave just like fire; in fact, in the shot in **Figure 14.21b** the explosion is fire, a huge ball of it where something very combustible must have gone up very quickly.

Some shots end up looking fake, however, because they use a gaseous explosion when a more chunky explosion is called for. A *debris explosion* is an explosion that also contains chunks of various types of exploding debris. The need for debris is one reason that exploding miniatures are still in use (or even, when possible, full-scale explosions).

The debris cues viewers to several important pieces of information about the shot. First of all, how big was the explosion? The slower moving and bigger the amount of debris, the bigger it probably was. For this reason, effects pyrotechnics tend to use miniatures shot with a high-speed camera. The resulting slow-motion effect makes the explosion seem much bigger than it was.

If your shot calls for a chunky explosion and you don't have any chunks in your source, you need to add them somehow. Many 3D programs these days include effective dynamics simulations; if you go that route, be sure to generate a depth map as well because each chunk will only be revealed as it emerges from the fireball. Many other concerns associated with this are beyond the scope of this discussion because they must be solved in other software.

One effect that seems to come close in After Effects is Shatter, but it's hard to recommend this unless it is specifically a pane of glass or other plane that breaks. Shatter isn't horrendous for a decade-old dynamics simulator, but its primary limitation is a huge one: It can only employ extruded flat polygons to model the chunks. A pane of glass is one of the few physical objects that would shatter into irregular but flat polygons, and Shatter contains built-in controls for specifying the size of the shards in the point of impact. Shatter was also developed prior to the introduction of 3D in After Effects; you can place your imaginary window in perspective space, but not using a camera or 3D controls.

Figure 14.23 Pyrotechnics footage is just the thing when you need a big explosion, filled with debris. (Images courtesy Artbeats.)

A wide selection of pyrotechnic explosions is also available as stock footage from such companies as Artbeats. In many cases, there is no substitute for footage of a real, physical object being blown to bits (**Figure 14.23**).

In a Blaze of Glory

With good reference and a willingness to take the extra step to marry your shot and effect together, you can create believable footage that would require danger or destruction if taken with a camera. Even in cases when you work on a project that had the budget to actually re-create some of the mayhem described in this chapter, you can use the After Effects techniques to enhance and build upon what the camera captured.

And remember, be careful out there.

Learning to See

Men in the game are blind to what men looking on see clearly.

— Chinese Proverb

Learning to See

In visual effects, we often speak of The Eye, as in, "She has a good eye," or "He's got good technical skills, but needs to develop his eye." Sure, we admire the luminary visual effects supervisors because they can field-strip a Mitchell camera movement blindfolded or code their own HDR exposure-merging Shake plug-in from scratch, but they are most revered because they have The Eye.

What exactly does that mean? It's simple: Having The Eye means knowing the answer to the Ultimate Question:

Why doesn't this shot look real?

It's the question you're implicitly seeking to answer with every tweak of a slider, every opacity adjustment, every key-frame nudge. And it's the hardest question to answer about a shot. Worse still, as the shot progresses from take 1 to 10 to nearly final, the answer becomes more and more elusive.

This chapter focuses on some techniques for honing your eye. These are not compositing techniques—things you'll do sitting in front of your workstation—these are lifestyle techniques. Much to the chagrin of those close to you, being a great compositor means thinking like one all the time. The answer to the Ultimate Question, the hardest question you'll ever face, is all around you in the real world, especially when you're not near your computer.

The only tools you'll need are your eyes, your brain, and a really, really expensive digital camera. C'mon, you were looking for an excuse to buy one, right? No? Fine, a cheap film camera is just as good, if not better. Funny, that.

Why Doesn't This Shot Look Real?

The ability to answer the Ultimate Question comes from developing two distinct skills:

- ▶ Seeing the shot every time as if for the first time
- ▶ Using the left brain to understand what the right brain sees

If those things sound easy, then this book worked better than I thought it would! Please send your resume to The Orphanage immediately.

Seeing the Shot

The first skill is perhaps the most elusive. It is something I observed sitting in dailies with the great visual effects supervisors of Industrial Light + Magic. Complex shots on their 40th take loop relentlessly on a 30-foot screen. The animator can't see anything but the keyframe tweak he finally nailed five minutes *after* submitting this take. The technical director stares relentlessly at his particle simulation, pondering coefficients of elasticity. The compositor is the last line of defense. She feels like she's done a pretty good job of putting the shot together, but knows that the motion track could use one more pass of fine-tuning.

Everyone in the room has what is known as *Familiarity Disorder*. This is the condition that prevents my health plan administrator from successfully explaining my coverage options: He understands the various plans so well that he cannot possibly put himself in my position, which is that I need it explained to me as if I was four years old and mildly retarded. He can never do that because he's too close to the details. In '80s action movie police-chief-speak, he's "in too deep." Everyone in dailies is in too deep. And that's why the chief needs to take each one's piece and badge and shout a spittle-drenched "You're off the case!"

But not Dennis Muren. His job is to remain objective, and this is a mighty challenge. But I would watch him do this—see the shot every time as if for the first time—and he would skip right past these nuances and details that the various contributors were sweating and say something like, "We should slip the sync of that explosion back a few frames. It will cut better with the next few shots that way."

Not that Dennis would ignore the details. But he would not focus on them when something bigger, something about the storytelling properties of the shot, was still not quite right.

How do you develop this skill? It is a matter of discipline. You need to be intimately familiar with the details of the shot in order to work it to perfection, but to keep it from getting overworked, you have to consciously remind yourself to stand back and at least try to see it objectively. So cure number one for Familiarity Disorder is

1. **Try.**

   As in, remind yourself that it's important. Take a deep breath, count to ten, and hear the chief's voice in your head, "You're in too deep!"

   This may seem obvious, but in the heat of battle, with deadlines approaching pointy-end first, it requires a conscious effort to step back and evaluate the shot from as objective a perspective as possible.

Cure number two is

2. **Look at it in the cut.**

   Check your shot in the context of the shots around it, preferably with sound and popcorn. I desperately wanted to add a very expensive, subtle enhancement to a shot I was compositing for Twister. An 18-frame shot. With four frame handles. Stefen Fangmeier showed me the cut sequence on the Avid and cured me of my desire in exactly half a second.

Cure number three is an easy one:

3. **Flop it.**

   This is a trick that designers and matte painters use. Flop your shot horizontally and loop it. You'll be amazed how different it feels, and if you're lucky, something new will jump out at you and the problem you've been slaving over will seem far less important.

None of these three cures work as well as the last one. The last one is your ace in the hole—but you have to be selective about how you play it:

4. Show it to someone who actually is seeing it for the first time.

> I know, duh. But it's amazing how often we forget to do this. We might even unconsciously not want our peers to point out the thing that we kind of suspect isn't quite working about the shot. Consult cure number one, swallow your pride, and show your buddy your shot.

One of the reasons that working against Familiarity Disorder is so important is, and I really hate to break this to you, there will always be something more you could do to make a shot better. But, chances are, you have a deadline to meet, so you have to pick your battles. I mentioned that Dennis Muren would be selective about how he would nitpick details. What I came to realize was that he was using his ability to emulate the audience's experience to pick which details to sweat. A well-designed shot leads a viewer's eye to specific places. When a defect in some remote corner of the frame was pointed out to Dennis, he'd say, "If they're looking there, we've lost them." He makes shots for the people who are engrossed in the film, and he prioritizes storytelling over immaculateness.

The discipline of maintaining your freshness to the work you're doing will be something you struggle with on every shot. But remembering to struggle with it puts you way ahead of the game. Keep at it.

Analyzing What You See

The second skill that is required when struggling with the Ultimate Question is the reason that the chapter is called "Learning to See."

Have you ever taken a life drawing class? You should. The supplies are cheap, and you get to look at naked people. Don't make me spell this out for you.

In life drawing you'll learn that you have to fight off the part of your brain that knows what an arm is. You know an arm is a long, skinny thing. But the model has an arm draped over a knee, aiming right at you. You see the arm heavily foreshortened or compressed in perspective. In fact, from your specific point of view, the elbow is directly in front of the shoulder, and the wrist is almost blocking it.

Now, of course your life drawing is perfect, but look what that idiot in front of you did. He drew the arm as a long, skinny thing. He did that because he *knows* that's what an arm looks like. He drew what he knew, not what he saw. And his arm be lookin' fonky.

Knowing What You Know

We do this all the time in visual effects without even realizing it. When asked to add an element, such as a haze effect, a lens flare, or a dust hit, you think "I know what that looks like" and add it to the shot. And it looks stupid. Why? Because in truth, we don't really know what things look like.

Let me use some theatrics here and ask you to read that last sentence again:

We don't really know what things look like.

Our brains are very complicated, sophisticated instruments that connect to our eyes in a slightly fancier way than an S-Video cable. When we visually absorb things, we don't see images, we recognize objects. We don't see colors and shapes, we see people and oncoming trains.

Don't believe me? Pop quiz: What color is the rearmost tomato in **Figure 15.1**?

Figure 15.1 What color is the rearmost tomato?

Did you say yellow? If so, you are correct. But check this out: **Figure 15.2** is a crop of that image, showing just the tomato.

Figure 15.2 Ok, *now* what color is the tomato?

That patch of color is clearly green. How did you know it was yellow? Your brain looked past the color on the screen and saw that the whole image has a blue tint to it. Knowing this, and knowing a little about tomatoes, your brain filed that as a yellow object.

Your brain second-guesses your eyes like this all the time. College students quizzed on the height of a guest speaker guessed taller when they were told he was a visiting professor than when told he was a grad student. Eyewitnesses to crimes report widely differing descriptions of the criminal depending on their personal experiences and associations.

As compositors, it's our job to know that our brains are unreliable image banks—they store ideas, not pictures. So we can therefore correlate that if we create images based on what we know, we will be basing them on bad data. This is where that digital camera comes into play.

All Hail Reference

We have a great luxury in our industry, which is that every image we create is meant to look as though it was photographed by a camera. Hey, you have a camera!

You should be taking pictures all the time. Take your camera with you wherever you go. I actually forged a pact with a friend that we would each take a photo every day for the entire year of 2002. Not every one of those was going to be a masterpiece, but it got me thinking about creating an image at least once every day.

The other thing it did was fill my FireWire drive with thousands of photos. Photos of all kinds of crazy things. And these photos are great reference.

The single key to creating believable visual effects is *reference*. If you were to worship a pagan god of visual effects, it would be named Reference.

Now that brings up a catch, which is that the whole reason we do visual effects tends to be to create images of impossible things. You can search your image database all day long for snapshots you may have taken of Nazis opening ancient artifacts and unleashing God's wrath, but chances are the closest thing you'll find is your friend blowing chunks behind a wurst stand in Linz.

But there's always something to look at to help you combat the misconception that you already know what something should look like. What should a star going supernova look like? Better it look like your friend blasting your Digital Elph with a LED keychain light than the default lens flare preset number 47. What does a helicopter look like flying through the Chunnel? Well, the reflections on its metal surfaces won't be terribly dissimilar from those on a Geo Metro stuck in traffic in the midtown tunnel.

Getting in the habit of taking pictures all the time, even of mundane things, and really looking at those photos—examining what's happening with light and surfaces and transparencies—will do more than supply you with reference for future projects. It will get you thinking about these things in ways that will have a direct impact on your work.

Putting Reference to Use

Check out **Figure 15.3**'s picture of the Golden Gate Bridge. Every once in a while this monument is half enshrouded in the "marine layer" like this. (I am told that to call it fog is blasphemous.) But what if it wasn't on the day when your shoot needed it to be, or what if you are compositing a matte painting of a future city with buildings so tall their tops get cut off by clouds?

Zooming way in, you can see how the cloud obscures the bridge in a way that is more complicated than a simple transparent overlay (**Figure 15.4**). The cloud actually acts like mist on your windshield, diffracting the light before completely occluding it.

When I first started seeing this in my photography, it changed the way I composited smoke elements. I got in

Figure 15.3 Here's some big, orange bridge I just found while walking around one day.

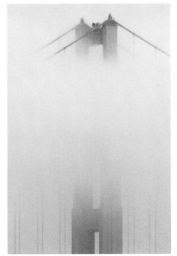

Figure 15.4 An enlargement of Figure 15.3 shows light diffraction through clouds.

Figure 15.5 The same bridge is bereft of brume.

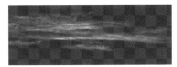

Figure 15.6 If the weather doesn't cooperate, extract a cloud element from another photo.

the habit of using the alpha channel of the fog or cloud or water spray element to drive a compound blur of the background.

Here's an example. **Figure 15.5** shows a clean photo of the bridge, and **Figure 15.6** is the cloud element to be composited over it.

If you do a simple A over B comp, you'll end up with something like **Figure 15.7**.

Now check out that same comp with a subtle compound blur in **Figure 15.8**.

Figure 15.7 The cloud element is simply layered over the bridge photo.

Figure 15.8 The same composite with Compound Blur. See the difference?

The blur simulates the diffraction of the light and ties the cloud element into the shot. This is a great example of how even the most basic layering requires precomposing in After Effects. Compound Blur uses the pixels from one layer to control how much to blur another layer. But the trick is that it uses the pixels before any effects or transformations. So you need a precomp where you reposition and possibly even animate the cloud layer. Here's how to set it up:

1. Create a Cloud Anim comp that features just the semi-transparent cloud with whatever animation you create.

2. Bring the Cloud Anim comp into a Cloud Over Bridge comp, and stack it on top of the bridge photo.

3. Because Compound Blur cannot directly use this layer's alpha channel as its Blur Layer (it uses Luminance of RGB), duplicate the Cloud Anim layer and apply Shift Channels, setting Alpha to Full On and Red, Green, and Blue to Alpha.

4. Because Compound Blur needs to see the pixels of a layer before any effects, precompose this layer (choosing the Move All Attributes option from the dialog), and name the precomp Cloud Blur Map.

5. Because Cloud Blur Map is used only to drive the Compound Blur, you can turn its visibility off in Cloud Over Bridge.

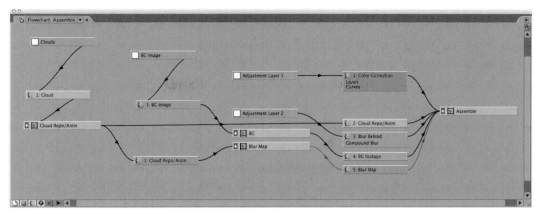

Figure 15.9 Take a look at the bridge composite in Flowchart view.

6. In Cloud Over Bridge, create a new adjustment layer between the cloud and the bridge and apply the Compound Blur effect. Choose Cloud Blur Map from the Blur Layer pull-down menu.

7. Adjust both the Maximum Blur and the Opacity of the adjustment layer to dial in the effect to match your reference.

If all goes well, your Flowchart view should look something like **Figure 15.9**. Now, if you move or even replace your cloud layer in the Cloud Anim comp, the rest of the comp will reflect those changes automatically.

Integration

In compositing, we talk about *integration* of elements. Yes, this means color correction, matching black levels, and tracking in the right motion, but the more advanced tricks of integration usually can be filed under the general idea of "everything in the scene affects everything else in the scene." Much of the reference you collect will yield revelations along these lines.

Check out **Figure 15.10**. Imagine it's your job to add an annoying CG alien next to this handsome guy. The 3D artist has lit the alien to match, but dropping him in A over B leaves the shot looking sad.

Take a closer look at the guy by extracting him from the shot (**Figure 15.11**).

Figure 15.10 What a handsome guy.

Figure 15.11 Isolate Handsome from his scene.

When you isolate him from the scene, it becomes very clear that he has a lot of contamination from the bright background behind him. Your eye can cancel this out in the same way it can allow you to see that the green tomato is really yellow, but when you isolate the guy you prevent your brain from "knowing" that it's right for the dude to look washed out if he's against a bright sky.

That CG alien is going to need more than just color correction, he's going to need *light wrap*, or a simulation of this contamination. This is a popular effect that is available as a plug-in and tempting to overuse. Because of the order of operations in After Effects layers, however, it's also very easy to use light wrap effect plug-ins incorrectly. For example, if you apply light wrap to a foreground layer and you tell it to wrap to the background, it will grab the pixels of the background before any color correction you may have done to it, which is not good. In the interest of becoming mightier, create a light wrap effect from scratch using only layer blend modes and the Fast Blur effect, using the process detailed back in Chapter 12, "Working with Light." Here it is in brief:

1. Create a precomp with your background and foreground elements.

2. Set the foreground to the Silhouette Alpha blend mode. This punches a hole in the background.

3. Add an adjustment layer at the top, and apply Fast Blur.

4. Turn Repeat Edge Pixels on, and crank up Blurriness until you really can see it.

5. Duplicate the foreground layer, move the copy to the top, and switch this new top layer to the Stencil Alpha blend mode. You are left with a halo of background color that matches the shape of the foreground.

And that's your light wrap element. Create a new comp that has this light wrap precomp on top of the foreground on top of your color-corrected background. As with the last example, it's both the blur size and the opacity of the layer that you use to dial in this effect. Generally you will use big blurs and small opacities, but there are times where you might use just the opposite. And you can play with various blend modes for the light wrap layer; Normal, Screen, Lighten, and Add are all good options.

Sometimes a photo will suggest a cool technique like this. Other times it will simply help you dial in the look of an effect. When I was asked to create the most dreaded of all compositing effects, a lens flare, for a shot in *Star Wars, Episode One: The Phantom Menace*, I asked John Knoll to shoot some reference the next time he was on the motion control stage. In between explosions and lightsaber sparks, John had the crew shoot a series of flare reference passes with various lenses. We picked the one we liked, and I spent three days (and about 17 nested After Effects comps) matching it exactly.

Emotional Truth

Photographic reference can help you get the facts straight in your shot. The highlights on your stompy robot look just like the ones on the live action car he's about to step on—no one can argue with the realism of that. But photos can also help us with another, far more nebulous concern.

Our clients are making movies, and movies are designed to do one thing: elicit an emotional reaction from the

Fast Blur and Gaussian Blur are the same (at Best quality), except that Gaussian Blur has no Repeat Edge Pixels option. So you might as well throw Gaussian Blur away. More about the difference between Gaussian, Fast, and Box Blurs is in Chapter 12.

audience. Even though our clients know that they are using technical tools to achieve this goal, they are still reacting emotionally to the images we show them. This is true whether you're working for a first time indie auteur or James Cameron. Clients react from the gut—as well they should. But here's the catch: They critique in technical terms.

This is a problem that I suspect jazz musicians do not have. When they are jamming and creating a new tune, I bet they are totally comfortable talking in emotional terms about their work. "Dude, this just isn't reminding me enough about the ills of society. We need to get more *strife* into this track!" OK, clearly I know as much about jazz as I know about running an oil refinery. The point is that our clients are not comfortable saying things like, "This shot isn't scary enough," or, "This shot just needs more umph!" That may well be their reaction, but rather than simply saying that, they feel compelled to suggest possible solutions. "Make his teeth more wet," or "Throw a lens flare in there."

At The Orphanage, we once had a very tech-savvy client who was obsessed with a shot that he felt was falling way short on photorealism. Every time it would come up, this client would explode with reasons why it was not realistic-looking. "This contact shadow isn't right." "There's not enough detail here." "These particles are too bright." We looked at shots that had finaled already and saw what our shot was missing. We made it darker, more blue, and we added contrast. The shot finaled. We addressed the emotional shortcomings of the shot and the technical problems, legitimate as they may have been, magically went away.

The lesson here is: Don't be afraid to make your shots beautiful. And your photography should help you. Chances are you've taken a hundred sunset shots that look like you shot them with a camera phone. Sunsets are hard, especially with digital cameras. But I bet you've got one sunset shot that you just nailed. It's a thing of beauty. Well, compare it to your hundred crappy sunsets and analyze the differences. And when the time comes to create a dusk shot of the enemy base, eyedropper the color palette straight out of your good one.

The matte paintings of Cloud City in *The Empire Strikes Back* are perfect examples of this. These paintings by Ralph McQuarrie are not very photoreal. But it so does not matter. You know why? Because they are purple and orange. They are beautiful, and they strike an emotional chord in the viewer. Have a smooth Colt 45 and watch your precious laserdiscs of the original *Star Wars* movies, because you truly belong here with us among the clouds.

If you take enough boring pictures of your car (**Figure 15.12**), one of them will eventually look decent (**Figure 15.13**).

The emotional resonance of a shot can also be linked to a common technical mistake. One of the biggest sins of visual effects shots that are built up from scratch is that they tend to contain no overexposed or underexposed elements. Skies are often a good example of this. Show me a shot with a perfectly exposed blue sky with no blown-out detail, and I'll show you a visual effect. The reason that the notorious car comp, in which the view out the window of a vehicle shot on a green-screen stage is replaced with moving scenery, usually looks wrong is often that the artist failed to slightly overexpose the exterior. **Figure 15.14** shows the kind of reference that can help you nail your next car comp.

Night exteriors are the worst culprits. In the middle of a sequence of inky black night shots set off by artificial but highly cinematic rim lighting, you can smell the matte painting coming from a mile away. It's the only shot where you can clearly see everything *except* where the light is coming from!

The eyedropper, the Info palette, and our friends Copy and Paste can help make tangible the intangible reasons why some images pop and some go thud. You are not just a technician assembling elements. You are a salesperson, trying to get the audience to buy the shot, warts and all. Use your reference and your dirty tricks, and close that deal.

Figure 15.12 A boring photo of a non-boring car.

Figure 15.13 Those are speed fangs.

Figure 15.14 Dare to overexpose the stuff you comp out the window.

Rolling Thine Own

When you use these techniques to start seeing the world, and then begin implementing your profound insights in your comps, you will begin to see the importance of this last point: It is almost always better to create effects from the basic toolkit of After Effects than to resort to an off-the-shelf, canned effect.

"Default" is a dirty word. Remember that week-long effort to re-create a photoreal lens flare? It's worth noting that this effort was supported fully by the guy whose name is synonymous with digital lens artifacts. But even John Knoll knew that to appear unflinchingly huge on the big screen, his schwings were going to need some nuancing.

I hope you do have Knoll Light Factory (Red Giant Software; a demo is on the book's disc) because its documentation is an excellent treatise on the importance of good reference. John points out some of the vital design aspects of flares that he noticed when scrutinizing the real thing.

In **Figure 15.15**'s real-life flare, the little septagonal reflections that slice through the center of the frame have seven sides because the camera's aperture has seven blades. The star-shaped core of the flare has 14 points (not counting the purplish CCD smear), each pair perpendicular to the edge of one of these blades. This is because the star is an artifact of light grazing off the edge of the aperture blades. This also means that if you were to defocus an element in this shot, you should use a five-sided camera blur shape for the proper boke effect for this lens.

Now, if you start throwing out terms like "boke" in dailies, even Dennis Muren will be impressed.

Most effects we use in After Effects are built up of smaller, simple filtering operations that themselves exist as effects. There's nothing about the built-in Glow effect, for example, that you cannot easily create on your own. You could wrestle with Glow all day long and never match the reference you shot of an F-18 afterburner, but with your homebrew glow not only will you have finer control, but you will also have a better understanding of how glows work (**Figure 15.16**).

Figure 15.15 I'm directly below the Earth's sun…now!

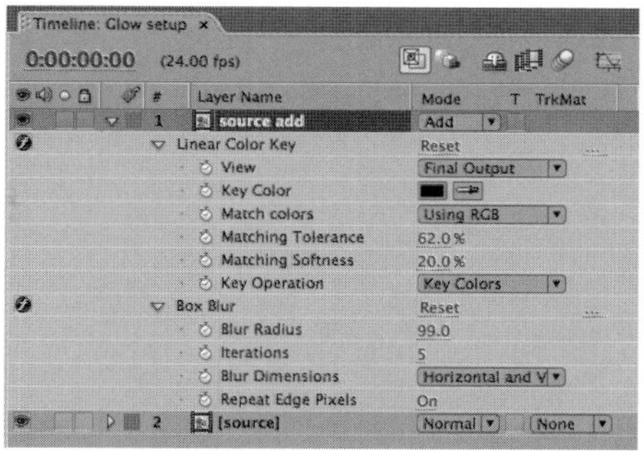

Figure 15.16 This simple glow outperforms the default.

After Effects ships with hundreds of effects. Apple's Shake ships with far fewer nodes but is viewed as "high end." Although some would say that the decision to eschew canned effects is one you arrive at after becoming an expert, I propose that the opposite is true: Skipping the all-in-one plug-ins and developing your own looks from scratch will propel you toward expert status.

Not a Conclusion

This chapter is not composed of conclusions. It is a dog-eared page in the lifelong process of one visual effects supervisor. We will all struggle with the answer to the Ultimate Question with each new shot. Keep taking pictures, remember your cures for Familiarity Disorder, and beg those close to you for forgiveness—for you are a compositor for life.

Index

Symbols and Numbers

string, 53
~ (tilde) key, 8
* (asterisk), 360
\ (backslash) key, 67
; key, 67
= (equal sign), 367
. (dot), 357
( ) (parentheses), 357
" " (quotation marks), 357
// marks, 377
2D
    arrays, 358
    fire layer, 502–503
    mixing 3D and, 324–326
    primary animation, 477
    rendering order of layers, 58
3:2 pulldown, 25
3D camera. *See also* cameras
    mixing effects from 2D and, 324–326
    parenting to background layer, 292, 294
    smoothing moving, 297–301, 365–368
3D effects
  animating heat distortion particles, 495
    fire element for, 503–504
    layers with Collapse Transformations on, 147
    protecting layers in subcomps, 146
    set recreations in, 241
    simulating shadows in, 441–444
3D motion tracking, 292–301, 305–308
    importing Maya scenes, 306–307
    parenting 3D camera to background, 292, 294, 296
    simulating, 292, 296–297
    smoothing moving cameras, 297–301, 365–368
    workflow for, 305
4:1:1 format, 234
4:2:2 format, 234
8 bpc images
    adjusting color effects to 32 bpc, 410–412
    pixel range for, 389
16:9 aspect ratio, 385–386
16 bpc images
    adjusting color effects to 32 bpc, 410–412
    pixel range for, 389
32 bpc images
    benefits of HDR images, 382, 400–403
    compositing sci-fi weapons as, 492–494
    limitations of, 383–384
  Linear blending mode with, 383
  using applied effects with, 410–414

A

absolute time measurement, 93–94
activating. *See* enabling
Adapt Feature If Confidence Is Below option
    (Motion Tracker Options dialog), 285
Adapt Feature on Every Frame option (Motion
    Tracker Options dialog), 284, 287
Add blending mode, 126, 127, 128, 453
Add Grain effect, 338, 339
Add mode for masks, 119, 120
Add Vertex tool, 254
add-a-negative number offset, 64
Adjust Tension pointer, 253
adjustment layers
    about, 148–149
    adding mattes or masks to, 149, 150
    effects on alpha channels vs., 149
Adobe After Effects 7.0. *See also* user interface;
  workflow
    Bridge in, 47
    brushes in Photoshop vs., 266–267
    cloning improvements in, 270
    color correction alternatives, 190–192
    expressions in, 352
    redundancy of features, 14
    rotoscoping in, 256
    running from OS X Terminal, 157
    running multiple copies of, 157–158
    time measurement in, 93–94
    workflow for, 4
Adobe Bridge, 47
Adobe Illustrator, 116
Adobe Photoshop
    brushes in After Effects vs., 266–267
    Curves dialog, 183
    file format, 28
    importing Photoshop files, 29–30
Adobe Premiere Pro
    importing images from, 30
    three-way color correction in, 430–431
Adobe Production Studio
    importing images from Premiere Pro, 30
    Three-Way Color Corrector, 192
Advanced 3D rendering plug-in, 147
Advanced tab (Composition Settings dialog), 31, 91,
  289
.aet files, 47
After Effects. *See* Adobe After Effects 7.0
Alpha Add blending mode, 131
alpha channel
    adjusting settings, 21–22
    applying Auto-trace to matte's, 258

alpha channel (*continued*)
    Difference Matte effects, 218
    display settings for, 114
    effects on adjustment layers vs., 149
    painting in black and white on, 266
    premultiplication and, 111–115
    saving in PNG format, 27
    touching up mattes as, 267
    track matte applied to layers with, 134
    using for selections, 105
    viewing matte detail in, 212–213
Alpha Channel mode (Levels effect), 175
Alpha Cleaner (Key Correct Pro), 243
alpha inverted track matte, 133
alpha track mattes, 132–133
Always Preview This View toggle (Composition panel), 140
Amount to Tint property, 353–354
anchor points, 89
Angle of View (Camera Settings dialog)
    adjusting, 317
    universal application of, 316
animation. *See also* keyframe eases
    adding variation in motion speed, 81
    animating clouds, 470
    eases for, 76–78
    indirect effects of wind, 477–478
    keyframe offsets, 88
    offsetting transform, 88–89
    primary and secondary, 477
    spatial keyframes and curves, 79–82
    using Graph Editor vs. Layer view for, 84–85
    working with wind, 475–476
animation presets
    about, 46, 47
    disabling, 46
animations
    looping, 361–365
    saving expressions without keyframes, 361
aperture
    adjusting settings, 333
    lens flare and, 437
    opening in video vs. linear space, 395, 396
    Super 35 film, 385
Apple Final Cut Pro, 15
application window
    illustrated, 6
    as part of new interface, 5
archiving projects, 16
arguments
    about loop effect, 361
    parentheses indicating, 357
arrays
    defined, 358
    identifying one portion with brackets, 358–359
articulated mattes, 249–255

    choosing Composition vs. Layer panel for, 249–251
    simplicity for, 249
artistic vision, 508–523
    about, 508
    analyzing what you see, 511–512
    combining techniques for new effects, 522–523
    developing visual objectivity, 509–511
    integrating elements with light wrap, 517–519
    overcoming brain's revision of images, 512–513
    portraying emotional resonance, 519–521
    reference as means to believable effects, 513–517
aspect ratios
    cinematography, 346
    Super 35 film format, 385
Assemble Master composition, 138
asterisk (*), 360
atmospheric conditions. *See* haze; weather conditions
attach points
    editing, 280–281
    setting up links between properties and, 356–357
Auto Levels effect, 178
Auto Select Graph Type option (Graph Editor), 73
Auto-Orientation dialog, 327
auto-save option, 18–20
auto-tracing masks, 106, 258–259
Auto-Zoom When Resolution Changes option (Preferences dialog), 32

A/V Features column (Timeline), 61, 62–63

B

backgrounds
    colors and plane of depth matched to, 460–461
    holdout mattes for, 222
    keyable, 238
    keying colors for, 210
    matching foreground elements to, 289
    multiplying into edge pixels, 110, 112
    previewing with custom, 37–38
    sampling pixels in, 225
    switching foreground swatch with, 269
    using with mattes, 211
backlighting
    adjusting with Curves, 188
    light wrap effects and, 432–435
backslash (\) key, 67
backward navigation in Timeline, 64
banding, 180–181
Beam effect, 492–494
Bezier masks, 118–119
Bias settings (Keylight), 232
billowing smoke, 469–475. *See also* smoke
    adding Liquify effects for swirling, 472–474

gradients for smoke trails, 475
Mesh Warp for distorting elements, 471, 472
simulating clouds with cotton puffs, 469–470
binoculars icon, 15
bitmap selection channel, 108
blending modes, 124–132
about, 124–125
Add, 126, 127, 128
Alpha Add and Luminescent Premultiply, 131–132
applying when Collapse Transformations on, 147
combining with mattes for selections, 107
compositing with, 106–107
Difference, 130
Hard Light, 126, 129
Hue, Saturation, and Brightness, 130
illustrated, 126
incompatible with linear blending and HDR values, 453
mathematical descriptions of, 125
Multiply, 126, 128–129
Overlay, 126, 129–130
preserving when precomposing, 145–146
Screen, 126, 127–128
selections vs., 106–107, 124–132
Silhouette Alpha, 433
Stencil and Silhouette, 130
types of Light, 129–130
Vivid Light, 129
blue channel, 235
blue screen. *See also* color keying
blue-screen keying, 219–228
using sky for, 463–465
blur, 332–337. *See also* motion blur
adding for rain or snow elements, 480–481
boke, 334–336
Box, Gaussian, and Fast, 435
camera shutter settings and motion, 92–93
matching tracking for motion, 288–290
boke blur, 334–336
boke images, 332
Bolles, Brendan, 382
Boujou, 305–306
Box Blur, 435
bracketing Input levels, 177, 178
breaking up shadows, 421
brightness. *See also* color spaces
adjusting with Curves, 184
formula for foreground/background, 110
gamma adjustments and, 172–173
Brightness & Contrast effect, 169
Brightness blending mode, 130
Browse command, 47
browsing .aet files, 47
Brush Tips panel, 266, 268, 269

brushes
adjusting on Brush Tips panel, 268, 269
After Effects vs. Photoshop, 266–267
bullet hits, 489–491

C

caching, 35–42
changing preview channel, 41–42
enabling disk, 35–36
grids and guides in workflow, 38–41
RAM previews, 37
textures on display card, 45
working with custom backgrounds, 37–38
Camera Mapper plug-in, 332
camera projection, 329–332
Camera Raw format, 28, 29
Camera Settings dialog
adjusting focal length and film size, 316
angle of view adjustments, 316, 317
aperture settings, 333
Comp Size settings, 317
depth of field and f-stop adjustments, 333
emulating real camera via settings in, 318–324
illustrated, 314
Zoom property, 317–318, 320
cameras, 313–326. *See also* grain
camera projection, 329–332
changing orientation of, 327
cinematography formats and aspect ratios, 346
emulating effects with Camera Settings dialog, 318–324
lens settings, 314–316
matching lens distortion, 320–324
mixing 2D and 3D, 324–326
push vs. zoom, 328
shortcuts for animation tools, 327
simulating camera blur, 332–337
single-node and targeted, 307
smoothing moving, 297–301, 365–368
storytelling with, 326–331
translating physical settings to virtual, 316–318
typical sizes of film formats, 321
user interface for, 313–314
working with grain, 337–343
channels. *See also* alpha channel
avoiding red tones in color keying, 238
bitmap selection, 108
changing for preview, 41–42
color matching in green, 198
isolating and adjusting saturation of, 190, 191
U luminance values in green, 235
using as luma matte, 215
V luminance values in blue, 235
Y luminance values in red, 235
child layers, 90

cinematography. *See* virtual cinematography
Cineon Converter, 386–387, 407
Cineon film format
    about, 28, 386
    log color space for, 390–393
    outputting 10-bit log for, 413–414
    working with, 386–387
Cineon log color space
    about, 390–393
    converting to video space, 386, 387
    expressed in logarithmic curve, 391–392
circles of confusion, 334
clean plate, 166, 217
click and drag interface, 67
climate. *See* weather conditions
Clip Back control (Keylight), 230
Clip Rollback value, 233
clipping
    black and white levels on output, 166
  maintaining high delta between Clip values, 232–233
clips
    cloning from separate, 270–271
    editing source, 271
    reversing with Time Remap, 98
Clone Stamp, 266
cloning
    about painting and, 265–266
    improvements to, 270
    tips for paint and, 271–272
    tools and techniques for, 270–271
Cloud Anim comp, 516, 517
clouds
    animating, 470
    simulating with cotton puffs, 469–470
CMYK color, 174
Collapse Transformations toggle, 146, 147
Collect Files dialog, 16
color. *See also* color correction; color keying; color matching
    adjusting user interface, 122, 159
    atmospheric haze and scene's, 460–461
    balancing, 426
    color-coding layers, 61–62
    customizing label, 62
    cycling for masks, 122
    depth adjustments of, 20
    effect on cinematography, 344, 346–347, 426–427
    giving overlapped mattes separate, 255
    indirect light and, 444
    removing for element, 429–430
    Rosco key, 231
    saturation adjustments for, 188–190, 191
color correction, 164–207. *See also* Curves effect; histograms; Levels effect

adjusting individual channels, 174–175
alternatives for, 190–192
clipping black/white output levels, 166
color matching, 193–194
gamma, 172–173, 184, 185–187
Hue/Saturation control for, 188–190, 191
setting contrast with input/output levels, 166–171
skill needed for, 164–165
three-way, 430–431
using histograms for, 172–173, 176–181
Color Difference Key, 219
Color Finesse, 191, 192
Color Key, 214
color keying, 210–245. *See also* Keylight
    about, 210–211
    avoiding matte holes, 243–244
    background colors used for, 210
    blue-screen and green-screen, 219–228
    choosing color for, 223–228
    edge selection, 242–243
    Extract tool for, 214–215
    fixing problems with, 238–245
    Linear Color Key effect, 214, 215–216
    matte fringing, 244
    methodology for, 220–223
    multiple passes for, 213, 220, 221
    optimizing Keylight, 228–237
    Rosco's Digicomp products used with, 238
    rotoscoping vs., 248
    sky used for, 463–465
    solving color spills, 244–245
    steps for, 220–223
    supervising on-set effects, 238–241
    tips for creating mattes, 211–213
    using difference mattes, 217–218
color matching, 193–194
    about, 192–194
    basics of, 193–194
    dramatic lighting and, 199–203
    gamma slamming, 205–207, 341
    ordinary lighting and, 194–199
    scenes with no clear reference, 203–204
Color Profile Converter effect, 408–410
Color Settings option (Project Settings dialog), 21, 404
color spaces. *See also* Cineon log color space
    encoding vs. compositing, 392
    selecting, 394–397, 405
    video gamma, 393–394
    working between multiple, 384
color spills
    defined, 236
    Spill Suppressor effect for, 244–245
    suppressing in Keylight, 236–237
color timing, 193

combining multiple masks, 119–121
comments in Timeline, 62
Comp Size (Camera Settings dialog), 317
compositing. *See also* color correction
    blending modes for, 106–107
    bullet hits, 491
    color matching in, 193
    color spaces, 392
    debugging shots in, 141
    fire, 499–500
    formula for foreground/background
    brightness, 110
    images with/without floating point, 398–399
    intuitive nature of, 108
    use of selections in, 104
Composition panel
    adjusting Timeline with closed, 140
    changing channel displayed in, 41–42
    changing display resolution of, 33
    defined, 5
    disabling vector outlines in, 41
    illustrated, 6
    rotoscoping in Layer vs., 249–251
    Timeline button on, 67
    working with opacity settings, 110–111
Composition section (Render Settings dialog), 49
Composition Settings dialog
    Advanced tab of, 31, 147–148, 289
    Shutter Angle and Shutter Phase settings on,
    91–93
compositions
    applying Time Stretch to, 96
    copying precomposed attributes to, 145
    fitting layers to width/height of, 66
    naming, 140–141
    organizing in standard templates, 137–138
    preserving frame rate of nested, 96–97
    trimming duration to work area, 65
    troubleshooting complicated shots, 141
    using proxies in, 155
    working with multiple, 137–141
Compound Blur effect, 475, 516
Compress-Expand Dynamic Range preset, 411
compression
    effect on output, 54
    ratios for digital video image, 234
conditional statements, 372, 375–376
conditional triggers, 377
Confidence settings for motion tracking, 285, 286
Consolidate All Footage command, 17, 18
Constant mode (Paint menu), 268
context menus
    Mask, 252
    opening and using, 13–14
context-clicking, 12–14
continue loops, 364–365

contrast
    adjusting, 169, 184
    color correcting, 167–169
    optimizing, 177
coplanar 3D layers, 329
copying
    data between keyframes, 355
    duplicating track matte layers, 134
    keyframes, 82–83
    masks, 123–124
    precomposed attributes to compositions, 145
core and edge mattes
    dividing mattes into, 238
    separating, 222, 227
    working with in Keylight, 232–233, 238
Corner Pin tracks
    about, 282
    applying to target layers, 283
    motion tracking and, 257
corners, tracking, 278–279
Correspondence Points (Reshape tool), 263
cropping compositions, 34
Current Time Indicator, 67
curve editor. *See* Graph Editor
Curves dialog (Photoshop), 183
Curves effect, 181–190
    color matching with, 194
    effects of adjustments on image, 183–184
    gamma adjustments with, 184, 185–187
    gamma slamming, 205–207, 341
    user interface for, 182–183
    uses for, 181–182
    using Hue/Saturation control vs., 189
custom backgrounds, 37–38
custom label colors, 62
Cycle Mask Colors option (Preferences dialog), 122, 255

cyclorama, 238–239

D

data
    adding random, 368
    copying and pasting between keyframes, 355
    expressions for linking animation, 355
    keyframe spatial, 79–82
    offsetting tracking, 357–358
    scale, 282, 284
    storing depth, 462
    types expressions can/can't evaluate, 351–352,
    353
day-for-night effect, 427–429
debris explosions, 505–506
default lens setting, 314, 315
Default Spatial Interpolation to Linear option
    (Preferences dialog), 76, 79–80
deleting workspaces, 11

density
    defined, 121
    managing mask, 121–122
    depth
    adding with atmospheric haze, 459–461
    adjusting color, 20
    recreating in 3D images, 461–462
Depth Cue plug-in, 332
depth maps, 462
depth of field, 318, 333
desaturating color for single elements, 429–430
deselecting active masks, 119
Deselecting Align option, 270
Despill Bias (Keylight), 226, 232, 237
Difference blending mode, 119, 120, 126, 130
difference mattes, 105, 217–218
digital source formats, 27–30. *See also* Cineon film
    format
    DV/HDV, 54
    about, 29
    Camera Raw, 28, 29
    Cineon and DPX, 28, 386
    comparison chart of, 28
    development of film formats, 385–386
    DPX, 28, 386
    .ffx, 47
    moving, 29
    OpenEXR, 28, 411
    Photoshop, 28
    PNG, 27
    sizes of, 321
    Super 35, 385
    Targa, 27
    TIFF, 27
    working with imported Adobe formats, 29–30
direction of light, 421, 422–423
disabling. *See also* enabling
    animation presets, 46
    auto-orientation, 327
    keyframes, 354
    Show Animation Presets, 46
    subpixel positioning, 288
    thumbnails in Project panel, 159
    vector outlines in Composition panel, 41
disk caching. *See* caching
display cards, 45
displays. *See* monitors
dissolves, 372
divider dragger, 8
dividers, 5
dot (.) in expressions, 357
double-gamma scenes, 452
DPX format, 28, 386
Draft quality, 32–33
drawing
    Bezier masks, 118–119
    ellipses and rectangles, 116–117

drop zones, 8
duration
    precomposing layers of different, 144–145
    setting for Paint panel, 268
    setting paint stroke, 268
    trimming to composition's work area, 65
DV/HDV formats, 54
dynamic range. *See also* HDR
    challenges with camera's, 388–389
    heightening, 447–452
    limitations enhancing, 445–447

E

E keyboard shortcut, 85
eases. *See* keyframe eases
Easy Ease, 76–78, 329
edge mattes
    creating for edge selection, 242–243
    separating core and, 222, 227, 238
    working with in Keylight, 232–233, 238
Edit Value Graph option (Graph Editor), 73
editing. *See also* Graph Editor
    anchor points, 89
    attach point, 280–281
    parent-child relationships, 90
    RotoBeziers, 252–253
    Smoother's destructive, 299, 300
    source clips, 271
    track points in Timeline, 288
Effect Controls panel
    applying expression from, 373
    Fractal Noise effects, 466–467
    Liquify effects, 472
    lock icon on, 83
effects. *See also specific effects*
    accessing on Effects & Presets panel, 45–46
    animation presets, 47
    making transparency selections from, 107
    reviewing order of paint and effects edits, 272
    types available, 46
Effects & Presets panel, 45–46
eight bit-per-channel images. *See* 8 bpc images
eLin, 382
ellipses, 116–117
Elliptical Mask tool, 425
embedded color profiles, 409
Enable Depth of Field checkbox (Camera Settings
    dialog), 333
enabling. *See also* disabling
    Bridge, 47
    Collapse Transformations toggle, 146
    depth of field settings, 333
    disk caching, 35–36
    expressions, 354
    Graph Editor, 71
    grids and rulers, 38–39

guide layers, 38
keyframes, 354
motion blur in Timewarp, 100
OpenGL, 42
Pen tool, 252, 254
proxies, 155
rulers, 39
Selection pointer, 254
storage overflow, 49–50
encoding color spaces, 392
environment reference shot of set, 241
equal sign (=), 367
Erodilation, 241
errors
out-of-memory, 160
in premultiplied images, 115
solving matte fringing problems, 244
Evolution animation, 466–467
explosions
bullet hits and, 489–491
gaseous and debris, 505–506
need for special effects with, 484–485
travel of, 488
Exponential Scale option, 328
exposure, 318
Exposure control, 402–403
expression controls, 359–360
expressions, 350–379
activating, 354
adding conditionals to loop, 375–376
building expression controls, 359–360
changing names of layers linked with, 360
checking values generated by, 368
conditional and trigger, 372–377
extending track with, 301–302
extraneous keywords in, 363
following equal sign with value in, 367
limitations of, 352, 353
linking animation data with, 355
logic and grammar of, 351–352
muting keyframes, 353–355
offsetting layers and time with, 368–371
offsetting tracking data, 357–358
saving, 361
scripting and, 353
smoothing and destabilizing camera with, 365–368
spaces in, 360
tracking brushes and effects, 356–357
uses for, 350–351
web resources on, 378–379
Expressions menu
selecting smooth expression, 300
working with, 361
external monitors, 37
Extract tool, 214–215

F

Familiarity Disorder, 509–511
Fast Blur
about, 519
comparing effect in video vs. linear space, 395, 396
using, 435
Fast Previews icon, 43
Feather options for mask, 117–118
feathered alpha, 108–109
feature regions, 278, 279
.ffx files, 47
Field of View values (Optics Compensation effect), 322–323
fields
add-a-negative number offset for, 64
interlacing, 24
files. See also digital source formats
adding file extensions, 15
collecting project, 16–17
digital source formats for source, 27–30
finding Project panel information for, 24
keeping source footage linked, 14–15
locating, 15
naming layers and instances of, 60
opening in program that created it, 16
storing depth data in RPF, 462
film
adding full-color tint for, 426–427
aperture of Super 35, 385
converting Cineon files for, 386–387
development of formats, 385–386
dynamic range of images, 388–389
replicating real-world effects on, 384–385
understanding Cineon log space, 390–393
film formats. See also digital source formats
development of, 385–386
sizes of, 321
Super 35, 385
Film Size value (Camera Settings dialog), 316
Final Cut Pro, 15
Final Output comp, 138
Find Missing Footage box (Find dialog), 15
fire. See also explosions; firearms; smoke
creating and using, 499–500
developing 3D element, 503–504
hang, 500–502
heat distortion, 494–498
need for special effects with, 484–485
simulating reflected firelight, 502
synthesizing, 498–504
using 2D layer for, 502–503
firearms, 486–491
bullet hits, 489–491
miming kick of, 486
muzzle flash and smoke from, 487–488
sci-fi weapons, 492–494

firearms (*continued*)
  simulating shells for, 488–489
First Vertex
  aligning points with, 124
  determining mask points with, 265
  matching animation shape with, 251
fisheye lens, 315, 321
Fit to Comp, 66
flag of Mars, 429–430
flip and flop options (Effects & Presets panel), 76
flipping mask on one axis, 117
floating windows, 5, 7, 9
Flowchart view
  projects in, 86–87
  viewing bridge composite in, 517
Focal Length value (Camera Settings dialog), 316
fog, 466–469
folders
  organizing workflow in, 12
  Redefinery, 62
  rendering projects from Watch, 156–157
  standardizing, 139
footage interlacing, 24–25
Force alphabetical order option, 11
foregrounds
  matching color and plane of depth to, 460–461
  mattes with, 211
  switching background swatch with, 269
  tracking and blurring multiple elements to match, 289
formulas
  foreground/background brightness, 110
  gamma adjustment, 172–173
Fractal Noise effect
  combining with Mesh Warp to create smoke, 473–474
  incompatible for billowing smoke, 469
  simulating movement through mist, 468–469
  smoke and mist with, 466, 467
Frame Blending effects, 95–96
frame rate
  adjusting settings for, 23–24
  compositions with differing, 146–147
  importance of, 344
  recommended settings for, 345–347
frames. *See also* frame rate
  calculating in expressions, 368
  cloning offset area of same, 270
  as part of new interface, 5
Frames option (Project Settings dialog), 21
Freeze Frame command, 96
fringing
  choking and, 235
  solving matte, 244
F-Stop settings (Camera Settings dialog), 333

G

gamma
  adding Color Profile Converter to output, 452
  adjusting with Curves, 184, 185–187
  Levels effect adjustments of, 172–173
  offsetting, 393–394
gamma curve, 172
gamma slamming, 205–207, 341
gamut, 406
garbage mattes, 220, 221, 303–304
gaseous explosions, 505–506
Gaussian Blur, 435, 519
glints
  examples of, 438–439
  lens flare vs., 437
Glow effect, 522–523
Go to Time dialog, 64
God rays, 440
gradients
  creating smoke trails with, 475
  Curves, 183–186
  emulating inverse square dissipation of intensity with, 425
  leveling hotspots with, 423–425
grain, 337–343
  about, 337–338
  adding with Despill Bias, 232
  expressions averaging, 369–371
  "film look" associated with, 343
  matching, 338–341
  Noise effect for adding, 340
  removing, 341–342
  strategies for using, 342–343
  triggers for excessive, 338
Graph Editor, 70–85
  animation in Layer view vs., 83–85
  copying and pasting keyframes, 82–83
  displaying Confidence graphs in, 285
  Easy Ease keyframe assistants, 76–78
  Graph Options icon and menu, 71, 72–74
  learning to use, 71
  results of smooth() expression in, 366–367
  roving keyframes, 82
  Show Properties options in, 71, 72
  Transform Box, 71, 74–75
  viewing tracking expression in, 302
Graph Options menu (Graph Editor), 71, 72–74
grayscale conversion
  for entire image, 189
  Hue/Saturation for, 429–430
green channel
  color matching, 198
  U luminance values of YUV displayed in, 235
green-screen keying. *See* color keying
GridIron Software, 156

grids, 38–39, 40
grip areas, 8
Grow Bounds effect, 146
Guess button (Interpret Footage dialog), 112, 114
guide layers
    appearing at render time, 150
    defined, 149
    effective uses for, 151
    using, 38
guides
    optimizing projects with, 138
    project workflow and, 38–41

H

hang fire, 500–502
Hard Light blending mode, 126, 129
hard vs. soft light, 419
haze
    adding plane of depth with atmospheric,
    459–460
    illustrated, 459
    visibility and, 457–458
HDR (high dynamic range). *See also* linear floating
    point
    benefits of, 382–384, 400–403
    compositing images with/without floating
    point, 398–399
    effects incompatible with, 435, 453
    heightening dynamic range with, 447–452
    lighting workflow for, 445–452
    limitations of 32 bpc compositing, 383–384
    techniques for creating, 389
    using images in 32 bpc, 382–383, 401–403
    working with linear blending, 403–404
heat distortion, 494–498
    defined, 494
    physics of, 495–496
    re-creating, 496–498
height, Fit to Comp shortcut for, 66
hiding layers, 63
high dynamic range. *See* HDR
high-contrast mattes
    about, 105
    combining with rotoscoping, 249
    defined, 213
histograms
    about Levels, 176–178
    displaying X across, 176
    Extract keying tool's use of, 214, 215
    gamma adjustments and, 172, 173
    problem solving with, 178–181
    viewing with Curves gradients, 183–186
Hold keyframes, 78
holdout mattes
    adding in Keylight, 227, 228

dividing mattes into, 238
    using, 222, 223
hotspots, 423–425
HSB color model, 189
Hue blending mode, 130
Hue/Saturation effect
    adjusting color with, 426
    adjusting saturation, 188–190, 191
    desaturating color, 245
    illustrated, 190
    removing color and grayscale conversion with,
    429–430

I

ICC profiles, 405–406
icons
    binoculars, 15
    Fast Previews, 43
    Graph Editor, 71
    lock, 5, 83
    pickwhip, 154, 355
    Preset, 271
    Time Stretch, 94
    Timeline, 59, 60
Illustrator, 116
images
    adjusting color of, 188–190
    banding in, 180–181
    chroma sampling and compression, 234
    converting to grayscale, 189
    correcting contrast of, 167–169
    effects of Curves adjustments on, 183–184
    gamma adjustments, 172–173, 184, 185–187
    histograms of, 176–178
    importing, 30, 114–115
    layering over opaque background, 110
    outputting 10-bit Cineon log, 413–414
    previewing morphed, 263–264
    removing color and grayscale conversion,
    429–430
    translating into pixels, 108–109
    troubleshooting with histograms, 178–181
importing
    footage with premultiplied images, 114–115
    images from Premiere Pro, 30
    Maya scenes for 3D tracking, 306–307
    one project into another, 17
    other Adobe formats, 29–30
    source materials, 11
    still sequences for moving footage, 23–24
Inferno, 143
Info panel
    entering mathematical values of blending
    modes, 125
    showing rendering in process in, 153

using during previews, 55
viewing values of sample pixels in, 224
Input Black controls (Levels effect), 167–169, 171, 177, 180
Input White controls (Levels effect), 167–169, 177
installing linear color ICC profiles, 405
interlaced fields, 24
Interpret Footage dialog, 21, 112, 114
interpreting footage, 21–27
adjusting alpha settings, 21–22
fields and footage interlacing, 24
frame rate settings, 23–24
Pixel Aspect Ratios, 25
removing pulldown, 25
working with imported Adobe formats, 29–30
Intersect mode for masks, 119, 120
inverse square law, 425
inverted layers, 65

J

J keyboard shortcut, 87

K

K keyboard shortcut, 87
Key Color eyedropper, 216
Key Correct Pro plug-ins, 242
keyable backgrounds, 238
keyboard shortcuts
adjusting brush size on fly, 268
camera animation tools, 327
cycling through brush tools with, 266
display resolution and size, 33
Easy Ease keyframe assistants, 76
enlarging panel to fill window, 8
keyframe navigation and selection, 87–88
layers, 65–66
opening files in program that created it, 16
Timeline navigation, 63–64
U/UU, 85
using, 13
working with masks, 254
zooming in floating windows, 10
keyframe eases
adding variation in motion speed, 81
animation with, 76–78
setting temporal ease on mask keyframes, 122–123
simulating camera push with, 329
keyframe markers, 279
keyframes. *See also* keyframe eases
allowing between frames, 74
controlling in Graph Editor, 70–71
copying and pasting, 82–83
destroyed by The Smoother, 299, 300
effect of time measurement on, 93–94
enabling/disabling, 354

history of, 249
Hold, 78
mask, 122–123
moving data between, 355
muting, 353–355
offsetting values of multiple, 88
putting rotoscope mask in motion via, 259
roving, 82
shortcuts for navigation and selection, 87–88
spatial data and curves for, 79–82
stretching, 95
translating set of, 75
keying. *See* color keying
Keylight, 228–237
about, 219–220
adding holdout mattes in, 227, 228
adjusting Screen Colour settings, 223–225
Bias settings in, 232
choosing color for keying, 223–228
Clip Back, 230
decision-making comparisons in, 230
Despill Bias, 226, 232, 237
handling fringing and choking, 235
looking at composite details for problems, 228–230
sampling pixels in backgrounds, 225
Screen Balance, 225, 231
Screen Gain, 226, 230, 231
Screen Preblur option, 233
spill suppression in, 236–237
version of, 223
working with core and edge mattes, 232–233
keys
;, 67
\, 67
linear, 213–216
previewing first pass, 220, 221, 222
Keys column (Timeline), 61
keywords
omitting extras in expressions, 363
syntax for, 357
Knoll Light Factory, 437, 451–452, 522
Kodak Vision film stock, 408

L

label colors, 62
Layer column (Timeline), 60
Layer Comments option, 62
layer markers, 372
Layer panel
creating masks in, 249–250
rotoscoping in Composition vs., 249–251
setting tracking points in, 278
Target and View menus of, 250–251
Layer Switches column (Timeline), 60

Layer view, 84–85
layers
    adjusting motion blur for, 289
    adjustment, 148–149
    applying expression to Opacity settings for, 370–371
    camera, 327
    color-coding, 61–62
    fog, smoke, and mist, 467–468
    guide, 138, 149–151
    hiding, 63
    highlighting masked, 117
    including static elements in, 64–65
    keyed, 212
    matching source and target masks for, 261–263
    mixing 2D and 3D camera effect, 324–326
    naming, 60
    null object, 291
    offsetting with expressions, 368, 370–371
    parenting 3D camera to, 292, 294
    precomposing, 141, 142, 144–145
    preset, 138
    relocating in Z space, 295
    remapping time for, 97–98, 99, 100
    renaming layers linked to expressions, 360
    rendering order and, 153
    replacing, 68
    reversing timing of, 96
    rotation and scale data for target, 282
    scaling 2D, 328
    scrolling stack of, 67
  selecting and duplicating track matte, 134
    selecting parent-child, 90
    shy, 63
    stabilizing, 292–293
    stretching, 95
    tips and shortcuts for, 65–66
    tracks as properties of, 288
    unlocking all, 63
    viewing render order of properties, 152
    working with Collapse Transformations on, 146, 147
LDR (low dynamic range) images, 402, 445–447
Leave All Attributes option (Pre-Compose dialog), 141, 143
lens angle, 318
Lens Blur effect, 336–337, 435
lens distortion
    emulating real, 318
    illustrated, 321
    matching, 320–324
lens flare
    about, 436–437
    difficulties working with, 345
    glints vs., 437–439
    illustrated, 436

    increase in popularity of, 436
lens settings, 314–316, 318
leveling uneven light, 423–425
Levels effect
    about, 166
    Alpha Channel mode for, 175
    bracketing Input levels, 177, 178
    color adjustments with, 426
    color matching with, 193–194
    contrast adjustments with, 166–171
    gamma adjustments with, 172, 173
    histograms in, 176–178
    Hue/Saturation vs., 189
    individual channel adjustments, 174–175
    tasks accomplished by, 174
    using expressions with, 353
Levels (Individual Controls) control, 174
light, 418–454. See also color spaces; lighting effects;
  reflected light; shadows
    adding full-color tint for film, 426–427
    backlighting and light wrap, 432–435
    changes in natural, 421, 422
    color matching with ordinary, 194–199
    day-for-night effect, 427–429
    desaturating color for single elements, 429–430
    emulating inverse square law for, 425
    firelight, 502
    glints and flares, 435–439
    hard vs. soft, 419
    heightening drama with, 420–422
    implying presence of water with, 480
    interrelationship with mass, 109
    leveling uneven, 423–425
    light scattering and volume, 439–440
    location and quality of, 419–420
    neutralizing direction of, 422–423
    reflected, 444, 480, 502
    shadows and, 441–444
    three-way color correction, 430–431
    uses in storytelling, 432
    volume and scattering of, 439–440
    workflow for HDR lighting, 445–452
Light blending modes, 129–130
light wrap, 517–519
lighting effects
    adjusting scene color with no clear reference, 203–204
    color matching with dramatic, 199–203
    supervising on-set, 239–241
Linear blending mode, 383
Linear Blending option (Project Settings dialog), 403–404
Linear Color Key effect
    about, 214, 215–216
    eyedropper tools for, 215–216
    using two instances of, 217

Linear Dodge blending mode, 127
linear floating point. *See also* HDR
    blooming out highlights with, 447
    bringing non-HDR footage into compositions
    using, 409
    compositing images with/without, 398–399
    formats supported by files with, 411
    future of, 453
    introduced in eLin, 382
    output for, 412
    pixel values for, 389
    setting up projects with color-managed, 405
linear keys. *See also* Linear Color Key effect
    defined, 213
    Extract tool for, 214–215
    usefulness of, 213–214
    using Linear Color Key effect, 214, 215–216
linear space, 394–397
linear(t, tMin, value1, value2) command, 373
Liquify effects (Effect Controls panel), 472–474
Live Update, 35
lock icon, 5, 83
Lock toggle (A/V Features column), 62, 63
log color space. *See* Cineon log color space
logarithmic curves
    about, 392
    Cineon log expressed in, 391–392
    illustrated, 390
loopIn() expression, 364
loopInDuration() expression, 364
loopOut() expression, 362, 363
loopOutDuration() expression, 364
loops
    animation, 361–365
    applying simple expressions for, 361–365
    continue, 364–365
    pingpong, 364
    preview, 55
lossless output, 53
low dynamic range (LDR) images, 402, 445–447
low-loss output, 54
luma inverted matte, 133
Luma Key, 214
luma mattes
    about, 133
    example of, 150
    simulating heat distortion with, 498
    using RGB channel as, 214–215
    luminance
        setting thresholds with Auto-trace, 258
        U values for, 235
        V values for, 235
        Y values for, 235
luminance keying, 214
Luminescent Premultiply blending mode, 131, 132

M
Macintosh platforms
    examples of OpenGL support in, 43
    forcing a crash for, 160
    memory management in, 159
    rendering with multiple copies of After Effects, 157
Magic Bullet Suite plug-ins, 347
managing workflow settings, 20–31
    composition settings, 30–31
    interpreting footage, 21–27
    project settings, 20–21
    working with digital source formats, 27–30
Marker dialog, 62
Mask context menu, 252
Mask Expansion option for mask, 118
Mask Shape dialog, 117
Mask Shape keyframes, 123–124
masks, 116–124
    adding to adjustment layers, 149, 150
    applying to track matte, 133
    auto-tracing, 106, 258–259
    Bezier, 118–119
    combining multiple, 119–121
    converting to RotoBeziers, 252
    creating in Layer panel, 249–250
    creating matching source and target, 261–263
    density of, 121–122
    deselecting active, 119
    determining corresponding points with First Vertex, 265
    developing smoke elements with feathered, 468
    keyframing, 249
    managing multiple, 122
    masking motion blur, 259
    matching animation shape with first vertex, 251
    moving, copying, and pasting with, 123–124
    naming and cycling color of, 122
    primary modes for, 119
    rotoscoping, 122–124
    setting temporal ease on mask keyframes, 122–123
    setting up to track, 256–257
    smoothing transitions between shapes, 124
    workflow for, 116–118
    working efficiently with, 254, 255
mass, 109
Master compositions
    about, 137, 139
    debugging shots from, 141
Match Grain effect, 338–341
match moving markers, 218
matrix, 358
matte boiling, 251
Matte Choker, 241
mattes

adding to adjustment layers, 149, 150
adjusting settings for shadow, 442
articulated, 249–255
assigning separate colors to overlapping, 255
avoiding matte holes, 243–244
cleaning up around, 232
combining with blending modes for selections, 107
depth, 462
difference, 217–218
edge, 242–243
fixing problems, 238
garbage, 220, 221
handling fringing and choking of, 235
holdout, 222, 223, 227, 228
protecting edge detail of, 212
pulling, 105
saving, 232
screen, 230
separating core and edge, 222, 227
tips for creating, 211–213
track, 132–134
usefulness of linear keying, 214
using, 220, 221
using Keylight core and edge, 232–233, 238
viewing detail in alpha channel, 212–213
visible fringing of, 244
Maxon Cinema 4D, 307
Maya 3D scenes, 306–307
Measure Film Size setting (Camera Settings dialog), 317
memory
displaying preferences for, 159
optimizing use of, 159–160
menus
Expressions, 300, 361
Graph Options, 71, 72–74
Mask context, 252
Motion Source pull-down, 289
opening and using context, 13–14
Random Numbers submenu, 368
reloading footage from context, 14
Target, 250–251
Time Control panel, 36
View, 250, 251, 272
View Layout pull-down, 314
Working Space drop-down, 404, 405
Mesh Warp effect
billowing smoke with, 471, 472
creating smoke with Fractal Noise and, 473–474
distortion in Liquify vs., 472
Microsoft Windows platforms
example of OpenGL support in, 43
memory management in XP, 160
rendering with multiple copies of After Effects,

157–158
Three-Way Color Corrector for, 192
Minimax, 241
mist
appearance of volume with, 469
effects creating, 466–467
rendering with Fractal Noise element, 467
simulating movement through, 468–469
misusing motion tracker, 276
monitors
adjusting resolution and size of, 33
broadcast output for, 405–407
floating panels in multiple, 9
output working in linear floating point, 412
previewing options for external, 37
theater preview output, 407–408
morphing, 260–265
about, 260
Reshape tool for image, 260–263
working with second morphs, 263–264
motion blur
adjusting for layers with keyframed motion, 289
adjusting settings for, 91–93
defined, 90
emulating real camera's, 318
enabling in Timewarp, 100
enhancing, 94
illustrated, 319
masking, 259
matching tracking for, 288–290
opening in video vs. linear space, 396, 397
premultiplication settings and, 112
preserving precomposing elements for, 145
Motion Blur toggle, 90–91
Motion Source pull-down menu (Tracker Controls panel), 289
Motion Tracker Options dialog
Adapt Feature If Confidence Is Below option, 285
Adapt Feature on Every Frame option, 284, 287
disabling subpixel positioning, 288
Track Fields option, 286
motion tracking, 276–309. *See also* 3D motion tracking
about, 277
attaching to paint stroke, 356–357
availability of, 277
choosing search and feature regions, 278
compensating for movement in sky element, 465
Confidence settings for, 285, 286
connecting tracker to paint stroke, 272
Corner Pin, 257, 282, 283
corners and, 278–279
editing track points in Timeline, 288
expression for, 356–357

motion tracking (*continued*)
    extending track with expressions, 301–302
    fixing tracks, 287–288
    grayed-out Options button on tracker, 286
    interactive controls for, 279
    matching motion blur, 288–290
    misuses of, 276
    nulls in, 290–291
    optimizing options for, 281–286
    reference point for, 277–280
    reverse, 284
    rig removal aided with, 273
    rotation and scale data for, 282, 284
    rotoscoping and, 248, 303–304
    search regions for, 279–280
    setting up to track masks, 256–257
    smoothing moving cameras, 297–301
    stabilizing layers, 292–293, 296
    subpixel positioning, 288
    SynthEyes 3D for, 308
    techniques misusing tracker, 276
    Transform tracks, 281
mouse
    using context-clicking with, 12–14
    using zoom wheel on, 33, 55, 67, 232
Move All Attributes option (Pre-Compose dialog), 143, 144
moving
    image formats, 29
    masks, 123–124
multiple masks
    combining, 119–121
    managing, 122
multiple monitors, 9
multiple passes for color keying, 213, 220, 221
Multiply blending mode, 126, 128–129, 425
muting keyframes, 353–355
muzzle flash from firearms, 487–488

N

naming
    brushes, 268, 269
    compositions descriptively, 140–141
    copied masks, 262
    layers and instances of source files, 60
    masks, 122
natural effects. *See* explosions; fire; weather conditions
navigation
    keyframe shortcuts for, 87–88
    layers and shortcuts for, 64–66
    from Project panel, 140
    Timeline shortcuts for, 63–64
negatives, film, 390–393
nesting

defined, 141
    preserving frame rate of nested compositions, 96–97
    time and, 146–148
network renders, 156–158
neutralizing direction of light, 422–423
No Repeat Edge Pixels option (Gaussian Blur), 519
noise
    adding grain with, 340
    expression averaging grain, 369–371
    suppression in Keylight, 233–235
None mode for masks, 119, 120
non-square PAR formats, 25–26
NTSC video
    frame rate settings for, 346
    NTSC DV compression ratio, 234
Nucleo plug-in, 156
nulls
    applying tracking data to, 290–291
    importing with Maya scenes, 307
number fields, 64
numbered image sequences, 53

O

offsetting
    gamma, 393–394
    layers and time with expressions, 368–371
    tracking data, 357–358
    transform animation, 88–89
opacity
    applying expression to, 361–362, 370–371
    calculating settings for, 110–111
OpenEXR source format, 28, 411
OpenGL Hardware plug-in, 44, 148
OpenGL workflow strategies, 31–45. *See also* caching; previewing
    about, 31–32
    caching and previewing, 35–42
    maintaining interactivity, 34–35
    OpenGL options, 42–45
    OpenGL unused in RAM Preview, 44
    resolution and quality, 32–34
opening
    context menus, 13–14
    files in program that created it, 16
Optics Compensation effect, 322–323, 324
optimizing projects, 136–160
    about, 136
    adjustment and guide layers, 148–151
    keeping Timeline tabs organized, 139–140
    memory management, 159–160
    navigating from Project panel, 140
    precomposing and nesting, 141–148
    setting preferences and project settings, 158–159

standardizing project templates, 137–139
understanding rendering order, 152–158
working with multiple compositions, 137–141
optimizing RAM previews, 36–37
Options section (Render Settings dialog), 48, 49
organizing
    files for imported projects, 17
    folders for workflow, 12
out-of-memory errors, 160
output. *See also* monitors
    10-bit log for Cineon film format, 413–414
    adding Color Profile Converter to gamma, 452
    adjusting render settings for, 48–50
    clipping black and white levels on, 166
    creating Output Module templates, 50–53
    effect of compression on, 54
    Final Output comp, 138
    guidelines for setting, 53–54
    linear floating point, 412
    lossless, 53
    low-loss, 54
    Render Queue, 47–54
    replacing output name with number, 53
    setting rendered output as proxies, 154
    settings for QuickTime, 54
Output Black control (Levels effect), 169–170, 171, 178
Output Module Settings dialog
    illustrated, 51
    Video Output section of, 113
Output Module templates, 50–53
Output White control (Levels effect), 169–170
Overlay blending mode, 126, 129–130
overlays
    grid, 38–39
    Title/Action Safe, 39, 41

P

Paint panel
    Duration setting of, 268
    illustrated, 266
    Paint on Transparent check box, 271, 272
    Preset icons for switching sources on fly, 271
    working in Single Frame mode, 268
painting. *See also* stroke
    about, 265–266
    guidelines for, 249
    reviewing order of paint and effects edits, 272
    setting stroke duration for, 268
    tips for paint and cloning, 271–272
    tools and techniques for, 266–269
PAL video
    frame rate settings for, 346
    PAL DVCPro compression ratio, 234
panels. *See also specific panels*

accessing OpenGL with Fast Previews icon on, 43
    docking, grouping, and adjusting, 7–8
    enlarging from drop zones, 8
    grip areas of, 8
    scrolling back and forth among, 9
    tearing off, 9
    turning into floating windows, 7, 9
    working with, 5–7
PAR (Pixel Aspect Ratio), 25–27
Parent column (Timeline), 61
parent-child relationships
    creating before animating, 89
    editing, 90
parentheses (), 357
parenthesized comp, 147
parenting
    3D camera to stabilized background, 292, 294, 296
    camera to null, 290–291
    linking properties with, 355
Particle Playground effect, 479, 496–498
Particular plug-in, 479
particulate matter, 457–463
    creating heat distortion with, 495–496
    illustrated, 459
    plane of depth with haze, 459–460
    recreating 3D image depth with, 461–462
    visibility and haze, 457–458
pasting masks, 123–124
Pen tool, 252, 254
performance
    deactivating Live Update for better, 35
    disadvantages of Draft quality on, 32–33
    multiple copies of After Effects while rendering, 157
    tracking points and, 279
Photoshop. *See* Adobe Photoshop
Photoshop format, 28
pickwhip
    attaching tracker to paint stroke, 356–357
    icon for, 154, 355
    selecting single channel properties with, 359
pingpong loop, 364
Pixel Aspect Ratio (PAR), 25–27
pixels
    choking and spreading in Minimax, 241
    entering values for blending modes, 125
    floating point values for, 389
    fringed, 235
    gamma adjustment formula, 172–173
    multiplying background into edge, 110, 112
    non-square formats for, 25–26
    problems translating images into, 108–109
    pushing edge, 212
    sampling background for keys, 225
    viewing values of sample, 224

plane of depth, 459–461
plate footage, 165–166
plug-ins
    Advanced 3D rendering, 147
    Camera Mapper, 332
    Depth Cue, 332
    Key Correct Pro, 242
    Nucleo, 156
    OpenGL Hardware, 44, 148
    Particular, 479
    Red Giant Software Key Correct Pro, 242
    Tracker Plug-in pull-down, 286
    Unmult, 115, 244, 500
    X-Factor, 156
PNG format, 27
points. *See also* linear floating point
    anchor, 89
    attach, 280–281, 356–357
    reference, 277–281
    setting First Vertex for aligning, 124
    track, 279–280, 288, 301–302
points of interest, 327
Position option (Tracker Controls panel), 281
Position tracks, 302
Post-Render Actions of Output Module templates, 53
post-render options, 154
precipitation
    about, 479
    compositing rain or snow element, 480–481
Pre-Compose dialog
    Leave All Attributes option, 141, 143
    Move All Attributes option, 143, 144
    moving some attributes to new composition, 145
precomposing, 141–148
    animation layers, 355
    defined, 141
    enabling Collapse Transformations for comp layers, 146
    layers of different duration, 144–145
    preserving data and blending modes when, 145–146
    rationale for, 142–143
    scripts for, 145
    undoing, 145
Preferences dialog
    adjusting user interface color, 122, 159
    Allow Scripts to Write Files and Access Network option, 74
    Auto-Save option in, 19
    designating importing preferences, 114–115
    disabling thumbnails in Project panel, 159
    Grids & Guides options, 40
    memory management options in, 159
    optimizing performance with, 158–159

restoring defaults, 159
setting spatial interpretations to linear, 76, 79–80
Switches Affect Nested Comps check box, 145
Premiere Pro, 30, 430–431
premultiplication, 111–115
    After Effects use of, 111
    defined, 112
    errors in, 115
    example of, 112–114
    importing footage with alpha channel, 114–115
    solving matte fringing problems of, 244
prerendering, 153
Preserve Frame Rate option (Composition Settings dialog), 147, 148
Preserve Resolution When Nested option (Composition Settings dialog), 147, 148
Preset icons (Paint panel), 271
previewing. *See also* OpenGL workflow strategies
    changing channel for, 41–42
    custom backgrounds for, 37–38
    first pass keys, 220, 221, 222
    looping previews, 55
    morphed images, 263–264
    with OpenGL, 44
    RAM previews, 37
    Render Final in Work Area, 65
    strategies for caching and, 35–42
Previews dialog, 42
primary animation, 477
Production Studio, 30, 192
Project Auto-Save option (Preferences dialog), 18–20
Project Flowchart view, 140
Project panel
    appearance of proxies in, 155
    defined, 5
    finding information for files in, 24
    imported projects and, 17
    navigating from, 140
Project Settings dialog, 20, 21, 404
projects. *See also* optimizing projects
    archiving, 16
    collecting files for, 16–17
    configuring for theater preview, 407–408
    Flowchart view of, 86–87
    importing one into another, 17
    navigating from Project panel, 140
    options for saving, 18–20
    reducing and consolidating footage in, 17–18
    saving when matte created, 232
    setting up color-managed floating point for, 405
    standardizing templates for, 137–139
    switching to SMPTE-C workspace, 405–407
    theater preview workspace for, 407–408
Proof Colors command, 412, 413
properties

animating, 69–70
defined, 68
Proportional Grids scale, 40
proxies
setting rendered output as, 154
using, 155
pulling mattes, 105
push
simulating with keyframe ease, 329
zoom vs., 328
pyrotechnics. *See also* fire; smoke
dangers producing, 484–486
stock footage for explosions, 506

Q

quality of light
assessing location and, 419–420
changes in natural light, 421, 422
queue. *See* Render Queue
QuickTime settings, 54
quotations indicating arguments, 357

R

rack focus shots, 332
rain, 480–481
RAM cache, 153
RAM previews
OpenGL options not used in, 44
optimizing, 36–37
Ramp effect
applying levels to layer containing, 167
leveling hotspots with, 424
Random Numbers submenu, 368
Raw tracks, 282, 283
Real Smart Motion Blur, 94
rectangles, 116–117
red channel
avoiding red tones in color keying, 238
Y luminance values of YUV displayed in, 235
Red Giant Software Key Correct Pro plug-ins, 242
Redefinery folder, 62
Reduce Project command, 17–18
reference for visual effects, 513–517
Reference Graph option (Graph Editor), 73
reference points
choosing for motion tracking, 277–280
editing attach point as, 280–281
reflected light
firelight, 502
implying water with, 480
interactive and, 444
refreshing histograms, 176
Region of Interest (ROI) tool, 33–34

reloading footage from context menu, 14
relocating layers in Z space, 295
removing
color for element, 429–430
color matting, 115
grain, 341–342, 369
OpenGL.aex if startup crashes, 44
pulldown, 25
tracking markers from alpha channel matte, 267
unused footage, 18
render farms, 156
render order, 152–158
2D layers and, 58
changing strokes, 272
fixing with precomposing, 142
showing current rendering in Info panel, 153
track matte, 134
understanding and optimizing, 152–158
Render Queue
adding items in, 48
workflow and output with, 47–54
Render Settings dialog, 44
settings for, 48–50
Use Comp Proxies Only option for, 155
rendering. *See also* render order
network, 156–158
post-render options, 154
running multiple copies of After Effects for, 157–158
showing guide layers at, 150
replacing
footage files, 14, 15
layers, 68
output name with number, 53
sky conditions, 463–465
reproducing weather conditions, 456–457
resetting
preferences, 11
workspaces to defaults, 7, 10
Reshape tool
determining corresponding points with First Vertex, 265
morphing images with, 260–263
resolution and quality strategies
keyboard shortcuts for display resolution and size, 33
speeding up previews without Draft quality, 32–33
using ROI tool, 33–34
restoring default workspace, 11
Reverse Lens Distortion option, 323, 324
reverse motion tracking, 284
reviewing
order of paint and effects edits, 272
rotoscopes, 249

RGB color
  color matching for, 197–198
  correspondence to CMYK color, 174
  displaying histograms for selected channels, 177
  individual channel display of, 174–175
  using luma matte for RGB channel, 215
rig removal, 273
ROI (Region of Interest) tool, 33–34
rotation and scale data for tracking, 282, 284
RotoBezier shapes
  converting masks to, 252
  creating masks that change over time, 251–255
  editing, 252–253
  matte boiling for, 251
rotoscoping, 122–124, 248–274. *See also* cloning; painting
  automated matte hole filling vs., 243
  Auto-trace masks, 258–259
  choice of Composition vs. Layer panel for, 249–251
  defined, 122
  elements out of shot, 222, 223
  guidelines for, 248–249
  limitations of After Effects, 256
  masking motion blur, 259
  morphing, 260–265
  motion tracking for, 303–304
  paint and cloning, 265–269
  plate restoration via cloning, 273–274
  setting up to track masks, 256–257
  using multiple masks during, 121
  wire removal in, 273
  working with RotoBezier shapes, 251–255
roving keyframes, 82
RPF files, 462
rulers, 39
Rush Render Queue, 156–157

S

sanity checking color conversion, 409–410
saturation. *See also* Hue/Saturation effect
  adjusting color, 188–190, 191
  desaturating color, 245
Saturation blending mode, 130
saving
  expressions, 361
  projects, 18–20
  projects once matte created, 232
  workspaces, 10
Scale and Letterbox Output to Fit Video Monitor option, 37
scale data for target layers, 282, 284
scaling
  2D layers, 328

values in Transform Box, 75
scene referred values, 395
sci-fi weapons, 492–494
Screen Balance (Keylight), 225, 231
Screen blending mode, 126, 127–128
Screen Colour (Keylight), 223–225
Screen Gain (Keylight), 226, 230, 231
Screen Grow/Shrink (Keylight), 235
screen mattes, 230
Screen Preblur (Keylight), 233
Screen Strength (Keylight), 230
Screen transfer mode, 397
scripts
  on companion CD, 379
  expressions and, 353
  precomposing layers with, 145
scroll wheel, 33, 55, 67, 232
scrolling between panels, 9
search regions
  choosing, 278
  illustrated, 279
  setting, 279–280
secondary animation, 477
Selection pointer, activating, 254
selections, 104–134. *See also* blending modes; compositing; masks
  alpha channels and premultiplication, 111–115
  bitmap selection channel, 108
  blending modes vs., 106–107, 124–132
  calculating opacity settings for, 110–111
  combining techniques to make, 107
  creating masks, 106, 116–124
  edge mattes for edge, 242–243
  feathered alpha, 108–109
  methods of creating, 104–107
  pulling a matte, 105
  shortcuts for keyframe, 87–88
  track mattes, 132–134
  transparency selections from effects, 107
  uses of in compositing, 104
  using existing alpha channel for, 105
semicolon (;) key, 67
Separate XYZ Position preset, 73
Set First Vertex command, 124
sets
  shooting environment reference of, 241
  supervising lighting effects of, 238–241
shadow mattes, 442
shadows
  breaking up, 421
  color matching for, 196
  keying out, 221
  simulating 3D, 441–444
Share View Options toggle, 314
shells for firearms, 488–489
Shift Channels effect, 215

shutter angle
  calculating, 92
  emulating, 318
  setting Shutter Phase to -50% of, 92–93
Shutter Angle setting (Composition Settings dialog), 91–93
Shutter Phase setting (Composition Settings dialog), 91–93
Shy toggle (A/V Features column), 62, 63
Silhouette Alpha blending mode, 433
Silhouette blending mode, 130
Silhouette FX, 303
Simple Choker, 241
Single Frame mode (Paint panel), 268
single-node cameras, 307
sixteen bit-per-channel images. *See* 16 bpc images
sky conditions, 463–465
  compensating for camera movement with new, 465
  importance to storytelling, 463
  replacing, 463–465
  simulating clouds with cotton puffs, 469–470
Slider Control (Expression Control panel), 359, 360
Slider dialog, 360
SLR cameras, 315–316
Smart Mask Interpolation command, 124
smoke. *See also* explosions; fire
  adding Liquify effects for swirling, 472–474
  appearance of volume with, 469
  billowing, 469–475
  creating with combined Mesh Warp and Fractal Noise effects, 473–474
  developing smoke trails, 474–475
  effects creating, 466–467
  firearm, 487–488
  gradients for smoke trails, 475
  Mesh Warp for emulating billowing, 471, 472
  rendering with Fractal Noise element, 467
  simulating with cotton puffs, 469–470
smoke trails, 474–475
smooth() expression
  applying, 366–368
  Smoother vs., 298, 299, 300
Smoother, The, 297–301
smoothing moving cameras
  applying smooth() expression, 366–368
  Smoother for, 297–301
SMPTE-C setting, 405–407
Snap button (Graph Editor), 74
snapshots of sample keying, 224
snow, 369–371, 480–481
Solid Footage Settings dialog, 18
Solo switch (A/V Features column), 62–63
Sound Keys, 353
source clips, editing, 271
Source column (Timeline), 60

Source folder, function of, 139
source footage
  digital formats for, 27–30
  importing, 11
  keeping linked, 14–15
  naming layers and instances of files, 60
spaces in expressions, 360
sparks for bullet hits, 489–490
spatial data and curves for keyframes, 79–82
spatial interpretations defaulting to linear, 76, 79–80
Spill Suppressor effect, 244–245
split layers, 66
split-screen view, 105, 107
squib hits, 489
squibs, 484
stabilizing
  3D camera to background, 292, 294, 296
  layers, 292–293
  tracks, 281–282
Standard workspace
  illustrated, 6
  panels in, 5
static elements in layers, 64–65
Stencil Alpha mode, 434
Stencil blending mode, 130
storage overflow, using, 49–50
storytelling
  cinematography as, 326–331
  developing visual objectivity for, 510–512
  heightening drama with light, 420–422
  portraying emotional resonance, 519–521
  sky's importance in, 463
  using light in, 432
stretching layers and keyframes, 95
stroke
  accumulating on Timeline, 269
  changing render order of, 272
  connecting motion tracker to, 272
  setting duration of paint, 268
studying shots, tips for, 54–55
subpixel positioning for tracker, 288
Subtract mode for masks, 119, 120
sunsets, difficulties working with, 345
Super 35 film format
  aspect ratio of, 385
  illustrated, 385
supervising on-set effects, 238–241
Switches Affect Nested Comps check box (General Preferences), 145
Switches column, 62–63
switching
  cloned sources on fly, 271
  foreground and background swatches, 269
syntax, keyword, 357
synthesizing fire, 498–504
SynthEyes, 308

T

Targa format, 27
target layers
    applying Corner Pin tracking to, 283
    rotation and scale data for, 282
Target menu (Layer panel), 250–251
targeted cameras, 307
tearing off panels, 9
Telecine process, 386
telephoto lens, 315, 458
templates
    Output Module, 50–53
    standardizing project, 137–139
temporal eases. *See* keyframe eases
texture maps, Fractal Noise, 467
Texture Memory option (OpenGL Info dialog), 42
textures, caching on display card, 45
thirty-two bit-per-channel images. *See* 32 bpc images
three-dimensional camera. *See* 3D camera
Three-Way Color Corrector, 192, 430–431
thumbnails, 159
TIFF format, 27
tilde (~) key, 8
time. *See also* timing
    absolute time measurement, 93–94
    nesting and, 146–148
    offsetting with expressions, 368–371
    remapping for layers, 97–98
    saving with subcomp prerendering, 153
Time Control panel, 36
Time Remap, 97–98, 99, 100
Time Sampling section (Render Settings dialog), 48, 49
Time Stretch, 60, 94–95, 96
TimeCode Base option (Project Settings dialog), 20, 21
Timeline, 58–101. *See also* Graph Editor
    about, 21, 58
    accumulating strokes on, 269
    animation methods, 68–70
    assigning color to layers, 61–62
    A/V Features column, 61, 62–63
    column views in, 59–61
    comments added in, 62
    defined, 5
    eases for animation, 76–78
    editing track points in, 288
    Frame blending effects on, 95–96
    icons for, 59, 60
    illustrated, 6
    keeping tabs organized, 139–140
    learning Graph Editor, 71
    method of time measurement, 93–94
    Motion Blur toggle, 90–91
    navigation keyboard shortcuts, 63–64

    preserving nested composition frame rate, 96–97
    property adjustments with closed Composition panel, 140
    reversing timing of layer, 96
    spatial data and curves for keyframes, 79–82
    Time Remap feature of, 97–98, 99, 100
    Time Stretch, 94–95
    Timewarp feature, 99–100
    using U/UU shortcuts with keyframes, 85
    view options for, 67
    viewing layer properties render order in, 152
Timeline button (Composition panel), 67
Timewarp feature, 99–100
timing. *See also* time
    color, 193
    retiming footage, 99–100
    reversing layer, 96
Tint
    adjusting color of shots with, 426
    creating day-for-night effect with, 429
Title/Action Safe overlay option, 39, 41
Toggle View masks button, 41
Track Fields option (Motion Tracker Options dialog), 286
    track mattes, 132–134
    advantages and disadvantages of, 133–134
    rendering order of, 134
    working with, 132–133
track points
    editing in Timeline, 288
    extending with expressions, 301–302
    illustrated, 279
    selecting, 279–280
Tracker Controls panel
    optimizing options, 281–286
    setting tracking points in, 278
    Stabilize option, 281–282
    Transform option, 281
Tracker Plug-in pull-down, 286
tracking. *See* motion tracking
tracking markers
    removing from alpha channel matte, 267
    visible on difference mattes, 218
tracks
    Corner Pin, 257, 282, 283
    fixing, 287–288
    Position, 302
    as properties of layers, 288
    Raw, 282, 283
    stabilizing, 281–282
    Transform, 281
Transform Box (Graph Editor), 71, 74–75
Transform controls (Timeline), 60, 68–70
triggers
    conditional, 377

dissolves with, 372
for excessive grain, 338
troubleshooting
footage with histograms, 178–181
forcing Macintosh crash, 160
premultiplication errors, 115
removing OpenGL.aex after startup crash, 44
shots from Master comp, 141
Twixtor, 100
two-dimensional. *See* 2D

U

U/UU keyboard shortcuts, 85
undoing
precompositions, 145
setting optimal levels of, 158–159
unlocking layers, 63
Unmult plug-in, 115, 244, 500
Use Comp Proxies Only option (Render Settings dialog), 155
user interface
adjust color of, 122, 159
camera, 313–314
Curves effect, 182–183
improving interactivity with, 34–35
workspaces and panels of, 5–10
User Interface Colors option (Preferences dialog), 122

V

Vector Paint effect, 267
vertices. *See also* First Vertex
preserving constant count of, 256
video gamma color space, 393–394
View Layout pull-down menu, 314
View menu (Layer panel), 250, 251, 272
viewing
bridge composite in Flowchart view, 517
layer properties render order, 152
matte detail in alpha channel, 212–213
options for Timeline, 67
views
Flowchart, 86–87
Layer, 84–85
vignette effect, 343, 424–425
virtual cinematography, 312–347
about, 312–313
After Effects' virtual camera, 313–314
camera projection, 329–332
changing camera orientation, 327
color in, 344, 346–347
effects producing "film and video look," 343–347
formats and aspect ratios for, 346
grain, 337–343

matching lens distortion, 320–324
mixing 2D and 3D elements, 324–326
motion blur and camera shutter settings, 92–93
push vs. zoom, 328
recommended frame rate settings for, 345–347
simulating camera blur, 332–337
storytelling with cameras, 326–331
strategies for using grain, 342–343
typical sizes of film formats, 321
Vivid Light blending mode, 129
volumetric light, 439–440

W

Watch Folder, 156–157
water, 478–481
compositing rain or snow element, 480–481
implying presence with reflected light, 480
importance of effects with, 478
physics of heat distortion from, 495–496
precipitation, 479
waterfalls, 479
Wave World effect, 480
weather conditions. *See also* mist; smoke
billowing smoke, 469–475
fog, smoke, or mist, 466–469
particulate matter in air, 457–463
reproducing, 456–457
simulating clouds with cotton puffs, 469–470
sky replacement, 463–465
water, 478–481
wind, 475–478
Web resources on expressions, 378–379
width, 66
wiggle() expression, 365–366, 367–368
wind, 475–478
adding and articulating elements to indicate, 476–477
indirect effects signifying, 477–478
noticing indications of, 475
Windows platforms. *See* Microsoft Windows platforms
wire removal, 273
wireframes, 314
Work Areas, 65
workflow, *see also* managing workflow settings;
OpenGL workflow strategies
3D motion tracking, 305
adjusting color with Curves, 188
collecting project files, 16–17
effects and presets, 45–47
HDR lighting, 445–452
importing source materials, 11
keeping source footage linked, 14–15
managing settings for, 20–31
masks, 116–118
options for saving projects, 18–20

workflow (*continued*)
    organizing folders for, 12
    output with Render Queue, 47–54
    previews and OpenGL, 31–45
    recommendations for Graph Editor, 83–85
    using workspaces and panels, 5–10
Working Space drop-down menu (Project Settings dialog), 404, 405
workspaces
    defining as theater preview, 407–408
    deleting, 11
    docking, grouping, and adjusting panels, 7–8
    resetting to defaults, 7, 10
    resolving color space issues in, 405
    saving, 10
    Standard, 5, 6
    switching project to SMPTE-C, 405–407

X

X across histogram, 176
X axis, 358
X-Factor plug-in, 156

Y

Y axis
    applying motion track only to, 358
    orientation in 2D and 3D, 327
Y'CrCb color format, 234
YUV format, 234–235

Z

Z space, 295
Zeno's Paradox, 110, 111
Zoom Control, 360
Zoom property (Camera Settings dialog)
    adjusting, 317–318
    expressions for, 320
zoom shots
    emulating real camera's, 318
    fake 3D tracking for, 295–297
    flares with zoom lenses, 437
zoom wheel on mouse, 33, 55, 67, 232
zooming
    illustrated, 319
    in/out on Timeline, 67
    with mouse scroll wheel, 33, 55, 67, 232
    pushing vs., 328
    shortcut for floating panels, 10
    viewing attach point with, 281

What's on the DVD?

Books are great for in-depth learning, but it's always good to investigate hands-on examples as well. Although this book is designed not to rely on tutorials, many of the techniques described in the text can be further explored via the dozens of projects and accompanying footage and stills included on the disc. Wherever possible, HD (1920×1080) clips from Pixel Corps and Artbeats are incorporated; other examples use NTSC footage and stills if that is all that's required to get the point across.

Additionally, the DVD includes demos of more than a dozen plug-ins and applications, including a demo of After Effects 7.0 itself. These demos are similar to the real software for everything but output, allowing you to experiment with your own footage.

▶ **Duplink** and **Merge Project** (*Redefinery*): Two scripts have been created specifically for this book, available only via this disc. **Duplink** allows you to create "instance" objects of existing ones, which are linked to the source so that anything you change in it, changes in them. **Merge Projects** is for After Effects users who like to use a specific and consistent directory structure in projects; it automatically places content found in nested folders in an imported project window into folders with the same names in the master project. More information on these is included as comments in the scripts themselves (which can be opened with any text editor).

▶ **After Effects 7.0** (*Adobe*): Shows you what you've been missing if you're still working with an earlier version, including the Graph Editor and the new, unified interface. Note that this is the Standard version; certain techniques described in the book, such as most of those in Chapter 6: "Color Keying," rely on effects included only with the Professional version of After Effects.

▶ **SynthEyes** (*Andersson Technologies*): Provides fully automatic, as well as user-controlled matchmoving for single or batch-processed shots; a stand-alone program that exports to After Effects.

▶ **Particular** (*Trapcode*): Designs 3D particle systems that simulate air resistance, gravity, and turbulence; provides real-time preview, as well as controls so you can freeze time and manipulate a camera in the scene.

▶ **Knoll Light Factory 2.0** (*Red Giant Software*): Includes such pre-built lighting effects as lens flares, sparkles, glows, and more; also provides individual lens components so you can create your own custom effects.

▶ **Primatte Keyer** (*Red Giant Software*): An alternative to Keylight. Extracts keys from any background and includes controls to handle uneven lighting, difficult shadows, light spill, and more.

▶ **Lux** (*Trapcode*): Simulates light reflection, using After Effects' built-in lights to create visible light that corresponds to your layers' lighting schemes.

▶ **Shine** (*Trapcode*): Produces a 2D light-ray effect that closely resembles volumetric light; includes controls for coloring and shimmering lights.

▶ **KeyCorrect** (*Red Giant Software*): Optimizes composites and automates color correction, blurring or feathering of edges, artifact removal, and more.

▶ **Magic Bullet Suite** (*Red Giant Software*): Manipulates digital video to look like film with tools for 24 p conversion, mimicking film artifacts and damage, creating film-like cross dissolves, removing DVD compression artifacts, and more.

▶ **Instant HD** (*Red Giant Software*): Provides higher-quality up-conversion of footage than is possible natively in After Effects.

- ▶ **Film Fix** (*Red Giant Software*): Full-featured restoration software; restores tears, removes dust and dirt, stabilizes footage transferred from film.

- ▶ **ReelSmart Motion Blur** (*RevisionFX*): Procedurally generates motion blur for moving elements in a shot which lack it (or lack enough of it); After Effects' built-in motion blur is available only on animated elements.

- ▶ **Echospace** (*Trapcode*): Creates any number of instanced objects whose animations follow those of the master object, but can be offset in time and space.

- ▶ **Erodilation** and **CopyImage** (*ObviousFX*): Not demos but freeware, these plug-ins allow for quick manipulation of matte data and quick production of stills, respectively.

- ▶ **Roto** (*SilhouetteFX*): Lets you quickly create sophisticated animated mattes using Rational B-Spline, NURB, or Bézier shapes.

- ▶ **Paint** (*SilhouetteFX*): As an add-on module to Roto, Paint is a high dynamic range 2D paint system for feature film and television production.

- ▶ **Starglow** (*Trapcode*): Produces an eight-pointed star-shaped glow around a sources' highlights; enables you to assign each direction of the star an individual color map and streak length.

- ▶ **Sound Keys** (*Trapcode*): Generates keyframes from audio energy; enables you to select a range in an audio waveform, then converts the frequencies into a stream of keyframes.

- ▶ Dozens of After Effects 7.0 project files demonstrating techniques described in the book. These range from simple demonstrations of single concepts to completed shots.

- ▶ Live Action, effects and graphics footage from Artbeats: four full-length professionally shot HD clips presented exactly as they would if licensed from Artbeats, free for use according to the terms described in the End User License Agreement (EULA) in the Artbeats folder.

- ▶ Effects footage from Pixel Corps: nearly a dozen HD clips, predominantly blue screen and green screen shots taken with a Sony F900 HD camera; they are presented on the disk as uncompressed QuickTime files. They can be found within individual source folders for each chapter in the Examples folder.